FORUM NON CONVENIENS

History, Global Practice, and Future Under the Hague Convention on Choice of Court Agreements

Ronald A. Brand
Professor of Law and Director
Center for International Legal Education
University of Pittsburgh School of Law

Scott R. Jablonski
The Law Firm of Scott R. Jablonski, P.L.
Miami Beach, Florida

OXFORD
UNIVERSITY PRESS

Oxford University Press, Inc., publishes works that further Oxford University's
objective of excellence in research, scholarship, and education.

Copyright © 2007 by Oxford University Press, Inc.
Published by Oxford University Press, Inc.
198 Madison Avenue, New York, New York 10016

Oxford is a registered trademark of Oxford University Press
Oceana is a registered trademark of Oxford University Press, Inc.

Cataloging-in-Publication information is available from the Library of Congress.
Library of Congress Control Number: 2006939348

ISBN: 978-0-19-532927-8 (Cloth)

Printed in the United States of America on acid-free paper.

Note to Readers:

This publication is designed to provide accurate and authoritative information in regard to the subject matter
covered. It is based upon sources believed to be accurate and reliable and is intended to be current as of
the time it was written. It is sold with the understanding that the publisher is not engaged in rendering
legal, accounting, or other professional services. If legal advice or other expert assistance is required, the
services of a competent professional person should be sought. Also, to confirm that the information has
not been affected or changed by recent developments, traditional legal research techniques should be used,
including checking primary sources where appropriate.

(Based on the Declaration of Principles jointly adopted by a Committee of the
American Bar Association and a Committee of Publishers and Associations.)

You may order this or any other Oxford University Press publication
by visiting the Oxford University Press website at www.oup.com

To students of the law who believe

there is a place for them

in the world of transnational practice

CILE Studies

CILE Studies is a series of monographs and edited volumes dedicated to the discussion of important issues and developments in public and private international law. Each volume is selected on the basis of its contribution to the literature in a manner that is likely to provide lasting commentary and innovative analysis. Potential authors may contact:

Center for International Legal Education
University of Pittsburgh
School of Law
Pittsburgh, PA 15260
U.S.A.
Phone: 412-648-7023
fax: 412-648-2648
email: cile@law.pitt.edu

Volumes 1 and 2 are available directly from the Center for International Legal Education at the above address. Volume 3 and later volumes are part of the catalogue of publications available from Oxford University Press.

The Series

VOLUME 1

The Draft UNCITRAL Digest and Beyond: Cases, Analysis, and Unresolved Issues in the U.N. Sales Convention, (Franco Ferrari, Harry M. Flechtner, and Ronald A. Brand, editors)

VOLUME 2

Private Law, Private International Law, and Judicial Cooperation in the EU-US Relationship, (Ronald A. Brand, editor)

VOLUME 3

Forum Non Conveniens—History, Global Practice, and Future Under the Hague Convention on Choice of Court Agreements, (Ronald A. Brand and Scott R. Jablonski)

Table of Contents

Forum Non Conveniens

History, Global Practice, and Future Under the Hague Convention on Choice of Court Agreements

PREFACE

Forum non conveniens is a legal doctrine first developed by the courts of Scotland, which by the twentieth century had gained acceptance in every major common law legal system. It allows courts to decline to exercise jurisdiction that otherwise exists in deference to litigation in a more appropriate forum in another state.

Three factors make the doctrine of forum non conveniens particularly relevant for comprehensive study at the beginning of the twenty-first century. First, while the doctrine of forum non conveniens is well-established in the four major common law nations, its application by the courts of each nation differs in ways that make over-generalization dangerous but that also elucidates important general distinctions among the legal systems of those nations. Second, the near complete absence of the doctrine of forum non conveniens (or anything like it) in civil law countries, and the presence in those legal systems of a rigid rule of lis alibi pendens requiring automatic deference to the court first seised of a case, creates a sharp contrast between the two major legal systems of the world. The doctrine of forum non conveniens—particularly when compared to lis alibi pendens—provides useful insight into those distinctions. Third, the completion of the *2005 Hague Convention on Choice of Court Agreements*, and the earlier consideration of a more comprehensive global treaty on jurisdiction and the recognition and enforcement of judgments, generated careful consideration of the intersection of the doctrines of forum non conveniens and lis alibi pendens and how different approaches to parallel litigation could be reconciled on a global basis. That discussion deserves note and should not be lost in future efforts to coordinate jurisdictional rules.

Our effort in this book is to provide a comprehensive comparative review of the doctrine of forum non conveniens, addressing both the history of the doctrine and possibilities for future development that will carry the doctrine into cooperative efforts to coordinate jurisdictional issues between common law and civil law legal systems. Thus, we first review the history and status of the doctrine of forum non conveniens in the four major common law jurisdictions: (1) the United Kingdom (with special attention to the history of the doctrine in Scotland), (2) the United States, (3) Canada, and (4) Australia. In each instance, we have endeavored to make clear the differing paths the courts of each nation have taken in addressing similar issues based on common legal history. We then provide a summary analysis of the similarities and differences in the application of the doctrine among the four major common law jurisdictions. That summary is followed by consideration of rules in civil law states that might allow courts to decline jurisdiction, as well as discussion of the more rigid, non-discretionary doctrine of lis alibi pendens that predominates in the continental civil law traditions.

After presenting the current status of the forum non conveniens doctrine in common law countries, and comparing the doctrine with its civil law counterparts, we turn to negotiations at the Hague Conference on Private International Law for a convention on jurisdiction and the recognition and enforcement of judgments. Those negotiations developed a compromise between the common law doctrine of forum non conveniens and the civil law doctrine of lis alibi pendens. A comprehensive treaty containing that compromise was not realized. Nonetheless, the work of the negotiators justifies further discussion so that the possibilities for common ground are not lost in the future. Our final chapter considers the text of the treaty that did result from those negotiations, the *2005 Hague Convention on Choice of Court Agreements*, and the manner in which that treaty deals with this tension between major legal systems.

It is our hope that a review of the historical development of the doctrine of forum non conveniens, followed by a discussion of the extraordinary work at the Hague Conference, might establish a starting point for further discussion of global development of the doctrine of forum non conveniens as well as of related doctrines addressing parallel proceedings and rules for declining jurisdiction. We also hope that this undertaking may serve as a useful reference tool for practitioners engaged in transnational litigation and cross-border contract drafting, as well as for courts and legislators around the world, as they continue to shape the development of rules for declining jurisdiction.

We express our special thanks to Alex Braden, Jamie Burchianti, Sarah Gordon, Andrew Lukashunas, and Greg Walker, whose assistance made the substance of this book better than it otherwise would have been, and to LuAnn Driscoll, Phyllis Gentille, Karen Knochel, Darleen Mocello, and Barbara Salopek, who helped make it much more readable.

April 2007
Ronald A. Brand
Scott R. Jablonski

CHAPTER 1

Common Law Forum Non Conveniens: Four Countries, Four Approaches

Forum non conveniens is a doctrine applied in common law judicial systems allowing the court seised of a case the discretion to decline to exercise jurisdiction because the interests of justice are best served if the trial takes place in another court. While Scottish courts are credited with first developing and applying the concepts underlying this doctrine, courts in other countries have joined in its evolution, resulting in familiarity with the doctrine throughout the common law world. This does not mean, however, that there is consistent application of the doctrine across legal systems. While there are similarities among national approaches, there are important differences in the inquiry, particularly in the way in which it intersects with basic jurisdictional rules.

Differences in legal systems can make consideration of the forum non conveniens doctrine a rather complex concept. First, as already noted, even in common law systems where the doctrine is a part of the procedural law, its application varies from country to country. One variation is the extent to which the doctrine is incorporated into basic jurisdictional analysis. In England and Canada, for example, the doctrine is applicable to basic jurisdictional analysis.[1] Thus, there are times when a forum non conveniens analysis comes into play even before the initial determination of jurisdiction is complete. This is sometimes referred to as a forum conveniens analysis.

---

[1] In England, CPR 6.20 of the Civil Procedure Rules of the Supreme Court (formerly Order 11, Rule 1(1), of the Rules of the Supreme Court) allows discretion in permitting service of a writ out of the jurisdiction. Through this system, service of process is fundamental to jurisdiction over a foreign defendant, and the exercise of discretion can bring in the forum non conveniens analysis.

Second, the strict lis alibi pendens approach of civil law jurisdictions both empha-sizes and enhances differences with common law systems that apply the forum non conveniens doctrine. While it may be considered appropriate (and even required) in civil law systems to decline jurisdiction in deference to a court earlier seised of the same case, it would not be considered appropriate to decline to exer-cise jurisdiction if it exists and no other court is seised of the case. Forum non conveniens is a doctrine requiring judicial discretion. Such discretion generally is not acknowledged in civil law systems where ostensibly comprehensive codes are intended to separate the legislative function of developing and declaring the law from the judicial function of applying the law. While judicial discretion is a neces-sary element of a court's function in common law systems, it is frowned upon in the civil law world.

A third factor making complete understanding of the doctrine of forum non con-veniens difficult is that it is only one part of a package of issues arising from con-cerns with parallel litigation in multiple judicial systems. Forum non conveniens applies when there are courts in at least two judicial systems with jurisdiction to hear the case. While civil law legal systems tend to prefer a lis alibi pendens approach to this problem, doing so encourages a race to the courthouse. The loser of the race is destined to have its filing rejected by a court that will defer to the court first seised. Another part of the package of procedural issues in parallel litigation is the anti-suit injunction (and even the anti-anti-suit injunction). Forum non conven-iens is thus only one part of the parallel litigation puzzle, and it may not be pos-sible to understand it completely without an analysis of the rest of the package.[2] As will become clear in later chapters, in some legal systems the same test may be applicable in analyzing jurisdiction, in applying the forum non conveniens doctrine, and in determining whether an anti-suit injunction should issue.

Despite the forum non conveniens doctrine's connection with related issues of parallel litigation, this book does not provide a comprehensive review of all the possibilities for declining jurisdiction in every legal system. Its focus is on the common law doctrine of forum non conveniens. While this may require some discussion of the doctrine of lis alibi pendens and of anti-suit injunctions, the detail of those topics is

---

[2]   In August 1994, a General Report and National Reports on "Rules for Declining to Exercise Jurisdiction in Civil and Commercial Matters: *Forum Non Conveniens, Lis Pendens* and Other Rules" were presented at the XIVth Congress of the International Academy of Comparative Law. These Reports provide useful analysis and are published in DECLINING JURISDICTION IN PRIVATE INTERNATIONAL LAW (James J. Fawcett ed., 1995).

left for others. At the same time, however, it is impossible to ignore the common issues of parallel litigation and the ultimate goal of having a case tried in the most appropriate court. Thus, when we reach a discussion of the future of forum non conveniens in Chapter 8, that future may also have implications for related doctrines. The foundation for that future, however, must deal with the doctrine of forum non conveniens as currently applied in common law legal systems; hence the focus of this book.

In Chapters 2 through 5, we explore whether and to what extent there exists a uniform modern doctrine of forum non conveniens. The current status of the doctrine throughout the common law world can be understood properly only in its historical context. Thus, we consider the evolution of the doctrine in four major common law jurisdictions: the United Kingdom, the United States, Canada, and Australia.[3]

In the United Kingdom, the current forum non conveniens test is stated in *Spiliada Maritime Corp. v. Cansulex Ltd.*:[4]

> [A] stay will only be granted on the ground of forum non conveniens where the court is satisfied that there is some other available forum, having competent jurisdiction, which is the appropriate forum for trial of the action, i.e., in which the case may be tried more suitably for the interests of all the parties and the ends of justice.[5]

In *Spiliada*, Lord Goff set up a two part analysis, with the first part focused on the appropriate forum and the second on considerations of justice. Thus, the initial burden is on the defendant to show that another available forum is clearly more appropriate than the British forum. If the defendant meets this burden, then the burden shifts to the plaintiff to show "circumstances by reason of which justice requires that a stay should nevertheless not be granted."[6]

---

[3] The forum non conveniens doctrine also exists in Israel, *see* Stephen Goldstein, *Israel*, *in* DECLINING JURISDICTION IN PRIVATE INTERNATIONAL LAW 259, 261–74 (James J. Fawcett ed., 1995); and New Zealand, *see* R.J. Paterson, *Forum Non Conveniens in New Zealand*, 13 N.Z. U. L. REV. 337 (1989); as well as in Ireland, Hong Kong, Brunei, Singapore, and Gibraltar, *see* PETER NORTH & JAMES J. FAWCETT, CHESHIRE AND NORTH'S PRIVATE INTERNATIONAL LAW 335 (13th ed. 1999).

[4] [1987] A.C. 460.

[5] [1987] A.C. 460, 476.

[6] [1987] A.C. 460, 478.

In the United States, the law on forum non conveniens has been developed largely through three major Supreme Court decisions: *Piper Aircraft Co. v. Reyno*,[7] *Gulf Oil Corp. v. Gilbert*,[8] and *Koster v. Lumbermens Mutual Casualty Co.*[9] These cases generally have been followed in both federal and state courts, and have been tracked in some instances in state legislation.[10] The analysis is similar to that in the United Kingdom. A court chosen by the plaintiff may decline to exercise its jurisdiction if it is a seriously inconvenient forum, another forum exists with jurisdiction, and a balancing of factors allows the court to determine that justice is best served by sending the case to the other, more convenient, available forum. Unlike the U.K. analysis, however, the U.S. procedure allows a consideration of public (as well as private) interest factors, and tends to place greater emphasis on a local plaintiff's choice of forum.

In *Amchem Products Inc. v. British Columbia (Workers' Compensation Board)*,[11] the Canadian Supreme Court largely followed the House of Lords' decision in *Spiliada* by delineating the forum non conveniens doctrine in a case involving jurisdictional service outside the forum state. The Court balanced private interest factors in determining that "the existence of a more appropriate forum must be *clearly* established to displace the forum selected by the plaintiff."[12]

Australia is the outlier in this comparison, rejecting what Professor von Mehren has called the "convenience-suitability approach" now applied in the other three systems and favoring an "abuse-of-process approach" to forum non conveniens.[13] Australia has rejected the "appropriate forum" approach applied by the House of Lords in *Spiliada*, and opted to continue the traditional requirement that the defendant demonstrate that the forum chosen by the plaintiff results in vexation

---

[7]   454 U.S. 235 (1981)

[8]   330 U.S. 501 (1947).

[9]   330 U.S. 518 (1947).

[10] *See, e.g.*, LA. CODE CIV. PROC. ANN. art. 123 (Supp. 2005) (allowing dismissal in circumstances similar to the federal standard enunciated in *Piper, Gilbert*, and *Koster*).

[11] [1993] 1 S.C.R. 897.

[12] [1993] 1 S.C.R. 897, 921.

[13] Arthur T. von Mehren, *Theory and Practice of Adjudicatory Authority in Private International Law: A Comparative Study of the Doctrine, Policies and Practices of Common- and Civil-Law Systems*, 295 RECUEIL DES COURS/COLLECTED COURSES OF THE HAGUE ACADEMY OF INTERNATIONAL LAW 326 (2002).

or oppression.[14] This may be demonstrated by a showing that the Australian court is clearly inappropriate.[15]

Chapter 6 explores whether there exists a uniform modern doctrine of forum non conveniens. There, we highlight the similarities and differences among the four legal systems previously considered. Throughout most of the twentieth century, courts in common law countries followed similar principles, often citing cases in other countries as justification for their own doctrine. Despite these similarities, however, significant differences in the application of the doctrine and its interplay with other jurisdictional rules preclude the categorical assumption that there exists a single common law doctrine of forum non conveniens. While the doctrine is applied in some courts only to the determination of whether jurisdiction should be exercised once it exists, in other courts it has worked its way into initial determinations of jurisdiction itself. The various differences in the use and application of the doctrine of forum non conveniens are important both in understanding the doctrine as it is applied in each judicial system, and in comparing common law systems with their civil law counterparts.

After discussing the similarities and differences among the forum non conveniens doctrine of common law legal systems, in Chapter 7 we briefly cover the concept of declining jurisdiction in civil law systems. We focus on Germany, Japan, and the effects of the *Brussels Convention* and the *Brussels I Regulation* in the European Union. This allows for the consideration of both the more rigid approach applied to parallel litigation issues in civil law systems and the general civil law choice to opt for a race to the courthouse as opposed to the common law race to judgment. It also allows discussion of Latin American legislative efforts to block application of the forum non conveniens doctrine in U.S. courts.

The lack of uniformity in common law forum non conveniens doctrine, and its rather sharp contrast with civil law rigidity in jurisdictional analysis, suggest the opportunity for multilateral developments that might make transnational litigation more orderly and predictable. Thus, in Chapters 8 and 9 we turn to the work at the Hague Conference on Private International Law, and specifically to the negotiation of conventions in which forum non conveniens must be considered.

---

[14] Oceanic Sun Line Special Shipping Co. Inc. v. Fay, (1988) 165 C.L.R. 197.
[15] Voth v. Manildra Flour Mills Pty. Ltd., (1990) 171 C.L.R. 538.

This includes a look at the *2005 Hague Convention on Choice of Court Agreements* negotiated by the Hague Conference on Private International Law, as well as the attempt at a more comprehensive convention on jurisdiction and judgments which preceded the *Hague Choice of Court Convention*.

Articles 21 and 22 of the *2001 Hague Interim Text* for a comprehensive convention represented a compromise between the discretionary common law forum non conveniens doctrine and the strict analysis of civil law lis alibi pendens, which may provide a foundation for the harmonization of procedure on the issue of declining jurisdiction. These articles deserve special attention in considering future approaches to the doctrine of forum non conveniens and where it fits in a global litigation context. They demonstrate the possibility of compromise between common law and civil law approaches to the declining jurisdiction question. At the same time, the *Hague Convention on Choice of Court Agreements* offers an initial step towards convergence by providing common rules when a choice of court agreement exists. By eliminating the possibility of an application of the doctrine of forum non conveniens when an exclusive choice of court agreement exists, the new *Hague Convention* initiates a process of global convergence of the rules for parallel litigation.

While it is difficult to predict the future in this area of the law, we can hope that more complete knowledge of both the history and current status of the forum non conveniens doctrine will facilitate a better understanding of global efforts to improve the transnational litigation framework, and that those efforts might ultimately result in both greater predictability for litigants and more uniform results.

CHAPTER 2

The United Kingdom

I.   Scotland: from forum non competens to most appropriate forum[1]

The term "forum non conveniens" was not used in the early seventeenth century Scottish decisions that are credited with originating the doctrine.[2] Those
courts assumed the authority, in the "interests of justice," to decline to hear a
case even when jurisdiction was otherwise proper. While this discretionary
authority originated as a part of the determination of jurisdiction and went
by the name "forum non competens",[3] by the mid-nineteenth century it had
evolved into a separate analysis, considered to be a question on the merits to

---

[1]   Although Scotland is a part of the United Kingdom, its legal system developed separately from that in
England. *See* ROBIN M. WHITE & IAN D. WILLOCK, THE SCOTTISH LEGAL SYSTEM 8–34 (1993).

[2]   The cases of *Vernor v. Elvies* 6 Dict. of Dec. 4788 (1610) (Scot.), and *Col. Brog's Heir v. . . . .* 6 Dict. of Dec.
4816 (1639) (Scot.) are most often cited as the source of the doctrine. *See, e.g.,* Edward L. Barrett, Jr., *The
Doctrine of Forum Non Conveniens*, 35 CAL. L. REV. 380, 387 n.35 (1947); Robert Braucher, *The Inconvenient
Federal Forum*, 60 HARV. L. REV. 908 (1947); Alexander Reus, *Judicial Discretion: A Comparative View
of the Doctrine of Forum Non Conveniens in the United States, the United Kingdom, and Germany*, 16
LOY. L.A. INT'L & COMP. L.J. 455 (1994). Reus notes, at 459, that the discretion to decline otherwise
valid jurisdiction arose "to balance undue hardship arising out of arrestment ad fundandum jurisdiction,
which existed when Scotland attached and seized foreign assets in order to force foreigners into Scottish
courts" (citing A. GIBB, THE INTERNATIONAL LAW OF JURISDICTION IN ENGLAND AND SCOTLAND 212–13
(1926)).

[3]   *See* Robert Braucher, *The Inconvenient Federal Forum*, 60 HARV. L. REV. 908, 909 (1947) ("Early Scottish
cases dealing with a plea of *'forum non competens'* suggest that the question litigated was one of power or
jurisdiction rather than discretion."). *See, e.g.,* Macmaster v. Macmaster, 11 S. 685 (Sess. Cas. 1833) (Scot.)
(declining to exercise jurisdiction in an estate case where the defendant executor resided abroad, even
though the court had jurisdiction through arrestment); Brown's Trustee v. Palmer, 9 S. 224 (Sess. Cas.
1830) (Scot.) (refusing jurisdiction where the defendant resided in India and the alleged harm occurred
there). *But see* Peters v. Martin, 4 S. 108 (Sess. Cas. 1825) (Scot.) (holding that even though the trial would
be more expedient in England, the court could not "deprive the pursuers of their legal right to sue a party
domiciled within their jurisdiction.").

be addressed after jurisdiction was established.[4] In the 1865 case of *Longworth v. Hope*,[5] Scotland's Court of Session acknowledged the power to stay proceedings in the interest of justice, but also emphasized the narrow scope of such power. The Court, in finding that Scotland was the more appropriate forum in which to entertain a libel action, stressed that deference should be given to a plaintiff's choice of forum, even while conceding that England was a more appropriate forum for assessing damages in the particular case.[6] Later in the nineteenth century, courts in Scotland explicitly replaced the term "forum non competens" with the phrase "forum non conveniens" to better reflect the nature of the plea.[7]

Some thirty years after *Longworth*, the Court of Session reaffirmed the limited scope of a forum non conveniens dismissal in *Sim v. Robinow*,[8] stating that "the Court has never refused to exercise its jurisdiction upon the ground of a mere

---

[4]   *See, e.g.*, Longworth v. Hope, 3 M. 1049, 1053 (Sess. Cas. 1865) (Scot.) ("Now the plea [of forum non competens] usually thus expressed does not mean that the forum is one in which it is wholly incompetent to deal with the question . . . and is frequently stated in reference to cases in which the Court may consider it more proper for the ends of justice that the parties should seek their remedy in another forum."); Parken v. Royal Exch. Assurance Co., 8 D. 365, 370 (Sess. Cas. 1846) (Scot.) (acknowledging that the court may stay proceedings when jurisdiction is otherwise valid and another forum is more appropriate); Tulloch v. Williams, 8 D. 657, 659 (Lord Fullerton) (Sess. Cas. 1846) (Scot.) ("This is not an incompetent but an inconvenient forum."); M'Morine v. Cowie, 7 D. 270, 272 (Lord Jeffrey) (Sess. Cas. 1845) (Scot.) ("[I]n such cases the question is not one of jurisdiction, but of *forum competens*, which is properly on the merits."). *See also* Robert Braucher, *The Inconvenient Federal Forum*, 60 HARV. L. REV. 908, 909 (1947), discussing how courts gradually began to recognize that the question "was one 'on the merits' rather than one of jurisdiction, and the English words 'inconvenient forum' were used to point out the inaccuracy of using the traditional Latin form of [forum non competens]."

[5]   3 M. 1049, 1052–55 (Sess. Cas. 1865) (Scot.).

[6]   3 M. 1049, 1059 (Sess. Cas. 1865) (Scot.). The Court denied the defendant's plea even though the parties were two English domiciliaries and the publication leading to the alleged injury originated in England. The case therefore suggested that the scope within which a court could exercise its discretion to decline otherwise valid jurisdiction was quite limited.

[7]   *See, e.g.*, Williamson v. North-Eastern Ry. Co., 21 Scot. L. R. 421 (1884) (Scot.); Brown v. Cartwright, 20 Scot. L.R. 818 (1883) (Scot.); Macadam v. Macadam, 11 M. 860 (Sess. Cas. 1873) (Scot.); Prescott v. Graham, 20 Scot. L.R. 573 (1883) (Scot.). *See also* John Bies, *Conditioning Forum Non Conveniens*, 67 U. CHI. L. REV. 489, 494 (2000) ("As the courts began to recognize convenience and expediency as distinct from competence of jurisdiction, they began to refer to this new discretionary refusal of jurisdiction as 'forum non conveniens'"). There was still not complete agreement among judges as to the viability of the doctrine. For an extreme view, see Lord Inglis in Clements v. Macaulay, 4 M. 583, 593 (Sess. Cas. 1866) (Scot.), stating that "in cases in which jurisdiction is competently founded, a Court has no discretion whether it shall exercise its jurisdiction or not." *But see* Williamson v. North-Eastern Ry. Co., 21 Scot. L. R. 421, 598 (1884) (Scot.) ("Apart . . . from the question of jurisdiction, we are always entitled to consider the question of *forum conveniens*, which includes, where jurisdiction exists in more than one country, whether this is the most convenient *forum* for trying the case.").

[8]   19 R. 665, 667–68 (Sess. Cas. 1892) (Scot.).

balance of convenience and inconvenience."[9] The *Sim* Court added that "the plea can never be sustained unless the court is satisfied that there is some other tribunal, having competent jurisdiction, in which the case may be tried more suitably for the interests of all the parties and for the ends of justice."[10] As in *Longworth*, the defendant had to prove that the plaintiff would gain some "unfair advantage" if the Scottish court maintained jurisdiction over the dispute.[11]

In 1926, the House of Lords, in *La Société du Gaz de Paris v. La Société Anonyme de Navigation "Les Armateurs Français,"*[12] considered the Scottish doctrine, finding the existence of a more appropriate forum to be the core of the forum non conveniens analysis. The Law Lords applied a balancing test to hold that France was the more appropriate forum and that a stay in Scotland was appropriate.[13] The original plaintiffs had no connection to Scotland, and the underwriters who proceeded with the action against the French defendants were from England, not Scotland.[14] The plaintiffs' damages resulted from the defendants' barge sinking at sea;[15] since most of the documentary evidence was written in French, the defendants would have been deprived of a limited liability defense in Scotland, and the

---

[9]   19 R. 665, 668 (Sess. Cas. 1892) (Scot.) (Lord Kinnear).

[10]   19 R. 665, 668 (Sess. Cas. 1892) (Scot.).

[11]   19 R. 665, 668 (Sess. Cas. 1892) (Scot.). The Court ultimately rejected the plea, despite the defendant's arguments that Scotland was an inconvenient forum, that the defendant was only temporarily in Scotland, that all of the transactions relating to the joint partnership at issue between the two parties occurred in South Africa, that all of the witnesses and documents were in South Africa, and that the plaintiff resided in England. 19 R. 665, 667–68 (Sess. Cas. 1892) (Scot.). The Court was not satisfied that there was another more "suitable forum" available to hear the case. It distinguished prior case law on these grounds, ruling that in cases where courts have granted the plea "there was one indispensable element present when the Court gave effect to the plea of *forum non conveniens*, namely, that the Court was satisfied that there was another Court in which the action ought to be tried as being more convenient for all the parties, and more suitable for the ends of justice." 19 R. 665, 669 (Sess. Cas. 1892) (Scot.).

In a case decided shortly after Sim, the Court sustained the defendant's plea for dismissal on grounds of forum non conveniens. In Fairweather and Others (Adamson's Ex'rs) v. Mactaggart, 20 R. 738 (Sess. Cas. 1893) (Scot.), all transactions, documents, and other evidence relating to the alleged injury were in India, and the defendant, although a Scottish citizen on visit to Scotland, lived in India. 19 R. 665, 740 (Sess. Cas. 1892) (Scot.). The Court held that India was a more suitable forum and was available, and it refused to give concession to the plaintiff's arguments that recovery of damages in India would hardly equal the expense of litigating there. 19 R. 665, 739 (Sess. Cas. 1892) (Scot.).

[12]   1926 Sess. Cas. 13 (H.L.).

[13]   1926 Sess. Cas. 13, 17 (H.L.).

[14]   1926 Sess. Cas. 13 (H.L.).

[15]   1926 Sess. Cas. 13, 14 (H.L.).

court did not view the prospect of taking the testimony of the few English witnesses in France as problematic.[16]

In *La Société du Gaz de Paris*, the court described the nature of the forum non conveniens plea as follows:

> [I]f in any case it appeared to the Court, after giving consideration to the interests of both parties and to the requirements of justice, that the case could not be suitably tried in the Court in which it was instituted, and full justice could not be done there to the parties, but could be done in another Court, then the former Court might give effect to the plea by declining jurisdiction and permitting the issues to be fought out in the more appropriate Court.[17]

Lord Sumner, in his concurring opinion, reasoned that, since a plaintiff is inherently deprived of some "convenience" when a court grants a motion to dismiss on grounds of forum non conveniens, the true purpose of the doctrine is not to find the most "convenient" forum, but rather to "find that *forum* which is the more suitable for the ends of justice, and is preferable because pursuit of the litigation in that *forum* is more likely to secure those ends."[18] *La Société du Gaz de Paris* demonstrated, nonetheless, that the forum non conveniens test was truly a balancing test applied to determine whether Scotland was the more appropriate forum. The defendant raising the plea carried the general burden of proof,[19] but did not have to prove that trial in Scotland would be an abuse of process or would be oppressive or vexatious to him (as was required in English courts at that time).[20] Subsequent cases indicate that *La Société du Gaz de Paris* firmly defined and established the doctrine of forum non conveniens as a part of Scottish common law.[21]

---

[16] 1926 Sess. Cas. 13, 16–17 (H.L.).
[17] 1926 Sess. Cas. 13, 17 (H.L.).
[18] 1926 Sess. Cas. 13, 22 (H.L.) (Lord Sumner).
[19] 1926 Sess. Cas. 13, 21 (H.L.).
[20] *See* Part II.B.1., below.
[21] *See, e.g.*, Balshaw v. Balshaw, 1967 Sess. Cas. 63, 73–75 (Scot.) (refusing to dismiss the case where a husband domiciled in Scotland brought a nullity proceeding against his English wife, holding that the dismissal would result in an unfair disadvantage to the plaintiff and the Court "would be declaring that 'for the ends of justice' a man domiciled in Scotland must have his action tried in England."); Argyllshire Weavers, Ltd. v. A. Macaulay (Tweeds), Ltd., 1962 Sess.. Cas. 388, 400–01 (Scot.) (refusing to decline jurisdiction, noting that lis alibi pendens was but only one factor to be considered in a forum non conveniens decision, and other factors such as applicable law and witnesses pointed to Scotland as the appropriate forum); Robinson v. Robinson and Others, 1930 Sess. Cas. 20, 24–26 (H.L.) (conceding that the appropriate forum is to be analyzed in "the whole of the circumstances," but refusing to sustain the plea where the

II.   England: from reticence to recognition

It was not until the twentieth century that English courts became comfortable with forum non conveniens as their own doctrine. Until that time, English courts avoided sending cases elsewhere on the premise that English courts were well-suited to entertain suits involving foreign parties.[22]

A.   First steps: the oppressive and vexatious principle

Movement towards the approach used in Scotland can be traced to the 1906 case of *Logan v. Bank of Scotland*,[23] where a Scottish plaintiff brought an action in England against a Scottish bank and various bank representatives, alleging corporate misrepresentation.[24] While jurisdiction existed by virtue of the defendant's London branch bank,[25] the court found that "all the circumstances upon which the plaintiff relies in the statement of claim took place in Scotland and not elsewhere, and that all the evidence with reference thereto will have to be obtained from Scotland."[26] The court granted the defendant's motion to stay the proceedings, with the court's President, Sir Gorell Barnes, stating:

> [I]t is true that the Courts of this country have not gone so far as to express themselves upon the question of convenience in terms similar to those used

---

parties were English and English law governed the will in dispute, because the trial involved a question of fact as to domicile that could be determined by either court, most witnesses were in Scotland, and Scottish law also applied with regard to a deed relevant to the case that had been executed by plaintiff). *Cf.* Sheaf Steamship Co., Ltd. v. The Compania Transmediterranea, 1930 Sess. Cas. 660, 667 (stating that the trial judge's decision to sustain the plea "is not lightly to be disturbed," and affirming the decision to dismiss where all witnesses and applicable laws were Spanish and the events giving rise to the action between the English plaintiff and Spanish defendant were at sea near Spain). *See generally* Alexander Reus, *Judicial Discretion: A Comparative View of the Doctrine of Forum Non Conveniens in the United States, the United Kingdom, and Germany*, 16 LOY. L.A. INT'L & COMP. L.J. 455, 460 (1994), noting that after *La Société du Gaz de Paris* "the use of *forum non conveniens* was limited . . . because courts did not apply it in favor of domestic defendants until the English case of *MacShannon v. Rockware Glass Ltd.* in 1978." (footnote omitted).

22   The traditional English view was that "it is impossible there ever could exist a doubt, but that a [foreign] subject born in Moraca . . . has as good a right to appeal to the King's Courts of Justice, as who is born without the sound of Bow Bell." Mostyn v. Fabrigas, 98 Eng. Rep. 1021, 1027 (K.B. 1775) (Lord Mansfield).

23   [1906] 1 K.B. 141 (C.A.).

24   [1906] 1 K.B. 141, 145 (C.A.) (Sir Gorell Barnes, President).

25   [1906] 1 K.B. 141, 145 (C.A.).

26   [1906] 1 K.B. 141, 146 (C.A.).

in the Scotch cases, though, as I have already noticed, it may be doubted whether there is any substantial difference between the two. Yet it seems to me clear that the inconvenience of trying a case in a particular tribunal may be such as practically to work a serious injustice upon a defendant and be vexatious.[27]

After noting that mere extra expense is not enough to create vexation, Sir Gorell went on to state:

> [W]here the difficulty for the defendant of trying in the country in which the action is brought is such that it is impracticable to properly try the case by reason of the difficulty of procuring the attendance of busy men as witnesses, and keeping them during a long trial, and of having to deal with masses of books, documents, and papers which are not in the country where the action is brought, and of dealing with law foreign to the tribunal, it appears to me that a case of vexation in some circumstances may be made.[28]

Thus, the *Logan* court adopted something similar to the forum non conveniens test used in Scotland, enumerating the various factors to be weighed in the analysis and even claiming to use a test similar to that applied by the Scottish courts, but at the same time noting that those courts were more prone to grant a stay on grounds of inconvenience rather than the more difficult-to-prove test of vexation to the defendant.[29] The English court also stressed the fact that the plaintiff in *Logan* would not be put at a juridical disadvantage as a result of the stay in England.[30]

---

[27] [1906] 1 K.B. 141, 151 (C.A.).

[28] [1906] 1 K.B. 141, 151–52 (C.A.).

[29] [1906] 1 K.B. 141, 149 (C.A.)

[30] [1906] 1 K.B. 141, 154 (C.A.). *See also* Egbert v. Short, [1907] 2 Ch. 205, 211 (C.A.) (staying on grounds that "the proceedings were entirely Indian proceedings," and because granting a stay would not result in injustice to the plaintiff, as there was no legitimate advantage or practical convenience to maintaining the action in England); *In re* Norton's Settlement, [1908] 1 Ch. 471, 484 (C.A.) (noting the validity of the holding in Egbert and granting the defendant's motion to stay the case in England on grounds that proceeding there would be an abuse of process, as all evidence and witnesses were in India, Indian law applied to the case, and the plaintiff did not lose any legitimate advantage as a result of dismissal).

Thirty years after *Logan*, the Court of Appeal reiterated the *Logan* test in *St. Pierre v. South American Stores (Goth & Chaves), Ltd.*:[31]

> (1.) A mere balance of convenience is not a sufficient ground for depriving a plaintiff of the advantages of prosecuting his action in an English Court if it is otherwise properly brought. The right to access to the King's Court must not be lightly refused. (2.) In order to justify a stay two conditions must be satisfied … (*a*) the defendant must satisfy the Court that the continuance of the action would work an injustice because it would be oppressive or vexatious to him or would be an abuse of process of the Court in some other way; and (*b*) the stay must not cause an injustice to the plaintiff. On both the burden of proof is on the defendant.[32]

The substantial deference accorded to a plaintiff's choice of forum under the English test demonstrated the difficult burden placed on the defendant in a motion to stay based on forum non conveniens. The *St. Pierre* court acknowledged that the alternative Chilean court was the more convenient forum.[33] The contract involved was written in Spanish, Chilean law applied to the contract, the events that gave rise to the suit occurred in Chile, all parties had a substantial connection with Chile, and the experts and witnesses would be found in Chile.[34] In the end, however, the court found that "these grounds only go to convenience," and did not evidence vexation to the defendant or abuse of process of the court if the action proceeded in England.[35]

The *St. Pierre* court interestingly disregarded the fact that parallel proceedings had already commenced in Chile, just as it disregarded the fact that the parties had previously agreed to resolve disputes arising from their contract in Chile.[36] Thus, the *St. Pierre* interpretation of *Logan* resulted in a much stricter test than the one then available in Scotland for obtaining a stay, opting for the "vexatious and oppressive" test rather than the Scottish doctrine that focused on the "more appropriate forum." It was not until the 1970s and early 1980s that several important forum non conveniens cases served to bridge the gap between the Scottish and English tests.

---

[31] [1936] 1 K.B. 382 (C.A.).
[32] [1936] 1 K.B. 382, 398 (C.A.).
[33] [1936] 1 K.B. 382, 397 (C.A.).
[34] [1936] 1 K.B. 382, 397 (C.A.).
[35] [1936] 1 K.B. 382, 397–98 (C.A.).
[36] [1936] 1 K.B. 382, 393 (C.A.).

B. The most suitable forum approach

The 1973 House of Lords decision in *The Atlantic Star*[37] began a movement toward relaxing the defendant's burden in a forum non conveniens analysis under English law.[38] Dutch barge owners brought suit against the Dutch owners of a container ship for damages resulting from the container ship's collision with the barge at sea.[39] The defendant argued that the case had absolutely no connection with England other than the container ship's occasional stops in English ports.[40] Lord Reid's opinion demonstrated a reluctance to adopt the Scottish doctrine:

> The appellant's counsel first referred to the law of Scotland, where for a very long time the plea of forum non conveniens has been recognized as valid. No doubt it is a desirable objective to diminish the remaining differences between the laws of the sister countries. But we must proceed with due caution. . . . I cannot foresee all the repercussions of making a fundamental change in English law and I am not at all satisfied that it would be proper for this House to make such a fundamental change or that it is necessary or desirable.[41]

Nevertheless, he indicated clear movement from a strict traditional test to a more liberal modern standard:

> I think that a key to the solution of the problem may be found in a liberal interpretation of what is oppressive on the part of the plaintiff. The position of the defendant must be put in the scales. In the end it must be left to the discretion of the court in each case where a stay is sought, and the question would be whether the defendants have clearly shown that to allow the case to proceed in England would in a reasonable sense be oppressive looking to all the circumstances including the personal position of the defendant.[42]

---

[37]   The Atlantic Star, [1974] A.C. 436 (H.L.) (appeal taken from Eng.).

[38]   *See* Kathryn N. Feldman & Susan M. Vella, *The Evolution of "Forum Conveniens": Its Application to Stays of Proceedings and Service Ex juris*, 10 ADVOCS. Q. 161 (Feb. 1989).

[39]   [1974] A.C. 436, 453 (H.L.) (Lord Reid).

[40]   [1974] A.C. 436, 453 (H.L.).

[41]   [1974] A.C. 436, 453–54 (H.L.).

[42]   [1974] A.C. 436, 454 (H.L.).

Lord Wilberforce provided a list of the factors that weighed in favor of granting the defendant's motion. The factors included that similar proceedings arising out of the collision had already been instituted in Belgium; that witnesses were in Belgium; that Belgian law applied to the action; and that none of the parties was English or had any connection with England other than occasional port stops.[43] While he opposed adopting the Scottish doctrine in England, he joined the move to a liberalization of the *St. Pierre* test:

> It is obvious that this important case depends upon a principle quite distinct from "forum non conveniens." It recognizes an exceptional power capable of being described by reference to "vexation" and "oppression" but shows that these words are to be widely interpreted in relation to the circumstances and in the light of the fact that the court's discretion is general.[44]

Lord Wilberforce found that "too close and rigid an application [of the test] may defeat the spirit which lies behind it and this is particularly true of the words 'oppressive' and 'vexatious.'"[45]

Atlantic Star represented the first major shift away from the strict *St. Pierre* rule, as well as the beginning of a gradual departure from the traditional English attitude that courts should only reluctantly decline to hear a case brought by a foreign plaintiff. The case decisively moved the House of Lords towards a forum non conveniens balancing test in English cases.[46]

The next milestone in English forum non conveniens law was the 1978 case of *MacShannon v. Rockware Glass Ltd.*,[47] where the House of Lords essentially "launched a de facto incorporation of *forum non conveniens* doctrine into English law."[48] In *MacShannon*, Scottish plaintiffs sued English defendants in England because the plaintiffs expected higher damages there, and because there

---

[43]   [1974] A.C. 436, 463 (H.L.) (Lord Wilberforce).

[44]   [1974] A.C. 436, 466 (H.L.).

[45]   [1974] A.C. 436, 468 (H.L.).

[46]   One commentator notes that the law in England on this matter actually was quite unstable after the *Atlantic Star* decision because the Court "had simply crammed a brand-new philosophy into an old vocabulary and conceptual apparatus." David Robertson, *Forum non conveniens in America and England: "A Rather Fantastic Fiction,"* 103 L.Q. REV. 398, 411 (1987).

[47]   [1978] A.C. 795 (H.L.).

[48]   Alexander Reus, *Judicial Discretion: A Comparative View of the Doctrine of Forum Non Conveniens in the United States, the United Kingdom, and Germany,* 16 LOY. L.A. INT'L & COMP. L.J. 455, 478 (1994).

would have been a longer delay in Scottish courts.[49] The Court of Appeal used the case to further refine the test for granting a forum non conveniens stay, moving closer to the Scottish doctrine:

> In order to justify a stay two conditions must be satisfied, one positive and the other negative: (*a*) the defendant must satisfy the court that there is another forum to whose jurisdiction he is amenable in which justice can be done between the parties at substantially less inconvenience and expense, and (*b*) the stay must not deprive the plaintiff of a legitimate personal or juridical advantage which would be available to him if he invoked the jurisdiction of the English court.[50]

While acknowledging the importance of a plaintiff's choice of forum, the *MacShannon* Court held that the plaintiff's advantage in proceeding in England "must be real," and that the plaintiff's genuine belief that he has an advantage is alone not enough.[51] Rather, "the advantage relied upon as a ground for diverting the action from its natural forum must be shown objectively and on the balance of probability to exist."[52] The Court moved from the traditional rule, which placed upon the defendant the burden of proving that the plaintiff would not suffer injustice as the result of dismissal, and instead shifted the burden to the plaintiff to demonstrate that a stay or dismissal would create an injustice.[53] The Court also reiterated Lord Wilberforce's *Atlantic Star* balancing factors, rejecting any requirement that the defendant show vexation or oppression, except to the extent that those terms are "to be broadly and liberally considered."[54]

The dramatic shift effected in *MacShannon* is especially interesting because the Court granted a stay of the action even though the defendant was an English resident. Finding that all the factors pointed to Scotland as "the only natural or appropriate forum,"[55] the Court stressed comity and the deterrence of forum shopping[56] in reformulating the English forum non conveniens test.

---

[49] MacShannon v. Rockware Glass Ltd., [1978] A.C. 795, 812 (H.L) (Lord Diplock).

[50] [1978] A.C. 795, 812 (H.L.).

[51] [1978] A.C. 795, 812 (H.L.).

[52] [1978] A.C. 795, 812 (H.L.).

[53] [1978] A.C. 795, 812 (H.L.).

[54] [1978] A.C. 795, 827 (H.L.). *See also* David Robertson, *Forum Non Conveniens in America and England: "A Rather Fantastic Friction,"* 103 L.Q. REV. 398, 411–12 (1987).

[55] [1978] A.C. 795, 812 (H.L.).

[56] [1978] A.C. 795, 812 (H.L.).

While *MacShannon* did liberalize the test for granting a stay, it was not completely effective in deterring forum shopping.[57] In applying the first prong of the test, subsequent courts seemed to consider whether there was a more natural forum that had the most substantial connection with the litigation.[58] Convenience and expense were important factors in this determination, but they were not always dispositive.[59] Factors such as applicable law, the location of evidence, the availability of witnesses, and the residence of the parties also received weight in the equation applied in determining the most appropriate forum.[60]

The most significant problems came in the application of the second part of the test. Although the House of Lords ruled that a plaintiff's advantages must be objective and real, courts actually gave greater weight to a plaintiff's juridical advantage in England, thus finding a way to refuse to grant forum non conveniens motions even when another forum was arguably more "appropriate."[61]

---

[57] *See* Rhona Schuz, *Controlling Forum Shopping: The Impact of* MacShannon v. Rockware Glass Ltd., 35 INT'L & COMP. L.Q. 374, 408 (1986).

[58] Rhona Schuz, *Controlling Forum Shopping: The Impact of* MacShannon v. Rockware Glass Ltd., 35 INT'L & COMP. L.Q. 374, 381–82 (1986). *See, e.g.*, The *"Forum Craftsman,"* [1985] 1 Lloyd's Rep. 291, 296 (C.A.) (affirming the trial court's analysis that "neither Japan nor England was *the* natural forum"); European Asian Bank A.G. v. Punjab & Sind Bank, [1982] 2 Lloyd's Rep. 356, 363–66 (C.A.) (addressing whether England, India, or Singapore was the natural forum).

[59] *See* Rhona Schuz, *Controlling Forum Shopping: The Impact of* MacShannon v. Rockware Glass Ltd., 35 INT'L & COMP. L.Q. 374, 381 (1986).

[60] *See* Rhona Schuz, *Controlling Forum Shopping: The Impact of* MacShannon v. Rockware Glass Ltd., 35 INT'L & COMP. L.Q. 374, 383 (1986). *See, e.g.*, The Abidin Daver, [1984] A.C. 398, 409 (C.A.) (residence); *The Jalakrishna*, [1983] 2 Lloyd's Rep. 628, 630–33 (Q.B. Adm. Ct.) (evidence); European Asian Bank A.G. v. Punjab & Sind Bank, [1982] 2 Lloyd's Rep. 356, 365 (C.A.) (applicable law).

[61] *See, e.g.*, Castanho v. Brown & Root (U.K.) Ltd., [1981] A.C. 557, 575 (H.L.) (holding that the test for determining whether to grant an anti-suit injunction was governed by *MacShannon*, and that the plaintiff's potential advantage of winning higher damages in the United States tipped the balance in favor of denying such an injunction). *See also* Kathryn N. Feldman & Susan M. Vella, *The Evolution of "Forum Conveniens": Its Application to Stays of Proceedings and Service Ex juris*, 10 ADVOCS. Q. 161, 169 (Feb. 1989) (in *Castanho*, "even though a Portuguese subject was asserting his right to proceed in an American court, the House of Lords was still prepared in the end to do all it could to give freedom to a plaintiff to proceed in his chosen jurisdiction."); Aratra Potato Co. Ltd. v. Egyptian Navigation Co. (The "El Amria"), [1981] 2 Lloyd's Rep. 119, 128–29 (C.A.) (refusing to grant a stay even though the parties had a forum selection clause in which they previously agreed to submit to Egyptian courts in the event of a dispute). *But see* Trendtex Trading Corp. v. Credit Suisse, [1982] A.C. 679, 696 (H.L.) (granting a stay where Switzerland was the more appropriate forum and the parties had previously agreed to submit to Swiss courts in a forum selection clause). This aspect of the development of the doctrine is discussed in Rhona Schuz, *Controlling Forum Shopping: The Impact of* MacShannon v. Rockware Glass Ltd., 35 INT'L & COMP. L.Q. 374, 386 (1986). *See also* Kathryn N. Feldman & Susan M. Vella, *The Evolution of "Forum Conveniens": Its Application to Stays of Proceedings and Service Ex juris*, 10 ADVOCS. Q. 161, 167 (Feb. 1989) ("Despite the softening of the defendant's burden to establish the criteria for a stay, the result of the decision in *MacShannon* was still to leave a plaintiff in the favored position on a stay application.").

The 1983 case of *Astro Exito Navegacion S.A. v. W.T. Hsu (The "Messiniaki Tolmi")*[62] demonstrates an interpretation of *MacShannon* that places emphasis on the plaintiff's juridical advantage. The Commercial Court viewed the test as a three stage process: (1) the defendant's burden to show that Taiwan was the more appropriate forum; (2) the defendant's burden to show that the plaintiffs would not lose any legitimate advantage in Taiwan; and (3) the court's ability to refuse a stay if England would afford the plaintiffs a juridical advantage, even if Taiwan was the more natural forum.[63] The court (even though it obviously interpreted the *MacShannon* test to give great weight to the plaintiffs' choice of forum) engaged in a classic balancing analysis on the first part of the test and ruled that England was the more appropriate forum, thus avoiding consideration of the other stages of the test.[64] The factors addressed by the court included the events giving rise to the action and the residence of the parties and witnesses.[65] The court also gave weight to the applicable law and the existence of multiple proceedings relating to the action already commenced in England, noting that such proceedings made trial in Taiwan inconvenient for the lawyers and parties.[66]

The 1983 case of *Amin Rasheed Shipping Corp. v. Kuwait Ins. Co.*[67] demonstrates the continuing relationship between the forum non conveniens doctrine and rules of jurisdiction. The House of Lords engaged in a forum non conveniens analysis to determine whether the court should exercise jurisdiction from the outset through leave to serve writ outside of England. The Liberian plaintiffs requested leave to serve writ from the English court in order to sue their Kuwaiti insurance company for reimbursement for the loss of the plaintiff's ship.[68] The Court stated:

> [T]he jurisdiction exercised by an English court over a foreign corporation which has no place of business in this country, as a result of granting leave [to serve writ outside of England], is an exorbitant jurisdiction. . . . Comity thus dictates that judicial discretion to grant leave [in this situation] should be exercised with circumspection in cases where there exists an alternative forum.[69]

---

[62] [1983] 1 Lloyd's Rep. 666 (Q.B. Comm. Ct.), *aff'd at* [1984] 1 Lloyd's Rep. 266 (C.A.).

[63] [1983] 1 Lloyd's Rep. 666, 671 (Q.B. Comm. Ct.).

[64] [1983] 1 Lloyd's Rep. 666, 671–74 (Q.B. Comm. Ct.).

[65] [1983] 1 Lloyd's Rep. 666, 671–74 (Q.B. Comm. Ct.).

[66] [1983] 1 Lloyd's Rep. 666, 671–74 (Q.B. Comm. Ct.).

[67] [1984] A.C. 50 (H.L.).

[68] [1984] A.C. 50, 58 (H.L.) (Lord Diplock).

[69] [1984] A.C. 50, 65 (H.L.) (Lord Diplock).

The exorbitance of the jurisdiction sought to be invoked ... is a factor capable of being outweighed if the would-be plaintiff can satisfy the English court that justice either could not be obtained by him in the alternative forum, or could only be obtained at excessive cost, delay or inconvenience.[70]

The opinion thus contains forum non conveniens undertones even though the issue was leave to serve a writ outside England. The major resulting difference came in placing the burden of proof on the plaintiff, with the court reserving discretion to exercise jurisdiction if the plaintiff would have extreme difficulty pursuing its action in another forum. In the end, the Lords refused to grant leave to serve the writ, determining that Kuwait was the most suitable forum, mainly because the only connection with England was the English language used in the insurance contract.[71]

The next major step by the House of Lords toward outright adoption of the more liberal Scottish approach to forum non conveniens came in 1984 in *The Abidin Daver*.[72] Essential to this development was the Court's incorporation of comity principles into its rationale, while at the same time denouncing the heavy weight traditionally given to a plaintiff's juridical advantages in English courts.[73] Cuban plaintiffs sued Turkish defendants in England after a vessel collision. The English defendants had already sued the English plaintiffs in Turkey. This resulted in a request that the English court prevent the second action by deferring to the first seised Turkish court through application of the doctrine of lis alibi pendens.[74] The collision had occurred in Turkish waters, none of the parties had connections with England, the cost of litigating in Turkey was considered to be the same as in England, witness convenience favored the Turkish forum, and the defendants

---

[70] [1984] A.C. 50, 68 (H.L.) (Lord Diplock).
[71] [1984] A.C. 50, 58 (H.L.) (Lord Diplock).
[72] [1984] A.C. 398 (H.L.). *See also* Alexander Reus, *Judicial Discretion: A Comparative View of the Doctrine of Forum Non Conveniens in the United States, the United Kingdom, and Germany*, 16 LOY. L.A. INT'L & COMP. L.J. 455, 478 (1994), noting that "in *The Abidin Daver*, the court confirmed the development towards the 'most suitable forum' approach and, thus, the *de facto* incorporation of the *forum non conveniens* doctrine into the English law."
[73] [1984] A.C. 398, 411.
[74] [1984] A.C. 398, 399.

put up security in England for a judgment in the Turkish court.[75] The Court gave great weight to the existing parallel action and granted the defendant's motion to stay the proceedings:

> The essential change in the attitude of the English courts to pending or prospective litigation in foreign jurisdictions . . . is that judicial chauvinism has been replaced by judicial comity to an extent which I think the time is now ripe to acknowledge . . . [that English law] is indistinguishable from the Scottish legal doctrine of forum non conveniens.[76]

The effect of *The Abidin Daver* was to diminish the strength of the first prong of the *St. Pierre* rule[77]—which *MacShannon* had not done—and to lay a common law foundation for deference to foreign litigation through application of the doctrine of lis alibi pendens.

Thus, it took nearly a century of judicial evolution for the House of Lords to become comfortable with the Scottish doctrine of forum non conveniens. The early twentieth-century English test had placed a heavy burden on the defendant, focusing on whether trial in England would be "oppressive" or "vexatious" to the defendant. While later cases demonstrate a reluctance to take away a plaintiff's right to litigate in England, they ultimately relaxed the heavy burden on the defendant. Cases dealing with issues of lis alibi pendens,[78] forum selection clauses,[79] and requests for leave to serve a writ outside England[80] also contributed to shifting the focus toward the "most suitable forum" balancing test at the core of the Scottish doctrine. This set the stage for the 1986 House of Lords decision that would firmly establish the forum non conveniens doctrine in England.

---

[75]   [1984] A.C. 398, 406.

[76]   [1984] A.C. 398, 411.

[77]   "A mere balance of convenience is not a sufficient ground for depriving a plaintiff of the advantages of prosecuting his action in an English Court if it is otherwise properly brought." St. Pierre v. South American Stores (Goth & Chaves), Ltd. [1936] 1 K.B. 382, 398 (C.A.).

[78]   *See, e.g.,* The Abidin Daver, [1984] A.C. 398 (H.L.).

[79]   *See, e.g.,* Trendtex Trading Corp. v. Credit Suisse, [1982] A.C. 679 (H.L.).

[80]   *See, e.g.,* Amin Rasheed Shipping Corp. v. Kuwait Ins. Co., [1983] 2 All E.R. 884 (H.L.).

C. Modern forum non conveniens doctrine in England

Current application of the doctrine of forum non conveniens in England is defined by *Spiliada Maritime Corp. v. Cansulex Ltd.*,[81] decided in 1986 by the House of Lords. Liberian plaintiffs brought an action in England against Canadian defendants. The Canadian defendants were already defendants in England in a related action (on a separate, but similar, claim) brought by English plaintiffs.[82] Although the issue before the court was whether to grant leave to serve process ex juris on the defendants, the Law Lords determined that the test for granting such leave is essentially the same as the forum non conveniens test for granting a stay of proceedings.[83] Thus, in approving the granting of the Liberian plaintiffs' request for leave to allow service ex juris, the House of Lords expressly acknowledged the doctrine of forum non conveniens as English law, authorizing service and the trial court's retention of the case.[84] Lord Goff of Chieveley summarized the modern English test, focusing on the following elements:

1) "[A] stay will only be granted on the ground of forum non conveniens where the court is satisfied that there is some other available forum, having competent jurisdiction, which is the appropriate forum for the trial of the action."[85]

2) "[I]n general the burden of proof rests on the defendant to persuade the court to exercise its discretion to grant a stay."[86]

3) If jurisdiction is a matter of right in England, as opposed to jurisdiction ex juris in which the plaintiff must request leave to serve the defendant outside the jurisdiction, then "the burden resting on the defendant is not just to show that England is not the natural or appropriate forum

---

[81]   [1987] A.C. 460 (H.L.).

[82]   [1987] A.C. 460, 467 (H.L.).

[83]   [1987] A.C. 460, 467 (H.L.).

[84]   "The Latin tag (sometimes expressed as forum non conveniens and sometimes as forum conveniens) is so widely used to describe the principle, not only in England and Scotland, but in other Commonwealth jurisdictions and in the United States, that it is probably sensible to retain it." [1987] A.C. 460, 474 (H.L.).

[85]   [1987] A.C. 460, 476 (H.L.).

[86]   [1987] A.C. 460, 476 (H.L.). "[I]f the court is satisfied that there is another available forum which is prima facie the appropriate forum for the trial of the action, the burden will then shift to the plaintiff to show that there are special circumstances by reason of which justice requires that the trial should nevertheless take place in this country."

for the trial, but to establish that there is another available forum which is clearly or distinctly more appropriate than the English forum. . . . [I]f in any case, the connection of the defendant with the English forum is a fragile one (for example, if he is served with proceedings during a short visit to this country), it should be all the easier for him to prove that there is another clearly more appropriate forum for the trial overseas."[87]

4) While not every case presents a "'natural forum' . . . 'with which the action had the most real and substantial connection,'"[88] the court must look at connecting factors including (a) the availability of witnesses, (b) the law governing the relevant transaction, and (c) the places where the parties reside or carry on business.[89]

5) If there is no other available forum "which is clearly more appropriate for the trial of the action," the court will refuse a stay.[90]

6) If "there is some other available forum which prima facie is clearly more appropriate for the trial of the action," the court ordinarily will grant a stay.[91] At this point, however, the burden of proof shifts to the plaintiff, who may prove "circumstances by reason of which justice requires that a stay should nevertheless not be granted."[92] Moreover, "[t]he court should [not] be deterred from granting a stay . . . simply because the plaintiff will be deprived of such an advantage, provided that the court is satisfied that substantial justice will be done in the available appropriate forum."[93]

The House of Lords thus applied a forum non conveniens analysis to the question of service ex juris. While it treated the two types of cases similarly, it nonetheless noted important distinctions. Lord Goff of Chieveley found three specific differences in the analysis to be applied in the two types of cases:

> The first is that . . . in the [service ex juris] cases the burden of proof rests on the plaintiff, whereas in the forum non conveniens cases that burden

---

[87]   [1987] A.C. 460, 477 (H.L.).

[88]   [1987] A.C. 460, 477–78 (H.L.) (quoting The Abidin Daver, [1984] A.C. at 415 (Keith of Kinkel, L.)).

[89]   [1987] A.C. 460, 478 (H.L.).

[90]   [1987] A.C. 460, 478 (H.L.).

[91]   [1987] A.C. 460, 478 (H.L.).

[92]   [1987] A.C. 460, 478 (H.L.).

[93]   [1987] A.C. 460, 482 (H.L.).

rests on the defendant. A second, and more fundamental, point of distinction (from which the first point of distinction in fact flows) is that in the
[service ex juris] cases the plaintiff is seeking to persuade the court to exercise its discretionary power to permit service on the defendant outside the
jurisdiction. Statutory authority has specified the particular circumstances
in which that power *may be* exercised, but leaves it to the court to decide
whether to exercise its discretionary power in a particular case, while providing that leave shall not be granted "unless it shall be made sufficiently
to appear to the court that the case is a proper one for service out of the
jurisdiction:"

Third, it is at this point that special regard must be had for the fact . . . that
the jurisdiction exercised under [service ex juris] may be "exorbitant." . . . .
The effect is, not merely that the burden of proof rests on the plaintiff to
persuade the court that England is the appropriate forum for the trial of
the action, but that he has to show that this is clearly so. In other words, the
burden is, quite simply, the obverse of that applicable where a stay is sought
of proceedings started in this country as of right.[94]

Cases immediately following *The Spiliada* yielded mixed results as courts
grappled with the new test.[95] One author finds explanation for these results "on
the basis that . . . 'appropriateness' is not a synonym for 'mere convenience.'
The forum should arguably be *legally* appropriate rather than merely factually
convenient."[96]

In a 1998 Canadian decision, the British Columbia Court of Appeal discussed
at length the history of English forum non conveniens, and aptly summarized

---

[94] [1987] A.C. 460, 480–81 (citations omitted).

[95] *See, e.g.,* De Dampierre v. De Dampierre, [1988] 1 A.C. 92 (H.L.) (granting a stay in favor of a French
forum despite plaintiff's argument that she would lose a juridical advantage in France, because according to French law she would lose all alimony if the court found the divorce was solely the result of her
actions); Charm Maritime Inc. v. Minas Xenophon Kyreakov, [1987] 1 Lloyd's Rep. 433, 447–48 (C.A.)
(refusing to grant a stay where English law applied and the plaintiff had a legitimate juridical advantage
in England, even though other factors such as convenience, events, and residence of parties weighed
heavily towards Greece as the more appropriate forum); DuPont v. Agnew, 2 Lloyd's [1987] L.R. 585,
593–95 (C.A.) (refusing to grant a stay and ruling that the case involved a determination of English public
policy because of an insurance policy at issue, even though there already were concurrent proceedings
in the United States, the events giving rise to the action occurred in the United States, and all witnesses,
evidence, and parties were in the United States).

[96] Helen Helston, *The Spiliada: From Convenience to Propriety,* DENNING L.J. 67, 72–73 (1988).

the major change in English jurisprudence resulting from *The Abidin Daver* and *The Spiliada* as follows:

> Comity, which played no part in the old rule, is now a major consideration. Parallel actions dealing with the same subject matter must now be avoided unless the party resisting the application to stay can demonstrate possible loss of a juridical advantage. The right of the plaintiff to sue in the court of his choice is not now a significant factor. . . . There is now no burden on the applicant to establish that the action would be vexatious, oppressive and/or an abuse of process of the court.[97]

With the *Spiliada* decision, England has joined Scotland, providing substantial uniformity in the application of the doctrine of forum non conveniens within the United Kingdom.

III. The impact of the Brussels Convention and Regulation

When the *Brussels Convention* became effective in U.K. law in 1987 as part of the *Civil Jurisdiction and Judgments Act of 1982*, a new regime of jurisdiction was initiated, and a new gloss was added to U.K. forum non conveniens law.[98] The *Brussels Regulation*,[99] which has since replaced the *Brussels Convention*, provides for uniform rules of jurisdiction within the European Union when a defendant is domiciled in a Member State.

---

[97] 472900 B.C. Ltd. v. Thrifty Can. Ltd., [1998] 168 D.L.R. 4th 602, ¶ 32. *See also* Kathryn N. Feldman & Susan M. Vella, *The Evolution of "Forum Conveniens": Its Application to stays of proceedings and Service Ex juris*, 10 Advocs. Q. 161, 174 (Feb. 1989), stating that "the most important innovation arising out of *The Spiliada* is the reduction in the emphasis and importance of the legitimate personal or juridical advantage of the plaintiff of proceeding in the home jurisdiction."

[98] European Convention on Jurisdiction and Enforcement of Judgments in Civil and Commercial Matters, done at Brussels, 27 September 1968, 41 O.J. Eur. Comm. C 27/1, 26 January 1998 (consolidated and updated version of the 1968 Convention and the Protocol of 1971, following the 1996 accession of the Republic of Austria, the Republic of Finland and the Kingdom of Sweden) [hereinafter Brussels Convention].

[99] On May 1, 1999, the Amsterdam Treaty became effective for the European Union Member States. The resulting amendment to Article 65 of the European Community Treaty transferred competence for coordination of internal rules on jurisdiction and recognition of judgments to the Community institutions. Pursuant to this authority, Council Regulation 44/2001 was promulgated on December 22, 2000 to replace the Brussels Convention. The Regulation became effective, except in Denmark, on March 1, 2002. Council Regulation 44/2001/EC of 22 December 2000 on Jurisdiction and the Recognition and Enforcement of Judgments in Civil and Commercial Matters, 2001 O.J. Eur. Comm. (L 12) 1 [hereinafter Brussels Regulation].

A. The basic framework

The provisions of the *Brussels Regulation* both restrict and cloud the application of the forum non conveniens doctrine. Some of the restrictions include the following:

1) Articles 23 and 24 provide for exclusive jurisdiction in the chosen court when the parties have entered into a valid choice of court agreement;

2) Article 22 lists certain types of cases in which the courts of only one Member State have exclusive jurisdiction;

3) Articles 8–14 provide special rules for jurisdiction in insurance cases;

4) Articles 15–17 provide special rules for jurisdiction in consumer contract cases;

5) Articles 18–21 provide special rules for jurisdiction in employment contract cases; and

6) Articles 27–30 set up a lis alibi pendens regime that requires courts second seised in a matter to defer to the court first seised, allowing no exercise of discretion.

Parallel litigation and forum shopping within the European Union are thus governed by specific *Brussels Regulation* rules when a case falls within its scope, and many of those rules prevent the application of a discretionary doctrine that allows a court to decline to exercise jurisdiction.[100] In a 1997 article, Professor Newman outlined the implications of these rules, categorizing the conflicts between the Regulation and the forum non conveniens doctrine. In doing so, he listed the

---

[100] One early discussion of the impact of the Brussels Convention suggested that:

> English courts *probably* retain a limited discretion to decline jurisdiction in the following situations (a) when a valid forum selection clause calls for litigation in a non-E.E.C. country; (b) when the lawsuit involves real property situated in a non-E.E.C. country; (c) when essentially the same action has already begun in the courts of a non-E.E.C. country; and (d) when suit in England would constitute an abuse of the court's process because seriously vexatious and oppressive to [the] defendant.

David Robertson, *Forum Non Conveniens in America and England: "A Rather Fantastic Fiction,"* 103 L.Q. REV. 398, 427 (1987).

following situations in which the question of the Regulation's effect on a court's ability to consider the forum non conveniens doctrine arises:

> (1) The defendant is domiciled in England, and the competing forum is the court of another [Member] State; (2) [t]he defendant is domiciled in England and the competing forum is the court of a non-[Member] State; (3) [t]he defendant is domiciled in a non-[Member] State, and the competing forum is the court of a non-[Member] State; (4) [t]he defendant is domiciled in a non-[Member] State, and the competing forum is the court of a [Member] State; (5) [t]he same situation obtains [as in (4)]—but the English court takes jurisdiction under a Convention on a particular matter.[101]

In the first category—when both forums involved are in EU Member States and the defendant is domiciled in an EU Member State—the application of forum non conveniens would be inconsistent with the Brussels system, and the doctrine is no longer available.[102] The third category also produces a straightforward answer. The primary nexus of the Convention and Regulation rules is that of the defendant's domicile in an EU Member State. Thus, when the defendant is not domiciled in an EU Member State, and the competing forum is not in a Member State, the Brussels system does not prevent a U.K. court from entertaining a forum non conveniens motion. Newman's second, fourth, and fifth categories present more difficulty.

The second and third categories—when a defendant domiciled in the United Kingdom requests a stay or dismissal in favor of a forum in a non-Member State—were both implicated in the decision by the Court of Appeal in *In Re Harrods (Buenos Aires) Ltd*.[103] The Court concluded that when the other forum is in a non-Member State, exercising discretion to decline valid jurisdiction under forum non conveniens is not inconsistent with the *Brussels Convention*.[104] One Swiss shareholder

---

[101] Justin J. Newman, *Forum Non Conveniens in Europe (Again)*, 3 LLOYD'S MAR. & COM. Q. 337, 338 (1997).

[102] *See, e.g.*, Viking Line ABP. v. The Int'l Transport Workers' Federation, [2005] EWHC 1222, 2005 WL 1410041 ¶ 71 (Q.B. Div (Comm. Ct.)) ("Where a Court has jurisdiction under the Regulation, it cannot refuse to exercise it on the ground that the Courts of another contracting state—or, indeed of a non-contracting state—would be a more suitable forum for resolution of the dispute. The common law notion of *forum non conveniens* has no place in the Regulation.").

[103] [1992] Ch. 72 (C.A.). For discussions of the *Harrods* decision, see Wendy Kennet, *Forum Non Conveniens in Europe*, 54 CAMBRIDGE L.J. 552, 561 (1995) and Trevor Hartley, *The Brussels Convention and* Forum Non Conveniens, 17 EUR. L. REV. 553 (1992).

[104] [1992] Ch. 72, 103 (C.A.).

petitioned for relief regarding an English corporation against the majority Swiss shareholder under the English *Companies Act of 1985* and the *Insolvency Act of 1986*, seeking leave to serve process ex juris on the majority shareholder from the English court.[105] The English corporation was a necessary party defendant to the proceedings.[106] When the Swiss defendant argued that Argentina was forum conveniens, the Court of Appeal applied the *Spiliada* test, holding that Argentina was the more appropriate forum because of the company's overwhelming connections with that forum.[107] This seemed a logical result, at least until the 2005 *Owusu* decision of the European Court of Justice, discussed below.

Professor Newman's fourth and fifth categories—when the defendant is domiciled in a non-Member State and the competing forum is in a Member State—have created further difficulty.[108] In line with *In re Harrods*, English courts presented with such situations continued to allow the plea of forum non conveniens in such cases.[109]

Cases subsequent to *Harrods* followed its analysis, finding the *Brussels Convention* and *Regulation* not to bar the application of the forum non conveniens doctrine when the alternative forum is not in an EU Member State.[110] In *Lubbe v. Cape PLC*,[111] the House of Lords considered an application to stay proceedings in

---

[105] [1992] Ch. 72, 90 (C.A.).

[106] [1992] Ch. 72, 91 (C.A.).

[107] [1992] Ch. 72, 108 (C.A.).

[108] *See* Justin J. Newman, *Forum Non Conveniens in Europe (Again)*, 3 LLOYD'S MAR. & COM. Q. 337, 338–43 (1997).

[109] *See, e.g.*, The "Xin Xang," [1996] 2 Lloyd's Rep. 217 (Adm. Ct.) (permitting Chinese defendants to plead forum non conveniens in favor of the Netherlands, a Member State).

[110] *See, e.g.*, Saab v. Saudi American Bank, [1999] 4 All E.R. 321 (C.A.) (stressing the authority of the trial judge to balance factors and retain jurisdiction or dismiss on forum non conveniens grounds, although Saudi Arabia was not a clearly more appropriate forum); Haji-Ioannou v. Frangos, [1999] 2 Lloyd's Rep. 337 (C.A.) (staying proceedings in England when Greece was a more appropriate forum); Connelly v. RTZ Corp. Plc. (No. 1), [1996] Q.B. 361 (C.A.) (denying a forum non conveniens request although Namibia had more of a connection with the action, because the plaintiff would not be able to try the case in Namibia due to the absence of legal aid).

[111] [2000] 2 Lloyd's Rep. 383, 394 (H.L.) (appeal taken from Eng.) (Lord Bingham of Cornhill). In the lead opinion, at 389, Lord Bingham stated:

> Where a plaintiff sues a defendant as of right in the English Court and the defendant applies to stay the proceedings on grounds of forum non conveniens, the principles to be applied by the English Court in deciding that application in any case not governed by art. 2 of the Brussels Convention are not in doubt.

He went on to cite with approval the forum non conveniens principles set forth in *The Spiliada*. For an in depth discussion of *Lubbe*, see C.G.J. Morse, *Not in the Public Interest?* Lubbe v. Cape PLC, 37 TEX. INT'L L.J. 541 (2002).

England in an action brought by several South African plaintiffs and one English plaintiff against a defendant domiciled in England. The House of Lords denied the application for a stay based on the second prong of the modern English test, finding that differences in systems of legal aid, contingent fee arrangements, and management of group claims rendered it unlikely that the plaintiffs would obtain justice in the alternative forum in South Africa.[112] The defendant argued that Article 2 of the *Brussels Convention* did not prevent the application of forum non conveniens to the case, but the Lords found it unnecessary to decide that issue.[113]

B. Owusu v. Jackson

The path traveled by the Court of Appeal in *Harrods* took an abrupt turn with the 2005 decision by the European Court of Justice in *Owusu v. Jackson*.[114] Mr. Owusu, a British national domiciled in the United Kingdom, brought suit in the United Kingdom against Mr. Jackson (also domiciled in the United Kingdom) and against other defendants domiciled in Jamaica, for injuries sustained by Mr. Owusu while on vacation in Jamaica.[115] After the trial court held that Article 2 of the *Brussels Convention* prohibited the court from staying the proceedings against the U.K. defendant,[116] the Court of Appeal referred the matter to the European

---

[112] [2000] 2 Lloyd's Rep. 383, 392–93 (H.L.).

[113] [2000] 2 Lloyd's Rep. 383, 394 (H.L.). Lord Bingham wrote:

> It is . . . unnecessary to decide whether the effect of art. 2 is to deprive the English Court of jurisdiction to grant a stay in a case such as this. Had it been necessary to resolve that question, I would have thought it necessary to seek a ruling on the applicability of art. 2 from the European Court of Justice, since I do not consider the answer to that question to be clear.

> [2000] 2 Lloyd's Rep. 383, 394 (H.L.). *See also* C.G.J. Morse, *Not in the Public Interest?* Lubbe v. Cape PLC, 37 TEX. INT'L L.J. 541, 556 (2002) (explaining that "the House of Lords did not have to pronounce upon the correctness of [*In re Harrods*] since, in refusing a stay, the court permitted the proceedings to continue in the court of the domicile of the defendant, which has jurisdiction according to Article 2 of the Convention.").

[114] Case C-281/02, Owusu v. Jackson, [2005] E.C.R. I-1383.

[115] Case C-281/02, Owusu v. Jackson, [2005] E.C.R. I-1383, ¶¶ 10–13.

[116] Case C-281/02, Owusu v. Jackson, [2005] E.C.R. I-1383, ¶¶ 17–18. Article 2 of the Brussels Convention provided as follows:

> Subject to the provisions of this Convention, persons domiciled in a Contracting State shall, whatever their nationality, be sued in the courts of that State.

> Persons who are not nationals of the State in which they are domiciled shall be governed by the rules of jurisdiction applicable to nationals of that State.

Court of Justice for a preliminary ruling on the interpretation of the *Brussels Convention*. The resulting decision, while not addressing or changing the basic analysis set forth in *Spiliada* when forum non conveniens is applicable, significantly diminishes the role of the doctrine in the United Kingdom by making it unavailable in Professor Newman's second category of cases (when the defendant is domiciled in the United Kingdom and the competing forum is not in an EU Member State). This, in turn, raises questions about the doctrine's survival in Newman's fourth and fifth categories (when the defendant is not domiciled in an EU Member State, and the competing forum is either in an EU Member State or in another state with which a jurisdiction and judgments convention exists).

The specific question referred to the Court of Justice in *Owusu* was the following:

1. Is it inconsistent with the Brussels Convention . . ., where a claimant contends that jurisdiction is founded on Article 2, for a court of a Contracting State to exercise a discretionary power, available under its national law, to decline to hear proceedings brought against a person domiciled in that State in favour of the courts of a non-Contracting State:

    (a) if the jurisdiction of no other Contracting State under the 1968 Convention is in issue;

    (b) if the proceedings have no connecting factors to any other Contracting State?[117]

The Court answered this question in the affirmative, demonstrating an expansive approach to the application of the *Brussels Convention* (and—it is to be assumed—the *Brussels Regulation*) that substantially diminishes the role of the forum non conveniens doctrine in the United Kingdom.

European Convention on Jurisdiction and Enforcement of Judgments in Civil and Commercial Matters, art. 2, done at Brussels, 27 September 1968, 41 O.J. Eur. Comm. C 27/1, 26 January 1998 (consolidated and updated version of the 1968 Convention and the Protocol of 1971, following the 1996 accession of the Republic of Austria, the Republic of Finland and the Kingdom of Sweden).

[117] Case C-281/02, Owusu v. Jackson, [2005] E.C.R. I-1383, ¶ 22. A secondary question was not reached by the Court: "If the answer to question 1(a) or (b) is yes, is it inconsistent in all circumstances or only in some and if so which?"

Rather than focusing on the fact that the dispute was between British and Jamaican parties, and that the events in question occurred largely in Jamaica, the Court began with a discussion of Article 2 of the *Brussels Convention*, which is the rule establishing general jurisdiction in the courts of the state of the defendant's domicile when the Convention applies.[118] Thus, the Court phrased the initial inquiry as:

> [w]hether Article 2 of the Brussels Convention is applicable in circumstances such as those in the main proceedings, that is to say, where the claimant and one of the defendants are domiciled in the same Contracting State and the case between them before the courts of that State has certain connecting factors with a non-Contracting State, but not with another Contracting State.[119]

In addressing this question, the Court could have found that the purpose of the Brussels Convention was to regulate jurisdiction when a dispute involves the interests of at least two Contracting States. This would have seemed consistent with standard treaty analysis, and with the original authority for the Convention, found in Article 220 (now Article 293) of the Rome Treaty creating the European Economic Community.[120] Article 220 addressed only the recognition and enforcement of judgments, and not jurisdiction. It was not until the completion of the *Brussels Convention* a decade later that a comprehensive system was adopted for the recognition of judgments that would include direct rules of jurisdiction in the originating court. Nonetheless, the Court based its decision in *Owusu* on a determination that the Brussels Convention applies to Contracting State judicial proceedings even when there is no involvement of any other Contracting State "either because of the subject-matter of the proceedings or the respective domiciles of the parties."[121]

While the Court noted that for the Convention to apply, there is the requirement of an "international element" in the case, it found that the "international nature

---

[118] The text of Article 2 is set out in footnote 115, above.

[119] Case C-281/02, Owusu v. Jackson, [2005] E.C.R. I-1383, ¶ 23.

[120] Treaty Establishing the European Community, art. 293 (ex art. 220), O.J. Euro. Comm. C 325/33, 24 Dec. 2002 ["TEC"] (declaring that the Member States of the Community should "enter into [further] negotiations with each other with a view to securing for the benefit of their nationals . . . the simplification of formalities governing the reciprocal recognition and enforcement of judgments of courts or tribunals and of arbitration awards").

[121] Case C-281/02, Owusu v. Jackson, [2005] E.C.R. I-1383, ¶ 26.

of the legal relationship at issue" need not derive from the presence of a party or interest from another Contracting State.[122] The fact that the defendant was from a Contracting State (even though the plaintiff was from the same Contracting State), brought the matter within Article 2, and the fact that other defendants were from Jamaica added the "international element" necessary to keep it within the Convention, even though neither of these relationships involved an interest of, or a party domiciled in, another Contracting State.

The Court justified this position in part by reference to its earlier decisions, stating that "the Court has already interpreted the rules of jurisdiction laid down by the *Brussels Convention* in cases where the claimant was domiciled or had its seat in a non-Contracting State while the defendant was domiciled in a Contracting State."[123] But each of those cases involved diversity of domicile between the plaintiff and a locally-domiciled defendant—not diversity of domicile among defendants in a case brought by a local plaintiff.[124] It is one thing to conclude that Article 2 of the *Brussels Convention* applies to protect persons domiciled in the various Contracting States when suit is brought by a party from another Contracting State or from a non-Contracting State. It is quite another to conclude that the same Article applies to protect a defendant domiciled in the United Kingdom in an action brought by a plaintiff also domiciled in the United Kingdom. The difference is reflected in the irony of the Court's own analysis when it described the purpose of Article 2 as protecting the interests of the defendant in providing predictability in the possible place of suit.[125] What the Court failed to note is that, in *Owusu*, the very defendant whose rights were to be protected by the predictability of Article 2 was the party requesting the application of the

---

[122] Case C-281/02, Owusu v. Jackson, [2005] E.C.R. I-1383, ¶¶ 25–26.

[123] Case C-281/02, Owusu v. Jackson, [2005] E.C.R. I-1383, ¶ 27.

[124] *See* Case C-190/89, Marc Rich & Co. AG v. Società Italiana Impianti PA, [1991] E.C.R. I-3855; Case C-406/92, The Tatry v. The Maciej Rataj, [1994] E.C.R. I-5439; and Case C-412/98, Group Josi Reinsurance Co. SA v. Universal General Ins. Co. (UGIC), [2000] E.C.R. I-5925.

[125] Case C-281/02, Owusu v. Jackson, [2005] E.C.R. I-1383, ¶¶ 40–41:

40. The Court has thus held that the principle of legal certainty requires, in particular, that the jurisdictional rules which derogate from the general rule laid down in Article 2 of the Brussels Convention should be interpreted in such a way as to enable a normally well-informed defendant reasonably to foresee before which courts, other than those of the State in which he is domiciled, he may be sued.

41. Application of the forum non conveniens doctrine, which allows the court seised a wide discretion as regards the question whether a foreign court would be a more appropriate forum for the trial of an action, is liable to undermine the predictability of the rules of jurisdiction laid down by the Brussels Convention, in particular that of Article 2, and consequently to undermine the principle of legal certainty, which is the basis of the Convention.

doctrine of forum non conveniens. The result is the defeat of the defendants' own claims (of forum non conveniens) by way of rules in treaties between states not involved in any way in the specific dispute, through an analysis that claims to be protecting that very defendant.

The *Owusu* Court ultimately determined that the civil law majority of Member State legal systems (those following the lis pendens approach to claims of alternative jurisdiction) wins out over the common law minority (those with a doctrine of forum non conveniens):[126]

> [A]llowing forum non conveniens in the context of the Brussels Convention would be likely to affect the uniform application of the rules of jurisdiction contained therein in so far as that doctrine is recognised only in a limited number of Contracting States, whereas the objective of the Brussels Convention is precisely to lay down common rules to the exclusion of derogating national rules.[127]

Thus,

> the Brussels Convention precludes a court of a Contracting State from declining the jurisdiction conferred on it by Article 2 of that convention on the ground that a court of a non-Contracting State would be a more appropriate forum for the trial of the action even if the jurisdiction of no other Contracting State is in issue or the proceedings have no connecting factors to any other Contracting State.[128]

The Court found it unnecessary to address the Court of Appeal's second question, whether the effect of the *Brussels Convention* is that application of the doctrine of forum non conveniens "is ruled out in all circumstances or only in certain circumstances."[129] Thus, the final death knell for the doctrine in the United Kingdom is left to a later date.

---

[126] This is a rather strange approach to treaty interpretation. The idea that entering into a treaty, with its specific provisions, will subject a state to the application of other rules simply because the majority of other contracting states prefer them in their internal law is contrary to the very contractual nature of treaties and not consistent with any existing rule of treaty interpretation.

[127] Case C-281/02, Owusu v. Jackson, [2005] E.C.R. I-1383, ¶ 43.

[128] Case C-281/02, Owusu v. Jackson, [2005] E.C.R. I-1383, ¶ 46.

[129] Case C-281/02, Owusu v. Jackson, [2005] E.C.R. I-1383, ¶¶ 47–52.

The full impact of *Owusu* may require further litigation and analysis. At the very least, however, it seems to mean that the doctrine of forum non conveniens in the United Kingdom no longer can be applied to any case in which the defendant is domiciled in the United Kingdom. Thus, the domicile of the plaintiff no longer has any bearing on the analysis. The only party that may be able to assert the doctrine may be a defendant domiciled in a state other than an EU Member State, in an action where no other defendant is domiciled in *any* Member State (including the forum state). This is a rather substantial limitation.[130]

IV. Current forum non conveniens analysis in the United Kingdom

While *Owusu* clearly limits the scope of application of the doctrine of forum non conveniens in the United Kingdom, it does not change the substance of that doctrine. As the above discussion indicates, modern U.K. forum non conveniens doctrine involves a blend of traditional Scottish forum non conveniens principles and twentieth century English concerns, often finding application in cases focusing on jurisdiction, service ex juris, anti-suit injunctions, or lis alibi pendens. All of this is further complicated by U.K. membership in the European Union and the existence of the Brussels system now found in the *Brussels Regulation*.

The substance of current U.K. forum non conveniens law involves an analysis designed to determine the most appropriate forum. That analysis is applicable not only after jurisdiction has been established, but also in determining when service ex juris is appropriate, and when an anti-suit injunction might be allowed. The factors to be considered in determining the most appropriate forum are summarized well by Professor Beaumont as follows:

1) The *applicable law* is a relevant factor whenever it has been agreed by the parties or would be the same in the alternative forum. It is a significant factor in favour of the forum that is applying its own law when the issues of law are important to determining the outcome of the case and are complex and disputable.

---

[130] For further discussion of *Owusu* as it relates to issues of party autonomy, see Ronald A. Brand, *Balancing Sovereignty and Party Autonomy in Private International Law: Regression at the European Court of Justice*, in LIBER MEMORIALIS PETAR ŠARČIVIČ: UNIVERSALISM, TRADITION AND THE INDIVIDUAL, 35, 46-51 (Vesna Tomljenovic, ed., 2006).

2) The *fact that litigation is pending in another forum* is a significant factor if the proceedings there have reached a stage which has had some impact upon the dispute between the parties.

3) The *convenience of witnesses* is a relevant factor unless the dispute is primarily one of law and there is little scope for oral evidence but it is rarely a significant factor unless the dispute is primarily factual rather than legal or a considerable amount of evidence is to be given in a foreign language.

4) The *convenience of the parties* is a relevant factor in making it difficult for a defendant to object to being sued in his own forum (the place where he is habitually resident or domiciled) or for a plaintiff to object to the alternative forum when that is his own forum.

5) The *geographical place with which the dispute is closely connected*, e.g., the place of performance of the contractual obligation in question, is a relevant factor.

6) If a *negative declaration is being sought* in one forum and a positive remedy in another forum then this is a factor in favour of the latter forum.

7) If *third parties or other defendants can be joined* to the action in one forum but not in the alternative forum then this is a significant factor in favour of the former.

8) If *related litigation has already taken place in one forum* and not in the alternative forum and this has enabled the lawyers in the former forum to acquire expertise of relevance to the present litigation then this is a relevant factor in favour of the former forum.

9) A forum will be reluctant to decline to exercise jurisdiction if it would require the alternative forum to rule on *questions of public policy* of the former forum that are central to a resolution of the litigation.

10) *Differences between one forum and the alternative forum* in terms of costs, damages and delays are of little or no relevance to determining appropriateness.

11) If the *defendant is unable to state an arguable defence on the merits* in the forum or in the alternative forum then this is a significant factor in favour of the former forum in order to avoid wasting time.

12) The *jurisdiction in which a tort or delict is committed* is prima facie the most appropriate forum to hear the tort or delict action.[131]

The substantive application of the forum non conveniens doctrine and the resulting most appropriate forum analysis remain alive. The *Owusu* decision and related jurisprudence of the European Court of Justice, however, have unequivocally imposed civil law concepts of lis pendens and jurisdictional "certainty" on the U.K. common law system.

The doctrine of forum non conveniens has continued to develop within the courts of the United Kingdom. Nonetheless, the case law of the European Court of Justice—interpreting the *Brussels Regulation* of the European Community—has hastened a trend toward the imposition of civil law concepts on the U.K. common law system. This process now seems overwhelming and is likely to continue to drain the doctrine of forum non conveniens of both purpose and effect in the United Kingdom. The doctrine may only continue to be relevant when a suit is filed against defendants not domiciled in European Union Member States and when the alternative forum is outside the European Union.

As U.K. courts become more accustomed to applying civil law concepts of jurisdiction, traditional common law doctrines such as forum non conveniens are likely to become less germane. Ironically, the courts of England in the early twentieth century first resisted application of the forum non conveniens doctrine—in part because of the belief that they were better-suited to hear international cases than other courts—U.K. courts today are in many cases required to resist application of the doctrine as a matter of European Community law.

---

[131] Paul Beaumont, "Forum Non Conveniens/Lis Pendens," paper presented at the International Association of Lawyers seminar on "The Draft Convention on Jurisdiction and Foreign Judgements in Civil and Commercial Matters", Edinburgh, Scotland, April 20–21, 2001, at 5–6 (paper on file with the authors). *See also* Paul Beaumont, *Great Britain, in* JAMES J. FAWCETT, DECLINING JURISDICTION IN PRIVATE INTERNATIONAL LAW 207 (1995).

CHAPTER 3

The United States

I.   Introduction

In the United States, the doctrine of forum non conveniens has a long history, beginning with cases in the nineteenth century that allowed discretionary dismissal when the parties and the subject matter were unrelated to the forum, gaining direction in a seminal law review article in 1929, and finding definition in two U.S. Supreme Court decisions in 1947. This evolutionary process has continued to the current-day analysis, which requires proof that an alternative forum is available and then follows with a balancing of private and public interests in order to determine whether the trial court should exercise its discretion to stay or dismiss in favor of that foreign forum. Along the way, a "transfer" statute has replaced the doctrine within the federal courts. Moreover, the focus, for the most part, has turned to nuances dealing with such issues as the plaintiff's residence, the extent to which specific factors are determinative in a court's decision to grant a stay or dismissal or simply part of the overall balancing test of convenience, and the order in which a court must address questions of jurisdiction and forum non conveniens.

II.   Early development

The term forum non conveniens first gained attention in the United States in a 1929 *Columbia Law Review* article by Paxton Blair, who noted that "it is apparent that the courts of this country have been for years applying the doctrine."[1]

---

[1]   Paxton Blair, *The Doctrine of Forum non conveniens in Anglo-American Law*, 29 COLUM. L. REV. 1, 22 (1929). While Blair noted that courts considered factors such as the availability of witnesses, the burden on the state's citizens, the possible differences between right and remedy, and the ability to enforce a judgment when a foreign law governed the dispute, he found that the most decisive factor among courts dismissing cases on such grounds was the "complexity of the governing foreign law." Paxton Blair, *The Doctrine of Forum non conveniens in Anglo-American Law*, 29 COLUM. L. REV. 1, 22–23 (1929).

Nonetheless, the practice of courts exercising discretion to decline to exercise jurisdiction can be traced to state and federal judicial decisions in the United States much earlier than was the case in England, Canada, or Australia. The concept was evident as early as 1801 in *Willendson v. Forsoket*,[2] where a federal district court in Pennsylvania declined to exercise jurisdiction over a Danish sea captain who had been sued for back wages by a Danish seaman. The court determined that "[i]f any difference should hereafter arise, it must be settled by a Danish tribunal."[3] The court's dismissal of the case was based on notions of justice and reciprocity, looking very much like the modern approach to forum non conveniens. Other nineteenth and early twentieth century state and federal cases, while acknowledging the existence of jurisdiction, refused to decide cases between foreign parties, arising on foreign soil, and/or requiring the application of foreign law.[4]

While most courts had declined jurisdiction without using the term "forum non conveniens" prior to 1929, at least one clearly referred to it. Bagdon v. Philadelphia & Reading Coal & Iron Co., 165 N.Y.S. 910 (App. Div. 1917) ("This demurrer raises the important question of the power of a state court to decline jurisdiction on the ground of forum non conveniens, or other reason rendering a trial here inexpedient.").

[2]   29 F. Cas. 1283 (D.C. Pa. 1801) (No. 17,682).

[3]   29 F. Cas. 1283, 1284 (D.C. Pa. 1801) (No. 17,682).

[4]   *See, e.g.,* Canada Malting Co. Ltd. v. Paterson Steamships, Ltd., 285 U.S. 413 (1932) (recognizing that discretion to decline otherwise valid jurisdiction was not exclusive to admiralty courts); Slater v. Mexican National R.R. Co., 194 U.S. 120 (1904) (affirming the lower court's decision to dismiss the case after reasoning that the events giving rise to the cause of action occurred in Mexico and Mexican law would govern the action, even though the plaintiffs were U.S. citizens residing in Texas); Collard v. Beach, 87 N.Y.S. 884, 885-86 (N.Y. App. Div. 1904) (stating that "the calendars of the courts of this state are congested, and it being difficult to administer speedy justice to litigants who are obliged to submit their controversies to our courts and have no other forum, it is eminently proper that we should refuse jurisdiction over actions for tort that properly belong in another forum."); The Infanta, 13 F. Cas. 37, 39 (S.D.N.Y. 1848) (No. 7,030) (commenting that the court often "discountenanced actions by foreign seamen against foreign vessels not terminating their voyages at this port, as being calculated to embarrass commercial transactions and relations between this country and others in friendly relations with it."); Johnson v. Dalton, 1 Cow. 543, 548 (N.Y. Sup. Ct. 1823) (stating that "[o]ur courts may take cognizance of torts committed on the high seas on board of a foreign vessel, where both parties are foreigners; but on principles of comity, as well as to prevent the frequent and serious injuries that would result, they have exercised a sound discretion"); Gardner v. Thomas, 14 Johns. 134, 137 (N.Y. Sup. Ct. 1817) (stating "[t]here may be cases . . . where the refusal to take cognizance of causes . . . may be justified by the manifest public inconvenience and injury which it would create to the community of both nations," and holding dismissal was appropriate where both parties were British and the suit arose out of a tort committed on a British vessel at sea); Mason v. Ship Blaireau, 6 U.S. (2 Cranch) 240, 264 (U.S. 1804) (deciding that a case filed in federal district court in Maryland should be heard, but recognizing the court's prerogative to weigh "public convenience" factors to decide whether to maintain jurisdiction where the parties were both foreign).

A. Admiralty roots in the federal courts

Many early federal court decisions declining to exercise jurisdiction involved admiralty jurisdiction.[5] In its 1869 decision in *The Maggie Hammond*,[6] the U.S. Supreme Court noted that, in admiralty cases, considerations of comity affected decisions on whether to exercise otherwise proper jurisdiction.[7] Such statements seemed to establish a clearer rule for declining jurisdiction in admiralty cases, even where a court had proper *in rem* jurisdiction. Limits on the lengths to which the Supreme Court would go in favoring adjudication in a foreign forum were indicated, however, when it stated that "in some cases [a court] will take jurisdiction to prevent loss and injustice, especially if no objection is made by the consul of the nation to which the vessel belongs."[8]

In 1885, in *The Belgenland*,[9] the Supreme Court elaborated on earlier reasoning by Chief Justice Marshall in *Mason v. Ship Blaireau*,[10] stating:

> [C]ircumstances often exist which render it inexpedient for the court to take jurisdiction of controversies between foreigners in cases not arising in the country of the forum; as, where they are governed by the laws of the country to which the parties belong, and there is no difficulty in a resort to its courts; or where they have agreed to resort to no other tribunals. The cases of foreign seamen . . . are often in this category; and the consent of their consul . . . is frequently required before the court will proceed to entertain

---

5   *See, e.g.*, The Infanta, 13 F. Cas. 37, 39 (S.D.N.Y. 1848) (No. 7,030); Mason v. Ship Blaireau, 6 U.S. (2 Cranch) 240, 264 (1804); Willendson v. Forsoket, 29 F. Cas. 1283, 1284 (D. Pa. 1801) (No. 17,682). *See also* John Bies, *Conditioning Forum Non Conveniens*, 67 U. CHI. L. REV. 489, 495 (2000) ("Many of the early cases in which U.S. courts declined jurisdiction arose in admiralty, where a party might obtain jurisdiction by the mere happenstance of a ship stopping at an American port . . . this might be more a function of the higher incidence of foreign parties and distant events in admiralty rather than a restriction of discretion to admiralty.").

6   76 U.S. (9 Wall) 435 (1869).

7   76 U.S. (9 Wall) 435, 450-51(1869):

    [I]n controversies wholly of foreign origin, and between citizens and subjects of the same foreign country, the admiralty courts of the United States will not, in general, entertain jurisdiction to enforce the maritime lien or privilege in favor of shipper or shipowner, in a case . . . where the contract was made or where the cause of action set forth in the libel accrued. . . . . [W]here the lien is given by the maritime law the question in such a case, in the admiralty courts of the United States, is not one of jurisdiction but of comity.

8   76 U.S. (9 Wall) 435, 452 (1869).

9   114 U.S. 355 (1885).

10   6 U.S. (2 Cranch) 240 (1804).

jurisdiction; not on the ground that it has not jurisdiction; but that, from motives of convenience or international comity, it will use its discretion whether to exercise jurisdiction or not.[11]

The Court noted that this determination lies within the discretion of the trial court, and that the trial judge's decision should not lightly be overturned.[12] The Court upheld the trial judge's decision to exercise jurisdiction,[13] even though none of the parties was from the United States and the events leading to the action occurred at sea, reasoning that the law governing the dispute was maritime law which the U.S. court could determine and apply.[14]

Thus, at least in federal admiralty cases, the ability of U.S. courts to decline available jurisdiction was clear throughout the nineteenth century when foreign parties were involved.[15] The position in non-admiralty cases was not so clear-cut, as evidenced by the Supreme Court's statement in 1821 that "[w]e have no more right to decline the exercise of jurisdiction which is given, than to usurp that which is not given."[16]

B. State courts and constitutional issues

Some early non-admiralty decisions in state courts employed discretion-based analysis to decline otherwise valid jurisdiction.[17] Other courts reasoned that discretion to decline valid jurisdiction was prevented by the Privileges and

---

[11]   114 U.S. 355, 363 (1885).

[12]   114 U.S. 355, 368 (1885).

[13]   114 U.S. 355, 368 (1885).

[14]   114 U.S. 355, 368-69 (1885).

[15]   "Even in admiralty, however, no case seems ever to have permitted dismissal of the claim of a United States citizen suing in his own right." Robert Braucher, *The Inconvenient Federal Forum*, 60 HARV. L. REV. 908, 925 (1947).

[16]   Cohens v. Virginia, 19 U.S. (6 Wheat.) 264, 404 (1821). For a list of cases in which the Supreme Court avoided acknowledgment of the authority of non-admiralty courts to decline otherwise valid jurisdiction, see Edward L. Barrett, Jr., *The Doctrine of Forum Non Conveniens*, 35 CAL. L. REV. 380, 394 (1947).

[17]   *See, e.g.*, Collard v. Beach, 87 N.Y.S. 884 (App. Div. 1904); Johnson v. Dalton, 1 Cow. 543 (N.Y. Sup. Ct. 1823); Gardner v. Thomas, 14 Johns. 134 (N.Y. Sup. Ct. 1817). *See* John Bies, *Conditioning Forum Non Conveniens*, 67 U. CHI. L. REV. 489, 496 (2000).

Immunities Clause.[18] This latter approach ultimately lost credence in 1929 with *Douglas v. New York, New Haven & Hartford R.R. Co.*,[19] in which the Supreme Court found constitutional a New York statute that permitted a state court to exercise discretion to decline jurisdiction over a nonresident where the parties and action were more connected with another forum. Nonetheless, the *Douglas* decision "did not result in any widespread movement by the states to adopt the doctrine of *forum non conveniens*,"[20] and most states did not permit discretionary-based dismissals until the mid-twentieth century, when the Supreme Court made clear that the forum non conveniens doctrine was a rule of federal common law.[21]

C. Extending the doctrine beyond admiralty cases

The Supreme Court's shift toward acceptance of the doctrine beyond admiralty cases began in a series of decisions in the first half of the twentieth century. In *Slater v. Mexican National R.R. Co.*,[22] the Court affirmed a dismissal on the basis of forum non conveniens even though the plaintiffs were U.S. citizens residing in Texas, reasoning that the events leading to the action occurred in Mexico and Mexican law would govern the action.[23]

When the *Douglas* decision implicitly removed constitutional concerns from discretionary dismissals, the stage was set for further development of the doctrine. [24]

---

[18] *See, e.g.*, Corfield v. Coryell, 6 Fed. Cas. 546, 552 (E.D. Pa. 1823). The Supreme Court at first implied approval of this position. *See, e.g.*, Ward v. Maryland, 79 U.S. (12 Wall.) 418, 430 (1870) (the Privileges and Immunities Clause "plainly and unmistakably secures and protects the right of a citizen of one State . . . to maintain actions in the courts of the State"). *See also* Edward L. Barrett, Jr., *The Doctrine of Forum Non Conveniens*, 35 CAL. L. REV. 380, 389–90 (1947).

[19] 279 U.S. 377 (1929).

[20] Edward L. Barrett, Jr., *The Doctrine of Forum Non Conveniens*, 35 CAL. L. REV. 380, 393 (1947).

[21] In his 1947 law review article, Barrett found that most states still had not considered the doctrine, that fourteen states had explicitly rejected it, and that only thirteen states had either adopted or selectively employed the doctrine. Edward L. Barrett, Jr., *The Doctrine of Forum Non Conveniens*, 35 CAL. L. REV. 380, 388-89 nn.40-41 (1947).

[22] 194 U.S. 120 (1904).

[23] 194 U.S. 120, 124–25 (1904).

[24] *See, e.g.*, Langnes v. Green, 282 U.S. 531, 544 (1931) ("while the courts of this country have and may entertain jurisdiction of actions between nonresident foreigners for torts committed in a foreign country, they will exercise such jurisdiction in their discretion and only in special cases").

In *Canada Malting Co. Ltd. v. Paterson Steamships, Ltd.*,[25] the Supreme Court explicitly recognized that discretion to decline otherwise valid jurisdiction was not exclusive to admiralty courts. When cargo owners sued in New York for damages resulting from a collision on Lake Superior, the defendants argued that jurisdiction should be declined because Canada was the proper forum for the action.[26] Citing numerous cases for the proposition that courts retain discretionary power to decline otherwise valid jurisdiction, the Court stated:

> Obviously, the proposition that a court having jurisdiction must exercise it, is not universally true; else the admiralty court could never decline jurisdiction on the ground that the litigation is between foreigners. Nor is it true of courts administering other systems of our law. Courts of equity and of law also occasionally decline, in the interest of justice, to exercise jurisdiction, where the suit is between aliens or non-residents or where for kindred reasons the litigation can more appropriately be conducted in a foreign tribunal.[27]

The Court affirmed the district court's decision to decline jurisdiction because, among other reasons, all parties were citizens of Canada, the vessels that collided were Canadian, and the witnesses resided in Canada.[28]

In 1933, the Supreme Court expanded its approach to discretionary authority over jurisdictional decisions in *Rogers v. Guaranty Trust Co. of N.Y.*[29] Shareholders brought suit in New York against the corporation's board of directors, alleging mismanagement.[30] The Court stated:

> While the district court had jurisdiction to adjudge the rights of the parties, it does not follow that it was bound to exert that power. It was free in the exercise of a sound discretion to decline to pass upon the merits of the controversy and to relegate plaintiff to an appropriate forum. . . . [I]t safely may be said that jurisdiction will be declined whenever considerations of convenience, efficiency and justice point to the courts of the State of the

---

25 285 U.S. 413 (1932).

26 285 U.S. 413, 417 (1932).

27 285 U.S. 413, 422–23 (1932).

28 285 U.S. 413, 423 (1932).

29 288 U.S. 123 (1933).

30 288 U.S. 123, 127 (1933).

domicile as appropriate tribunals for the determination of the particular case.[31]

The action in *Rogers* clearly dealt with the internal affairs of the corporation, which were matters governed by New Jersey law, and thus justified the lower court's dismissal of the action in New York.[32]

In 1935, the Supreme Court explicitly stated that a state court could apply the doctrine of forum non conveniens in certain circumstances without violating the Constitution.[33] Nevertheless, the Supreme Court did not yet categorically acknowledge such power for the federal courts. In *Baltimore & Ohio R.R. v. Kepner*,[34] an action against a railroad was brought in New York under the *Federal Employers' Liability Act*, consistent with the venue provision in the Act.[35] The railroad argued that the plaintiff was "acting in a vexatious and inequitable manner in maintaining the federal court suit in a distant jurisdiction when a convenient and suitable [Ohio] forum [was] at [the plaintiff's] doorstep."[36] The Court refused to permit dismissal of the action, stating, "[w]hatever burden there is here upon the railroad, because of inconvenience or cost, does not outweigh the plain grant of privilege for suit in New York."[37]

These cases indicate a tendency on the part of the Supreme Court in the early twentieth century to expand the conditions under which federal courts could

---

[31]   288 U.S. 123, 130–31 (1933) (citations omitted).

[32]   288 U.S. 123, 132 (1933).

[33]   Broderick v. Rosner, 294 U.S. 629, 642-43 (1935). For an extensive list of Supreme Court cases extending situations in which federal courts could decline jurisdiction on forum non conveniens grounds, see Edward L. Barrett, Jr., *The Doctrine of Forum non conveniens*, 35 CAL. L. REV. 380, 395-96 (1947).

[34]   314 U.S. 44 (1941).

[35]   314 U.S. 44, 47 (1941).

[36]   314 U.S. 44, 51 (1941).

[37]   314 U.S. 44, 54 (1941). In his dissenting opinion, Justice Frankfurter argued that the "familiar doctrine of *forum non conveniens*" was "firmly embedded" in United States law. 314 U.S. 44, 55 (1941). Using language strikingly similar to modern day forum non conveniens terminology, he added:

> It does not comport with equity and justice to allow a suit to be litigated in a forum where, on the balance, unnecessary hardship and inconvenience would be cast upon one party without any compensatingly fair convenience to the other party, but where, on the contrary, the suit might more conveniently be litigated in another forum available equally to both parties.

> This doctrine of justice applies with especially compelling force where the conveniences to be balanced are not merely conveniences of conflicting private interests but where there is added the controlling factor of public interest.

314 U.S. 44, 57–58 (1941).

decline otherwise valid jurisdiction for the purposes of convenience and justice, even though such expansion did not go unchecked.[38] Matters were clarified in 1947, however, when the Court took the opportunity provided by a pair of cases to establish the clear foundation of modern forum non conveniens doctrine in the United States.

III. Modern forum non conveniens doctrine

Modern forum non conveniens doctrine in the United States is anchored in three Supreme Court decisions: two in 1947 (*Gulf Oil Corp. v. Gilbert*,[39] *Koster v. Lumbermens Mutual Casualty Co.*),[40] and one in 1981 (*Piper Aircraft Co. v. Reyno*).[41] More recent cases have developed the nuances of the tests they established, but these three decisions continue to provide the core of the analysis.

A. *Gilbert* and *Koster*: the foundations of current doctrine

In *Gilbert*, the Supreme Court for the first time directly faced the question of "whether the United States District Court has inherent power to dismiss a suit pursuant to the doctrine of *forum non conveniens*."[42] A Virginia resident sued a Pennsylvania corporation in federal court in New York, alleging negligence resulting in a fire that did considerable damage to the plaintiff's warehouse in Virginia.[43] The defendant did business in both New York and Virginia, and was properly subject to jurisdiction in both states.[44] The district court dismissed the case on a forum non conveniens motion, finding that the case could be better tried in Virginia.

---

38   *See, e.g.,* Williams v. Green Bay & Western R.R. Co., 326 U.S. 549 (1946) (holding that for a federal court to dismiss a case involving the internal affairs of a corporation, there must be evidence that the suit in the original court would be vexatious and oppressive to the defendant); Meredith v. Winter Haven, 320 U.S. 228, 234 (1943) (holding that a federal court may not dismiss a diversity case on grounds of mere inconvenience or the complexity of ascertaining state law); Baltimore & Ohio R.R. v. Kepner, 314 U.S. 44 (1941) (refusing to grant dismissal on convenience grounds where a federal statute granted venue to the forum at issue).

39   330 U.S. 501 (1947).
40   330 U.S. 518 (1947).
41   454 U.S. 235 (1981).
42   330 U.S. 501, 502 (1947).
43   330 U.S. 501, 502 (1947).
44   330 U.S. 501, 503 (1947).

The Second Circuit Court of Appeals reversed, but the Supreme Court ultimately agreed with the trial court.[45] Justice Jackson stated that, in U.S. courts, "the proposition that a court having jurisdiction must exercise it, is not universally true."[46] He also found the doctrine of forum non conveniens to apply specifically when jurisdiction does exist, noting that it "can never apply if there is absence of jurisdiction or mistake of venue."[47]

The *Gilbert* decision made clear that when more than one forum is available the doctrine of forum non conveniens gives the trial court substantial discretion. It also set the basic parameters for the application of the doctrine:

> In all cases in which the doctrine of *forum non conveniens* comes into play, it presupposes at least two forums in which the defendant is amenable to process; the doctrine furnishes criteria for choice between them.

> The principle of *forum non conveniens* is simply that a court may resist imposition upon its jurisdiction even when jurisdiction is authorized by the letter of a general venue statute.

> . . . .

> Wisely, it has not been attempted to catalogue the circumstances which will justify or require either grant or denial of remedy. The doctrine leaves much to the discretion of the court to which plaintiff resorts, and experience has not shown a judicial tendency to renounce one's own jurisdiction so strong as to result in many abuses.[48]

Such discretion is to be used judiciously, however, and while "the plaintiff may not, by choice of an inconvenient forum, 'vex,' 'harass,' or 'oppress' the defendant by inflicting upon him expense or trouble not necessary to his own right to pursue his remedy . . . unless the balance is strongly in favor of the defendant, the plaintiff's choice of forum should rarely be disturbed."[49]

---

[45] 330 U.S. 501, 503 (1947).

[46] 330 U.S. 501, 504 (1947) (quoting from the decision of Justice Brandeis in Canada Malting Co., Ltd. v. Paterson Steamships, Ltd., 285 U.S. 413, 422–23 (1932)).

[47] 330 U.S. 501, 504 (1947).

[48] 330 U.S. 501, 506–08 (1947) (citation omitted).

[49] 330 U.S. 501, 508 (1947).

As guidance for determining when a court should stay or dismiss a case in favor of another forum, the *Gilbert* decision set out factors to be considered, grouping them into private and public interest categories:

> An interest to be considered, and the one likely to be most pressed, is the private interest of the litigant. Important considerations are the relative ease of access to sources of proof; availability of compulsory process for attendance of unwilling, and the cost of obtaining attendance of willing, witnesses; possibility of view of premises, if view would be appropriate to the action; and all other practical problems that make trial of a case easy, expeditious and inexpensive. There may also be questions as to the enforcibility of a judgment if one is obtained. The court will weigh relative advantages and obstacles to fair trial. It is often said that the plaintiff may not, by choice of an inconvenient forum, "vex," "harass," or "oppress" the defendant by inflicting upon him expense or trouble not necessary to his own right to pursue his remedy. But unless the balance is strongly in favor of the defendant, the plaintiff's choice of forum should rarely be disturbed.
>
> Factors of public interest also have place in applying the doctrine. Administrative difficulties follow for courts when litigation is piled up in congested centers instead of being handled at its origin. Jury duty is a burden that ought not to be imposed upon the people of a community which has no relation to the litigation. In cases which touch the affairs of many persons, there is reason for holding the trial in their view and reach rather than in remote parts of the country where they can learn of it by report only. There is a local interest in having localized controversies decided at home. There is an appropriateness, too, in having the trial of a diversity case in a forum that is at home with the state law that must govern the case, rather than having a court in some other forum untangle problems in conflict of laws, and in law foreign to itself.[50]

The Court ultimately held that the district court's decision to dismiss on forum non conveniens grounds was correct because neither party was from New York; all events leading to the action occurred in Virginia; all witnesses were in Virginia; and trial in New York would be a burden on the citizens and the district court in

---

[50] 330 U.S. 501, 508–09 (1947) (footnote omitted).

New York, specifically with regard to jury duty and conflict of laws analyses.[51] Like both the original Scottish doctrine and the modern U.K. approach, the *Gilbert* decision indicates that any attempt to provide an exhaustive list of factors to be balanced is quite difficult.

In *Koster v. Lumbermens Mutual Casualty Co.*,[52] decided the same day as *Gilbert*, the Court addressed questions about the application of the forum non conveniens doctrine with regard to the relationship between parties and the forum. A policyholder of a mutual insurance company brought a derivative action in a New York federal district court against defendants from Illinois, alleging breach of fiduciary duties.[53] With Justice Jackson again writing for the majority, the Court emphasized the strong deference usually accorded to the plaintiff's choice of forum:

> Where there are only two parties to a dispute, there is good reason why it should be tried in the plaintiff's home forum if that has been his choice. He should not be deprived of the presumed advantages of his home jurisdiction except upon a clear showing of facts which either (1) establish such oppressiveness and vexation to a defendant as to be out of all proportion to plaintiff's convenience, which may be shown to be slight or nonexistent, or (2) make trial in the chosen forum inappropriate because of considerations affecting the court's own administrative and legal problems. In any balancing of conveniences, a real showing of convenience by a plaintiff who has sued in his home forum will normally outweigh the inconvenience the defendant may have shown.[54]

---

[51] 330 U.S. 501, 510–11 (1947). In his dissent, Justice Black expressed favor for a court exercising jurisdiction if it exists, and for the proposition that any authority to do otherwise should emanate from the legislature. He characterized the majority's holding as a clear balancing of conveniences:

> The Court does not suggest that the federal district court in New York lacks jurisdiction under this statute or that the venue was improper in this case. But it holds that a district court may abdicate its jurisdiction when a defendant shows to the satisfaction of a district court that it would be more convenient and less vexatious for the defendant if the trial were held in another jurisdiction.

330 U.S. 501, 512–13 (1947) (Black, J., dissenting) (citations omitted).

[52] 330 U.S. 518 (1947).

[53] 330 U.S. 518, 519 (1947).

[54] 330 U.S. 518, 524 (1947). Professor Robertson has criticized the Court's fashioning of the *Forum Non Conveniens* test in *Gilbert* and *Koster* as being too limited and similar to the Scottish doctrine and what was then used in English courts, rather than the more modern "appropriate forum" test:

> In its narrow holding, *Gilbert* was probably an abuse of process decision. . . . [T]he Court's opinion was vague, and it was ambiguous as well, setting forth a "private interest" approach

Despite such deference to the plaintiff's choice, however, the Court ultimately held dismissal on forum non conveniens grounds to be proper in the trial court since in a derivative suit the individual plaintiff acts on behalf of all similarly situated persons, and in a matter involving internal affairs of a corporation, the conveniences often weigh in favor of the forum in which the corporation is located. While such suits are not required to be resolved in the home forum of the corporation, "the ultimate inquiry is where trial will best serve the convenience of the parties and the ends of justice,"[55] and the "plaintiff was utterly silent as to any reason of convenience to himself or to witnesses and as to any advantage to him in expense, speed of trial, or adequacy of remedy if the case were tried in New York."[56]

A close reading of *Gilbert* and *Koster* together indicates that while a plaintiff's choice of forum is important, it can be overridden in the name of justice.[57] This sharply diverged from English jurisprudence at the time regarding discretionary dismissals.[58]

B. Federal transfer rules

In 1947, *Gilbert* and *Koster* settled the questions of (1) whether forum non conveniens was the law in the United States, and (2) the structure of its application in federal courts. The following year, a major legislative development narrowed the

---

approximately tracking the abuse of process version of *forum non conveniens* right alongside a "public interest" approach that reflected the most suitable forum philosophy. . . . Thus, *Gilbert* opened the way for development of a transnational *forum non conveniens* doctrine, but offered almost no guidance as to its proper scope.

David W. Robertson, *Forum Non Conveniens in America and England: "A Rather Fantastic Friction,"* 103 L.Q. REV. 398, 401 (1987). Nonetheless, while the *Gilbert* court used words such as "vexatious" and "abuse of process" to describe the required effect on the defendant, the incorporation of private and public balancing factors, and the heavy emphasis in *Koster* on public factors, more closely approximate a "more suitable forum" approach than an "abuse of process" approach.

[55] 330 U.S. 518, 527 (1947).

[56] 330 U.S. 518, 531 (1947).

[57] *See* Douglas W. Dunham & Eric F. Gladbach, *Forum Non Conveniens and Foreign Plaintiffs in the 1990s,* 24 BROOK. J. INT'L L. 665, 669 (1999) (noting that while both cases emphasized that a plaintiff's chosen forum should not be easily disturbed, "this presumption in favor of the plaintiff's choice may be overcome by a showing that the relevant private and public interest factors clearly outweigh the deference to be afforded to plaintiff's selected forum").

[58] *See* Chapter 2, Part II.A., above.

scope of the doctrine in the federal courts when Congress enacted section 1404(a) of Title 28 of the *U.S. Code*—a venue provision that transformed the way in which federal courts handle problems of forum shopping and docket congestion. Section 1404(a) provides that "[f]or the convenience of parties and witnesses, in the interest of justice, a district court may transfer any civil action to any other district or division where it might have been brought."[59] This provision had a significant effect on both the role and scope of forum non conveniens in diversity cases, virtually eliminating dismissals based on forum non conveniens in federal courts where all parties to the suit are from the United States. Under section 1404(a), a transfer is both easier to obtain (its requirements are more liberal than the test for granting a dismissal based on forum non conveniens) and more available (while only the defendant may request dismissal based on forum non conveniens, either party may move for a transfer of venue under section 1404(a)) than dismissal on grounds of forum non conveniens.[60]

C. Jurisdictional developments limiting the need for forum non conveniens

Two additional developments relating to jurisdiction have further limited the scope of application of the forum non conveniens doctrine in U.S. courts.[61]

---

[59] 28 U.S.C. § 1404(a) (2001).

[60] *See* Alexander Reus, *Judicial Discretion: A Comparative View of the Doctrine of Forum Non Conveniens in the United States, the United Kingdom, and Germany*, 16 Loy. L.A. Int'l & Comp. L.J. 455, 466 (1994) (stating that "venue transfers deprived *forum non conveniens* of its foundation, necessity and original designation as domestic law, causing an unintended extension of the doctrine's applicability to mainly international cases."). In Norwood v. Kirkpatrick, 349 U.S. 29 (1955), the Court explained the difference between venue transfers under section 1404(a) and forum non conveniens dismissals. Under forum non conveniens a court dismisses entirely a case upon a clear showing that the case would be best adjudicated in another more appropriate forum, whereas a court may transfer a case (without dismissal) to another forum "upon a lesser showing of inconvenience." 349 U.S. 29, 31–32 (1955). Thus, the venue-transfer statute was not "a mere codification of *forum non conveniens*." *See also* Cunningham v. Ford Motor Co., 413 F. Supp. 1101, 1105 (D.C.S.C. 1976) (noting that section 1404(a) is much more liberal than the forum non conveniens test); Simon v. Silfen, 247 F. Supp. 762, 763 (S.D.N.Y. 1965) (commenting that section 1404(a) is an improvement over forum non conveniens because a plaintiff is guaranteed another forum in which to sue, and the provision does not limit the authority of federal courts to dismiss a case on forum non conveniens grounds where a state court is the more convenient forum).

[61] For summaries of how jurisdictional developments affected forum non conveniens in the United States by decreasing the number of situations in which a plaintiff could sue a defendant in an "inconvenient" forum, see John Bies, *Conditioning Forum non conveniens*, 67 U. Chi. L. Rev. 489, 498 (2000), and Jacqueline Duval-Major, *One-Way Ticket Home: The Federal Doctrine of Forum Non Conveniens and the International Plaintiff*, 77 Cornell L. Rev. 650, 663–70 (1992).

The refinement of the "minimum contacts" due process analysis, which limits the reach of state long-arm statutes through cases such as *International Shoe Co. v. Washington*,[62] *World-Wide Volkswagen Corp. v. Woodson*,[63] and *Asahi Metal Industry Co., Ltd. v. Superior Court of California*,[64] can result in jurisdictional dismissals that preempt any forum non conveniens analysis.[65] In addition, the Supreme Court's decision in *Shaffer v. Heitner*[66]—holding that jurisdiction over a nonresident defendant may not be based solely on the presence of the defendant's intangible property in the state where that property is unrelated to the cause of action—has limited *in rem* jurisdiction over a nonresident defendant having scarce connections with a forum, thus eliminating a major category of cases in which forum non conveniens might be alleged.

D. Refinement in the Supreme Court: *Piper Aircraft*

The 1981 Supreme Court decision in *Piper Aircraft Co. v. Reyno*[67] served to refine further the modern U.S. doctrine of forum non conveniens. Scottish plaintiffs brought a wrongful death action in California state court against the defendants Piper and Hartzell, two American corporations who had manufactured the engine and propellers of the plane involved in the crash that killed the plaintiffs' decedents.[68] The plaintiffs admitted to forum shopping in order to obtain the most favorable laws regarding liability, capacity to sue, and damages.[69] The case

---

[62]   326 U.S. 310 (1945).

[63]   444 U.S. 286 (1980).

[64]   480 U.S. 102 (1987).

[65]   *See* Jacqueline Duval-Major, *One-Way Ticket Home: The Federal Doctrine of Forum Non Conveniens and the International Plaintiff*, 77 CORNELL L. REV. 650, 663 (1992) (citations omitted):

> The doctrine of *forum non conveniens* has diminished in importance given the modern development of the "minimum contacts" test for personal jurisdiction. The increased reliance by courts on the "minimum contacts" notion of personal jurisdiction, when taken in concert with modern applications of venue and subject matter jurisdiction, satisfies requirements of fairness and reasonableness embedded in the Due Process Clause of the Fifth Amendment. A proper personal jurisdiction inquiry should dispose of many cases in which the choice of forum is truly inconvenient.

> For a discussion of the evolution of the "minimum contacts" test generally, see Ronald A. Brand, *Due Process, Jurisdiction, and a Hague Judgments Convention*, 60 U. PITT. L. REV. 661, 669-87 (1999).

[66]   433 U.S. 186 (1977).

[67]   454 U.S. 235 (1981).

[68]   454 U.S. 235, 239 (1981).

[69]   454 U.S. 235, 240 (1981).

was removed to a California federal district court under 29 U.S.C. § 1441, and then transferred to a Pennsylvania federal district court under Section 1404(a), where the defendants moved for dismissal on forum non conveniens grounds.[70] The district court engaged in a classic *Gilbert* balancing analysis and determined that Scotland was an alternative, appropriate forum, despite the fact that the law there was less favorable to the plaintiff.[71] As a condition to the dismissal, the defendants agreed to waive any statute of limitation defenses and to submit to the jurisdiction of the courts of Scotland.[72] The Third Circuit Court of Appeal determined that dismissal was inappropriate because Scottish law would be less favorable to the plaintiff.[73]

The Supreme Court rejected the idea that differences in substantive law should prevent dismissal:

> The Court of Appeals erred in holding that plaintiffs may defeat a motion to dismiss on the ground of *forum non conveniens* merely by showing that the substantive law that would be applied in the alternative forum is less favorable to the plaintiffs than that of the present forum. The possibility of a change in substantive law should ordinarily not be given conclusive or even substantial weight in the *forum non conveniens* inquiry.[74]

Thus, "dismissal on grounds of *forum non conveniens* may be granted even though the law applicable in the alternative forum is less favorable to the plaintiff's chance of recovery."[75] This does not, however, prevent a difference in substantive law from being a factor in the forum non conveniens analysis. Notably, "if the remedy provided by the alternative forum is so clearly inadequate or unsatisfactory that it is no remedy at all, the unfavorable change in law may be given substantial weight; the district court may conclude that dismissal would not be in the interests of justice."[76]

---

[70] 454 U.S. 235, 241 (1981).
[71] 454 U.S. 235, 241 (1981).
[72] 454 U.S. 235, 242 (1981).
[73] 454 U.S. 235, 244 (1981).
[74] 454 U.S. 235, 247 (1981).
[75] 454 U.S. 235, 250 (1981).
[76] 454 U.S. 235, 254 (1981).

In refining the forum non conveniens inquiry, the *Piper* decision makes clear that the first step is a determination that an adequate alternative forum exists.[77] If it does, then the court must apply the private interest and public interest analysis set out in *Gilbert*. The *Piper* majority read *Koster* to require that the "plaintiff's choice of forum is entitled to greater deference when the plaintiff has chosen the home forum,"[78] thus justifying more favorable treatment of a resident or citizen plaintiff than of a foreign plaintiff. This distinction, however, does not appear to have been based on the nationality of the party so much as on the determination of convenience in applying the private factors test of *Gilbert*:

> When the home forum has been chosen, it is reasonable to assume that this choice is convenient. When the plaintiff is foreign, however, this assumption is much less reasonable. Because the central purpose of any *forum non conveniens* inquiry is to ensure that the trial is convenient, a foreign plaintiff's choice deserves less deference.[79]

The Court weighed the private interest factors, finding it particularly important that the witnesses and the accident site were in Great Britain, that only some evidence would be found in the United States, and that the most interested plaintiffs were Scottish.[80] With regard to the public interest factors, the Court noted that the necessary application of the laws of both nations would result in complex applicable law determinations, and that the trial would be costly and result in burdens to the citizens of Pennsylvania who had no real interest in the litigation.[81]

The Supreme Court's next major pronouncement on the modern doctrine of forum non conveniens came in *American Dredging Co. v. Miller*.[82] Writing for the majority, Justice Scalia stated that the doctrine "is nothing more or less than a supervening venue provision, permitting displacement of the ordinary rules of venue when, in light of certain conditions, the trial court thinks that jurisdiction ought to be declined."[83] He emphasized that the doctrine has developed in response

---

[77]   454 U.S. 235, 254 n.22 (1981).

[78]   454 U.S. 235, 255 (1981).

[79]   454 U.S. 235, 255–56 (1981).

[80]   454 U.S. 235, 242 (1981).

[81]   454 U.S. 235, 242–43 (1981).

[82]   510 U.S. 443 (1994).

[83]   510 U.S. 443, 455 (1994).

to court administration and private litigant problems that often result from a plaintiff's misuse of venue. Thus, the doctrine serves to discourage plaintiffs from forum shopping.[84] Yet, as Justice Scalia noted, "[t]he discretionary nature of the doctrine, combined with the multifariousness of the factors relevant to its application . . . make uniformity and predictability of outcome almost impossible."[85] This lack of uniformity is accepted, however, because the doctrine serves as a procedural rule, and not as a substantive rule affecting the primary conduct of litigants.[86]

Piper thus elaborated on concepts of forum non conveniens as derived from Scotland and adopted in *Gilbert* and *Koster*, while at the same time refining the doctrine as it now applies in courts of the United States. Any forum non conveniens analysis must begin with a finding that there is an alternative, appropriate forum,[87] and the court may condition a dismissal on grounds that guarantee the practical availability of such a forum.[88] The next step is to engage in the *Gilbert* balancing of private interest[89] and public interest[90] factors. The plaintiff's choice

---

[84]   510 U.S. 443, 450 (1994).

[85]   510 U.S. 443, 463 (1994).

[86]   510 U.S. 443, 454 n.4 (1994).

[87]   Only on rare occasion is this requirement not satisfied. *See, e.g.*, Bhatnagar v. Surrendra Overseas Ltd., 52 F.3d 1220 (3d Cir. 1995) (holding that excessive delay in processing the action in the alternative Indian jurisdiction was extreme enough to render that forum inadequate); *In re* Silicone Gel Breast Implants Product Liability Litigation, 887 F. Supp. 1469 (N.D. Ala. 1995) (dismissing actions brought by some foreign plaintiffs against various United States-based manufacturers for harm caused from defective breast implants, but retaining a New Zealand plaintiff's action because a New Zealand statute prevented a remedy in her home forum).

[88]   *See* David W. Robertson, *Forum Non Conveniens in America and England: "A Rather Fantastic Friction,"* 103 L.Q. REV. 398, 408 (1987) ("Nowadays dismissal is almost always conditioned on defendant's promise to submit to the jurisdiction of the foreign tribunal, waive the benefit of any statute of limitations that has accrued during the pendency of the United States action, and abide by the judgment of the foreign court."); Douglas W. Dunham & Eric F. Gladbach, *Forum Non Conveniens and Foreign Plaintiffs in the 1990s*, 24 BROOK. J. INT'L L. 665, 690–91 (1999) (noting that courts often impose conditions on service of process, statutes of limitation defenses, and enforcement of judgments, although discovery remains an area of dispute among courts). *See also In re* Union Carbide Corp. Gas Plant Disaster at Bhopal, 809 F.2d 195 (2d Cir. 1986), *cert. denied*, 484 U.S. 871 (1987) (letting stand the District Court's conditions that the defendant submit to the jurisdiction of India and waive any statute of limitations defenses, but rejecting conditions that the defendant agree in advance to the enforceability of an Indian judgment and accept discovery in India according to the Federal Rules of Civil Procedure).

[89]   *See* Baumgart v. Fairchild Aircraft Corp., 981 F.2d 824 (5th Cir. 1993) for an example of the modern trend in assessing private interest factors.

[90]   Public interest factors usually found to favor dismissal include lack of local interest in the dispute, complex choice of law determinations, and administrative burdens. *See* Douglas W. Dunham & Eric F. Gladbach, *Forum Non Conveniens and Foreign Plaintiffs in the 1990s*, 24 BROOK. J. INT'L L. 665, 675–78 (1999).

of a forum with more favorable law is not dispositive, and the presence of a foreign plaintiff necessarily makes the forum less convenient than if the plaintiff is domestic.[91]

E. Forum non conveniens and international comity

A party to U.S. litigation will sometimes raise both forum non conveniens and international comity as parallel doctrines supporting dismissal in favor of a foreign forum. While the two doctrines are related in terms of demonstrating respect for foreign forums, they differ somewhat in their application.

The doctrine of international comity originated in the writings of seventeenth century Dutch scholars, was imported into English common law by Lord Mansfield,[92] and crystallized in U.S. law by Joseph Story, who described comity between nations as "an imperfect obligation" which "cannot be reduced to any certain rule,"[93] which is appropriately applied due to "mutual interest and utility."[94] In 1895, the U.S. Supreme Court provided its oft-cited definition of comity in *Hilton v. Guyot*:[95] "the recognition which one nation allows within its territory to the legislative, executive or judicial acts of another nation, having due regard both to international duty and convenience, and to the rights of its own citizens or of other persons who are under the protection of its laws."[96]

Discussions of comity arise in three principal contexts implicating judicial relations with foreign states. The most prominent context, in which the doctrine has been most notably developed, is in the recognition of foreign judgments.[97] The second is in determining when it is appropriate to apply U.S. law extraterritorially— the question of jurisdiction to prescribe.[98] Here, a balancing test is often

---

[91]   *See* the discussion of Iragorri v. United Technologies Corp., 274 F.3d 65 (2d Cir. 2001), below.

[92]   *See* Joel R. Paul, *Comity in International Law*, 32 HARV. INT'L L.J. 1, 13–19 (1991).

[93]   JOSEPH STORY, COMMENTARIES ON THE CONFLICT OF LAWS §§ 28, 33 (8th ed. 1883) (*quoting* Saul v. His Creditors, 5 Mart. (n.s.) 569, 5950596 (La. 1827)).

[94]   *Id.* § 35.

[95]   159 U.S. 113 (1895).

[96]   159 U.S. 113, 164.

[97]   *See, e.g.*, Hillton v. Guyot, 159 U.S. 113 (1895); Somportex Ltd. v. Philadelphia Chewing Gum Corp., 453 F.2d 435, 440 (3d Cir. 1971), *cert. denied*, 405 U.S. 1017 (1972).

[98]   *See* RESTATEMENT (THIRD) FOREIGN RELATIONS LAW §§ 402–04 (1986).

applied to determine whether it is appropriate to apply domestic law to parties or events occurring outside the United States.[99]

The third use of comity deals directly with the issue of declining to exercise jurisdiction, and occurs most often when there is parallel foreign litigation to which the U.S. court is asked to defer.[100] Thus, when "adjudication of [the] case by a United States court would offend 'amicable working relationships' with" another country,[101] such "comity among courts" is viewed as "a discretionary act of deference by a national court to decline to exercise jurisdiction in a case properly adjudicated in a foreign state."[102] This type of comity is often applied in bankruptcy proceedings when a matter is appropriately left to insolvency proceedings already filed in a foreign court.[103]

The existence of parallel foreign litigation to which the U.S. court is asked to defer is a principal difference between the concept of international comity and the doctrine of forum non conveniens. Forum non conveniens is appropriately raised even when no foreign action has been commenced, while the application of international comity involves a stay or dismissal when there is parallel litigation already filed in a foreign forum.

> Similar to the doctrine of forum non conveniens, principles of international comity allow a . . . court to exercise its discretion and dismiss a case over which it has subject matter jurisdiction in deference to the laws and interests of another nation. . . . . These principles permit a court to engage in "a spirit of international cooperation." . . . . They do not, however, extend judicial deference to those cases whose dismissal would be contrary to

---

[99] See, e.g., Hartford Fire Ins. Co. v. Calif., 509 U.S. 764 (1993); Mannington Mills, Inc. v. Congoleum Corp., 595 F.2d 1287 (3d Cir. 1979); Timberlane Lumber Co. v. Bank of Am. Nat'l Trust & Savings Ass'n, 549 F.2d 597 (9th Cir. 1976).

[100] Some would place comity analysis within a forum non conveniens analysis as part of the review of public interest factors to be considered once it is determined that an alternative appropriate forum exists. See, e.g., Radeljak v. DaimlerChrysler Corp., ___ N.W.2d ___, 2006 WL 2022233 at *9–*12 (Mich. 2006) (Markman, J., concurring).

[101] Bigio v. Coca-Cola Co., 448 F.3d 176, 178 (2d Cir. 2006).

[102] See, e.g., In re Maxwell Comm. Corp., 93 F.3d 1036, 1047 (2d Cir. 1996); Cornfeld v. Investors Overseas Services, Ltd., 471 F. Supp. 1255 (1979).

[103] See, e.g., JP Morgan Chase Bank v. Altos Hornos de Mexico, S.A. de C.V., 412 F.3d 418, 423 (2d Cir. 2005).

domestic public policy. . . . . Nor do they compel dismissal when the suits in question are neither duplicative nor parallel.[104]

A foreign action is considered to be "parallel" to the U.S. litigation when

substantially all the same parties are contemporaneously litigating substantially the same issues in another forum. . . . . While the cases are not required to be identical, 'the issues must be sufficiently similar, in that there must be a 'substantial likelihood that the [foreign] litigation will dispose of all claims presented in the [U.S.] case."[105]

Once it is determined that a parallel case exists, additional factors are considered:

Even the existence of a "parallel" case, however, need not compel dismissal. "[A] district court should exercise jurisdiction over an action even where identical subject matter is concurrently before a foreign court." . . . . Dismissal for reasons of international comity is appropriate only in "extraordinary circumstances." Such circumstances include: (i) duplicative litigation, (ii) inconvenience of the domestic forum, (iii) the governing law, (iv) the order in which jurisdiction was obtained, (v) the relative progress of each proceeding, and (vi) the "contrived nature' of the domestic claim."[106]

It is not necessary that all of these factors exist in order for a court to grant deference to foreign proceedings under an international comity analysis. As with forum non conveniens, where the law of the foreign court governs the proceedings, this seems to weigh quite heavily.[107]

---

[104] Lexington Ins. Co. v. Forrest, 263 F. Supp. 2d 986, 1002 (E.D. Pa. 2003), *quoting* Paraschos v. YBM Magnex Int'l, Inc., 2000 WL 325945 at *5–*6 (E.D. Pa. 2000).

[105] Hay Acquisition Co., I, Inc. v. Schneider, 2005 WL 1017804 at *11 (E.D. Pa. 2005) *quoting from* Paraschos v. YBM Magnex Int'l, Inc., 2000 WL 325945 at *5 (E.D. Pa. 2000) and Lumen Constr., Inc. v. Brant Constr. Co., 780 F.2d 691, 695 (7th Cir. 1985).

[106] Lexington Ins. Co. v. Forrest, 263 F. Supp. 2d 986, 1002 (E.D. Pa. 2003), *quoting* Paraschos v. YBM Magnex Int'l, Inc., 2000 WL 325945 at *5–*6 (E.D. Pa. 2000).

[107] *See, e.g.,* Hay Acquisition Co., I, Inc. v. Schneider, 2005 WL 1017804 (E.D. Pa. 2005); Paraschos v. YBM Magnex Int'l, Inc., 130 F. Supp. 2d 642 (E.D. Pa. 2000).

F. Discretion to Dismiss in Whole or in Part

While the doctrine of forum non conveniens most often is used to seek full dismissal of all aspects of an action before a court, nothing in that doctrine (or in the doctrine of international comity) prevents a court from dismissing part of the case and retaining other parts of the case when it is appropriate to do so. A number of state statutes—based on the now-withdrawn *Uniform Interstate and International Procedure Act*[108]—specifically authorize dismissal of part of an action at the discretion of the trial court,[109] and both state and federal courts have acknowledged the authority to dismiss some claims under the doctrine of forum non conveniens while retaining others, or to dismiss claims against some parties while retaining claims against others.[110]

---

[108] Uniform Interstate and International Procedure Act, 13 U.L.A. 355 (1986 ed.).

[109] *See, e.g.,* ARK. CODE ANN. § 16-4-101 ("When the court finds that in the interest of substantial justice the action should be heard in another forum, the court may stay or dismiss the action in whole or in part on any conditions that may be just."); CAL. CIV. PROC. CODE § 410.30(a) ("the court shall stay or dismiss the action in whole or in part on any conditions that may be just"); MASS. GEN. LAWS ANN. ch. 223A § 5 (2006) ("the court may stay or dismiss the action in whole or in part on any conditions that may be just"); MD Code, Courts and Judicial Proceedings, § 6-104 ("the court may stay or dismiss the action in whole or in part on any conditions it considers just"); NEB. REV. STAT. § 25-538 ("the court may stay or dismiss the action in whole or in part on any conditions it considers just"); N.Y. C.P.L.R. § 327(a) ("the court on the motion of any party, may stay or dismiss the action in whole or in part on any conditions that may be just"); 12 OKLA. STAT. ANN. § 1701.05 ("the court may stay or dismiss the action in whole or in part on any conditions it considers just"); 42 PA. CONS. STAT. ANN. § 5322(e) ("the tribunal may stay or dismiss the matter in whole or in part on any conditions that may be just"); TEX. CODE ANN., CIVIL PRACTICE & REMEDIES CODE § 71.051 (Vernon's) ("the court may stay or dismiss the action in whole or in part on any conditions it considers just").

[110] *See, e.g.,* Bacardi v. De Lindzon, 728 So. 2d 309 (1999), *review granted,* 743 So. 2d 11 (Fla. 1999), *decision approved,* 845 So. 2d 33 (Fla. 2002) ("We disagree with the contention that the trial court is compelled to dismiss the action in favor of one alternative forum when severance of the disparate claims is appropriate. . . . . A trial court is accorded 'substantial flexibility' in ruling on a forum non conveniens issue. . . . Thus, the trial court may consider discrete claims in dismissing a portion of a case pursuant to a forum non conveniens motion."); Banco Latino v. Lopez, 17 F. Supp. 2d 1327 (S.D. Fla. 1998) (ordering severance of claims and granting dismissal based on forum non conveniens as to the claims of some plaintiffs but not as to others); Ciba-Geigy Ltd. v. Fish Peddler, Inc., 691 So. 2d 1111, 1116–17 (Fla. Dist. Ct. App. 1997) (reversing district court's denial of fourth-party defendants' motion to dismiss on forum non conveniens grounds only against certain of the plaintiffs); Cooper Industries v. Continental Ins. Co., No L-15947-91 (N.J. Super. Essex County, May 14, 1993), *reported in* Mealey's Litigation Reporter-Insurance, July 1, 1993, at § F (rejecting Cooper's argument that forum non conveniens may not be used to dismiss portions of a larger insurance coverage dispute); Hsu v. Chang, 606 N.Y.S.2d 1009 (1993) (granting plaintiff's motion to dismiss parts of defendant's counterclaims—but not all—on the basis of forum non conveniens, under N.Y. C.P.L.R. § 327(a)). *See also* Duha v. Agrium, Inc., 448 F.3d 867, 886 (6th Cir. 2006) (Cole, J., dissenting) ("I have found no requirement that a district court, when faced with a motion on *forum non conveniens* grounds, either dismiss the entire complaint on *forum non conveniens* gounds or none of it.").

G. The nationality of the plaintiff

The idea that lesser weight should be given to the forum choice of a non-resident plaintiff was an issue in *Piper*, where the Court stated that the forum choice of a foreign plaintiff "deserves less deference" than does the choice of a domestic plaintiff.[111] Courts and commentators have wrestled with the role of this factor in current-day forum non conveniens analysis. The issue first appeared in the Supreme Court in *Swift & Co. Packers v. Compania Colombiana del Caribe*,[112] when the Court stated that the "[a]pplication of *forum non conveniens* principles to a suit by a United States citizen against a foreign respondent brings into force considerations very different from those in suits between foreigners."[113] In *Piper*, it is important to note that the Court's statement about reduced deference was not a naked statement, but rather tied to the issue of convenience:

> When the home forum has been chosen, it is reasonable to assume that this choice is convenient. When the plaintiff is foreign, however, this assumption is much less reasonable. Because the central purpose of any forum non conveniens inquiry is to ensure that the trial is convenient, a foreign plaintiff's choice deserves less deference.[114]

More recently, in *Iragorri v. United Technologies*,[115] the Second Circuit Court of Appeals rendered an *en banc* decision in which it explained its rationale for the difference in treatment of domestic and foreign plaintiffs in the forum non conveniens analysis. In that opinion, the Court stated:

> Based on the Supreme Court's guidance, our understanding of how courts should address the degree of deference to be given to a plaintiff's choice of a U.S. forum is essentially as follows: The more it appears that a domestic or foreign plaintiff's choice of forum has been dictated by reasons that the law recognizes as valid, the greater the deference that will be given to the plaintiff's forum choice. Stated differently, the greater the plaintiff's or the lawsuit's bona fide connection to the United States and to the forum of choice and the more it appears that considerations of convenience favor

---

[111] Piper Aircraft v. Reyno, 454 U.S. 235, 257 (1981).

[112] 339 U.S. 684 (1950).

[113] 339 U.S. 684, 697 (1950).

[114] Piper Aircraft v. Reyno, 454 U.S. 235, 257 (1981).

[115] 274 F.3d 65 (2d Cir. 2001).

the conduct of the lawsuit in the United States, the more difficult it will be for the defendant to gain dismissal for *forum non conveniens*. Thus, factors that argue against *forum non conveniens* dismissal include the convenience of the plaintiff's residence in relation to the chosen forum, the availability of witnesses or evidence to the forum district, the defendant's amenability to suit in the forum district, the availability of appropriate legal assistance, and other reasons relating to convenience or expense. On the other hand, the more it appears that the plaintiff's choice of a U.S. forum was motivated by forum-shopping reasons—such as attempts to win a tactical advantage resulting from local laws that favor the plaintiff's case, the habitual generosity of juries in the United States or in the forum district, the plaintiff's popularity or the defendant's unpopularity in the region, or the inconvenience and expense to the defendant resulting from litigation in that forum—the less deference the plaintiff's choice commands and, consequently, the easier it becomes for the defendant to succeed on a *forum non conveniens* motion by showing that convenience would be better served by litigating in another country's courts.[116]

---

[116] 274 F.3d 65, 71–72 (2d Cir. 2001). The Second Circuit had invited the U.S. Attorney General to file an amicus curiae brief on this issue, including comments on "how, if at all, the question presented is affected by treaty obligations of the United States, including any treaty obligations concerning reciprocal access to courts by nationals of other countries." 274 F.3d 65, 69 n.2 (2d Cir. 2001). The Justice Department declined the request, but provided some comment in a letter in response to the request. The *Iragorri* opinion summarizes the Department's letter as follows:

> The DOJ began by acknowledging that "the United States is a party to a number of treaties that include various obligations regarding access to courts, including in some treaties an obligation to grant 'national treatment,'" generally meaning that "nationals of the other party to the treaty are entitled to access to U.S. courts on terms no less favorable than those enjoyed by U.S. nationals 'in like situations.'".... The DOJ then articulated three points that it believed pertinent to our framing of standards for forum non conveniens analysis. First, the DOJ noted that "the Supreme Court has already made clear that the fact that the plaintiff is a citizen or resident of the United States is relevant but not dispositive in a forum non conveniens analysis.".... Second, the DOJ observed that "any right to court access afforded to a foreign national plaintiff by treaty will generally be only a right to the same access that would be accorded to a U.S. national plaintiff who is otherwise similarly situated.".... Third, the DOJ posited that "even if citizenship or nationality per se were held to be dispositive in otherwise evenly balanced cases, and even if national treatment provisions were interpreted under some circumstances to require that the same tie-breaking rule be applied in favor of those non-national plaintiffs who are entitled to the benefit of treaties that include such provisions, ... it is not obvious that applying such provisions in that way would necessarily be either unworkable or inappropriate."

274 F.3d 65, 69 n.2 (2d Cir. 2001) (quoting from Letter from Att'y Michael J. Singer, Appellate Staff, Civil Div., U.S. Dep't of Justice, to Roseann B. MacKechnie, Clerk of Court, of 5/15/01).

Such an analysis seems to provide proper balance between the impact of a local plaintiff's choice of a local forum on determinations of convenience and questions of discrimination against foreign plaintiffs in a forum non conveniens analysis. Recent cases are likely to continue to fuel the debate about proper balancing or improper discrimination, however. The Eleventh Circuit found a clear presumption in favor of a domestic plaintiff's choice of forum, reversing the District Court's determination of an equal balance of private interest factors:

> This presumption in favor of the plaintiffs' initial forum choice in balancing the private interests is at its strongest when the plaintiffs are citizens, residents, or corporations of this country. . . . [I]n this Circuit we have long mandated that district courts "require positive evidence of unusually extreme circumstances, and should be thoroughly convinced that material injustice is manifest before exercising any such discretion as may exist to deny a United States citizen access to the courts of this country."[117]

This analysis does not necessarily mean that a foreign plaintiff's choice of forum should be given lesser weight as a matter of arbitrary discriminatory practice. A recent Second Circuit opinion in fact reversed the district court's forum non conveniens dismissal precisely because the district court appeared "to have given the [foreign] plaintiff's choice of forum no weight whatsoever."[118] Citing its decision in *Iragorri*, the court stated:

> [T]he more that a plaintiff, even a foreign plaintiff, chooses to sue in a United States court for "legitimate reasons," the more deference must be given to that choice. . . . . Furthermore, even where the degree of deference is reduced, "[t]he action should be dismissed only if the chosen forum is shown to be genuinely inconvenient and the selected forum significantly preferable."[119]

If the Second Circuit has come down on the side of consideration of the nationality of the plaintiff simply as one factor in a convenience analysis, the Sixth Circuit has staked out the position most strongly favoring a domestic plaintiff.

---

[117] SME Racks v. Sistemas Mecanicos Para Electronica, 382 F.3d 1097, 1001 (11th Cir. 2004) (internal citations omitted).

[118] Bigio v. Coca-Cola Co., 448 F.3d 176, 179 (2d Cir. 2006).

[119] 448 F.3d 176, 179.

In *Duha v. Agrium, Inc.*,[120] the majority revisited an earlier decision that had appeared to be consistent with the Second Circuit analysis in *Iragorri*,[121] and instead relied on language from the Supreme Court's opinion in *Koster* to determine that "the standard of deference for a U.S. plaintiff's choice of a home forum permits dismissal only when the defendant 'establish[es] such oppressiveness and vexation to a defendant as to be out of all proportion to plaintiff's convenience, which may be shown to be slight or nonexistent.'"[122] Thus, the Sixth Circuit seemed to hold not only that a U.S. plaintiff is entitled to a heightened level of deference in its choice of forum, but that, when the plaintiff is domestic, the otherwise abandoned "oppressiveness and vexation" test is resurrected.[123] Judge Cole, dissenting in the *Duha* decision, provides a rather convincing argument that the majority not only misapplied *Piper*, but its own Sixth Circuit precedent.[124]

The Supreme Court, in its 2007 decision in *Sinochem Int'l Co. Ltd. v. Malaysia Int'l Shipping Corp.*,[125] seemed to come down on the side of the Second Circuit in this distinction, when Justice Ginsburg included the following passage in her opinion written for a unanimous court:

> A defendant invoking *forum non conveniens* ordinarily bears a heavy burden in opposing the plaintiff's chosen forum. When the plaintiff's choice is not its home forum, however, the presumption in the plaintiff's favor "applies with less force," for the assumption that the chosen forum is appropriate is in such cases "less reasonable."[126]

This language supports the position that the relevant dicta in *Piper* simply means that when there is a local plaintiff there is a greater likelihood of a connection

---

[120]   448 F.3d 867 (6th Cir. 2006).

[121]   Kryvicky v. Scandinavian Airlines Sys., 807 F.2d 514, 517 (6th Cir. 1986).

[122]   448 F.3d at 873–74, *quoting* Koster v. Lumbermens Mutual Casualty Co., 330 U.S. 518, 524 (1947).

[123]   *See also* DiRienzo v. Philip Servx. Corp., 294 F.3d 21, 30 (2d Cir. 2002) (in a suit brought by a U.S. plaintiff, stating "plaintiffs should not have been deprived of their choice of forum except upon defendants' clear showing that a trial in the United States would be so oppressive and vexatious to them as to be out of all proportion to plaintiffs' convenience").

[124]   *See* Duha v. Agrium, Inc., 448 F.3d 867, 884 (6th Cir. 2006) (Cole, J., dissenting) (citing Kryvicky v. Scandinavian Airlines Sys., 807 F.2d 514, 517 (6th Cir. 1986) and Stewart v. Dow Chem. Co., 865 F.2d 103, 105 (6th Cir. 1989) as being "clear in their requirement that a 'high standard would constitute a misreading of *Piper* and its progeny'").

[125]   ___ U.S. ___, 127 S.Ct. 1184 (2007).

[126]   *Id.* at 127 S.Ct. 1191, quoting Piper Aircraft Co., 454 U.S., at 255–256.

with the forum than when there is a foreign plaintiff. While the presumption in favor of the plaintiff's choice of forum has "less force" when the plaintiff is foreign, it nonetheless applies.

A special group of cases on this issue involves application of *Treaties of Friendship, Commerce and Navigation* (FCN Treaties). FCN treaties consistently include a provision requiring nondiscriminatory treatment of each state's nationals in the courts of the other state. Some courts have applied a domestic plaintiff standard to foreign plaintiffs from countries that are party to such a treaty with the United States. These courts have reasoned that the plaintiff's residence cannot be a factor in the analysis if it is in a country that has an FCN treaty with the United States.[127] While some commentators have tried to advance this approach,[128] Professor Weintraub provides a convincing rebuttal when he states that, "if a treaty guarantees citizens of other countries equal access to our courts with U.S. citizens, a court that would deny access to a non-resident U.S. citizen is free to deny access to a non-resident citizen of another country."[129] The Second Circuit Court of Appeals has adopted this rule as well:

> Plaintiffs are only entitled, at best, to the lesser deference afforded a U.S. citizen living abroad who sues in a U.S. forum. This was precisely the level of deference the district court assigned plaintiffs' choice of forum: it gave them the same initial deference in choosing a United States court as it would a United States citizen discounted by the fact that plaintiffs are not residents of the United States.[130]

---

[127] *See, e.g.,* Irish Nat'l Ins. Co. Ltd. v. Aer Lingus Teoranta, 739 F.2d 90 (2d Cir. 1984) (giving the foreign plaintiff's choice of forum the same weight as that of a domestic plaintiff because the United States had such a treaty with Ireland); Complaint of Maritima Aragua, S.A., 823 F. Supp. 143, 150 (S.D.N.Y. 1993) ("[b]ecause [an FCN] treaty exists between the United States and Venezuela . . . no discount may be imposed upon the initial choice of a New York forum solely because certain of the plaintiffs are Venezuelan corporations."); Roman v. Aviateca, 120 F.3d 265 (5th Cir. 1997), 1996 U.S. Dist. LEXIS 21789 (1996) (not giving plaintiff equal access rights to the United States court because an FCN Treaty between the United States and Nicaragua had been abolished). *Compare* Murray v. British Broad. Corp., 81 F.3d 287 (2d Cir. 1996) (refusing to give a foreign plaintiff's choice of forum the same deference as a domestic plaintiff's choice even though an international convention provided that any copyright action would be governed by the laws of the jurisdiction in which a plaintiff sought relief).

[128] *See, e.g.,* Jordan J. Paust, *"Equal Treaty Rights," Resident Status & Forum Non Conveniens*, 23 Hou. J. Int'l L. 405 (2004).

[129] Russell J. Weintraub, *"Equal Treaty Rights": A Response to Professor Paust*, 27 Hous. J. Int'l L. 241, 242–43 (2005).

[130] Pollux Holding Ltd. v. Chase Manhattan Bank, 329 F.3d 64, 73 (3d Cir. 2003), *cert. denied*, 540 U.S. 1149 (2004).

While such logic would seem to put the matter to rest, it is likely that some courts and commentators will keep the issue open.

The Second Circuit's analysis in *Iragorri* is both logical and consistent with the language of the Supreme Court in both *Gilbert*[131] and *Sinochem*.[132] Nonetheless, the debate on whether considering the plaintiff's nationality or domicile in balancing private interests is appropriate probably will continue, especially where the defendant is a U.S. corporation.[133] Forum non conveniens is often an issue when a U.S. corporate defendant is sued by foreign plaintiffs in connection with personal injuries resulting from corporate activities abroad. A significant number of decisions in federal courts have found that the defendant in such circumstances has satisfied its burden of proof, and have dismissed with conditions.[134] The effect of a forum non conveniens dismissal may be outcome determinative, meaning that the suit is never brought in the alternative, more "appropriate" forum. Some commentators have viewed this as an unfair reaction by courts hoping to deter plaintiffs from forum shopping in already congested courts.[135]

---

[131] 454 U.S. 235, 255–56 (1981).

[132] ___ U.S. ____, S.Ct. 1184, 1191 (2007).

[133] *See, e.g.,* Douglas W. Dunham & Eric F. Gladbach, *Forum Non Conveniens and Foreign Plaintiffs in the 1990s,* 24 Brook. J. Int'l L. 665, 666–67 (1999):

> American courts have become . . . "extremely attractive" to foreign plaintiffs because of the availability of jury trials, liberal discovery rules, malleable choice of law rules, contingency fees and potentially large compensatory and punitive damage awards. . . . [T]he clear trend in the 1990s has been for American courts to dismiss actions brought by foreign plaintiffs under products liability theories of recovery.

See also Jacqueline Duval-Major, *One-Way Ticket Home: The Federal Doctrine of Forum Non Conveniens and the International Plaintiff,* 77 Cornell L. Rev. 650, 658 (1992), stating that "in most modern applications of forum non conveniens, foreign plaintiffs' forum choices now face a presumption of inconvenience in suits against United States-based MNCs."

[134] For a discussion of these cases, see John Bies, *Conditioning Forum Non Conveniens,* 67 U. Chi. L. Rev. 489, 500–01 (2000).

[135] *See* David W. Robertson, *Forum Non Conveniens in America and England: "A Rather Fantastic Friction,"* 103 L.Q. Rev. 398, 417-21 (1987) (arguing that "American courts' overt reliance on calendar congestion as a standard reason for dismissing cases tips the scales far too heavily against retaining jurisdiction, [which] comes into obvious conflict with the system's need for 'justice.'"). *See also* Jacqueline Duval-Major, *One-Way Ticket Home: The Federal Doctrine of Forum Non Conveniens and the International Plaintiff,* 77 Cornell L. Rev. 650, 671–72 (1992), discussing the various scenarios that may render it infeasible or impossible for a foreign plaintiff to sue a U.S. company in an available alternative forum. Forum non conveniens in this context, she argues, is simply an effective tool used by U.S. corporate

The frequency of forum non conveniens dismissals in cases involving foreign plaintiffs and U.S. corporate defendants remains a contested topic. Despite judicial analysis, such as that in *Iragorri* and *Sinochem*, tending to make this simply one factor in the convenience analysis when an alternative forum is available, some commentators question whether application of the modern doctrine by U.S. courts produces just results in a wide range of tort claims against U.S. corporations.[136]

H. Parallel litigation and forum selection clauses

While the test fashioned by the U.S. Supreme Court turns on appropriateness and convenience—with the latter of these determined by a balancing of public and private interest factors—two additional considerations may also come into play in a forum non conveniens analysis. These are the existence of parallel litigation in a foreign court, and the presence of a forum selection clause. The existence of parallel proceedings abroad is not dispositive in a forum non conveniens analysis, but may be an important factor.[137] Thus, the lis pendens approach of the *Brussels Regulation*, discussed in Chapter 2, is not followed in U.S. courts.

The presence of a valid forum selection clause, however, often has primary significance in the analysis. The Supreme Court, in two major decisions on the

---

defendants to avoid trial for harm caused by their products in foreign countries. 77 CORNELL L. REV. 650, 679-80 (1992). *But cf.* William L. Reynolds, *The Proper Forum for a Suit: Transnational Forum Non Conveniens and Counter-Suit Injunctions in the Federal Courts*, 70 TEX. L. REV. 1663, 1704 (1992) (discussing the expansion of long-arm jurisdiction, and arguing that "[t]he effect of that expansion has been to make it possible to bring litigation in a forum that has significantly less connection with the cause of action than other forums where it might have been brought.").

136   *See, e.g.*, Phillip I. Blumberg, *Asserting Human Rights Against Multinational Corporations Under United States Law: Conceptual and Procedural Problems*, 50 AM. J. COMP. L. 493 (2002); Matthew R. Skolnick, *The Forum Non Conveniens Doctrine in Alien Tort Claims Act Cases: A Shell of its Former Self After WIWA*, 16 EMORY INT'L L. REV. 187 (2002); Malcolm J. Rogge, *Towards Transnational Corporate Accountability in the Global Economy: Challenging the Doctrine of Forum Non Conveniens in* In Re Union Carbide, Alfaro, Sequihua, and Aguinda, 36 TEX. INT'L L.J. 299 (2001).

137   *See* William L. Reynolds, *The Proper Forum for a Suit: Transnational Forum Non Conveniens and Counter-Suit Injunctions in the Federal Courts*, 70 TEX. L. REV. 1663, 1676 (1992) ("The presence of related litigation abroad is another powerful factor favoring dismissal. There are significant advantages in having all the parties interested in apportioning a limited source of recovery assert their claims in one forum, not only to avoid inconsistent factual findings, but also 'to spare the litigants the additional costs of duplicate lawsuits.' . . . Superior American interests and a belief that the plaintiff only filed the action abroad as a 'defensive measure' may persuade the court to keep the action at home.") (footnote omitted).

viability of forum selection clauses, has emphasized that such clauses are presumptively valid, thus limiting situations in which a defendant may obtain dismissal based on forum non conveniens.[138] Although there is no bright line rule regarding the interplay of forum selection clauses with forum non conveniens, cases indicate that such clauses, especially when they are exclusive, often require favoring the chosen court, regardless of convenience factors.[139] This is an important issue, and is discussed in detail in Chapter 9, below.

---

[138] Carnival Cruise Lines, Inc. v. Shute, 499 U.S. 585 (1991); The Bremen v. Zapata Off-Shore Co., 407 U.S. 1 (1972).

[139] *See, e.g.*, General Elec. Co. v. G. Siempelkamp GmbH & Co., 29 F.3d 1095 (6th Cir. 1994) (dismissing the case on forum non conveniens grounds in favor of German courts in accordance with the choice of court clause in the sales contract); Omron Healthcare Inc. v. Maclaren Exports, Ltd., 28 F.3d 600 (7th Cir. 1994) (applying forum non conveniens analysis to enforce an English choice of court clause in a distributorship contract); Mercier v. Sheraton Int'l, Inc., 981 F.2d 1345 (1st Cir. 1992) (applying forum non conveniens analysis despite an apparently exclusive choice of court clause, but dismissing in favor of the Turkish court named in the clause); Northwestern Nat'l. Ins. Co. v. Donovan, 916 F.2d 372, 378 (7th Cir. 1990) (holding that the agreement to an exclusive forum selection clause constituted a waiver of objections to venue on the basis of cost or inconvenience to the party); Royal Bed & Spring Co. v. Famossul Industria E Comercio de Moveis Ltda., 906 F.2d 45 (1st Cir. 1990) (enforcing a Brazilian choice of court clause in a distributorship agreement under a *Bremen* analysis and granting dismissal); Heller Financial, Inc. v. Midwhey Powder Co., 883 F.2d 1286 (7th Cir. 1989) (denying a motion for dismissal or transfer under 28 U.S.C. § 1404(a) in the face of a forum selection clause); ACEquip, Ltd. v. Am. Eng'g Corp., 153 F. Supp. 2d 138 (D. Conn. 2001) (denying a motion to dismiss in favor of a Japanese court when a mandatory choice of court clause designated a Connecticut forum); Poddar v. State Bank of India, 79 F. Supp. 2d 391 (S.D.N.Y. 2000) (denying dismissal where a clause created mandatory jurisdiction in courts in both India and the United States); Skyline Steel Corp. v. RDI/Caesars Riverboat Casino, LLC, 44 F. Supp. 2d 1337, 1337-38 (N.D. Ala. 1999) (sending the case to the chosen forum under 28 U.S.C. § 1404(a), while stating that "the law of the Eleventh Circuit is that forum selection clauses are virtually impossible to overcome by an application of the general principles of *forum non conveniens*."); A.C. Sudduth v. Occidental Peruana, Inc., 70 F. Supp. 2d 691 (E.D. Tex. 1999) (denying the defendant's motion to dismiss on forum non conveniens grounds only after determining that a mandatory choice of court clause was invalid under the *Bremen* standards); Cambridge Nutrition A.G. v. Fotheringham, 840 F. Supp. 299 (S.D.N.Y. 1994) (enforcing a New York choice of court clause despite a motion to dismiss brought by the Spanish defendant for whom trial in New York was inconvenient); TUC Electronics, Inc. v. Eagle Telephonics, Inc., 698 F. Supp. 35 (D. Conn. 1988) (dismissing a case brought in Connecticut in the face of a New York state court choice of court clause, applying a combination of *Bremen* and forum non conveniens factors). *But see* Blanco v. Banco Industrial de Venezuela, S.A., 997 F.2d 974 (2d Cir. 1993) (affirming a dismissal on forum non conveniens grounds even though New York was one of three jurisdictions named in a non-exclusive choice of court clause); Magellan Real Estate Inv. Trust v. Losch, 109 F. Supp. 2d 1144 (D.C. Ariz. 2000) (denying dismissal in favor of the Ontario court named in a non-exclusive clause); S & D Coffee, Inc. v. GEI Autowrappers, 995 F. Supp. 607 (M.D.N.C. 1997) (denying dismissal in favor of the English court named in a non-exclusive clause).

I. State or federal law?

The Supreme Court has not provided a clear answer to the question of whether forum non conveniens is a matter of state or federal law. In *Piper Aircraft Co. v. Reyno*, the Court specifically noted this issue, but left it unresolved.[140]

In *American Dredging Co. v. Miller*,[141] the Supreme Court considered the nature of the doctrine of forum non conveniens in the context of a maritime case in a Louisiana state court. The Court described the doctrine of forum non conveniens as "procedural," reasoning that "[a]t bottom, the doctrine of forum non conveniens is nothing more or less than a supervening venue provision. . . . . But venue is a matter that goes to process rather than substantive rights—determining which among various competent courts will decide the case."[142] While this language did not involve a clear determination of whether the forum non conveniens doctrine should be considered procedural for *Erie* purposes, five Federal Circuit Courts of Appeal have conducted *Erie* doctrine inquiries in the context of forum non conveniens motions in diversity cases, and all have decided that the matter is to be governed by federal common law.

The Eleventh Circuit first addressed this question in *Sibaja v. Dow Chemical Co.*,[143] and recently reaffirmed its position in *Esfeld v. Costa Crociere, S.p.A.*[144] In *Esfeld*, the court determined that it was not clear under *Erie* whether the doctrine of forum non conveniens was purely procedural or purely substantive law.[145] Following the Supreme Court's analysis in *Guaranty Trust Co. v. York*,[146] it then

---

[140] Piper Aircraft Co. v. Reyno, 454 U.S. 235, 248 n.13 (1981):

> In previous *forum non conveniens* decisions, the Court has left unresolved the question whether under *Erie R. Co. v. Tompkins*, 304 U.S. 64 (1938), state or federal law of *forum non conveniens* applies in a diversity case. The Court did not decide this issue because the same result would have been reached in each case under federal or state law. The lower courts in these cases reached the same conclusion: Pennsylvania and California law on *forum non conveniens* dismissals are virtually identical to federal law. Thus, here also, we need not resolve the *Erie* question.

> 454 U.S. 235, 249 n.13 (citations omitted).

[141] 510 U.S. 443 (1994).

[142] 510 U.S. 443, 453 (1994). Justice Scalia stated that "[f]ederal courts will continue to invoke *forum non conveniens* to decline jurisdiction in appropriate cases, whether or not the State in which they sit chooses to burden its judiciary with litigation better handled elsewhere." 510 U.S. 443, 454 n.4 (1994).

[143] 757 F.2d 1215 (11th Cir. 1985).

[144] 289 F.3d 1300 (11th Cir. 2002).

[145] *Esfeld*, 289 F.3d 1300, 1306 (11th Cir. 2002).

[146] 326 U.S. 99 (1945).

determined that the difference between state and federal law on forum non conveniens could be outcome-determinative, which weighed in favor of classifying the doctrine as a substantive law.[147] Several "federal countervailing interests" were found to tip the scales in favor of classifying the forum non conveniens doctrine as a procedural rule so that federal common law could apply.[148] These interests included (1) the relationship of the doctrine of forum non conveniens to "the court's inherent power, under article III of the Constitution, to control the administration of the litigation before it and to prevent its process from becoming an instrument of abuse, injustice and oppression,"[149] (2) the interest of federal courts in "ensuring that, as a general rule, United States citizens have access to courts of this country for resolution of their disputes,"[150] (3) an understanding that "foreign relations are implicated in the *forum non conveniens* calculus,"[151] and (4) the federal interest in the "protection of a national, unified set of venue rules within the federal judicial system."[152] Taking these countervailing federal interests into account, the Eleventh Circuit concluded that federal law must govern issues of forum non conveniens in diversity cases.[153]

Other Circuits have taken similar approaches. After a lengthy *Erie* doctrine analysis, the Fifth Circuit described the problem as "a difficult *Erie* choice":

> We must choose between maintaining important internal administrative and equitable powers of our courts at the cost of disuniformity of result between state and federal diversity courts, or uniformity at the cost of giving up part of our self-regulatory powers. It is fashionable to call a difficult choice between important objectives a "balancing" test, but we decline to resort to this metaphor. It is simply a matter of choice, and choose we must.

> We hold that the interests of the federal forum in self-regulation, in administrative independence, and in self-management are more important than

---

[147] *Esfeld*, 289 F.3d 1300, 1307–08 (11th Cir. 2002).

[148] *Esfeld*, 289 F.3d 1300, 1308–15 (11th Cir. 2002).

[149] *Sibaja*, 757 F.2d 1215, 1218 (11th Cir. 1985).

[150] *Esfeld*, 289 F.3d 1300, 1311 (11th Cir. 2002).

[151] *Esfeld*, 289 F.3d 1300, 1312 (11th Cir. 2002).

[152] *Esfeld*, 289 F.3d 1300, 1313 (11th Cir. 2002) (*citing In re* Air Crash Disaster, 821 F.2d 1147, 1158 (5th Cir. 1987)).

[153] *Esfeld*, 289 F.3d 1300, 1315 (11th Cir. 2002).

the disruption of uniformity created by applying federal *forum non conveniens* in diversity cases.[154]

Courts in other Circuits following this reasoning include the Ninth Circuit in *Ravelo Monegro v. Rosa*,[155] the Tenth Circuit in *Rivendell Forest Products v. Canadian Pacific Ltd.*,[156] and the First Circuit in *Royal Bed and Spring Co. v. Famossul Industria E Commercio de Moveis*.[157]

Given the consensus among the Circuits that have addressed this issue, it is likely that most federal courts today would find that the doctrine of forum non conveniens should be governed by federal common law in diversity cases. Although the Supreme Court has not decided the issue definitively, its silence on these decisions can be interpreted as a tacit approval.

J. Jurisdiction and forum non conveniens

One particular element of the forum non conveniens analysis remained in dispute in the federal courts until the 2007 *Sinochem* decision of the U.S. Supreme Court. That was the question of whether a court may dismiss or stay an action based on the doctrine of forum non conveniens without first deciding whether jurisdiction exists. The Second Circuit and the D.C. Circuit both held that a court may dismiss on forum non conveniens grounds without first determining whether personal jurisdiction exists.[158] The Third, Fifth, Seventh, and Ninth Circuits, on the other hand, held that the doctrine of forum non conveniens may be applied only after personal jurisdiction is first determined to exist.[159] Two of these cases also considered the order for addressing subject matter jurisdiction and forum non conveniens, with the Second and D.C. Circuits finding that a case may be decided on the basis of forum non conveniens without addressing subject matter

---

[154]   *In re* Air Crash Disaster, 821 F.2d 1147, 1159 (5th Cir. 1987).

[155]   211 F.3d 509, 511–12 (9th Cir. 2000).

[156]   2 F.3d 990, 992 (10th Cir. 1993).

[157]   906 F.2d 45 (1st Cir. 1990).

[158]   *In re* Arbitration Between Monegasque de Reassurances S.A.M. v. Nak Naftogz of Ukraine, 311 F.3d 488, 497–98 (2d Cir. 2002); *In re* Papandreou, 139 F.3d 247, 255–56 (D.C. Cir. 1998), *superseded by statute on other grounds.*

[159]   Malaysia Int'l Shipping Corp. v. Sinochem Int'l Co. Ltd., 436 F.3d 349 (3d Cir, 2006) *reversed*, ___ U.S. ___, 127 S. Ct. 1184 (2007). Dominguez-Cota v. Cooper Tire & Rubber Co., 396 F.3d 650, 654 (5th Cir. 2005); Kamell v. Hill-Rom Co., 108 F.3d 799 (7th Cir. 1997); Patrickson v. Dole Food Co., 251 F.3d 795 (9th Cir. 2001), *aff'd in part, cert. dismissed in part*, 538 U.S. 468 (2003).

jurisdiction,[160] and the Fifth Circuit holding that forum non conveniens goes to the merits of a case and cannot be addressed until the district court has established subject matter jurisdiction.[161]

This debate among the circuits hinged largely on two Supreme Court decisions that did not involve the doctrine of forum non conveniens. In *Steel Co. v. Citizens for a Better Env't*,[162] the Court held that a court must first determine whether subject matter jurisdiction exists before considering the merits of a case. *Steel* was followed by the decision in *Ruhrgas AG v. Marathon Oil Co.*,[163] in which the Court applied the same principle to personal jurisdiction, stating that "[p]ersonal jurisdiction . . . is an essential element of the jurisdiction of a district . . . court, without which the court is powerless to proceed to an adjudication."[164] The *Ruhrgas* decision also determined that "[i]t is hardly novel for a federal court to choose among threshold grounds for denying audience to a case on the merits,"[165] and thus, while *Steel* required that subject matter jurisdiction be determined to exist before addressing the merits, it did not "dictate a sequencing of jurisdictional issues."[166]

This issue was addressed directly by the Supreme Court in its 2007 decision in *Sinochem Int'l Co. Ltd. v. Malaysia Int'l Shipping Corp.*[167] Sinochem, a Chinese state-owned importer, successfully petitioned a Chinese admiralty court for the arrest of a vessel owned by Malaysia International, claiming that Malaysia International had fraudulently backdated a bill of lading regarding cargo loaded in Philadelphia. Malaysia International, after unsuccessfully contesting jurisdiction in the Chinese court, brought an action in the United State District Court for the Eastern District of Pennsylvania claiming misrepresentation and seeking damages for the loss of its vessel.

Sinochem moved for dismissal of the second action based on lack of jurisdiction and under the doctrine of forum non conveniens. The District Court determined

---

[160]   *In re* Arbitration Between Monegasque de Reassurances S.A.M. v. Nak Naftogz of Ukraine, 311 F.3d 488, 497-98 (2d Cir. 2002); *In re* Papandreou, 139 F.3d 247, 255-56 (D.C. Cir. 1998), *superseded by statute on other grounds.*

[161]   Dominguez-Cota v. Cooper Tire & Rubber Co., 396 F.3d 650 (5th Cir. 2005).

[162]   523 U.S. 83, 101–02 (1998).

[163]   526 U.S. 574 (1999).

[164]   526 U.S. at 584.

[165]   526 U.S. at 585.

[166]   526 U.S. at 584.

[167]   ___ U.S. ___, 127 S.Ct. 1184, (2007).

(1) that it had subject-matter jurisdiction, and (2) that it lacked personal jurisdiction over Sinochem under Pennsylvania law, but that limited discovery might demonstrate jurisdiction under Federal Rule of Civil Procedure 4(k)(2). Nonetheless, it dismissed based on forum non conveniens without first resolving the latter aspect of personal jurisdiction. The Third Circuit Court of Appeals held that the District Court could not dismiss on forum non conveniens grounds without first providing a definitive determination on the issue of personal jurisdiction. The Supreme Court granted certiorari, in part to resolve the split among the Circuits.

Justice Ginsburg, writing for a unanimous court, held that the doctrine of forum non conveniens "may justify dismissal of an action though jurisdictional issues remain unresolved."[168] Her opinion acknowledged that a federal court generally may not rule on the merits of a case without first determining that it has both subject-matter and personal jurisdiction, but went on to note that "jurisdiction is vital only if the court proposes to issue a judgment on the merits."[169] Thus, "[a] district court therefore may dispose of an action by a *forum non conveniens* dismissal, bypassing questions of subject-matter and personal jurisdiction, when considerations of convenience, fairness, and judicial economy so warrant."[170]

The major obstacle to the *Sinochem* holding was language in *Gulf Oil* stating that "the doctrine of *forum non conveniens* can never apply if there is absence of jurisdiction,"[171] and that "[i]n all cases in which . . . *forum non conveniens* comes into play, it presupposes at least two forums in which the defendant is amenable to process."[172] The *Sinochem* Court, however, drew a distinction between asking "whether a court fully competent to adjudicate [a] case . . . could nevertheless dismiss the action under the *forum non conveniens* doctrine,"[173] (for which the *Gulf Oil* answer was "yes"), and "whether a federal court can dismiss under the *forum non conveniens* doctrine before definitively ascertaining its own jurisdiction"[174] (the question presented in *Sinochem*). The Third Circuit had expressed concern that, unless a court first determines that it has jurisdiction, it cannot

---

168 *Id.* at 127 S.Ct. 1190.
169 *Id.* at 127 S.Ct. 1191–92, *quoting* Intec USA, LLC v. Engle, 467 F.3d 1038, 1041 (7th Cir. 2006).
170 *Id.* at 127 S.Ct. 1192.
171 330 U.S. at 504.
172 *Id.* at 506–507.
173 ___ U.S. ___, 127 S.Ct. 1193.
174 *Id.*

condition a forum non conveniens dismissal on the defendant's waiver of a statute of limitations defense, something commonly done in successful assertions of forum non conveniens.[175]

The Supreme Court was able to avoid the concerns of lack of jurisdiction through a holding limited to the facts of the *Sinochem* case, which included the pre-existing submission of the defendant to jurisdiction in China as plaintiff in that action. Thus, the Court found it unnecessary to "decide whether a court conditioning a *forum non conveniens* dismissal on the waiver of jurisdictional or limitations defenses in the foreign forum must first determine its own authority to adjudicate the case."[176] That matter was left for another day. Determining that the District Court would have dismissed on forum non conveniens grounds even if it had both subject-matter and personal jurisdiction, the Court found that "[j]udicial economy is disserved by continuing litigation in the Eastern District of Pennsylvania given the proceedings long launched in China."[177] Thus, "where subject-matter or personal jurisdiction is difficult to determine, and *forum non conveniens* considerations weigh heavily in favor of dismissal, the court properly takes the less burdensome course."[178]

The limited nature of the *Sinochem* holding leaves open the question of whether it will apply directly in very many future cases. While it clearly allows a court to dismiss based on forum non conveniens grounds without first determining the existence of subject-matter and personal jurisdiction, it does so only in limited circumstances. Without jurisdiction, a court does not have the authority to bind the parties to the types of conditions normally attached to a forum non conveniens dismissal. Thus, in cases in which such conditions are requested, the *Sinochem* holding is likely to be of limited value.

K. Non-uniformity among the states

Although many states have adopted the federal doctrine subsequent to *Gilbert*, other states have followed their own paths.[179] The Texas Supreme Court abolished

---

[175] *Id.*

[176] *Id.* at 1193–94.

[177] *Id.* at 1194.

[178] *Id.*

[179] For discussions of state forum non conveniens law, see John W. Joyce, *Forum Non Conveniens in Louisiana*, 60 LA. L. REV. 293 (1999), and Karolyn King, *Open "Borders"—Closed Courts: The Impact of* Stangvik v. Shiley, Inc., 28 U.S.F. L. REV. 1113 (1994).

its state doctrine on grounds that a state statute precluded such discretionary dismissals.[180] The Texas legislature responded by enacting legislation permitting state courts to apply the doctrine where foreign plaintiffs sue United States defendants for personal injuries suffered abroad resulting from violations of Texas or U.S. law.[181] The Supreme Court of Washington State, like the Second Circuit in *Iragorri*,[182] has specifically rejected any claim that a foreign plaintiff's choice of forum is presumptively inconvenient.[183] New York decisions have been read to eliminate the first prong of the federal analysis—proof of an alternative, appropriate forum.[184] One commentator suggests that Delaware's doctrine "is the most restrictive . . . in the United States," requiring "overwhelming hardship and inconvenience" for a dismissal.[185] Thus, while U.S. federal law has moved toward a rather consistent approach to the doctrine of forum non conveniens, significant distinctions exist in the individual states.

An example of the separation between state and federal law on forum non conveniens is found in the 2006 decision of the Michigan Supreme Court in *Radeljak v. DaimlerChrysler Corp.*[186] The Michigan court provided its own list of private and public interest factors that, though much like the U.S. Supreme Court's list in *Gilbert*,[187] has some differences. It also adopted what it considered to be the *Piper* rule that "a foreign plaintiff's choice is entitled to less deference than that accorded to a domestic plaintiff's choice of forum,"[188] and overruled earlier Michigan common law that would require that the private and public interest factors be considered only if the defendant first proved that the local court is a "seriously inconvenient" forum.[189] Thus, the law of the various states may both move away from, and back to, the federal standard.

---

[180] Dow Chemical Co. v. Castro-Alfaro, 786 S.W.2d 674 (Tex. 1990). *See also* Karolyn King, *Open "Borders"— Closed Courts: The Impact of* Stangvik v. Shiley, Inc., 28 U.S.F. L. REV. 1113, 1124–26 (1994).

[181] TEX. CIV. PRAC. & REM. CODE ANN. § 71.051(a) (West Supp. 1994).

[182] *See* Part III.E., above.

[183] Myers v. Boeing Co., 794 P.2d 1272 (Wash. 1990). *See also* Karolyn King, *Open "Borders"—Closed Courts: The Impact of* Stangvik v. Shiley, Inc., 28 U.S.F. L. REV. 1113, 1127–28 (1994).

[184] *See* John W. Joyce, *Forum Non Conveniens in Louisiana*, 60 LA. L. REV. 293, 310 (1999).

[185] Phillip I. Blumberg, *Asserting Human Rights Against Multinational Corporations Under United States Law: Conceptual and Procedural Problems*, 50 AM. J. COMP. L. 493, 525 (2002).

[186] ___ N.W.2d ___, 2006 WL 2022233 (Mich. 2006).

[187] Gulf Oil Corp. v. Gilbert, 330 U.S. 501, 510–11 (1947).

[188] ___ N.W.2d ___, 2006 WL 2022233, *5 (Mich. 2006).

[189] ___ N.W.2d ___, 2006 WL 2022233, *6–*7 (Mich. 2006).

IV. Conclusion

The development of the doctrine of forum non conveniens began early in the nineteenth century in the United States. It has crystallized through significant decisions of the U.S. Supreme Court in the twentieth century and remains a viable and dynamic tool for defendants faced with litigation in U.S. courts when an alternative foreign forum is available. It is viewed as a legitimate instrument for the exercise of judicial discretion in order to place a dispute in the most appropriate court. In this regard, it diverges from the civil law preference for strict application of a lis alibi pendens rule that favors the first party to reach the courthouse door. It represents a clear choice for equity over efficiency, and for fairness in a particular case over predictability of procedural status.

The Supreme Court has honed the contours of its two-step analysis of the forum non conveniens doctrine—requiring proof first of an available alternative forum, and then turning to a balancing of private and public interest factors to determine the most appropriate forum. Nonetheless, the parameters of the doctrine remain subject to the common law evolutionary process. While the Supreme Court has opted to apply federal doctrine, even in diversity cases, states have adopted divergent approaches on matters of nuance in their forum non conveniens analyses. Debate continues on the role of the plaintiff's nationality as a factor in the balance of interests. Both existing parallel litigation in a foreign court and the existence of a choice of court agreement between the parties present issues not fully resolved in terms of their effect on a court's exercise of discretion.

Despite debate on aspects of nuance, the doctrine of forum non conveniens is well-ensconced in U.S. law, at both the state and federal level. While the availability of the federal venue transfer rule of 28 U.S.C. § 1404(a) reduces the impact of the doctrine in moving cases among federal courts, it retains life in cases of alternative state fora and particularly in cases involving alternative fora outside the United States.

CHAPTER 4

Canada

I. Common law development of forum non conveniens

In Canada, the doctrine of forum non conveniens developed first in the common law provinces and later in Québec. While Canadian forum non conveniens principles developed from English law,[1] "[a]s a practical matter, forum non conveniens achieved general acceptance at an earlier time in both Canada and the United States than in England where it was dismissed as a civil law principle of Scots law."[2] As early as 1925, Canadian courts recognized that "when once the admission is made that the Court has jurisdiction it becomes a matter of mere discretion on the part of the Court whether it will or will not exercise it."[3]

A. One doctrine, three purposes

In Canada, as in other common law legal systems based on the English model, jurisdiction is closely connected with concepts of service of process. Thus, in order to fully understand the development of the forum non conveniens doctrine

---

[1] *See* Amchem Prods. Inc. v. British Columbia (Workers' Comp. Bd.), [1993] 1 S.C.R. 897, 915, 918. Canada received its official independence from England in 1931, with judicial subservience to England lasting into the mid-twentieth century. *See* Ralph Folsom & W. Davis Folsom, Understanding NAFTA and Its International Business Implications 33 (1999):

> As a rule, English law was supreme during Canada's colonial period. This supremacy embraced British legislation directed towards Canada as well as its historic body of Common Law as developed by the courts and customary practices. Supremacy meant that no law adopted in Canada could alter any British statute or judicial doctrine. This subservient state of affairs lasted until 1931 when the British Parliament adopted the Statute of Westminster, eliminating its power to legislate for Canada unless requested to do so. Judicial subservience continued formally until 1949 when the Canadian Supreme Court finally became the court of last resort in the Canadian legal system.

[2] J.P. McEvoy, *International Litigation: Canada,* Forum Non Conveniens *and the Anti-Suit Injunction,* 17 Advocs. Q. 1, 5 (1995).

[3] The Jupiter (No. 2), (1925) P. 69, 75, [1925] 69 Sol. J. 547.

in Canada, it becomes necessary to consider three types of cases: (1) those in which an action is commenced by service within the jurisdiction, (2) those in which the action is commenced by service ex juris, and (3) those involving parallel litigation of the same or a related action in a foreign forum (*i.e.*, cases considering the doctrine of lis alibi pendens and questions of anti-suit injunctions). Early cases in the first of these categories relied on "the tortured phrase 'oppressive' or 'vexatious' as the appropriate standard,"[4] while the other two categories can be seen as leading to the more modern doctrine of forum non conveniens in Canada.[5] For a time, consideration of similar concepts in differing contexts created inconsistency and "a large body of diverse and conflicting jurisprudence."[6] This had changed by the end of the twentieth century, with the Canadian courts applying forum non conveniens concepts with greater consistency in all three types of cases.

An example of a case involving a defendant's challenge to service ex juris is *Antares Shipping Corp. v. Capricorn*,[7] in which the Canadian Supreme Court outlined the forum non conveniens principles applicable in such a case:

> The factors affecting the application of this doctrine . . . include the balance of convenience to all the parties concerned . . . the undesirability of trespassing on the jurisdiction of a foreign State, the impropriety and inconvenience of trying a case in one country when the cause of action arose in another where the laws are different, and the cost of assembling foreign witnesses. . . . [T]he overriding consideration . . . must . . . be the existence of some other forum more convenient and appropriate for the pursuit of the action and for securing the ends of justice. Each such case must of necessity turn upon its own particular facts.[8]

---

[4] J.P. McEvoy, *International Litigation: Canada,* Forum Non Conveniens *and the Anti-Suit Injunction*, 17 Advocs. Q. 1, 5 (1995).

[5] *See, e.g.*, Van Vogt v. All-Canadian Group Distributors Ltd., [1969] 9 D.L.R.3d 407 (dismissing plaintiff's breach of employment contract action in Manitoba on forum non conveniens grounds because the employer's head office and records were in Montreal and Québec law governed the contract at issue, even though the plaintiff lived and worked in Manitoba).

[6] J.P. McEvoy, *International Litigation: Canada,* Forum Non Conveniens *and the Anti-Suit Injunction*, 17 Advocs. Q. 1, 5 (1995). *See also* Ellen L. Hayes, Forum Non Conveniens *in England, Australia and Japan: The Allocation of Jurisdiction in Transnational Litigation*, 26 U.B.C. L. Rev. 41, 42 (1992) (noting that, at the time, "the status of the doctrine of *forum non conveniens* in Canada [was] unclear.").

[7] [1976] 65 D.L.R.3d 105.

[8] [1976] 65 D.L.R.3d 105, 123.

The Court held that the lower court should have exercised its jurisdiction and issued service ex juris on the defendant, because even though both parties were foreign and the laws of the United States and England seemingly governed the dispute, Canada appeared to be the most appropriate forum.[9] The plaintiffs had little chance of successfully pursuing their action in those other forums, and the defendants had already become actively involved in the litigation in Canada before they moved to strike the order for service ex juris.[10]

The British Columbia Court of Appeal decision in *Avenue Properties Ltd. v. First City Development Corp.*[11] is an example of a case applying forum non conveniens principles to a situation involving parallel litigation. When an Ontario real estate transaction went bad, the seller initiated suit in Ontario and the buyer brought a parallel action in British Columbia. The seller then moved to stay the British Columbia action brought by the buyer.[12] The lower court granted the stay, but the Court of Appeal reversed, relying on the test as set forth in the *MacShannon* decision in England.[13]

The *Avenue Properties* court listed several forum non conveniens principles as being applicable to parallel proceedings: the trial court retains broad discretion to grant or refuse a motion to stay proceedings; the appellate court should not easily overturn the trial court's decision; the court should not imprudently deny a plaintiff's first choice of forum; the defendant must demonstrate that he will suffer great inconvenience and oppression if litigation continued in the forum; situations of lis alibi pendens are alone not sufficient grounds for the court to grant a stay; and the court should not grant a stay if there would be undue prejudice to the plaintiff in proceeding in an alternative forum.[14] Ultimately, the proper test for granting a stay in situations of lis alibi pendens was determined to be whether the defendant establishes that he is amenable to the jurisdiction of an appropriate, alternative forum, in which the proceeding would be more convenient and less expensive for the parties. Nonetheless, the plaintiff may still prevent a stay if he proves there is a fair possibility that he will lose a juridical advantage if forced to proceed in an alternative forum.

---

9   [1976] 65 D.L.R.3d 105, 125, 128–29.
10 [1976] 65 D.L.R.3d 105, 125.
11 [1986] B.C.L.R. (2d) 45.
12 [1986] B.C.L.R. (2d) 45, ¶ 1.
13 [1986] B.C.L.R. (2d) 45, ¶¶ 17–24.
14 [1986] B.C.L.R. (2d) 45, ¶¶ 17–21.

The court held that the action and the parties had a valid connection to British Columbia because the law of that province governed the contract solicitation and the purchaser's only assets were in that province.[15] Interestingly, the court disregarded a forum selection clause in the written sales contract in which the parties agreed to "attorn to the jurisdiction of the Province of Ontario."[16] Moreover, the possible inconvenience of inconsistent decisions for the defendant due to parallel proceedings in sister provinces was not alone enough to dissuade the court from overturning the lower court and refusing to grant the stay.[17]

B. *Amchem Products*: Clarifying the modern doctrine

In 1993, the Supreme Court of Canada provided greater clarity regarding the modern application of the doctrine of forum non conveniens in *Amchem Products Inc. v. British Columbia Workers' Compensation Board*.[18] *Amchem* was not a typical forum non conveniens case in which a defendant to a suit moves to stay the proceedings in favor of another forum, but rather continued the development of forum non conveniens concepts in the context of a request for an anti-suit injunction.

Multiple plaintiffs, many of whom were residents of British Columbia, brought an action in a Texas federal district court against the defendant asbestos companies, seeking damages for injuries resulting from prolonged exposure to asbestos.[19] The asbestos companies did business in Texas, and had no connection with British Columbia.[20] The Texas court found that it had jurisdiction, and many of the defendants moved for dismissal on grounds of forum non conveniens. This motion was denied, and the Texas Supreme Court denied the defendants' request for leave to file a writ of mandamus.[21] The asbestos companies then filed an action in British Columbia seeking an anti-suit injunction against the plaintiffs in Texas in order to prevent the Texas action from proceeding.[22] In response, the Texas

---

15   [1986] B.C.L.R. (2d) 45, ¶ 34.
16   [1986] B.C.L.R. (2d) 45, ¶ 34.
17   [1986] B.C.L.R. (2d) 45, ¶ 35.
18   [1993] 1 S.C.R. 897.
19   [1993] 1 S.C.R. 897, 905.
20   [1993] 1 S.C.R. 897, 905.
21   [1993] 1 S.C.R. 897, 907.
22   [1993] 1 S.C.R. 897, 907–08.

plaintiffs who were not residents of British Columbia obtained a Texas anti-anti-suit injunction against the defendants in order to prevent the defendants from obtaining anti-suit injunctions in the Canadian forum.[23] The British Columbia court granted the defendants' request for an anti-suit injunction, and the Court of Appeal affirmed.[24] On further appeal, the Supreme Court of Canada determined that "in order to arrive at more specific criteria" on the granting of anti-suit injunctions,

> it is necessary to consider when a foreign court has departed from our own test of forum non conveniens to such an extent as to justify our courts in refusing to respect the assumption of jurisdiction by the foreign court and in what circumstances such assumption amounts to a serious injustice.[25]

Thus, the Canadian Supreme Court applied its own concepts of forum non conveniens in determining whether the Texas court had properly retained jurisdiction, all for purposes of determining whether a Canadian court should grant an anti-suit injunction. It was in this context that the Canadian Supreme Court set forth its modern doctrine of forum non conveniens.[26]

The *Amchem* Court adopted the forum non conveniens test announced by the House of Lords in *Spiliada*,[27] noting the importance of a review of "connecting factors" in order to determine the appropriateness of the forum chosen by the plaintiff.[28] Like the House of Lords in *Spiliada*, the Canadian Court stated that "the existence of a more appropriate forum must be *clearly* established to displace the forum selected by the plaintiff."[29] It then added two purely Canadian modifications

---

[23] [1993] 1 S.C.R. 897, 907–08.
[24] [1993] 1 S.C.R. 897, 908.
[25] [1993] 1 S.C.R. 897, 915.
[26] [1993] 1 S.C.R. 897, 919–20. *See also* Genevieve Saumier, Forum Non Conveniens: *Where Are We Now?*, 12 SUP. CT. L. REV. (2d) 121, 124 (2000) (stating that "because the anti-suit injunction test elaborated by Sopinka J. was directly based on a *forum non conveniens* analysis, this doctrine became a central focus of the decision. The Supreme Court explicitly recognized the need for a restatement of the doctrine given the state of confusion surrounding the doctrine in common law Canada.").
[27] In *Spiliada*, Lord Goff of Chiveley stated that where the defendant could prove the existence of another available forum which prima facie is clearly more appropriate for the trial of the action, the court ordinarily will grant a stay unless the plaintiff prove by more than simple loss of a juridical advantage that justice requires that a stay should not be granted. Spiliada Maritime Corp. v. Cansulex Ltd., [1987] A.C. 460, 478–82 (H.L.). *See* Chapter 2, Part II.C., above.
[28] [1993] 1 S.C.R. 897, 915, 917.
[29] [1993] 1 S.C.R. 897, 921.

to the *Spiliada* test. First, in weighing the relevant factors, it determined that "there is no reason in principle why the loss of juridical advantage should be treated as a separate and distinct condition rather than being weighed with the other factors which are considered in identifying the appropriate forum."[30] Second, the Canadian court determined that the same test is applicable both to questions of service ex juris and to traditional questions of forum non conveniens.[31]

This second contribution of the *Amchem* decision to the forum non conveniens doctrine clearly sets Canadian law apart from its cousins in other common law jurisdictions. Thus, in Canada:

> [T]he test for establishing jurisdiction and the test for deciding whether or not to exercise that jurisdiction are the same. . . .

> The effect of this similarity of criteria may well explain why some courts in common law provinces examine the forum non conveniens issue without a prior consideration of their jurisdictional competence. In other words they jump directly to the forum non conveniens discussion, even where the defendant is contesting jurisdiction simpliciter.[32]

Considerations applied to motions to dismiss based on forum non conveniens grounds are therefore also taken into account in determining jurisdiction in the

---

30   [1993] 1 S.C.R. 897, 919. Note that under the English test, the defendant first has the burden of establishing that there is another appropriate forum. If this burden is met, then the court considers whether the plaintiff will lose a juridical advantage if a stay is granted. *See* Chapter 2, above. For a post-*Amchem* example of this application in Canada, see *Upper Lakes Shipping Ltd. v. Foster Yeoman Ltd.*, [1993] 14 O.R.3d 548 (ruling that even if the court accepted the plaintiff's arguments of juridical advantages, they are but one factor in the forum non conveniens analysis).

31   [1993] 1 S.C.R. 897, 920 (Sopinka J.) ("It seems to me that whether it is a case for service out of the jurisdiction or the defendant is served in the jurisdiction, the issue remains: is there a more appropriate jurisdiction based on the relevant factors."). *Bushell v. T & N PLC*, [1992] 67 B.C.L.R. (2d) 330, is an example of a Canadian court applying the stricter test for cases of service ex juris before *Amchem*, in which the plaintiff had the burden of proof, but greater weight was given to the plaintiff's choice of forum. In *Bushell*, the defendant asbestos companies requested that the British Columbia court stay the plaintiffs' action on grounds of forum non conveniens because the injuries had occurred in Québec; the defendants had no connections with British Columbia; and there was a possibility that the defendants would not get the same statute of limitation defense in British Columbia as they would in Québec. [1992] 67 B.C.L.R. 330, ¶ 30. The court, however, refused to grant the stay, giving greater weight to the plaintiffs' choice of forum and juridical advantage in British Columbia. [1992] 67 B.C.L.R. (2d) 330, ¶ 60.

32   Genevieve Saumier, Forum Non Conveniens: *Where Are We Now?*, 12 SUP. CT. L. REV. (2d) 121, 131 (2000).

first instance (jurisdiction simpliciter), and the analysis in each instance appears to be the same.[33] Anti-suit injunctions are treated differently, however. The *Amchem* Court held that the test for granting an anti-suit injunction, although derived from forum non conveniens principles, involves a higher threshold because of the comity element,[34] and reversed the lower courts' decision to grant the defendants an anti-suit injunction.

Canadian cases subsequent to *Amchem* have both confirmed its approach and clarified its analysis. In *472900 B.C. Ltd. v. Thrifty Canada Ltd.*,[35] the British Columbia Court of Appeal applied the *Amchem* test to a request that the trial court decline to accept jurisdiction over a case having ties to both British Columbia and Ontario. Examining the House of Lords decision in *Spiliada*, the court referred to Lord Sumner's comments that "it is wiser to avoid use of the word 'convenience' and to refer rather, as Lord Dunedin did, to the appropriate forum."[36] Importantly, however, the court also clearly noted the shift from the traditional standard of the forum non conveniens doctrine to the modern rule, stating that "[t]here is now no burden on the applicant to establish that the action would be vexatious, oppressive and/or an abuse of the process of the court."[37] The case ultimately was decided on the basis of a non-exclusive Ontario choice of forum clause and the fact that an action had also been filed in Ontario, where the court had first refused a stay. The "great significance which must now be given to the matter of comity between provinces" favored holding that the stay in British Columbia be granted.[38]

---

[33] In *Spiliada*, Lord Goff of Chieveley specifically found the U.K. doctrine to require three distinctions between a pure forum non conveniens analysis and the application of the doctrine to cases of service ex juris. Spiliada Maritime Corp. v. Cansulex Ltd., [1987] A.C. 460, 480–81 (H.L.).

[34] [1993] 1 S.C.R. 897, 924.

[35] 168 D.L.R. 4th 602 (1998).

[36] 168 D.L.R. 4th 602, 617 (1998) (citing Spiliada Maritime Corp. v. Cansulex Ltd., 1 A.C. 460, (H.L. 1987) ("[T]he Latin tag, however inapt to describe the principle, is so widely used that it is sensible to retain it. But it is important to keep in mind that it refers, not to the more convenient forum, but to the appropriate forum.").

[37] 168 D.L.R. 4th 602, 617–18 (1998) ("Such matters can, of course, still be relied on in aid of the application to stay because, if they can be established, the jurisdiction in which that would occur can hardly be the appropriate one. But the absence of such factors is no longer a basis for refusing the application to stay.").

[38] 168 D.L.R. 4th 602, 628–29 (1998). *See also* Sannes v. Canada, [1994] 23 C.P.C (3d) 30 (holding that the plaintiff's juridical advantage is only one factor in the forum non conveniens balancing analysis and staying the action on grounds that the Canadian federal court was more suitable to deal with the immigration and constitutional law implications at issue); Bank Van Parijs en de Nederlanden Belgie N.V. v. Cabri, (1993) 41 A.C.W.S.3d 1132, 19 C.P.C 3d 362 (holding that Belgium was the more appropriate forum because most events giving rise to the action occurred in that country, and a forum selection clause arguably favored Belgium).

The combination of jurisdiction simpliciter and forum non conveniens was dealt with explicitly in *Westec Aerospace Inc. v. Raytheon Aircraft Co.*,[39] a British Columbia case that illustrates both the jurisdiction/forum non conveniens distinction and the application of the *Amchem* test. Westec (a British Columbia corporation) licensed to Raytheon (a Kansas corporation) the right to use certain computer software.[40] Upon termination of the license the parties disputed whether all hardware and software were properly returned to Westec.[41] Raytheon first brought an action in Kansas seeking a declaration that it had not breached the agreement.[42] Westec then filed suit in British Columbia claiming breach.[43] The British Columbia trial court first ruled that jurisdiction simpliciter existed because Westec had demonstrated that "either Raytheon or the subject matter of the dispute has a real and substantial connection with" British Columbia, and that there was a "good arguable case that brings the action within the Rule relied on for effecting service *ex juris*."[44] The real question for the trial court then became "whether this court should exercise its discretion and take jurisdiction given that largely parallel proceedings [have] been commenced and advanced to the close of pleadings in Kansas."[45] The trial court's test was stated as follows:

> Where jurisdiction *simpliciter* exists, a defendant that contends the action should not be entertained bears the onus of demonstrating that the courts of another jurisdiction are sufficiently more appropriate for the resolution of the dispute to displace the forum the plaintiff has selected. . . . The factors commonly considered are the parties' residences and places of business, the jurisdiction where the cause of action arose and where the damage was suffered, juridical advantages and disadvantages, convenience and expense, the governing law and the difficulty of its proof, and the existence of any parallel proceedings.[46]

Of particular interest was the trial court's approach to the location of witnesses, which it dealt with by stating that "the facilities for video conferencing

---

[39] 173 D.L.R. 4th 498 (B.C.C.A. 1999), *affirmed at* 197 D.L.R. 4th 211 (2001).
[40] 173 D.L.R. 4th 498, 501 (B.C.C.A. 1999).
[41] 173 D.L.R. 4th 498, 501 (B.C.C.A. 1999).
[42] 173 D.L.R. 4th 498, 501 (B.C.C.A. 1999).
[43] 173 D.L.R. 4th 498, 501 (B.C.C.A. 1999).
[44] Westec Aerospace Inc. v. Raytheon Aircraft Co., 1998 Carswell B.C. 2684, ¶ 4 (B.C. Sup. Ct.).
[45] 173 D.L.R. 4th 489, 502 (B.C.C.A. 1999).
[46] 173 D.L.R. 4th 489, 502–03 (B.C.C.A. 1999).

on a world-wide basis that are now available in this court go a long way to rendering the expense and convenience of bringing witnesses to trial a consideration of declining importance in an application of this kind."[47] In the end, the court relied on the fact that Westec was the natural or "true plaintiff," and Raytheon "claims only a declaration that it owes nothing."[48] Westec was entitled to the benefit of the juridical advantage, and Raytheon's motion for a forum non conveniens stay was dismissed.

Cases subsequent to *Amchem* have thus confirmed and applied its definition of the current approach to forum non conveniens doctrine in Canada. The result is very close to the analysis applied in the United Kingdom, but with no special consideration given to the possible loss of juridical advantage as compared to other factors, and with no apparent distinction between a pure forum non conveniens analysis and its application to questions of service ex juris (jurisdiction simpliciter).

II. Discretion to decline jurisdiction in the Québec Civil Code

Québec, unlike the other Canadian provinces, is a civil law jurisdiction drawing upon French legal traditions. It would thus be expected not to have adopted the doctrine of forum non conveniens. Recent changes in the Québec *Civil Code* defy this expectation, however, with three provisions that bear on the question of a court's discretionary authority to decline to exercise jurisdiction. First, Article 3135 explicitly adopts a forum non conveniens analysis:

> Even though a Québec authority has jurisdiction to hear a dispute, it may exceptionally and on an application by a party, decline jurisdiction if it considers that the authorities of another country are in a better position to decide.[49]

Contrary to the blending of forum non conveniens and jurisdiction issues in other Canadian provinces, this provision requires that a Québec court first decide whether it has jurisdiction before it entertains a motion for dismissal on grounds that there is another, more appropriate forum.

---

47   Westec Aerospace Inc. v. Raytheon Aircraft Co., Inc. v. Raytheon Aircraft Co. (1999), 173 D.L.R. (4th) 503 (B.C.C.A.); 1999 Carswell B.C. 825, ¶ 7 (B.C.C.A.).

48   1999 Carswell B.C. 825, ¶ 10 (B.C.C.A.).

49   Art. 3135 Civ. Code Que. (2001).

Québec Civil Code Article 3137 on lis alibi pendens illustrates a second codification of a court's discretionary power to decline jurisdiction when a parallel action is pending in a foreign court:

> On application of a party, a Québec authority may stay its ruling on an action brought before it if another action, between the same parties, based on the same facts and having the same object is pending before a foreign authority, provided that the latter action can result in a decision which may be recognized in Québec, or if such a decision has already been rendered by a foreign authority.[50]

This discretionary authority to defer to a foreign court provides a middle ground between the traditional, strict civil law approach to lis alibi pendens and common law discretion based upon forum non conveniens principles.

The third relevant provision in the Québec *Civil Code* pertains to forum selection clauses. Article 3148 provides:

> [A] Québec authority has no jurisdiction where the parties, by agreement, have chosen to submit all existing or future disputes between themselves relating to a specified legal relationship to a foreign authority or to an arbitrator, unless the defendant submits to the jurisdiction of the Québec authority.[51]

Thus, when a choice of court clause leads to a forum outside Québec, not only will the Québec court not entertain a forum non conveniens analysis, it simply will not have jurisdiction to hear the case.[52]

---

[50]   Art. 3137 Civ. Code Que. (2001). This approach is, of course, much narrower than the general common law approach in Canada.

[51]   Art. 3148 Civ. Code Que. (2001).

[52]   Interestingly, a strict reading of Articles 3148 and 3135 together would make a forum non conveniens analysis technically unnecessary when a defendant proves the existence of a choice of court clause directing the case to a foreign court. The Québec court would not have jurisdiction, so it could not decline to exercise it under Article 3135. The irony is that Article 3148 would not appear to prevent a forum non conveniens analysis when combined with Article 3135 where the plaintiff brings the case in a Québec court based on a choice of court clause directing the case to Québec. The court would then have jurisdiction, and the defendant could assert the right to discretionary declination of that jurisdiction under Article 3135. For further discussion of these provisions, see Genevieve Saumier, Forum Non Conveniens: *Where Are We Now?*, 12 SUP. CT. L. REV. (2d) 121, 129–33 (2000).

The codification of forum non conveniens in Québec law has not escaped criticism. By its very nature, the doctrine is a discretionary tool for courts, and therefore inconsistent with traditional civil law expectations of predictability based on legislative rules. This tension has been noted by civil law scholars in Québec:

> Unfortunately, the Québec jurisprudence reveals few guidelines to help lawyers predict whether the Québec Court will choose to decline its jurisdiction. The jurisprudence in Québec is problematic because it does not reflect a clear, Québecois version of *forum non conveniens*: the cases offer no clear understanding of the term "exceptional" in article 3135 C.c.Q. As a result of this uncertainty, *forum non conveniens* is raised with great frequency by defendants, and thus plays a more prominent role in determining the appropriateness of the Québec forum than it otherwise should in international and inter-provincial cases. This development is troublesome in that it leads to the replacement of the rule of law with informal and intuitive judicial decision-making.[53]

At this point, however, the Québec experiment with concepts of forum non conveniens is in place, and provides important comparative opportunities.

---

[53] Jeffrey Talpis & Shelley L. Kath, *The exceptional as commonplace in Québec* forum non conveniens *law: Cambior, a case in point*, 34 Revue Juridique Themis 761, 796–97 (2000) (discussing what the authors list as seven different interpretations by Québec courts of the word "exceptional" in Article 3135, ranging from requiring that the court engage in a balancing analysis to a "clearly more appropriate" forum test). 34 Revue Juridique Themis 761, 798 (2000).

CHAPTER 5

Australia

I.   Between "vexation and oppression" and the "most appropriate forum"

The Australian High Court first clearly adopted forum non conveniens principles in its 1908 decision in *Maritime Insurance Co. Ltd. v. Geelong Harbor Trust Commissioners*,[1] where it followed the "vexation and oppression" test of the House of Lords in *Logan v. Bank of Scotland*.[2] This meant that relief from suit in an Australian court would be granted if "the exercise of the jurisdiction would [subject the defendant to] injustice."[3] As in Canada, the United States, and the United Kingdom, more recent cases have revisited this strict traditional test. However, while the other three countries have moved to a more liberal "most appropriate forum" standard, Australia has remained closer to the original test, moving forward from a strict vexation and oppression test, but clinging to an analysis focusing primarily on whether the Australian forum is clearly inappropriate. This test acknowledges the developments in the House of Lords' opinions in *Spiliada*, but nonetheless results in a unique approach.

II.   The "clearly inappropriate forum" test

Three cases provide insight into the current forum non conveniens test applied by the Australian High Court. They are the 1988 decision in *Oceanic Sun Line Special Shipping Co. Inc. v. Fay*,[4] the 1990 decision in *Voth v. Manildra Flour Mills Pty. Ltd.*,[5] and the 2002 decision in *Dow Jones & Co., Inc. v. Gutnick*.[6]

---

[1]   6 C.L.R. 194 (1908).

[2]   [1906] 1 K.B. 141 (C.A.). *See* Chapter 2, Part II.A., above.

[3]   6 C.L.R. 194, 198 (1908), *quoting* Logan v. Bank of Scotland [1906] 1 K.B. 141, 150.

[4]   165 C.L.R. 197, 79 A.L.R. 9 (1988).

[5]   171 C.L.R. 538 (1990).

[6]   210 C.L.R. 575, [2002] H.C.A. 56, 194 A.L.R. 433 (2002).

A. *Oceanic Sun Line Special Shipping Co. Inc. v. Fay*

In *Oceanic Sun Line*, an Australian who had been injured aboard a Greek ship owned by Oceanic Sun while on a cruise off the Greek islands brought an action for damages in the Supreme Court of New South Wales.[7] When the court granted leave to serve the shipping company in Greece, the company moved to stay the proceedings, arguing the applicability of a clause contained in the passenger ticket designating Greek courts as the proper forum, and that Greece was clearly the "more appropriate" forum.[8] Both the trial court and the Court of Appeal denied the motion to stay.[9]

The High Court affirmed by a slim majority, but with no majority as to the appropriate test. The two dissenting justices argued for Australian adoption of the modern English test.[10] The other justices opted for varying degrees of the old English test. Most notably, Justice Deane articulated what he called the "clearly inappropriate forum" test, based on a combination of *St. Pierre*[11] and

---

[7] *Oceanic Sun Line*, 165 C.L.R. 197, 198 (1988).

[8] 165 C.L.R. 197, 199 (1988).

[9] 165 C.L.R. 197, 198 (1988).

[10] Justices Wilson and Toohey argued against maintaining an "abuse of process" test:

> [T]his century has witnessed such a transformation in communications and travel, coupled with a greater importance attaching to considerations of international comity as the nations of the world become more closely related to each other as to render the *St. Pierre* principle, fashioned as it was in the nineteenth century, inappropriate to modern conditions. . . . The *St. Pierre* principle places such a tight rein on the discretion of a court as to render it unable to deal justly with the problem of forum shopping, even in blatant cases.

165 C.L.R. 197, 212 (1988) (citations omitted). They went on to outline the modern English test as pronounced in *Spiliada*, arguing that Australia should follow other common law jurisdictions in liberalizing its test:

> [I]n an area of law involving the courts of other countries it is expedient to preserve as much consistency as possible between the common law countries. The doctrine of *forum non conveniens* has long formed part of the law of Scotland and of the United States of America. It is now the law of England. It would seem to be the law of Canada. . . . In our view, the *Spiliada* approach should henceforth chart the course for the common law of Australia in relation to the inherent jurisdiction of a court to stay proceedings when there is a more appropriate forum in a foreign country.

165 C.L.R. 197, 212–13 (1988).

[11] St. Pierre v. South American Stores (Gath & Chaves) Ltd., [1936] 1 K.B. 382 (C.A.).

The Atlantic Star.[12] Under that test, as interpreted by Justice Deane:

> The power of a court whose jurisdiction has been regularly invoked to dis-
> miss or stay proceedings on the ground that they should have been brought
> in some tribunal in another country is limited to the case where the court
> is persuaded that it is such an unsuitable or inappropriate forum for their
> determination that their continuance would work a serious injustice in
> that it would be oppressive and vexatious to the defendant. On that tradi-
> tional approach, the clear inappropriateness of the local forum may justify
> dismissal or a stay. The mere fact that some foreign tribunal would repre-
> sent a "more appropriate" forum will not.[13]

Justice Deane did acknowledge that the words "vexatious and oppressive" should
not be construed literally.[14]

The Court held that the choice of court clause found in the cruise ticket was inapplicable, and that the plaintiff's initial purchase of the exchange order for the
cruise ticket in New South Wales was the only contract of carriage. Thus, Australia
was the "locus contractus."[15] For Justice Deane, the courts in both jurisdictions
"would have competing claims to be considered as the most appropriate forum,"
and New South Wales was thus not a clearly inappropriate forum.[16] Justice
Gaudron agreed with Justice Deane's formula, but argued that the applicable

---

[12]   The Atlantic Star, [1974] A.C. 436 (H.L.).

[13]   Oceanic Sun Line, 165 C.L.R. 197, 242 (1988). Justice Deane repeated the traditional English objection to
limiting a plaintiff's right to litigate in his chosen forum:

A party who has regularly invoked the jurisdiction of a competent court has a prima facie right to insist
upon its exercise and to have his claim heard and determined. . . . In this country, [certain] special categories of cases have not traditionally encompassed a general judicial discretion to dismiss or stay proceedings
in a case within jurisdiction merely on the ground that the local court is persuaded that some tribunal in
another country would be a more appropriate forum.

165 C.L.R. 197, 241 (1988).

[14]   165 C.L.R. 197, 244–47 (1988).

[15]   165 C.L.R. 197, 256 (1988).

[16]   165 C.L.R. 197, 256 (1988). Interestingly, "[o]ne aspect of the Ocean Sun decision which . . . caused much
confusion is that for reasons which were not articulated, the majority dealt with the case as one of juris-
diction as of right when in fact jurisdiction was exorbitant. It has never been the law in England or
Australia that service out is always to be sustained unless the proceedings are vexatious and oppressive."
Ellen L. Hayes, *Forum Non Conveniens in England, Australia and Japan: The Allocation of Jurisdiction in
Transnational Litigation*, 26 U.B.C. L. REV. 41, 50 (1992) (footnote omitted). *See also* Voth v. Manildra

substantive law should be a major factor in determining whether a forum is inappropriate.[17] Justice Brennan, on the other hand, argued that Australia should retain the strict test as pronounced in *St. Pierre*, according literal meaning to the words "oppressive" and "vexatious."[18] Thus, while the *Ocean Sun* decision provided a specific outcome, it left Australian law on forum non conveniens in a state of uncertainty.

B. *Voth v. Manildra Flour Mills Pty. Ltd.*

In its 1990 decision in *Voth v. Manildra Flour Mills Pty. Ltd.*,[19] the High Court reviewed both its own decision in *Oceanic Sun*, and the decision of the House of Lords in *The Spiliada*,[20] in developing its unique Australian approach. An action by two Australian companies was brought in New South Wales against an accountant from Missouri, alleging professional negligence regarding tax advice that resulted in financial loss to the companies in both Australia and the United States.[21] The defendant moved for a stay of proceedings in Australia on grounds that Missouri was the more appropriate forum.[22] The trial court, applying the English test pronounced by the House of Lords in *MacShannon*,[23] denied the defendant's motion, determining that "the factors in favour of maintenance of the litigation in Missouri were not such as obviously to outweigh the factors in favour of allowing the litigation to remain in New South Wales," and further, that

---

Four Mills, 171 C.L.R. 538, 553 (1990) (stating that since *Oceanic Sun Line*, "[a]lthough . . . courts . . . have applied the 'clearly inappropriate forum' test, the application of that test has given rise to disagreement and disconformity, particularly in cases where leave has been granted to serve originating process outside the jurisdiction").

17   165 C.L.R. 197, 264–66 (1988).

18   165 C.L.R. 197, 236 (1988).

19   171 C.L.R. 538 (1990).

20   Spiliada Maritime Corp. v. Cansulex Ltd., [1987] A.C. 460 (H.L.).

21   *Voth*, 171 C.L.R. 538, 544 (1990).

22   It is interesting to note that if the facts were reversed, with the plaintiffs in the United States, the defendant in Australia, and the case brought in the United States, the U.S. court would find itself without personal jurisdiction over the defendant under the Due Process Clause. *See, e.g.*, Ronald A. Brand, *Due Process, Jurisdiction and a Hague Judgments Convention*, 60 U. PITT. L. REV. 661 (1999). This highlights the dual focus of (1) the defendant's challenge to service outside the jurisdiction of Australia and (2) the defendant's claim that if service was proper the court should nonetheless decline to exercise jurisdiction based on the doctrine of forum non conveniens. It also indicates why in the United States the forum non conveniens doctrine does not fold into the analysis of jurisdiction in the same way that it does in the United Kingdom, Canada, and Australia. The Due Process Clauses in the United States operate to prevent jurisdiction in cases that in Commonwealth courts become the subject of a forum non conveniens analysis because of the broader jurisdictional reach that results from not having a due process limitation on jurisdictional reach.

23   MacShannon v. Rockware Glass Ltd., [1978] A.C. 795 (H.L.).

allowing defendant's motion "would operate to deprive the respondents of a legitimate juridical advantage in relation to the measure of damages and the awarding of costs in Missouri."[24] By the time the Court of Appeal heard the case, the High Court had rejected the *Spiliada* test in its decision in *Oceanic Sun*. The Court of Appeal thus could no longer apply English law, but had to decide which of the differing tests expressed in *Oceanic Sun* it should apply. It ultimately affirmed the trial court's decision, holding "that the majority approach in *Oceanic Sun* would 'result in the present case in a refusal of a stay of proceedings on the general basis of forum non conveniens.'"[25]

The High Court rejected the petitioner's argument that Australia should adopt the modern "most appropriate forum" test announced for England in *The Spiliada*, and held that the "clearly inappropriate forum" test pronounced by Justice Deane in *Oceanic Sun* should be the law in Australia.[26] In explaining its reasons for adopting the "clearly inappropriate forum" test, as opposed to the "most appropriate forum" test of the House of Lords, the Court noted that both tests are likely to result in similar decisions in a majority of cases, and that differences in result would probably only occur where the alternative forum is more appropriate but the Australian forum is not clearly inappropriate. According to the court, the latter situation gives even more justification for a court to deny a motion to set aside service or stay proceedings, because "in those cases in which the ascertainment of the natural forum is a complex and finely balanced question, the court may more readily conclude that it is not a clearly inappropriate forum," and thus not enmesh itself with often time consuming forum non conveniens determinations.[27]

---

[24]   *Voth*, 171 C.L.R. 538, 548 (1990).

[25]   171 C.L.R. 538, 550 (1990) (footnote omitted). The court stressed that the plaintiffs were local residents, that this was not a case of forum shopping, that some of the damages at issue occurred in Australia, that the substantive law to be applied was probably that of New South Wales, and that the dispute was "transnational in character, and it is inappropriate to describe the State of Missouri as 'the natural forum' for the resolution of the dispute."

[26]   In reaching this result, the High Court rejected the argument that the English test in *The Spiliada* has been generally accepted in other common law countries:

> [I]t would obviously be desirable in the interests of international comity that this Court, in common with the courts of other countries, should adopt a common approach. However, we are not persuaded that there exists any real international consensus favouring a particular solution to the question. Nor are we persuaded that any consensus exists among countries of the common law world.

171 C.L.R. 538, 560 (1990).

[27]   171 C.L.R. 538, 558 (1990).

Applying this test, the High Court reversed the Court of Appeal, and ordered a stay of the proceedings in New South Wales.[28] In doing so, the Court provided useful distinctions between its "clearly inappropriate forum" test and both the traditional "vexatious and oppressive" test and the modern "clearly more appropriate forum" test of *The Spiliada*:

> The content of the "clearly inappropriate forum" test is more expansive than the traditional test applied by Brennan J. The former test, unlike the latter, recognizes that in some situations the continuation of an action in the selected forum, though not amounting to vexation or oppression or an abuse of process in the strict sense, will amount to an injustice to the defendant when the bringing of the action in some other available and competent forum will not occasion an injustice to the plaintiff. Thus, in order to obtain a legitimate advantage, the plaintiff may commence an action in the selected forum though the subject-matter of the action and the parties have little connexion with that forum and the defendant may be put to great expense and inconvenience in contesting the action in that forum. On the application of traditional principles, a stay would be refused in such a case, notwithstanding that the selected forum was a clearly inappropriate forum. Since the traditional test is apt to produce such an extreme result, the "clearly inappropriate forum" test is to be preferred to the traditional test. In this respect, it is significant that the traditional test is no longer applied in the United Kingdom, New Zealand, Canada or the United States.
>
> . . . .
>
> Likewise, in England, the movement away from the traditional principles to the adoption in *Spiliada* of the "clearly more appropriate forum" test began with a recognition that those principles did not always produce acceptable results and that the key to the solution of the problem was to be found "in a liberal interpretation of what is oppressive on the part of the plaintiff," to use the words of Lord Reid: see *The "Atlantic Star."* From this beginning, Lord Diplock restated the traditional principles and, in restating them, required the defendant to satisfy the court that there is another forum (the "natural forum") in which justice can be done between the parties at substantially less

---

28   171 C.L.R. 538, 571 (1990).

inconvenience or expense: see *MacShannon*. That restatement has since given way to the *Spiliada* formulation in which the "natural forum" and "more appropriate forum" are treated as interchangeable expressions: see *Spiliada*. The natural forum has been understood to mean "that with which the action [has] the most real and substantial connexion": *The "Abidin Daver."*[29]

Moreover, the Court noted that in practice the "clearly inappropriate forum" and "more appropriate forum" tests are most often "likely to lead to the same results":[30]

> The difference between the two tests will be of critical significance only in those cases—probably rare—in which it is held that an available foreign tribunal is the natural or more appropriate forum but in which it cannot be said that the local tribunal is a clearly inappropriate one. But the question which the former test presents is slightly different in that it focuses on the advantages and disadvantages arising from a continuation of the proceedings in the selected forum rather than on the need to make a comparative judgment between the two forums.[31]

The Court then outlined the major points of its clearly inappropriate forum test for forum non conveniens in Australia:

> First, a plaintiff who has regularly invoked the jurisdiction of a court has a prima facie right to insist upon its exercise. Secondly, the traditional power to stay proceedings which have been regularly commenced, on inappropriate forum grounds, is to be exercised in accordance with the general principle empowering a court to dismiss or stay proceedings which are oppressive, vexatious or an abuse of process and the rationale for the exercise of the power to stay is the avoidance of injustice between the parties in the particular case. Thirdly, the mere fact that the balance of convenience favours another jurisdiction or that some other jurisdiction would provide a more appropriate forum does not justify the dismissal of the action or the

---

[29]   171 C.L.R. 538, 556–57 (1990).
[30]   171 C.L.R. 538, 558 (1990).
[31]   171 C.L.R. 538, 558 (1990).

grant of a stay. Finally, the jurisdiction to grant a stay or dismiss the action is to be exercised "with great care" or "extreme caution."[32]

The High Court explained that the test for granting a defendant's motion to stay should be the same as the test for consideration of leave to serve outside of the jurisdiction.[33] Not only does this burden lie with the plaintiff at the outset in a case of service ex juris, but it remains with the plaintiff if the defendant challenges the leave.[34]

In discussing the factors to be balanced, the High Court in *Voth* looked to *The Spiliada* as providing "valuable assistance" in Australia[35] and found that virtually all factors weighed heavily in favor of Missouri. It also found that there was no concrete juridical advantage to the plaintiff that should prevent allowance of the stay. New South Wales was an inappropriate forum.[36] The Court did, however,

---

[32]   171 C.L.R. 538, 554 (1990) (Mason, C.J., Deane, Dawson, and Gaudron, JJ.).

[33]   171 C.L.R. 538, 563–64 (1990).

[34]   "In such a case the onus should remain on the plaintiff on a subsequent application to set aside the service outside the jurisdiction." 171 C.L.R. 538, 564 (1990). *See also* Lawrence Collins, *The High Court of Australia and Forum Conveniens: The Last Word?*, 107 LAW Q. REV. 182, 187 (1991) ("[C]onstrained by *Oceanic Sun*, the High Court in *Voth* formulated a new test for service out of the jurisdiction cases which had never been applied in England or Australia. The effect is to shift the balance in favour of plaintiffs suing defendants outside the jurisdiction further than in any other Commonwealth country.").

This particular aspect of the High Court's approach has been widely criticized. Ellen Hayes, *Forum Non Conveniens in England, Australia and Japan: The Allocation of Jurisdiction in Transnational Litigation*, 26 U.B.C. L. REV. 41, 53 (1992) argues that "it is illogical to allocate the burden based upon the location of service in any event because service within the jurisdiction does not guarantee that the case has substantial contacts with the state; the defendant could be merely in transit" (footnote omitted). She notes that the approach taken in *Voth* is perplexing given that different Australian states have different leave requirements, as opposed to the situation in England, where judicial permission is uniformly required for service ex juris. Another commentator also questions the *Voth* court's approach, given that "[t]he common practice today is to allow a plaintiff to serve originating process outside the jurisdiction without prior leave of the court." Peter Brereton, *Forum Non Conveniens in Australia: A Case Note on* Voth v. Manildra Flour Mills, 40 INT'L & COMP. L.Q. 895, 900 (1991) (in Australia, "the absence of a hearing about leave to serve will mean that in an application to set aside service on inappropriate forum grounds, the onus of proof will rest on the defendant").

[35]   *Voth*, 171 C.L.R. 538, 565 (1990).

[36]   171 C.L.R. 538, 571–72 (1990). As to the loss of a plaintiff's juridical advantage, the High Court again diverged from the English test. As in England, an Australian court is to assess such an advantage in terms of "damages, costs, and limitation periods." However, where English courts assess the adequacy of an alternative forum's legal system in determining whether a plaintiff would lose an advantage, Australian courts are not to form subjective views about the adequacy of courts in foreign jurisdictions. Peter Brereton, *Forum Non Conveniens in Australia: A Case Note on* Voth v. Manildra Flour Mills, 40 INT'L & COMP. L.Q. 895, 896–97 (1991).

require that the stay be with the condition that the defendant agree to waive any statute of limitations defenses available in Missouri.[37] In this respect, the Australian doctrine is similar to that found in the United Kingdom, the United States, and Canada.

Subsequent to *Voth*, the High Court has dealt with the application of forum non conveniens in the face of exclusive choice of court clauses,[38] child custody matters,[39] anti-suit injunctions,[40] and lis alibi pendens. In *Henry v. Henry*,[41] a case involving parallel divorce litigation, the High Court affirmed the viability of the *Voth* test, but seemed to take strides towards liberalizing the forum non conveniens test in Australia. There the husband initiated divorce proceedings in Australia after proceedings were already underway in Monaco, and the wife moved for a stay of the Australian proceedings on grounds of forum non conveniens.[42] The *Henry* Court granted the appellant's motion to stay the divorce proceedings in Australia on grounds that Australia was clearly an inappropriate forum, holding that under *Voth* "[i]t is prima facie vexatious and oppressive, in the strict sense of those terms, to commence a second or subsequent action in the

---

[37]   Voth, 171 C.L.R. 538, 591 (1990).

[38]   *See, e.g.,* Akai Pty. Ltd. v. People's Ins. Co. Ltd., 141 A.L.R. 374 (1996) (denying defendant's motion to stay on grounds of public policy because Australian insurance law would not apply in England and thus a stay would deprive plaintiff of a legitimate juridical advantage, despite the presence of an exclusive jurisdiction clause pointing to England as the proper forum for litigation); Leigh-Mardon Pty. Ltd. v. PRC Inc., 44 F.C.R. 88 (1993) (holding that although an Australian court has discretion to stay proceedings in the face of an exclusive choice of court clause designating a foreign forum, it should only do so where strong cause is shown for maintaining the action in Australia).

[39]   *See, e.g.,* ZP v. PS, 122 A.L.R. 1 (1994) (holding that when the jurisdiction of the Family Court is invoked for settlement of a child custody dispute the court has no discretion to decline jurisdiction based on appropriateness of forum, and therefore the doctrine of forum non conveniens is inapplicable in such matters).

[40]   *See, e.g.,* CSR Ltd. v. Cigna Ins. Australia Ltd., 146 A.L.R. 402 (1997) (dismissing the respondents' motion for an anti-suit injunction and staying the action in Australia in favor of the United States forum, holding that while the court's power to issue an anti-suit injunction does not necessarily involve a forum non conveniens analysis and can be based on other principles of "equity," if a court determines that it is a "clearly inappropriate forum" it will not grant the injunction). Prior to *CSR*, the Federal Court of Australia, General Division, considered the application of *Voth* in the context of an application for an anti-suit injunction, holding that an anti-suit injunction is to be granted cautiously, and in doing so there must be strong evidence that suit in the forum about which the injunction is sought would be oppressive and vexatious to the petitioning party. Evidence that a court is the natural forum is simply not enough. Allstate Life Ins. v. Anz Banking Group Ltd., 142 A.L.R. 412 (Federal Court of Australia 1996).

[41]   185 C.L.R. 571 (1996).

[42]   185 C.L.R. 571, 581–82 (1996) (Dawson, Gaudron, McHugh and Gummow, JJ.).

courts of this country if an action is already pending with respect to the matter in issue."[43]

The Court in *Henry* warned against placing undue emphasis on a plaintiff's "prima facie" right to his chosen forum,[44] finding the purpose of the statement of such a right in *Voth* to be to allocate the burden to the defendant, rather than to shift unreasonable weight to a plaintiff's choice of forum. Professor Nygh summarized the effect of *Henry* on the evolution of modern forum non conveniens law in Australia as follows:

> In the first place, it has lowered the hurdle which the applicant for a stay has to overcome. The court does not start with a presumption that the plaintiff has a right to the selected forum once formal jurisdiction is established. This was an unfortunate interpretation of *Voth* which led to the denial of a stay in almost all cases decided in lower courts since. Secondly, where there is a *lis alibi pendens*, the forum must start from the point of view that this is undesirable. Once it concludes that each has jurisdiction, it must compare the competing *fora* and the effectiveness, including recognition and enforcement, of the resulting judgment as well as the degree of connection of each forum with the parties and the subject matter.
>
> In other words, it must determine which is the more appropriate forum. If there is an even balance, the determining factor should not be the selection of the home town plaintiff, but which proceeding is prior in time. In redefining *Voth* the High Court has moved away from the apparent advantage which its previous policy gave to the forum shopper. It has certainly sent a strong message to those who walk away from existing foreign proceedings to try their luck in Australia.[45]

---

43 185 C.L.R. 571, 591 (1996) (footnote omitted). The Court also reiterated that the point of the *Voth* test is to determine whether the Australian forum chosen is clearly inappropriate in the sense that it would be vexatious and oppressive to the defendant if the action continued there—with those words being liberally construed. 185 C.L.R. 571, 587 (1996).

44 185 C.L.R. 571, 591 (1996).

45 Peter Nygh, Voth *in the Family Court re-visited: the High Court pronounces forum non conveniens and lis alibi pendens*, 1996 Austl. J. Family L. LEXIS 10, 20 (July 23, 1996) (footnote omitted). *See also* Richard Garnett, *Stay of Proceedings in Australia: A "Clearly Inappropriate" Test?*, 23 Melb. U. L. Rev. 30 (1999) (noting that a great majority of cases in lower courts following *Voth* have rejected applications for a stay).

C. *Dow Jones & Co., Inc. v. Gutnick*

Subsequent to *Voth*, the High Court has declined to liberalize the Australian doctrine further so as to bring it closer to that in other common law jurisdictions. In *Dow Jones & Co., Inc. v. Gutnick*,[46] a well-known Australian businessman with substantial financial ties to the United States filed a claim in the Supreme Court of Victoria for damages resulting from the defendant's allegedly defamatory remarks about the plaintiff and his business activities.[47] These statements were found in an article in *Barron's Magazine*, published by Dow Jones.[48] Gutnick based his claim on both the internet publication of the article in question and the paper editions containing the article sold in Victoria.[49] Dow Jones moved for dismissal on several grounds, including that Victoria was a clearly inappropriate forum.[50]

The Supreme Court of Victoria refused to grant a stay in favor of the New Jersey forum,[51] based largely on its own Rule 7.05(2)(b), which allows a stay if Victoria "is not a convenient forum for the trial of the proceeding."[52] The defendant argued that the wording of the Rule indicates that the test for granting a stay in Victoria is less stringent than the "clearly inappropriate forum" test announced in *Voth* and, instead, leans more toward the *Spiliada* approach. The lower court, however, considered the language of Rule 7.05(b)(2) to do "no more or less than, in an English-literal form, convey the meaning and substance of the concept of forum non conveniens considered by the High Court in [*Voth*]."[53] Victoria was found to be "both the appropriate and convenient forum" for the case.[54]

---

[46] 210 C.L.R. 575 (2002).
[47] 210 C.L.R. 575, 594–95 (2002).
[48] 210 C.L.R. 575, 594–95 (2002).
[49] 210 C.L.R. 575, 594–95 (2002).
[50] 210 C.L.R. 575, 595–96 (2002).
[51] 210 C.L.R. 575, 632–33 (2002).
[52] 210 C.L.R. 575, 640 (2002).
[53] 210 C.L.R. 575, 622–23 (2002).
[54] 210 C.L.R. 575, 632 (2002).

On appeal, both the Victoria Court of Appeal[55] and the High Court affirmed the trial court.[56] The High Court found that determining where the allegedly defamatory publication was published would also "determine[] ... whether proceedings in the Supreme Court of Victoria should, as Dow Jones contended, be stayed on

---

[55]   Dow Jones Co., Inc. v. Gutnick, (2001) V.S.C.A. 249 (Sup. Ct. Vict., App. Ct.). With regard to the forum non conveniens issue, the Court of Appeal stated, at ¶ 10:

> [W]e think the decision is plainly correct. Publication took place in Victoria. The plaintiff resides and carries on business in Victoria. He wishes to restore his reputation in Victoria, and has undertaken to sue in no other place. The illegal activities in which the plaintiff is said to have participated took place principally in Victoria.

In Regie National des Usines Renault S.A. v. Zhang, 210 C.L.R. 491 (2001), decided several months before the High Court had rendered its decision in Gutnick, there was some indication by the dissenting justices that legislative intent should serve to replace the Voth "clearly appropriate forum" test where applicable. The plaintiff, an Australian citizen, had filed an action for damages in the Supreme Court of New South Wales against Renault, a French automobile manufacturer whose only connections with Australia were through its sales in Australia. 210 C.L.R. 491, 496–97 (2001). The plaintiff had suffered serious injury while driving one of the defendant's vehicles in New Caledonia. 210 C.L.R. 491, 497 (2001). Renault moved for a stay of the proceedings pursuant to the language in Pt 10, r 2A, on grounds that New South Wales was an "inappropriate forum." 210 C.L.R. 491, 499–500 (2001). The rule omits the word "clearly" from the test for a stay, and therefore presented the court with the almost identical issue dealt with by the Supreme Court of Victoria in Gutnick. The Supreme Court of New South Wales granted the stay in favor of New Caledonia, with conditions, based on an "inappropriate forum" test, but the Court of Appeal dismissed holding that the defendant "had not discharged the onus of showing that New South Wales was a 'clearly inappropriate forum.'" 210 C.L.R. 491, 500 (2001).

In affirming the Court of Appeal and refusing to stay, the High Court majority in Zhang adopted an approach similar to that taken by the lower court in Gutnick:

> Because a court's power to stay proceedings is an aspect of its inherent or implied power to prevent its own processes being used to bring about injustice, the same concepts and consideration necessarily inform the test of "inappropriate forum"... as inform the "clearly inappropriate forum" test adopted in Voth. And because the ultimate consideration is the prevention of injustice, they inform it in the same way.

210 C.L.R. 491, 503 (2001). The two dissenting justices, however, argued that legislative intent demonstrated an "inappropriate forum" test in place of the Voth test in New South Wales, and, accordingly, under that "less stringent" test New Caledonia was the more appropriate forum for the action. Justice Kirby stated this position in the following language:

> Whether or not, subjectively, the Rule Committee of the Supreme Court of New South Wales in 1988 intended to modify the previous common law is irrelevant. Until Pt 10 r 6A of the Rules was introduced, the language of the Rules committed a discretion to the Supreme Court in general terms ("may"). Such language was apt to invite incorporation of the common law elaboration as expounded by this Court. It was in this circumstance that the "clearly inappropriate forum" found its way into Australian law. But rule-makers had already begun introducing their own particular standards. Those standards now govern the field. The "clearly inappropriate forum" test had to give way to the applicable Rule. The specificity of statutory language expels the generality of the common law.

210 C.L.R. 491, 544 (2001) (Kirby, J., dissenting).

[56]   Dow Jones & Co., Inc. v. Gutnick, 210 C.L.R. 575 (2002).

the ground that that Court was a clearly inappropriate forum for the determination of the action."[57] As to the test for forum non conveniens, the High Court firmly endorsed the "clearly inappropriate forum" test set forth in *Voth*:

> [I]t is now established that an Australian court will decline, on the ground of *forum non conveniens*, to exercise jurisdiction which has been regularly invoked by a plaintiff, whether by personal service or under relevant long-arm jurisdiction provisions, only when it is shown that the forum whose jurisdiction is invoked by the plaintiff is clearly inappropriate.[58]

Upon finding that Victoria was the forum where the alleged tort occurred, the High Court ruled that Victoria law applied to the substantive issues at bar, and affirmed the lower court's decision to deny a stay.[59]

In his concurrence, Justice Kirby reiterated his preference for adopting a forum non conveniens doctrine in Australia more aligned with the modern English doctrine, but conceded that:

> [A]lthough the formulation by the House of Lords has found favour in most Commonwealth jurisdictions, and is more harmonious with the rules of public international law respectful of comity between nations and their courts, I must accept that this Court has adopted an approach more defensive of the exercise of properly invoked jurisdiction by Australian courts.[60]

III. Internal case allocation: The Cross-Vesting Act

The *Jurisdiction of Courts (Cross-Vesting) Act 1987* permits the transfer of a case between States of the Australian Commonwealth on convenience grounds under a less stringent test than that established for forum non conveniens in *Voth*. In Australia, this statute has served to limit forum non conveniens applications to

---

57   210 C.L.R. 575, 595 (2002).

58   210 C.L.R. 575, 596 (2002). Dow Jones argued that Victoria was clearly an inappropriate forum on grounds that the alleged defamatory article was published in New Jersey, and because of this New Jersey law would apply and hence a New Jersey court should preside over the substantive issues.

59   210 C.L.R. 575, 608 (2002).

60   210 C.L.R. 575, 641 (Kirby, J., concurring). Justice Kirby then found that the lower court correctly applied the "clearly inappropriate forum" test set forth in *Voth*, giving due weight to the fact that Victoria law applied to the dispute. 210 C.L.R. 575, 642 (2002).

those cases involving a foreign forum. This development is similar to the relationship between 28 U.S.C. § 1404(a) and forum non conveniens in the United States.[61]

IV. Summary and conclusion

Oceanic Sun Line, *Voth*, and *Gutnick* demonstrate that the Australian High Court has moved away from the strict "vexation and oppression" test adopted when it originally embraced the forum non conveniens doctrine in the *Maritime Insurance* case in 1908. Nonetheless, while the High Court has found "valuable guidance" in the House of Lords' decision in *The Spiliada*, and has demonstrated a tendency toward a more "liberal" approach in the *Henry* case, it has maintained its "clearly inappropriate forum" test as evidenced most recently in *Gutnick*. It may be that many cases would come out the same under this test and the "most appropriate forum" approach that is at the core of the doctrine in the United Kingdom, the United States, and Canada. Other cases in the High Court demonstrate, however, that Australia continues to place heavy emphasis on a plaintiff's right to a given forum, and remains the most difficult common law jurisdiction in which to succeed on a forum non conveniens motion.

---

[61] *See, e.g.,* Schmidt v. Won, 3 V.R. 435 (1998) (stating that *Voth* no longer applies to questions of venue concerning two Australian states, "and should in practice be confined to cases where it is arguable that a foreign court should be preferred").

CHAPTER 6

Similarities and Differences in Common Law Forum Non Conveniens Doctrine

I.   Introduction

While the four legal systems discussed in Chapters 2 through 5 are not the only ones with a forum non conveniens doctrine,[1] they represent the major common law legal systems and provide a reasonably comprehensive review of the development and application of the doctrine at the beginning of the twenty-first century. While each of these four countries has its own approach to forum non conveniens, there are important common elements to those approaches. In order to facilitate a consideration of how the doctrine can be dealt with in the context of global efforts at judicial cooperation and procedural harmonization, it is useful to clarify both the similarities and differences in the application of the doctrine in these four countries.

II.   Similarities in forum non conveniens doctrines

It is easiest to find similarities among the United Kingdom, the United States, and Canada, as indicated by the decisions in *Spiliada*,[2] *Piper*,[3] and *Amchem*,[4] respectively.

---

[1]   *See, e.g.*, Stephen Goldstein, *Israel, in* DECLINING JURISDICTION IN PRIVATE INTERNATIONAL LAW 259 (James J. Fawcett ed., 1995); Laurette Barnard, *New Zealand, in* DECLINING JURISDICTION IN PRIVATE INTERNATIONAL LAW 341 (James J. Fawcett ed., 1995); and PETER NORTH & JAMES J. FAWCETT, CHESHIRE AND NORTH'S PRIVATE INTERNATIONAL LAW 335 (13th ed. 1999) (noting the existence of the doctrine also in Brunei, Gibraltar, Hong Kong, Ireland, and Singapore).

[2]   Spiliada Maritime Corp. v. Cansulex Ltd., [1987] A.C. 460 (H.L.).

[3]   Piper Aircraft Co. v. Reyno, 454 U.S. 235 (1981).

[4]   Amchem Prods. Inc. v. British Columbia (Workers' Comp. Bd.), [1993] 1 S.C.R. 897.

The decisions of the Australian High Court in *Oceanic Sun Line*[5] and *Voth*,[6] on the other hand, make that country's forum non conveniens doctrine more difficult to reconcile fully with the others. Nonetheless, there remain common elements in the application of the doctrine in all four major common law systems.

A. The requirement of an available, alternative forum

In all four legal systems the core element of the forum non conveniens doctrine is the requirement that there be an available alternative forum for litigation of the dispute. The House of Lords made this clear in *Spiliada* in the statement that "a stay will only be granted on the ground of forum non conveniens where the court is satisfied that there is some other available forum, having competent jurisdiction, which is the appropriate forum for the trial of the action."[7] In the United States, the Supreme Court held in *Piper* that the first step in a forum non conveniens inquiry is the determination that an adequate alternative forum exists,[8] and stated in *Gilbert* that "[i]n all cases in which the doctrine of forum non conveniens comes into play, it presupposes at least two forums in which the defendant is amenable to process; the doctrine furnishes criteria for choice between them."[9] The same was made clear in the *Amchem* case in Canada when the Supreme Court adopted this element of the House of Lords' forum non conveniens test from *Spiliada*, and stated that "the existence of a more appropriate forum must be clearly established to displace the forum selected by the plaintiff."[10]

While Australia's "clearly inconvenient forum" test focuses more on the inappropriateness of the local forum than on the appropriateness of an alternative foreign forum, the requirement of an available alternative forum remains nonetheless an aspect of the analysis. This is clear from the statement of the High Court in *Voth* that "considerations relating to the suitability of the alternative forum are relevant to the examination of the appropriateness or inappropriateness of the selected forum."[11]

---

5   Oceanic Sun Line Special Shipping Co. Inc. v. Fay, 165 C.L.R. 197, 79 A.L.R. 9 (1988).

6   Voth v. Manildra Flour Mills Pty Ltd., 171 C.L.R. 538 (1990).

7   *Spiliada*, [1987] A.C. 460, 476 (H.L.).

8   *Piper*, 454 U.S. 235, 255 n.22 (1981).

9   *Gilbert*, 330 U.S. 501, 506–07 (1947).

10   *Amchem*, [1993] 1 S.C.R. 897, 921.

11   *Voth*, 171 C.L.R. 538, 558 (1990).

B. Allocation of the general burden of proof on the defendant

While it is possible that the burden may shift at certain stages of the analysis, in all four systems the defendant generally has the burden of proving the elements required to stay or dismiss the case in the initial forum. In the United Kingdom, "the burden resting on the defendant is not just to show that England is not the natural or appropriate forum for the trial, but to establish that there is another available forum which is clearly or distinctly more appropriate than the English forum."[12] This element of the doctrine appears to have been so clearly assumed in the cases before the U.S. Supreme Court that it has received scant discussion. It is clear, however, in the decisions of lower courts.[13] In Canada, the burden is perhaps best captured by the language of the British Columbia Court of Appeal in the *Westec Aerospace*[14] case, stating that "[w]here jurisdiction *simpliciter* exists, a defendant that contends the action should not be entertained bears the onus of demonstrating that the courts of another jurisdiction are sufficiently more appropriate for the resolution of the dispute to displace the forum the plaintiff has selected."[15] In Australia, the differences in the test make the burden even higher for the defendant to show that the plaintiff's chosen court is a clearly inappropriate forum.[16]

Differences in approach to the type of case in which a forum non conveniens analysis may be applied, including its application to basic issues of jurisdiction, result in nuanced distinctions in the allocation of the burden of proof. Nonetheless, on the basic issue in a straightforward forum non conveniens analysis, once jurisdiction is established (*i.e.*, excluding cases of service ex juris), the burden is on the defendant in all four common law systems.

---

[12] *Spiliada*, [1987] A.C. 460, 477 (H.L.).

[13] *See, e.g., In re* Air Crash Disaster near New Orleans, 821 F.2d 1147, 1164 (5th Cir. 1987):

> A defendant of course bears the burden of invoking the doctrine and moving to dismiss in favor of a foreign forum. This burden of persuasion runs to all the elements of the forum non conveniens analysis. Therefore, the moving defendant must establish that an adequate and available forum exists as to all defendants if there are several. If the moving defendant carries this initial burden, it must also establish that the private and public interests weigh heavily on the side of trial in the foreign forum.

[14] Westec Aerospace Inc. v. Raytheon Aircraft Co., 173 D.L.R. 4th 498 (B.C.C.A. 1999), *affirmed at* 197 D.L.R. 4th 211 (2001).

[15] 173 D.L.R. 4th 498, 502–03 (B.C.C.A. 1999).

[16] *See, e.g.,* Regie National des Usines Renault S.A. v. Zhang, (2002) 210 C.L.R. 491, 187 A.L.R. 1, ¶¶ 13–14, (H.C.) (stating that the defendant "had not discharged the onus of showing that New South Wales was a 'clearly inappropriate forum'").

C. Consideration of private interest factors

While only the United States explicitly applies public interest factors to the forum non conveniens analysis, all four systems specifically consider factors going to the private interests of the parties to the litigation. In *Spiliada*, the House of Lords stated that "connecting factors … will include not only factors affecting convenience or expense (such as availability of witnesses), but also other factors such as the law governing the relevant transaction … and the places where the parties respectively reside or carry on business."[17] The private interest factors are most specifically listed in the U.S. Supreme Court's decision in *Gilbert*:

> Important considerations are the relative ease of access to sources of proof; availability of compulsory process for attendance of unwilling, and the cost of obtaining attendance of willing, witnesses; possibility of view of premises, if view would be appropriate to the action; and all other practical problems that make trial of a case easy, expeditious and inexpensive. There may also be questions as to the enforcibility of a judgment if one is obtained. The court will weigh relative advantages and obstacles to fair trial.[18]

In Canada, "[t]he factors commonly considered are the parties' residences and places of business, the jurisdiction where the cause of action arose and where the damage was suffered, juridical advantages and disadvantages, convenience and expense, the governing law and the difficulty of its proof, and the existence of any parallel proceedings."[19] While these factors have not been so clearly itemized by the High Court of Australia, in *Voth* the Court effectively brought them into the analysis by noting the "valuable assistance" of the relevant connecting factors discussed in *Spiliada*, and then proceeding to discuss such factors in its own analysis.[20]

---

[17] *Spiliada*, [1987] A.C. 460, 478 (H.L.).
[18] *Gilbert*, 330 U.S. 501, 508 (1947).
[19] Westec Aerospace, Inc. v. Raytheon Aircraft Co. (1999), 173 D.L.R. (4th) 498, 503 (B.C.C.A.). *See also* Joost Blom, *Canada*, *in* DECLINING JURISDICTION IN PRIVATE INTERNATIONAL LAW 121, 130 (James J. Fawcett ed., 1995) ("resolving the question of *forum conveniens* may require the consideration of any factor that bears on the interests of the parties in obtaining the most success at the least cost").
[20] *Voth*, 171 C.L.R. 538, 564–65 (1990).

D. Trial court discretion in applying forum non conveniens analysis

In all four systems, it is considered important that the trial court has broad discretion in making a forum non conveniens determination, and that such a determination will not lightly be overturned on appeal. In *Spiliada*, the House of Lords specifically noted "the limited grounds upon which an appellate court may interfere with the exercise of a trial judge's discretion."[21] In *Gilbert*, the U.S. Supreme Court justified deference to the trial court's determination by stating that "[t]he doctrine leaves much to the discretion of the court to which plaintiff resorts, and experience has not shown a judicial tendency to renounce one's own jurisdiction so strong as to result in many abuses."[22] In Canada, courts have made clear that "[w]here the judge of first instance has exercised his discretion one way or the other, the grounds on which an appellate court is entitled to interfere with the decision which he has made are of limited character," and an appellate court "cannot simply interfere because its members consider that they would, themselves sitting at first instance, have reached a different conclusion."[23]

This element of the doctrine recognizes the substantial deference given by higher courts to the balancing of relevant factors by the trial judge who is best positioned to consider them. It may appear at first that the greater deference given in Australia to the plaintiff's choice of forum brings with it an enhanced opportunity for a review of the forum non conveniens decision on appeal. Nonetheless, in *Voth*, the High Court specifically stated that "the question is pre-eminently one for the trial judge, and appeal should be rare and an appellate court should be slow to intervene."[24]

E. Ability to impose conditions on a stay or dismissal

In all four legal systems, a court may impose conditions on a stay or dismissal granted on forum non conveniens grounds, including the defendant's submission

---

[21] *Spiliada*, [1987] A.C. 460, 471.

[22] *Gilbert*, 330 U.S. 501, 508 (1947). The level of trial court discretion was emphasized by Justice Scalia's majority opinion in *American Dredging Co. v. Miller*, 510 U.S. 443, 455 (1994), when he noted that "[t]he discretionary nature of the doctrine, combined with the multifariousness of the factors relevant to its application . . . make uniformity and predictability of outcome almost impossible."

[23] Avenue Properties Ltd. v. First City Development Corp., (1986) 7 B.C.L.R.(2d) 45, ¶ 18 (B.C.C.A.).

[24] *Voth*, 171 C.L.R. 538, 570 (1990).

to jurisdiction in the alternative forum and waiver of any time bar in that forum. In the United Kingdom, Lord Goff's opinion in *Spiliada* specifically suggested that the lower court require that the defendant waive the statute of limitations as a condition of granting its forum non conveniens request.[25] In the United States, prominent examples include *Piper*, where dismissal was conditioned on the defendants' agreement to waive any statute of limitation defenses and to submit to the jurisdiction of Scotland.[26] In the *Bhopal* case, the Second Circuit Court of Appeal approved conditions that the defendant submit to the jurisdiction of India and waive any statute of limitations defenses, but rejected conditions that the defendant agree in advance to the enforceability of an Indian judgment and accept discovery in India according to the Federal Rules of Civil Procedure.[27] In Canada, the British Columbia Court of Appeal has stated that "if a court has jurisdiction but declines it under *forum non conveniens*, the court may condition the stay of proceedings on, among other things, the defendant agreeing to submit to the jurisdiction of the more proper forum or to waive a statute of limitations defence in the other forum."[28] In Australia, the High Court in *Voth* specifically noted that an undertaking by the defendant not to raise a statute of limitations bar in the alternative forum "may be made a condition of any order staying the action."[29]

F. Benefits of existing similarities in comparative analysis

These similarities provide substantial common ground in the application of the forum non conveniens doctrine in the common law world, and allow a more focused discussion of how the doctrine might appropriately be dealt with in global efforts at legal harmonization. Before moving on to those efforts, however, it is worth considering differences that exist in order to address their impact as well.

---

[25] *Spiliada*, [1987] A.C. 460, 484 ("The appropriate order, where the application of the time bar in the foreign jurisdiction is dependent upon its invocation by the defendant, may well be to make it a condition of the grant of a stay, or the exercise of discretion against giving leave to serve out of the jurisdiction, that the defendant should waive the time bar in the foreign jurisdiction....").

[26] *Piper*, 454 U.S. 235, 242 (1981).

[27] *In re* Union Carbide Corp. Gas Plant Disaster at Bhopal, 809 F.2d 195 (2d Cir. 1987), *cert. denied*, 484 U.S. 871 (1987).

[28] Jordan v. Schatz, 2000 B.C.C.A. 409, 77 B.C.L.R.3d 134, ¶ 25 (2000).

[29] *Voth*, 171 C.L.R. 538, 571 (1990).

III. Differences in forum non conveniens doctrines

The differences in substance and application of the forum non conveniens doctrine among the four legal systems discussed here are best indicated by the ways in which the approaches in Australia and the United States diverge from the other three states. Differences in Canada and the United Kingdom generally are more nuanced, and best discussed after consideration of the more significant distinctions found in Australia and the United States.

A. Distinctions setting Australia apart

1. *The clearly inappropriate forum test*

The most notable distinction in considering the forum non conveniens doctrine in these four countries is the Australian preference for a "clearly inappropriate forum" test, as opposed to what can generally be called the "more appropriate forum" test applied in the three other common law systems.[30] Australia's different approach in this regard represents a tendency to hold on to elements of the strict "vexatious and oppressive" standard while the other three systems have evolved to a more liberal approach. Even so, the Australian High Court's retention of a "clearly inappropriate forum test" in *Voth*[31] was accompanied by an explanation that the words "oppressive" and "vexatious" are to be liberally construed.[32] Nonetheless, this test brings with it significant distinctions, the most important of which involves the test itself.

As noted in Chapter 5, the test in Australia diverges both from the traditional "vexatious and oppressive"/"abuse of process" test and from the more appropriate forum test applied in some manner in the other three common law systems studied here. The abuse of process test of the early twentieth-century placed the highest burden on a defendant seeking to move the case to another forum, and the more appropriate forum test represents a substantial liberalization of the

---

[30] Professor von Mehren has referred to this as the distinction between an "abuse-of-process" and a "convenience-suitability approach." Arthur von Mehren, *Theory and Practice of Adjudicatory Authority in Private International Law: A Comparative Study of the Doctrine, Policies and Practices of Common- and Civil-Law Systems*, 295 RECUEIL DES COURS 326 (2002).

[31] *Voth*, 171 C.L.R. 538, 556–57 (1990).

[32] *Voth*, 171 C.L.R. 538, 555 (1990) (noting that in *Oceanic Sun Lines*, "Deane J. agreed with the caution uttered by Lord Wilberforce in *The Atlantic Star* against construing 'oppressive' and 'vexatious' too rigidly in the context of dismissing or staying an action on inappropriate forum grounds.").

forum non conveniens doctrine in this regard. Thus, while changes have occurred, the evolutionary process has not gone as far in Australia as it has in the other three countries. The real difference is found in the level of deference given to the plaintiff's choice of forum, with Australia imposing a more difficult burden on the defendant while at the same time moving away from the traditional test that would require a strict showing of vexation and oppression.

It is interesting to note that the Australian High Court in *Voth* suggested that its rejection of the more appropriate forum approach of *Spiliada* resulted in a closer relationship between the U.S. and Australian approaches than between Australia and either the United Kingdom or Canada.[33] For this conclusion, the Court relied on the use in *Piper* of the oppressive and vexatious language of the traditional forum non conveniens doctrine.[34] Regardless of this U.S.-Australian connection, the Australian High Court has chosen to set itself apart from the other three common law countries considered here, in a manner that imposes a heavier burden on the defendant seeking authorization to move the case to another jurisdiction.

2. *The plaintiff's juridical advantage from its choice of forum*

The second Australian distinction comes in the consideration of the plaintiff's juridical advantage that may result from its chosen forum. This is a major forum shopping issue, and the distinction indicates a choice regarding the extent to which the doctrine of forum non conveniens works to encourage or discourage forum shopping in each legal system. While in the other three countries a plaintiff's advantage from trial in its chosen forum is only one factor to be considered in determining whether a court should decline to exercise jurisdiction, in Australia a plaintiff's juridical advantage from its choice of forum is given significant deference in the forum non conveniens analysis, and weighs much more heavily against stay or dismissal.

---

[33] *Voth*, 171 C.L.R. 538, 561 (1990).

[34] *Piper*, 454 U.S. 235, 241 (1981) (quoting from Koster v. (American) Lumbermens Mut. Cas. Co., 330 U.S. 518, 524 (1947)):

[W]hen an alternative forum has jurisdiction to hear the case, and when trial in the chosen forum would "establish . . . oppressiveness and vexation to a defendant . . . out of all proportion to plaintiff's convenience," or when the "chosen forum [is] inappropriate because of considerations affecting the court's own administrative and legal problems," the court may, in the exercise of its sound discretion, dismiss the case.

In *Spiliada,* Lord Goff dealt with the juridical advantage issue by noting that a court should not avoid a forum non conveniens stay simply because damages might be lower in the alternative forum.[35] In the United States, the Supreme Court specifically determined in *Piper* that the fact that Scottish law was less favorable to the plaintiff was not in itself enough to justify a forum non conveniens dismissal.[36] Similarly, in Canada, the Supreme Court in *Amchem* stated that "there is no reason in principle why the loss of [a plaintiff's] juridical advantage should be treated as a separate and distinct condition rather than being weighed with the other factors which are considered in identifying the appropriate forum."[37]

The Australian High Court in *Voth* made clear its added deference to a plaintiff's juridical advantage. In its discussion of the first element of what it considered to be "common ground" in the opinions from *Oceanic Sun,* the Court stated that "a plaintiff who has regularly invoked the jurisdiction of a court has a prima facie right to insist upon its exercise."[38] This was later tempered a bit in *Henry v. Henry,*[39] when the High Court warned against placing undue emphasis on a plaintiff's "prima facie" right to his chosen forum, and found the purpose of the statement of such a right in *Voth* to be to allocate the burden to the defendant, rather than to shift unreasonable weight to a plaintiff's choice of forum.[40] Nonetheless, the extent to which the Australian doctrine gives more weight to the plaintiff's juridical advantage than is done in the other three countries is further indicated by the fourth "common" aspect of the *Oceanic Sun* opinions highlighted in *Voth,* namely that "the jurisdiction to grant a stay or dismiss the action is to be exercised 'with great care' or 'extreme caution.'"[41] Thus, two of the four important common elements carried forward from *Oceanic Sun* to *Voth* require significant deference to the plaintiff's choice of forum.[42]

---

[35] *Spiliada,* [1987] A.C. 460, 482.
[36] *Piper,* 454 U.S. 235, 249 n.15 (1981) (noting that the Court in *Gilbert* "held that dismissal may be warranted where a plaintiff chooses a particular forum, not because it is convenient, but solely in order to harass the defendant or take advantage of favorable law.").
[37] *Amchem,* [1993] 1 S.C.R. 897, 919.
[38] *Voth,* 171 C.L.R. 538, 554 (1990).
[39] 185 C.L.R. 571 (1996).
[40] 185 C.L.R. 571, 591 (1996).
[41] *Voth,* (1990) 171 C.L.R. 538, 554.
[42] In *Voth,* the Court specifically considered the argument that granting the defendant's forum non conveniens motion "would operate to deprive the respondents of a legitimate juridical advantage in relation to the measure of damages and the awarding of costs in Missouri." 171 C.L.R. 538, 548 (1990).

The question of juridical advantage also serves to highlight an important distinction between U.K. and Canadian law. In *Spiliada*, Lord Goff set out a two-stage process of analysis:

> Since the question is whether there exists some other forum which is clearly more appropriate for the trial of the action, the court will look first to see what factors there are which point in the direction of another forum. . . .

> If the court concludes at that stage that there is no other available forum which is clearly more appropriate for the trial of the action, it will ordinarily refuse a stay; . . . it is difficult to imagine circumstances where, in such a case, a stay may be granted.

> If however the court concludes at that stage that there is some other available forum which prima facie is clearly more appropriate for the trial of the action, it will ordinarily grant a stay unless there are circumstances by reason of which justice requires that a stay should nevertheless not be granted. In this inquiry, the court will consider all the circumstances of the case, including circumstances which go beyond those taken into account when considering connecting factors with other jurisdictions.[43]

The Canadian Supreme Court has effectively rejected such a two-stage analysis, especially where the consideration in the second stage is of a plaintiff's juridical advantage. Thus, Justice Sopinka stated in *Amchem* that:

> [T]here is no reason in principle why the loss of juridical advantage should be treated as a separate and distinct condition rather than being weighed with the other factors which are considered in identifying the appropriate forum. . . . The weight to be given to juridical advantage is very much a function of the parties' connection to the particular jurisdiction in question. If a party seeks out a jurisdiction simply to gain a juridical advantage rather than by reason of a real and substantial connection of the case to the jurisdiction, that is ordinarily condemned as "forum shopping." On the other hand, a party whose case has a real and substantial connection with a forum has a legitimate claim to the advantages that that forum provides.

---

43   *Spiliada*, [1987] A.C. 460, 477–78.

The legitimacy of this claim is based on a reasonable expectation that in the event of litigation arising out of the transaction in question, those advantages will be available.[44]

While U.K. courts may consider a plaintiff's juridical advantage as one element in determining, at a second stage, that justice requires that a stay not be granted, Canadian courts treat it merely as one of the factors to be balanced in determining the more appropriate forum. In either event, the matter is given less weight in both Canada and the United Kingdom than is the case in Australia.

B. Distinctions setting the United States apart

While the adherence of U.S. Courts to a more appropriate forum approach places it closer to the doctrine applied in the United Kingdom and Canada than to the clearly inconvenient forum approach applied in Australia, the U.S. doctrine has a number of elements that distinguish it from that of the other three legal systems. While substantively the Australian doctrine is most unique among the four, the U.S. doctrine demonstrates special procedural distinctions.

1. Consideration of public interest factors

The list of factors considered in a forum non conveniens analysis in U.S. courts continues to be that stated in *Gulf Oil Corp. v. Gilbert*.[45] These explicitly include both private interest and public interest factors. While cases from the other three legal systems may include consideration of issues of comity and applicable law,[46] the United Kingdom explicitly denies that public interest factors are a part of the forum non conveniens analysis. Thus, U.K. courts have specifically stated that "public interest considerations not related to the private interests of the parties

---

[44] *Amchem*, [1993] 1 S.C.R. 897, 919–20.

[45] 330 U.S. 501, 508–09 (1947).

[46] *See, e.g.,* Joost Blom, *Canada, in* DECLINING JURISDICTION IN PRIVATE INTERNATIONAL LAW 121, 131–32 (James J. Fawcett ed., 1995) ("Typically, the fact that the litigation concerns a contract or a tort that is governed by the law of a particular country is mentioned only as a supplementary reason for favouring the hearing of the action in that country. Occasionally it may be treated as a dominant factor.").

and the ends of justice have no bearing on the decision which the Court has to make" in a forum non conveniens analysis.[47]

Canadian and Australian cases tend not to be as clear on whether public interest factors are appropriate for consideration. The heavy reliance of Canadian courts on U.K. authorities would appear to place Canada with the United Kingdom on this issue. Nonetheless, it is difficult to find explicit authority for this proposition. It is the case, however, that the list of factors considered by most Canadian courts is limited to traditional private interest factors.[48] In its decision in *Voth*, the Australian High Court specifically noted that its test differed from that in the United States, which "takes account of the selected forum's administrative problems, e.g., congested lists and lack of judicial resources, these being matters of a kind to which our courts do not usually have regard."[49] In the earlier *Oceanic Sun* decision, Justice Deane specifically rejected consideration of public interest factors in his choice of the U.K. approach over that in the United States.[50]

While some courts in the other three countries have considered factors such as administrative inconvenience in hearing the case in a particular forum, as well as issues of complex applicable law analyses, the United States clearly places greater emphasis on factors involving public interests. This may result in part from a history of docket congestion in the United States, especially in federal courts.

---

[47]   Lubbe v. Cape PLC, [2000] 2 Lloyd's Rep. 383, 394 (H.L.) (Lord Bingham of Cornhill) and 397–98 (Lord Hope of Craighead) (H.L.):

> [T]he principles on which the doctrine of forum non conveniens rest leave no room for considerations of public interest or public policy which cannot be related to the private interests of any of the parties or the ends of justice in the case which is before the Court. . . . So, if the plea of forum non conveniens cannot be sustained on the ground that the case may be tried more suitably in the other forum, . . . "for the interests of all the parties and for the ends of justice," the jurisdiction must be exercised—however desirable it may be on grounds of public interest or public policy that the litigation should be conducted elsewhere and not in the English Courts.

[48]   *See, e.g.,* Antares Shipping Corp. v. The Capricorn, [1977] 65 D.L.R.3d 105, 123 (S.C.).

> The factors affecting the application of this doctrine. . . include the balance of convenience to all the parties concerned . . . the undesirability of trespassing on the jurisdiction of a foreign State, the impropriety and inconvenience of trying a case in one country when the cause of action arose in another where the laws are different, and the cost of assembling foreign witnesses."

[49]   *Voth*, 171 C.L.R. 538, 561 (1990).

[50]   *Oceanic Sun*, 165 C.L.R. 197, 250 (1988) (Deane, J). *But see* Joost Blom, *Canada, in* DECLINING JURISDICTION IN PRIVATE INTERNATIONAL LAW 121, 130 (James J. Fawcett ed., 1995) ("[R]esolving the question of *forum conveniens* [in Canada] may require the consideration of any factor that bears on the interests of the parties in obtaining the most success at the least cost, *as well as on the interests of the administration of justice in the affected countries*."). Emphasis added.

Docket congestion has traditionally not existed in the United Kingdom,[51] and appears not to be as great an issue in Australia and Canada.

2. *The post-jurisdiction nature of the doctrine*

Subsequent to the *Sinochem* decision by the U.S. Supreme Court, forum non conveniens doctrine may be applied to dismiss or stay an action even before a final determination of personal jurisdiction.[52] Nonetheless, no U.S. court to date has applied a forum non conveniens analysis to the determination of jurisdiction. In the United States, a forum non conveniens challenge will not be considered as part of the basic jurisdictional analysis.[53] This differs rather substantially from the scope of the doctrine in the other three countries, where similar analysis can influence the initial consideration of jurisdiction, questions of service outside the forum territory, declination of existing jurisdiction, and the analysis of anti-suit injunction issues. Because Canadian jurisdiction tests are so similar to the forum non conveniens test, Canadian common law courts often blend the initial jurisdictional inquiry, blurring the distinction between jurisdiction as of right and the concept of forum non conveniens. In the United Kingdom and Australia, special rules concerning shifting of burden of proof result from distinctions in jurisdictional analysis and incorporation of concepts of service into the jurisdictional decision. This also leads to differences in the application of the forum non conveniens doctrine, but those differences are more appropriately discussed in the context of the burden of proof.

---

[51]   *See* David Robertson, *Forum non conveniens in America and England: "A Rather Fantastic Friction,"* 103 L.Q. Rev. 398, 417 (1987):

> England's courts are simply not that crowded, and the kind of transnational litigations that does tend to flow to England is highly desirable stuff. Furthermore, overtly stating that a case is being dismissed because of the court's own administrative problems would seem completely inconsistent with British judicial traditions. The courts of Scotland have explicitly disapproved docket congestion as a justification for forum non conveniens dismissal, and England can confidently be expected to follow Scotland's lead in this.

[52]   *See* Chapter 3, Part III.J., above.

[53]   It has been suggested that courts in the United States should combine various "gatekeeping" doctrines, including forum non conveniens, in a manner that would make the U.S. system in some ways more like that of the three other common law systems in their application of forum non conveniens and forum conveniens principles. *See, e.g.*, Spencer Weber Waller, *A Unified Theory of Transnational Procedure*, 26 Cornell Int'l L.J. 101, 101–02 (1993) (suggesting that "questions of subject matter jurisdiction or jurisdiction to prescribe, antisuit injunctions, service of process, personal jurisdiction, venue, choice of law, choice of discovery rules, forum non conveniens, and other preliminary questions" should all be dealt with under a common procedure so that similar doctrines do not result in repetitive analysis, and so that "the real issue of whether the United States has any direct and substantial interest in the resolution of the dispute" can be the singular focus).

3. The false distinction: assumed bias against foreign plaintiffs

It often is assumed that in the United States the forum non conveniens doctrine accords more weight to a domestic plaintiff's choice of a U.S. forum than to a similar choice by a foreign plaintiff. This has developed from language analyzing convenience in the discussion of balancing factors in the *Koster*[54] and *Piper*[55] cases. In final analysis, however, it is inappropriate to assume that the Supreme Court has authorized a type of discrimination against foreign plaintiffs in the forum non conveniens analysis. In *Koster*, the Court commented not on any disadvantage to a foreign plaintiff, but rather on the balance of conveniences when the plaintiff is local and when there is one plaintiff as compared to multiple plaintiffs:

> Where there are only two parties to a dispute, there is good reason why it should be tried in the plaintiff's home forum if that has been his choice. He should not be deprived of the presumed advantages of his home jurisdiction except upon a clear showing of facts which either (1) establish such oppressiveness and vexation to a defendant as to be out of all proportion to plaintiff's convenience, which may be shown to be slight or nonexistent, or (2) make trial in the chosen forum inappropriate because of considerations affecting the court's own administrative and legal problems. In any balancing of conveniences, a real showing of convenience by a plaintiff who has sued in his home forum will normally outweigh the inconvenience the defendant may have shown.[56]

This language was picked up in *Piper*, and extended to produce the following analysis when a foreign plaintiff is involved:

> The District Court's distinction between resident or citizen plaintiffs and foreign plaintiffs is fully justified. In *Koster*, the Court indicated that a plaintiff's choice of forum is entitled to greater deference when the plaintiff has chosen the home forum. . . . When the home forum has been chosen, it is reasonable to assume that this choice is convenient. When the plaintiff is foreign, however, this assumption is much less reasonable. Because the central purpose of any *forum non conveniens* inquiry is to

---

54   *Koster v. (American) Lumbermens Mut. Casualty Co.*, 330 U.S. 518 (1947).
55   *Piper Aircraft Co. v. Reyno*, 454 U.S. 235 (1981).
56   *Koster*, 330 U.S. 518, 524 (1947).

ensure that the trial is convenient, a foreign plaintiff's choice deserves less deference.[57]

This aspect of the analysis seems most properly explained in the Second Circuit decision in *Iragorri v. United Technologies Corp.*,[58] where the court explained its rationale for any difference in treatment of domestic and foreign plaintiffs as follows:

> Based on the Supreme Court's guidance, our understanding of how courts should address the degree of deference to be given to a plaintiff's choice of a U.S. forum is essentially as follows: The more it appears that a domestic or foreign plaintiff's choice of forum has been dictated by reasons that the law recognizes as valid, the greater the deference that will be given to the plaintiff's forum choice. Stated differently, the greater the plaintiff's or the lawsuit's bona fide connection to the United States and to the forum of choice and the more it appears that considerations of convenience favor the conduct of the lawsuit in the United States, the more difficult it will be for the defendant to gain dismissal for *forum non conveniens*. Thus, factors that argue against *forum non conveniens* dismissal include the convenience of the plaintiff's residence in relation to the chosen forum, the availability of witnesses or evidence to the forum district, the defendant's amenability to suit in the forum district, the availability of appropriate legal assistance, and other reasons relating to convenience or expense. On the other hand, the more it appears that the plaintiff's choice of a U.S. forum was motivated by forum-shopping reasons—such as attempts to win a tactical advantage resulting from local laws that favor the plaintiff's case, the habitual generosity of juries in the United States or in the forum district, the plaintiff's popularity or the defendant's unpopularity in the region, or the inconvenience and expense to the defendant resulting from litigation in that forum— the less deference the plaintiff's choice commands and, consequently, the easier it becomes for the defendant to succeed on a forum non conveniens motion by showing that convenience would be better served by litigating in another country's courts.[59]

---

[57] *Piper*, 454 U.S. 235, 255–56 (1981).
[58] 274 F.3d 65 (2d Cir. 2001).
[59] 274 F.3d 65, 71–72 (2d Cir. 2001).

Under this analysis, it is not a matter of discrimination against foreign plaintiffs that results in the difference in treatment, but rather simple recognition that the presence of a foreign plaintiff will make a forum less convenient than will the presence of a local plaintiff.[60]

Great Britain (England in particular) has a long history of encouraging foreign plaintiffs to sue there, and has not attached a "presumption of inconvenience" to a foreign plaintiff's selection of a U.K. forum. Canada similarly does not disfavor a foreign plaintiff's choice of forum in a forum non conveniens analysis.[61] Australia's "clearly inconvenient forum" analysis seems not to attach any explicit or implicit disadvantage to a foreign plaintiff. Given a proper analysis of this issue in U.S. case law, it would seem that the difference between a local plaintiff and a foreign plaintiff is simply one element of the balancing of private interest factors, and no real substantive doctrinal distinction exists in this regard; or if it does it is at best quite limited.

C. Other distinctions

1. A shifting burden of proof

As noted above,[62] the general principle that the defendant bringing a forum non conveniens motion bears the burden of proof is common among all four jurisdictions. Nonetheless, other distinctions in the application of the doctrine result in the burden shifting between the parties as different tests are considered.

In the United Kingdom, the focus of the proceedings determines which party has the initial burden, and the burden may shift as the analysis progresses. At the outset, if service must be effected on a defendant outside the jurisdiction (service ex juris), then jurisdiction is considered "exorbitant,"[63] and "[t]he intention must be to impose upon the plaintiff the burden of showing good reasons why service of a writ, calling for appearance before an English court, should, in the circumstances, be permitted upon a foreign defendant."[64] On the other hand, if service may be effected within the jurisdiction, then the issue is first raised by the

---

60 This analysis appears to have been confirmed by the Supreme Court in Sinochem Int'l Co. Ltd. v. Malaysia Int'l Shipping Corp., _U.S._ 127 S.Ct. 1184, 1191 (2007).

61 *See* Genevieve Saumier, *Forum Non Conveniens: Where Are We Now?*, 12 SUP. CT. L. REV. (2d) 121, 143 (2000).

62 See Part II. B, above.

63 *Spiliada*, [1987] A.C. 460, 478 (H.L.).

64 *Spiliada*, [1987] A.C. 460, 479 (H.L.).

defendant, and the burden is on the defendant. Even then, however, that burden may be shifted to the plaintiff. The two-stage analysis of Lord Goff in *Spiliada* places the initial burden in such a case on the defendant to show that there is another available forum that is distinctly more appropriate.[65] If that burden is not met, then no stay is granted. If that burden is met, however, then "the burden of proof shifts to the plaintiff to show 'circumstances by reason of which justice requires that a stay should nevertheless not be granted.'"[66]

In Canada, the first distinction found in the United Kingdom appears also to apply, but with a further distinction between service outside the jurisdiction as a matter of right, and service that requires leave of the court. Thus as one commentator puts it,

> [i]n the cases where a plaintiff must have leave to serve *ex juris*, the Canadian courts have assumed on the basis of tradition, rather than any express reference to this issue in the rules of court, that the plaintiff has the burden of persuading the local court that it is *forum conveniens*. Where the requirement of leave has been removed, so that service *ex juris* is available as of right, it is arguable that the burden of proof has been altered as well, so that it is for the defendant who challenges such service to show that the court is *forum non conveniens*.[67]

This conclusion appears to be consistent with the language of *Amchem*, where Justice Sopinka stated:

> Whether the burden of proof should be on the plaintiff in *ex juris* cases will depend on the rule that permits service out of the jurisdiction. If it requires that service out of the jurisdiction be justified by the plaintiff, whether on an application for an order or in defending service *ex juris* where no order is required, then the rule must govern.[68]

---

65   *Spiliada*, [1987] A.C. 460, 477–78 (H.L.).

66   James J. Fawcett, *General Report*, *in* DECLINING JURISDICTION IN PRIVATE INTERNATIONAL LAW 11 (James J. Fawcett ed., 1995). This distinction in the English test is not difficult to grasp when placed in the context of history. English courts traditionally encouraged forum shopping by foreign plaintiffs. Thus, it may be argued that when the House of Lords decided *Spiliada* and pronounced the modern English test, it was still reluctant to completely abandon the strong historical protection given to a plaintiff's choice of forum in England.

67   Joost Blom, *Canada*, *in* DECLINING JURISDICTION IN PRIVATE INTERNATIONAL LAW 121, 128–29 (James J. Fawcett ed., 1995). Blom's analysis indicates, however, that case law on the burden when service ex juris is a "matter of right" goes both ways.

68   *Amchem*, [1993] 1 S.C.R. 897, 921, ¶ 38.

Nonetheless, it was immediately stated in the same opinion that "[t]he burden of proof should not play a significant role in these matters as it only applies in cases in which the judge cannot come to a determinate decision on the basis of the material presented by the parties."[69]

Once the initial burden is allocated, there is no shifting in Canada similar to that in the United Kingdom under *Spiliada*. The *Amchem* rejection of the two-stage analysis of *Spiliada* effectively leaves only a single question before the appropriate forum and thus results in no burden-shifting.

In Australia, the allocation of the burden of proof also depends upon whether service *ex juris* is required. In *Voth*, the High Court specifically stated that "[o]n an application for leave to serve outside the jurisdiction, the onus is on the plaintiff to satisfy the court that the case is a proper one for service out of the jurisdiction."[70] Other cases and commentary have determined that the burden is on the plaintiff "irrespective of whether the proceedings involved an ex parte application by the plaintiff for leave or a subsequent application by the defendant to set aside service out of the jurisdiction."[71] This of course tempers the Australian clearly inconvenient forum test, which otherwise places a higher burden on the defendant than the more convenient forum test applied in the other three countries.

In the United States, the forum non conveniens doctrine is not tied into basic jurisdictional analysis and service of process. Thus, the burden of proof question arises only after jurisdiction is established, and a defendant moves to have the case dismissed because an alternative, more appropriate forum exists. This is the classic forum non conveniens analysis. The burden at this stage is on the defendant, as is the case in other common law countries. Similar to the doctrine's application in Canada and Australia, there is no possibility for shifting this burden as there is under *Spiliada* in the United Kingdom.[72]

---

69 *Amchem*, [1993] 1 S.C.R. 897, 921, ¶ 38.
70 *Voth*, 171 C.L.R. 538, 587 (1990).
71 Judd Epstein, *Australia, in* DECLINING JURISDICTION IN PRIVATE INTERNATIONAL LAW 79, 86 (James J. Fawcett ed., 1995).
72 There is at least one notable aberration, however. In the District of Columbia, a line of cases has focused on the plaintiff's choice of forum, the residence of the parties, and the place where the cause of action arose. Thus, "[w]here it is shown that neither party resides in the District [of Columbia] and the plaintiff's claim has arisen in another jurisdiction which has more substantial contacts with the cause of action, the burden normally allocated to the defendant to demonstrate why dismissal is warranted for

2. The Brussels Regulation in the United Kingdom

Neither Canada, the United States, nor Australia is party to a regional treaty that plainly limits when courts in those countries may exercise discretion to decline jurisdiction. The applicability of the *Brussels Regulation* in the United Kingdom will continue to produce complex jurisdictional questions regarding the use of forum non conveniens. The European Court of Justice has indicated that these questions will generally be answered by determining that the doctrine is no longer available in the United Kingdom.[73] Thus, while forum non conveniens is clearly part of the common law of the United Kingdom, the *Brussels Convention*, and now the *Brussels Regulation*, appear to have rendered its application obsolete not only when both parties to litigation are from European Union Member States, but whenever the defendant is domiciled in the United Kingdom.

IV. Conclusions: Similarity with distinctions

As the above discussion indicates, there are both important common elements of the doctrine of forum non conveniens in the four legal systems considered, and important differences. Core concepts that remain consistent across legal systems, as well as substantive and procedural variations, provide perspective in considering any effort toward global harmonization of rules governing a court's ability to decline jurisdiction. The prospect of any such effort, however, is complicated further by the contrasting civil law approach to discretionary dismissals and parallel litigation.[74] Nonetheless, if any agreement on harmonization—or even cooperation—is to be reached on a global basis, it must involve consideration of the consistent elements of the forum non conveniens doctrine found in the major common law legal systems.

---

forum non conveniens rests instead upon the plaintiff to show why it is not." Mills v. Aetna Fire Underwriters Ins. Co., 511 A.2d 8, 11 (D.C. App. 1986). "To avoid dismissal in such a case, the plaintiff must 'show some reasonable justification for his institution of the action in the . . . [District of Columbia] rather than in a state with which the defendant or the res, act or event in suit is more significantly connected." Rolinski v. Lewis, 828 A.2d 739, 748 (D.C. App. 2003) (quoting from *Mills*, 511 A.2d 8, 11 (D.C. App. 1986)).

[73] *See* Chapter 2, Part III, above.

[74] These are matters considered further in Chapter 7, below.

CHAPTER 7

Related Doctrines in Civil Law Systems[1]

I. Introduction

The concept of forum non conveniens is generally inconsistent with civil law systems in which there is a belief in the predictability of comprehensive procedure codes created by the legislature and the absence of all but minimal discretion in the role of the judge. Thus, it normally is thought in such systems that when an action has been filed and jurisdiction exists, that jurisdiction must be exercised.[2] This is tempered by the jurisdiction-defeating rule of lis alibi pendens, which requires a court to defer to another court first seised of the same case.[3] The result is a clear choice for a race to the courthouse (first-seised wins the jurisdictional competition), rather than the corresponding race to judgment in common law legal systems that tend to allow parallel litigation combined with the discretion to decline jurisdiction where it is deemed appropriate to do so. A brief review of several examples serves to highlight the more rigid civil law approach to issues of declining jurisdiction, as well as the limited possibilities for exception.

---

[1] Portions of this chapter originally appeared in Ronald A. Brand, *Comparative Forum Non Conveniens and the Hague Convention on Jurisdiction and Judgments*, 37 TEX. INT'L L.J. 467 (2002) copyright 2002 Ronald A. Brand.

[2] See the reports on civil law jurisdictions in DECLINING JURISDICTION IN PRIVATE INTERNATIONAL LAW (James J. Fawcett ed., 1995).

[3] *See, e.g.*, Council Regulation 44/2001/EC of 22 December 2000 on Jurisdiction and the Recognition and Enforcement of Judgments in Civil and Commercial Matters, 2001 O.J. Eur. Comm. (L 12) 1, art. 27 [hereinafter Brussels Regulation].

II. Germany

No express provision of German law allows for a forum non conveniens doctrine,[4] and "German law of jurisdiction is distinguished by strict, clearly defined, statutory rules which generally do not give discretion to the judge."[5] Nonetheless, some German courts have declined jurisdiction in cases using reasoning in some ways similar to common law forum non conveniens. In 1961, the *Oberlandesgericht Nurnberg* (Court of Nuremburg) declined jurisdiction when a less expensive trial was available in an alternative forum.[6] Similarly, a court in Hamburg required a "sufficient domestic element" as a prerequisite to upholding a choice of court clause selecting that court in a contractual agreement, choosing instead to treat the clause as a mere presumption of the forum's appropriateness.[7] A Frankfurt court even went so far as to refer explicitly to the forum non conveniens doctrine in declining jurisdiction in a non-contentious matter with *perpetuatio fori* jurisdiction (a child custody matter).[8]

Article 101(1) of the *German Federal Constitution*, designed to prevent manipulations in determining the judge in a particular case, states that "[n]o one may be removed from the jurisdiction of his lawful judge."[9] Thus, it has been said that "an integration of the forum non conveniens doctrine would only be permissible if the specific legal judge could be determined with sufficient degree of certainty."[10]

---

[4] *See* Alexander Reus, *Judicial Discretion: A Comparative View of the Doctrine of Forum Non Conveniens in the United States, the United Kingdom, and Germany*, 16 LOY. L.A. INT'L & COMP. L.J. 455, 490–509 (1994).

[5] Haimo Schack, *Germany, in* DECLINING JURISDICTION IN PRIVATE INTERNATIONAL LAW 189, 190 (James J. Fawcett ed., 1995).

[6] Oberlandesgericht Nurnberg, IPRspr. 1960/61 No. 207; 1961 AWD 18.

[7] Landgericht Hamburg, Recht der Internationalen Wirtschaft [RIW], 22 (1976) 228.

[8] Oberlandesgericht Frankfurt, Praxis des Internationalen Privat-und-Verfahrens-Rechts [IPRax], 3 (1983) 294. One commentator has gone so far as to suggest that the German system for appointing a guardian for an incompetent "closely resembles the doctrine of forum non conveniens," but that comparison seems more appropriate with substantive family law in the United States than with the procedural doctrine of forum non conveniens. *See* Gregoire Andrieux, *Declining Jurisdiction in a Future International Convention on Jurisdiction and Judgments—How Can We Benefit from Past Experiences in Conciliating the Two Doctrines of Forum Non Conveniens and Lis Pendens?*, 27 LOY. L.A. INT'L & COMP. L. REV. 323, 331 (2005).

[9] Grundgesetz für die Bundesrepublik Deutschland (German Federal Constitution), art. 101(1).

[10] Alexander Reus, *Judicial Discretion: A Comparative View of the Doctrine of Forum Non Conveniens in the United States, the United Kingdom, and Germany*, 16 LOY. L.A. INT'L & COMP. L.J. 455, 504 (1994). *See also* Haimo Schack, *Germany, in* DECLINING JURISDICTION IN PRIVATE INTERNATIONAL LAW 189 (James J. Fawcett ed., 1995) ("It is hard for a judge to forgo exercising the international jurisdiction that is extended to him by law: the plaintiff's expectations of domestic legal protection will not be met.") and 194 ("Article 101, I, 2 . . . requires a predictable jurisdiction which cannot be manipulated under any circumstances whatsoever.").

Some have gone so far as to argue that dismissals based on forum non conveniens would violate the right of a person to have recourse to a court of law (*Justizgewahrungsanspruch*), which is derived from the principle that a state is to be governed by the rule of law (*Rechtsstaatsprinzip*).[11] This is consistent with a rigid view of jurisdiction favored by many in Germany:

> [T]he majority view favors legal certainty against the individual flexibility offered by the *forum non conveniens* doctrine. The majority bases its opinion on the patent rigidity of German procedural law, which acknowledges few and exclusive exceptions. The legislature intends to provide little discretion at the jurisdictional level.[12]

> *Legal certainty* requires clear and foreseeable jurisdictional rules. Adopting the doctrine of *forum non conveniens* into the German system, which rests on statutorily standardized jurisdictional interests, would be paramount to breaking that system.[13]

It has been suggested that the procedural requirement of a "legitimate interest to take legal action" (*Rechtsschutzbedürfnis*) might be an indirect route to a concept of forum non conveniens, if it could be shown that a German judgment would not be enforced abroad and would therefore demonstrate a lack of legitimate interest.[14] But this approach has been generally rejected,[15] and the desire for legal certainty plays such an important role in Germany that courts have upheld and retained jurisdiction even when it is clear that the plaintiff has manipulated the rules of jurisdiction.[16]

---

[11] Alexander Reus, *Judicial Discretion: A Comparative View of the Doctrine of Forum Non Conveniens in the United States, the United Kingdom, and Germany*, 16 LOY. L.A. INT'L & COMP. L.J. 455, 505 (1994).

[12] Alexander Reus, *Judicial Discretion: A Comparative View of the Doctrine of Forum Non Conveniens in the United States, the United Kingdom, and Germany*, 16 LOY. L.A. INT'L & COMP. L.J. 455, 503 (1994).

[13] Haimo Schack, *Germany, in* DECLINING JURISDICTION IN PRIVATE INTERNATIONAL LAW 189, 194 (James J. Fawcett ed., 1995).

[14] *Id.* at 191.

[15] *Id.*

[16] *See, e.g.*, Bundesgerichtshof, 4 June 1971 [1971] FamRZ 519, 520, *cited in* Haimo Schack, *Germany, in* DECLINING JURISDICTION IN PRIVATE INTERNATIONAL LAW 189, 192 (James J. Fawcett ed., 1995) (holding that no abuse of process existed where the plaintiff obtained German nationality just sixteen days prior to filing a divorce suit in Germany).

III. Japan

Japan also takes a rather rigid civil law approach to jurisdictional issues.[17] Still, a 1986 case applied the doctrine of "special circumstances" to reach a result very similar to that found in common law forum non conveniens cases. In *Sei Mukoda v. Boeing*,[18] the family of a victim of a Taiwanese airline accident in Taiwan sued two U.S. companies (Boeing and United Airlines). The Tokyo District Court held that "if a venue for local territorial competence provided in the *Code of Civil Procedure* ('CCP') is located in Japan, it would accord with the principle of justice and reason to sustain the jurisdiction of the Japanese court, unless we find some special circumstances."[19] The court went on to state that "[s]uch special circumstances exist where, in light of the concrete facts of the case concerned, sustaining the Japanese court's jurisdiction would result in contradicting the ideas of promoting impartiality between the parties and fair and prompt administration of justice."[20] Finding that it would be difficult to secure a fair trial in Japan, since crucial evidence in Taiwan would not be available due to a lack of diplomatic relations, the court focused on four factors to determine the fairness of continuing the proceedings in Japan:

1) whether Taiwanese courts should dismiss on account of lack of international jurisdiction,[21]

2) whether the plaintiffs had enough money to bring an action in Taiwan,[22]

3) whether a Taiwanese court should not dismiss the claim on account of prescription,[23] and

4) whether the plaintiffs could enforce the judgment they might obtain in Taiwan.[24]

---

[17] *See* Masato Dogauchi, *Japan, in* DECLINING JURISDICTION IN PRIVATE INTERNATIONAL LAW 303 (James J. Fawcett ed., 1995).

[18] Sei Mukoda v. The Boeing Co., 604 HANREI TAIMUZU 138 (Tokyo Dist. Ct., June 20, 1986), *reprinted in* 31 JAPANESE ANN. INT'L L. 216 (1988).

[19] Sei Mukoda v. The Boeing Co., 31 JAPANESE ANN. INT'L L. 216, 217 (1988).

[20] *Id.*

[21] *Id.* at 218

[22] *Id.* at 218–19.

[23] *Id.* at 219.

[24] *Id.*

The court ultimately dismissed the case on the grounds that special circumstances made the assertion of jurisdiction by a Japanese court unreasonable.[25]

In one aspect, the Japanese doctrine of special circumstances and the common law doctrine of forum non conveniens in the United Kingdom, Canada, and Australia look rather similar. The court in Japan considered only private interest factors in the application of its doctrine of special circumstances.[26] These private factors include the "relative ease of access to sources of proof, availability of compulsory process for attendance of unwilling witnesses, the cost of obtaining attendance thereof, the enforceability of a judgment, and other relative advantages and obstacles to a fair, proper and prompt trial."[27]

Another aspect of the special circumstances doctrine in Japan sets it apart from the common law doctrine of forum non conveniens: Japanese courts cannot stay a case or dismiss with conditions. "[T]here are only two choices for a Japanese courts: either sustain jurisdiction or dismiss the case completely."[28] Finally, it appears that a Japanese court may dismiss a case even where it has not first determined that another more appropriate forum exists.[29]

IV. The Brussels Regulation

Current European continental civil law practice is perhaps best demonstrated by the provisions of the *Brussels Regulation*[30] that has now replaced the *European*

---

[25] Sei Mukoda v. The Boeing Co., 31 JAPANESE ANN. INT'L L. 216, 219 (1988). For a more complete discussion of this case, see Masato Dogauchi, *The Hague Draft Convention on Jurisdiction and Foreign Judgments in Civil and Commercial Matters from the Perspective of Japan*, 3 JAPANESE Y.B. PRIV. INT'L L. 80, 88–90 (2001).

[26] *See* Masato Dogauchi, *The Hague Draft Convention on Jurisdiction and Foreign Judgments in Civil and Commercial Matters from the Perspective of Japan*, 3 JAPANESE Y.B. PRIV. INT'L L. 80, 89 (2001).

[27] *Id.*

[28] Masato Dogauchi, *The Hague Draft Convention on Jurisdiction and Foreign Judgments in Civil and Commercial Matters from the Perspective of Japan*, 3 JAPANESE Y.B. PRIV. INT'L L. 80, 90 (2001). One further distinction may be considered to create a third difference. The "special circumstances" doctrine can be applied to sustain jurisdiction as well as to deny it. 3 JAPANESE Y.B. PRIV. INT'L L. 80, 90 (2001) (citing D. Kono v. Taro Kono, Minshu, Vol. 50, No. 7, p. 1451 (Sup. Ct., June 24, 1996), *reprinted in* 40 JAPANESE ANN. INT'L L. 132 (1997) (sustaining jurisdiction in a divorce case in accordance with principles of justice, where the case could not be refiled in Germany)).

[29] *See* Masato Dogauchi, *Japan, in* DECLINING JURISDICTION IN PRIVATE INTERNATIONAL LAW 303, 310 (James J. Fawcett ed., 1995).

[30] Council Regulation 44/2001/EC of 22 December 2000 on Jurisdiction and the Recognition and Enforcement of Judgments in Civil and Commercial Matters, 2001 O.J Eur. Comm.. (L 12) 1.

Convention on Jurisdiction and Enforcement of Judgments in Civil and Commercial Matters, better known as the *Brussels Convention*.[31] First created in 1968 by the six original Member States of the European Economic Community (EEC), the *Brussels Convention* became effective in all Member States as enlargement occurred. While the numbering of articles has changed, the Brussels Regulation now contains rules applicable throughout the European Union as internal legislation. These rules are for the most part identical to those in the *Brussels Convention* it replaced.

The *Brussels Regulation* provides a comprehensive approach to jurisdiction and the recognition and enforcement of judgments. In doing so, it makes no provision for the doctrine of forum non conveniens, thereby operating to prohibit the application of the doctrine within the European Union system.[32] Instead, the *Brussels Regulation* establishes both a rule on jurisdiction through contractual choice of court clauses in Article 23[33] and a strict rule of lis pendens in Article 27. This lis pendens rule reads as follows:

1. Where proceedings involving the same cause of action and between the same parties are brought in the courts of different Member States, any court other than the court first seised shall of its own motion stay its proceedings until such time as the jurisdiction of the court first seised is established.

2. Where the jurisdiction of the court first seised is established, any court other than the court first seised shall decline jurisdiction in favour of that court.[34]

With this rule, the Brussels system creates a strict race to the courthouse. The first court seised captures jurisdiction, and an action filed in the court of a second

---

[31]   European Convention on Jurisdiction and Enforcement of Judgments in Civil and Commercial Matters, done at Brussels, 27 September 1968, 41 O.J. Eur. Comm. C 27/1, 26 January 1998 (consolidated and updated version of the 1968 Convention and the Protocol of 1971, following the 1996 accession of the Republic of Austria, the Republic of Finland and the Kingdom of Sweden) [hereinafter Brussels Convention].

[32]   *See* Chapter 2, Part III, above.

[33]   Brussels Regulation, 2001 O.J. Eur. Comm. (L 12) 1, art. 23.

[34]   Brussels Regulation, 2001 O.J. Eur. Comm. (L 12) 1, art. 27.

Member State must be stayed, and ultimately dismissed, in favor of the first action.[35] The importance of Article 27 was emphasized most recently in the *Gasser* case,[36] where the court gave precedence to the lis pendens concept over recognition of a purported choice of court agreement between the parties to the action. When an action was first instituted in Italy by one party, and then a second action was begun in Austria under a choice of court agreement by the other party, the European Court of Justice held that Article 21 of the *Brussels Convention* (the equivalent of Article 27 of the subsequent *Brussels Regulation*) requires that "a court second seised whose jurisdiction has been claimed under an agreement conferring jurisdiction must nevertheless stay proceedings until the court first seised has declared that it has no jurisdiction," even where "the duration of proceedings before the courts of the Contracting State in which the court first seised is established is excessively long."[37] Italian courts are notoriously slow in moving cases to conclusion, resulting in the "Italian torpedo" tactic of filing first in Italy to prevent a natural plaintiff from bringing a successful action elsewhere.[38]

---

[35] Brussels Regulation, 2001 O.J. Eur. Comm. (L 12) 1. Provisions affecting this process include the following:

Article 28

1. Where related actions are pending in the courts of different Member States, any court other than the court first seised may stay its proceedings.

2. Where these actions are pending at first instance, any court other than the court first seised may also, on the application of one of the parties, decline jurisdiction if the court first seised has jurisdiction over the actions in question and its law permits the consolidation thereof.

3. For the purposes of this Article, actions are deemed to be related where they are so closely connected that it is expedient to hear and determine them together to avoid the risk of irreconcilable judgments resulting from separate proceedings.

Article 29

Where actions come within the exclusive jurisdiction of several courts, any court other than the court first seised shall decline jurisdiction in favour of that court.

Article 30

For the purposes of this Section, a court shall be deemed to be seised:

1. at the time when the document instituting the proceedings or an equivalent document is lodged with the court, provided that the plaintiff has not subsequently failed to take the steps he was required to take to have service effected on the defendant, or

2. if the document has to be served before being lodged with the court, at the time when it is received by the authority responsible for service, provided that the plaintiff has not subsequently failed to take the steps he was required to take to have the document lodged with the court.

[36] Case C-116/02, Erich Gasser GmbH v. MISAT Srl., [2003] E.C.R. I-14693 (9 Dec. 2003).

[37] Case C-116/02, Erich Gasser GmbH v. MISAT Srl., [2003] E.C.R. I-14693 (9 Dec. 2003).

[38] *See, e.g.,* Trevor C. Hartley, *The European Union and the Systematic Dismantling of the Common Law of Conflict of Laws,* 15 INT'L COMP. L.Q. 813, 815–21 (2005).

Granting priority to a rule of lis pendens serves to exacerbate this problem by preventing either parallel litigation or the resolution of the case in an expeditious manner in the natural forum.

V.   Latin American efforts to frustrate common law forum non conveniens

One of the more interesting developments regarding the forum non conveniens doctrine has been the effort in Latin America to frustrate the application of the doctrine in the United States by enacting laws designed to make courts unavailable for cases that have been filed outside the legislating country and then dismissed on the basis of forum non conveniens.

A. The foundations of Latin American concern

Two basic rules of Latin American civil procedure, like those in the continental European systems from which they developed,[39] provide the basis for this concern with the application of the forum non conveniens doctrine in the United States. First, it is a basic rule of jurisdiction in Latin America that a person (legal or natural) may be sued at his place of domicile or residence.[40] Second, like the lis pendens rule in Europe, once a plaintiff has chosen a court that has jurisdiction on this ground, that court generally does not have discretion to refuse to hear the case, and all other courts are considered to have lost jurisdiction over the case.[41] This legal tradition obviously comes into conflict with the U.S. forum non conveniens doctrine which allows courts to reject the plaintiff's choice of forum and dismiss a case over which it has both personal and subject-matter jurisdiction.

---

[39]   *See* Chapter 2, Part III.A., above.

[40]   Many Latin American nations, including Bolivia, Brazil, Chile, Costa Rica, Cuba, the Dominican Republic, Ecuador, El Salvador, Guatemala, Haiti, Honduras, Nicaragua, Panama, and Peru, have adopted the Bustamante Code, art. 323 of which provides that "the judge competent for hearing personal causes shall be the one of the place where the obligation is to be performed, and in the absence thereof the one of the domicile or nationality of the defendants and subsidiarily that of their residence." Those jurisdictions that have not adopted the Bustamante Code have procedural codes that also reflect this civil law rule. *See* Henry Saint Dahl, *Forum Non Conveniens, Latin America and Blocking Statutes*, 35 U. MIAMI INTER-AM. L. REV. 21, 26 n.25 (2003–2004); Dante Figueroa, *Are There Ways Out of the Current Forum Non Conveniens Impasse Between the United States and Latin America?*, 1 BUS. L. BRIEF (Am. U.) 42, 44 (2005).

[41]   *See* Dante Figueroa, *Are There Ways Out of the Current Forum Non Conveniens Impasse Between the United States and Latin America?*, 1 BUS. L. BRIEF (Am. U.) 42, 44-45 (2005).

It is not difficult to see how these differences in legal systems lead to serious conflict in specific litigation. Critics of the forum non conveniens doctrine charge that it is used by U.S. corporations as a tool to escape liability when they are sued in U.S. courts for injuries caused in Latin America.[42] In many cases, it is not forum non conveniens itself that is found offensive so much as the fact that its operation denies plaintiffs access to U.S. courts and their liberal discovery rules; proximity to the assets of U.S. corporate defendants; perceived higher damage awards; punitive damages; jury trials; favorable products liability laws; the contingent fee system; and the lack of a loser-pays rule for attorney fees. Nonetheless, the doctrine of forum non conveniens serves as a gatekeeper to these benefits.

When this gate closes, it can have a significant effect on the litigants. Commentators report that very few cases dismissed on forum non conveniens grounds are refiled in the alternative Latin American court.[43] Some cases are settled out of court for far less than similar cases in the United States.[44] Others are never resolved at all.[45] Such results have spurred a deeper criticism: that application of the forum non conveniens doctrine is used to protect U.S. corporations from liability for harm caused in Latin America.

As in other cases, those involving Latin American plaintiffs in U.S. courts have faced questions about bias against foreign plaintiffs and the role of treaties. Any case involving at least one foreign party will naturally result in less convenience than a case involving only domestic parties.[46] U.S. courts consider this not a matter of discrimination but a natural result of the balancing of private interest factors.[47] Nonetheless, this issue has been a source of irritation in cases brought by Latin American plaintiffs. Both the treaties of Friendship, Commerce and Navigation and the *International Covenant on Civil and Political Rights* have been cited as prohibiting

---

[42] *See, e.g.*, Dante Figueroa, *Are There Ways Out of the Current Forum Non Conveniens Impasse Between the United States and Latin America?*, 1 Bus. L. Brief (Am. U.) 42 (2005).

[43] Dante Figueroa, *Are There Ways Out of the Current Forum Non Conveniens Impasse Between the United States and Latin America?*, 1 Bus. L. Brief (Am. U.) 42, 45 (2005).

[44] *See* Winston Anderson, *Forum Non Conveniens Checkmated?—The Emergence of Retaliatory Legislation*, 10 J. Transnat'l L. & Pol'y 183, 184 n.7 (2001). In one case, *Delgado v. Shell Oil Co.*, 890 F. Supp. 1324 (S.D. Tex. 1995), plaintiffs coming from the Caribbean settled their claims for approximately $2,000 each, while the average award made to American victims of the same product was approximately $500,000 each.

[45] *See* Dante Figueroa, *Are There Ways Out of the Current Forum Non Conveniens Impasse Between the United States and Latin America?*, 1 Bus. L. Brief (Am. U.) 42, 45 (2005).

[46] *See* Chapter 3, Part III.E., above.

[47] *See* Iragorri v. United Technologies Corp., 274 F.3d 65, 71–72 (2d Cir. 2001).

a preference for domestic plaintiffs in a forum non conveniens analysis.[48] In 1997, the Attorney General of Ecuador issued an Official Opinion in a letter addressed to U.S. Attorney General Janet Reno asserting that closing American courts to Ecuadoran plaintiffs through the doctrine of forum non conveniens was a violation of the *Peace, Friendship, Navigation, and Commerce Treaty* between the two nations:

> If according to this Treaty, the access to the courts is open and free, it is not clear how the application of a judicial theory ("forum non conveniens"), inferior in ranking to international treaties, can close the doors of American courts to citizens of my country . . . . It would seem that citizens of my country, just for being foreign, are considered as second class citizens and receive a less favorable treatment than that afforded to American nationals.[49]

This argument assumes, of course, that any difference of treatment in the balancing of interest factors in a forum non conveniens analysis is singularly responsible for any resulting dismissal based on the doctrine. While foreign plaintiffs tend to argue that the application of the doctrine results in discrimination against foreign plaintiffs, as discussed earlier,[50] the nationality of the plaintiff generally is simply one factor in weighing conveniences—a factor that does weigh in favor of hearing the case in the plaintiff's home court.

B. *Delgado v. Shell Oil* and increased expressions of concern

Concern with the application of the doctrine of forum non conveniens to dismiss cases involving Latin American plaintiffs crystallized in the mid-1990s with

---

[48] *See, e.g.*, Treaty of Peace, Friendship, Navigation, and Commerce, art. 13, June 13, 1839, U.S.-Ecuador, 8 Stat. 534 ("Both the contracting parties promise and engage, formally, to give their special protection to the persons and property of the citizens of each other . . . leaving open and free to them the tribunals of justice, for their judicial recourse, on the same terms which are usual and customary with the natives or citizens of the country in which they may be."); International Covenant on Civil and Political Rights, art. 14(1) *opened for signature* Dec. 16, 1966, 999 U.N.T.S. 171, 176 (*entered into force* Mar. 23, 1976) ("All persons shall be equal before courts and tribunals."). *See also* Henry Saint Dahl, *Forum Non Conveniens, Latin America and Blocking Statutes*, 35 U. MIAMI INTER-AM. L. REV. 21, 30–31 (2003–2004); Paul Santoyo, *Bananas of Wrath: How Nicaragua May Have Dealt Forum Non Conveniens a Fatal Blow Removing the Doctrine as an Obstacle to Achieving Corporate Accountability*, 27 HOUS. J. INT'L L. 703, 725–26 (2005).

[49] Official Opinion of the Attorney General's Office, signed by Don Leonidas Plaza Verduga, on 15/1/97, in a letter addressed to the US Attorney General, Ms. Janet Reno, *available at*: http://www.iaba.org/LLinks_forum_non_Ecuador.htm.

[50] *See* Chapter 3, Part III.E., above.

Delgado v. Shell Oil Co.[51] Citizens of twelve countries, including nine in Latin America, brought products liability actions against U.S. chemical manufacturers for injuries allegedly caused by exposure to hazardous chemicals while working on farms in 23 countries. The case was first filed in Texas state court, but removed to federal court. After removal, the defendants sought dismissal on the grounds of forum non conveniens. In a lengthy opinion, the Federal District Court for the Southern District of Texas dismissed the case after determining that alternative fora were available in the plaintiffs' home countries, where the injuries had occurred, and that the application of private and public interest factors weighed in favor of litigation in those fora. At the end of its decision, the court stated:

> Notwithstanding the dismissals that may result from this Memorandum and Order, in the event that the highest court of any foreign country finally affirms the dismissal for lack of jurisdiction of any action commenced by a plaintiff in these actions in his home country or the country in which he was injured, that plaintiff may return to this court and, upon proper motion, the court will resume jurisdiction over the action as if the case had never been dismissed for f.n.c.[52]

Many of the attempts by the *Delgado* plaintiffs to refile their cases in the alternative fora in Latin America were unsuccessful because of basic civil law objections to a court declining to exercise jurisdiction once seised of a case. One case was dismissed in Costa Rica, with the court noting that it had no jurisdiction: "A procedural decision, issued by a Court of the United States of America, cannot determine the territorial jurisdiction within this country, to adjudicate the present case, since that would violate National Sovereignty."[53] Similarly, a court in Nicaragua reasoned:

> The fact that the Nicaraguan plaintiffs in this case have filed the same lawsuit, requesting the same damages, before the Honorable Federal Court in Texas, amounts to a jurisdictional submission. According to Art. 255 of the Code of Civil Procedure, once jurisdiction attaches it cannot be modified. Finally, . . . our procedural system does not recognize, and therefore it does

---

[51]   890 F. Supp. 1324 (S.D. Tex. 1995).

[52]   890 F. Supp. 1324, 1375 (S.D. Tex. 1995).

[53]   Decision of the Juzgado Civil y de Trabajo de Limon, signed by the Honorable Javier Viquez Herrara, (May 20, 1996), *available at*: http://www.iaba.org/LLinks_forum_non_Costa_Rica.htm.

not accept nor does it admit, the imposition of the Forum Non Conveniens Theory by foreign courts.[54]

Latin American governments also issued opinions stating that they would not recognize or respect the doctrine of forum non conveniens. For example, an Official Opinion issued by the Attorney General of Guatemala stated:

> Guatemala does not recognize the Forum Non Conveniens theory. . . . The jurisdictional standards in our system are mandatory and do not lend themselves to being manipulated by any tribunal whether domestic or foreign. Once the plaintiffs have exercised the right to bring suit in the domicile of the defendants, whether in this country or abroad, it is illegal for a Guatemalan judge to disturb this choice of tribunal. . . . We trust that, in the same way that a Guatemalan court would not dare to require an American judge to violate American law, the American Judiciary Power would also abstain from requesting that the Guatemalan Judiciary Power violate Guatemalan law.[55]

C. The emergence of forum non conveniens blocking statutes

The most significant response to the *Delgado* case was the creation of model legislation developed by a non-official organization calling itself the "Latin American Parliament" or "PARLATINO." This group created a *Model Law on International Jurisdiction and Applicable Law to Tort Liability*, containing two articles:

> *Art. 1. National and international jurisdiction.* The petition that is validly filed, according to both legal systems, in the defendant's domiciliary court, extinguishes national jurisdiction. The latter is only reborn if the plaintiff desists of his foreign petition and files a new petition in the country, in a completely free and spontaneous way.

> *Art. 2. International tort liability. Damages.* In cases of international tort liability, the national court may, at the plaintiff's request, apply to damages

---

54 Decision of the Second District Civil Court of León, signed by the Honorable Teresa de Jesus Bustamante (Aug. 21, 1995), *available at:* http://www.iaba.org/LLinks_forum_non_Nicaragua.htm.

55 Official Opinion of the Attorney General's Office, signed by Don Acisclo Valladares Molina, Attorney General for Guatemala (May 3, 1995), *available at* http://www.iaba.org/LLinks_forum_non_Guatemala.htm.

and to the pecuniary sanctions related to such damages, the relevant standards and amounts of the pertinent foreign law.[56]

The basic thrust of the first article of the Model Law is to favor litigation in the court of the defendant's domicile (consistent with article 323 of the *Bustamante Code*), and prevent reference to another court, even if the court at the defendant's domicile considers that other court the more appropriate forum. Comments with the Model Law include the following:

> Article 1 makes sure that if the plaintiff chooses a foreign court with jurisdiction, such judge will not be able to close the doors of the court on him as, for instance, has been happening with the theory of forum non conveniens. Article 2 also favors the victims of ecological wrongs since it strengthens the possibility that the indemnity and pecuniary sanctions be in accordance with foreign law.
>
> In summary, what the law clarifies is that those who incur an international tort liability, will not be able to escape their domiciliary courts and, additionally, that they will be sanctioned, at the victim's option, whether by the law of the place where the wrong is suffered, or by the law of the place where damages are generated.[57]

Proponents of such statutes hope that Latin American plaintiffs will be able to use these laws in U.S. courts to prove that they have no available alternative forum in which to file their cases.

Similar statutes have been enacted in Latin American nations, including the 1997 Guatemalan *Law for the Defense of Procedural Rights of Nationals and Residents*, which provides that: "The personal action that a plaintiff validly establishes abroad before a judge having jurisdiction, forecloses national jurisdiction, which is not revived unless a new lawsuit is filed in the country, brought spontaneously and freely by the plaintiff."[58] Ecuador adopted such a statute, but it was declared

---

[56] The Model Law is available in English at: http://www.iaba.org/LLinks_forum_non_Parlatino.htm.

[57] Introduction to Model Law on International Jurisdiction and Applicable Law to Tort Liability, *available at*: http://www.iaba.org/LLinks_forum_non_Parlatino.htm.

[58] Law for the Defense of Procedural Rights of Nationals and Residents, Guatemala, May 14, 1997, *available at*: http://www.iaba.org/LLinks_forum_non_Guatemala.htm.

unconstitutional for its failure to allow any basis for regaining national jurisdiction.[59] The *Panama Judicial Code* provides that "Lawsuits filed in the country as a consequence of a *forum non conveniens* judgment from a foreign court, do not generate national jurisdiction. Accordingly they must be rejected *sua sponte* for lack of jurisdiction because of constitutional reasons or due to the rules of preemptive jurisdiction."[60]

Latin American nations have also adopted statutes making their courts a less attractive alternative forum for U.S. corporate defendants in an attempt to dissuade them from moving to dismiss based on forum non conveniens in the first place. Article 2 of the *PALATINO Model Law* would allow courts to assess damages against U.S. corporate defendants according to the legal standards of the defendant's domicile, including punitive damages in amounts commensurate with American jury awards. The *Dominican Transnational Causes of Action (Product Liability) Act of 1997* uses this approach. It applies exclusively to "transnational causes of action brought against a foreign defendant" when the action has been dismissed by a foreign court on the basis of forum non conveniens, comity, or similar doctrines.[61] Section 12 of this statute allows its courts to "consider and be guided by awards made in similar proceedings or for similar injuries in other jurisdictions, in particular damages awarded in the Courts of the country with which the defendant has a strong connection." Section 5 also requires the defendant to post a bond "in the amount of one hundred and forty percent per claimant of the amount proved by plaintiff to have been awarded in similar foreign proceedings." Finally, Section 8 imposes strict products liability on such foreign defendants. Rather than blocking jurisdiction in cases dismissed by U.S. courts on the basis of forum non conveniens, this legislation seeks to deter the corporate defendant from seeking dismissal in the United States by imposing strict liability and harsh remedies when the plaintiff must refile the case in the Dominican Republic.

---

[59] *See* Henry Saint Dahl, *Forum Non Conveniens, Latin America and Blocking Statutes*, 35 U. MIAMI INTER-AM. L. REV. 21, 48 (2003-2004).

[60] Judicial Code of Panama, art. 1421-J, Law 32 of August 1, 2006.

[61] Transnational Causes of Action (Product Liability) Act of 1997, the Dominican Republic, Sec. 3, *available at*: http://www.iaba.org/LLinks_forum_non_Dominica.htm.

D. A mixed reception for Latin American blocking statutes in U.S. courts

It is uncertain whether any of these statutes will have their intended effect. Two cases have determined that the laws of Guatemala and Ecuador do not preclude a conditional forum non conveniens dismissal. In each of these cases, after expressing skepticism about interpretations of the foreign law, the court dismissed the case on forum non conveniens grounds subject to the condition that the plaintiffs could resume their case in the U.S. if the highest courts of the alternative forum refused to hear it. In *Polanco v. H.B. Fuller Co.*,[62] the court stated:

> Plaintiff argues that Guatemalan law forbids disturbing a plaintiff's choice of forum. Consequently, Guatemalan courts will not recognize jurisdiction that has been "manipulated" by a forum non conveniens transfer. However, a quick and decisive solution to this potential problem was reached in *Delgado*. . . . [T]he court directed that "in the event that the highest court of any foreign country finally affirms the dismissal for lack of jurisdiction" of any plaintiff's case, that plaintiff may return, and the court will resume jurisdiction.[63]

In *Aguinda v. Texaco, Inc.*,[64] the plaintiffs argued that Interpretive Law 55 of Ecuador extinguished the jurisdiction of Ecuador's courts as soon as the plaintiffs chose to file their claim in the United States. That law states that "the claimant will be able to choose freely between filing the lawsuit in Ecuador or abroad. . . . . Should the lawsuit be filed outside Ecuadorian territory, this will definitely terminate national competency as well as any jurisdiction of Ecuadorian judges over the matter."[65] The court concluded that Interpretive Law 55 would not deprive courts in Ecuador of jurisdiction over cases that had been dismissed on forum non conveniens grounds:

> This [result] seems highly doubtful, since the ostensible purpose of the law is to require plaintiffs to proceed in a single forum, not to be deprived of any forum whatever. . . . [T]he unlikelihood that Ecuadorian courts would

---

[62]   941 F. Supp. 1512 (D. Minn. 1996).
[63]   941 F. Supp. 1512, 1525 (D. Minn. 1996).
[64]   142 F. Supp. 2d 534, 546–47 (S.D.N.Y. 2001).
[65]   142 F. Supp. 2d 534, 546–47 (S.D.N.Y. 2001).

ultimately adopt [this result] makes Law 55 an insufficient basis for concluding that the Ecuadorian forum is unavailable.[66]

The *Aguinda* District Court also chose to make its dismissal conditional on the acceptance of jurisdiction by the Ecuador courts. The Second Circuit affirmed this reasoning and noted that Interpretive Law 55 had since been declared unconstitutional by Ecuador's Constitutional Court, providing further support for the dismissal.[67]

Other plaintiffs have had greater success in persuading U.S. courts that the alternative fora in their home countries are unavailable when statutes provide a lis pendens rule that effectively blocks the foreign court from taking jurisdiction of a case first filed in the United States. In *Canales Martinez v. Dow Chemical Co.*,[68] the Federal District Court for the Eastern District of Louisiana concluded that there was no available alternative forum in Costa Rica after a close examination of Costa Rican procedural law. The court relied primarily on Article 31 of the *Costa Rica Code of Civil Procedure*, which states: "If there were two or more courts with jurisdiction for one case, it will be tried by the one who heard it first at the plaintiff's request."[69] The court held:

> Under this rule, in cases in which there might initially have been concurrent jurisdiction in two or more fora, once a plaintiff has chosen a particular forum, all other possible fora are divested of jurisdiction. Thus, when plaintiffs filed suit against defendants in this Court, by operation of CCP 31, as of that filing, the Costa Rican courts—if they ever had jurisdiction—were divested of jurisdiction in favor of this Court. Because the courts of Costa Rica may no longer assert jurisdiction over plaintiffs' claims, they must be considered unavailable.[70]

The *Canales Martinez* court also noted that Articles 122 and 477 of the *Costa Rica Code of Civil Procedure* provide that claims are only valid if they are filed "freely and voluntarily." As a result of these laws, the court concluded that it could not

---

66 *Id.*
67 Aguinda v. Texaco, Inc., 303 F.3d 470, 477 (2d Cir. 2002).
68 219 F. Supp. 2d 719 (E.D. La. 2002).
69 *Id.* at 728.
70 *Id.*

dismiss the case on forum non conveniens grounds since doing so would force the plaintiffs to file a claim in Costa Rican courts against their will:

> Were this court to dismiss the action conditioned on plaintiffs' refiling it in Costa Rica and having the Costa Rican court accept the case (as was done by the district court in *Delgado*), the Court would be forcing the plaintiffs to try to file the lawsuit in Costa Rica in violation of articles 122 and 477.[71]

Thus, the court rejected the solution employed by other district courts, on the basis that a conditional dismissal would result in a conflict with Costa Rican law.

The Federal District Court for the Southern District of Indiana reached a similar result in *In re Bridgestone/Firestone, Inc.*,[72] determining that a Venezuelan court could not exercise jurisdiction over a case that had been dismissed on forum non conveniens grounds. Under Article 40(4) of the *Statute on Private International Law*, the courts of Venezuela can exercise jurisdiction over cases filed against non-domiciliaries if both parties have submitted to such jurisdiction.[73] The defendants offered to consent to jurisdiction in Venezuela and argued that this alone satisfied the requirements of the statute. The court disagreed with this approach, relying heavily on the plaintiffs' expert testimony that the statute also requires that the plaintiffs expressly submit to the jurisdiction of the Venezuelan courts. The court accepted the plaintiffs' argument that "by bringing their cases in the United States, they are not expressly submitting to the jurisdiction of Venezuelan courts, and that the unilateral submission of [the defendants] to Venezuelan jurisdiction is insufficient to create jurisdiction."[74] There was thus no available alternative forum, and the forum non conveniens motion was denied.

In spite of the plaintiffs' success in the *Bridgestone/Firestone* case, at least two subsequent courts faced with products liability claims by Venezuelan plaintiffs have followed the *Delgado* approach, granting forum non conveniens dismissals subject to the condition that the courts in Venezuela accept jurisdiction. They did not find that the *Bridgestone/Firestone* interpretation of Venezuelan law was persuasive. In *Rivas v. Ford Motor Co.*,[75] the Federal District Court for the Middle District

---

71 *Id.*
72 190 F. Supp. 2d 1125 (S.D. Ind. 2002).
73 190 F. Supp. 2d 1125, 1130 (S.D. Ind. 2002).
74 *Id.* at 1131.
75 2004 WL 1247018 (M.D. Fla. 2004).

of Florida accepted defendant's expert testimony as rebutting that offered by the plaintiffs, which had simply been recycled from the *Bridgestone/Firestone* case:

> In *Bridgestone* I, the Indiana District Court based its finding of unavailability on competing Venezuelan law expert affidavits and testimony. This Court is now asked to make the same determination based on the same testimony from the [*Bridgestone/Firestone* case]. However, plaintiffs do not acknowledge Ford's new expert affidavits submitted specifically in this case. Plaintiffs have had ample time to depose Ford's new witnesses (18 months). Defendant's burden to show availability is not a heavy one and under the circumstances of *this* case, the Court is not persuaded by the [*Bridgestone/ Firestone*] decision.[76]

The defendant in *Rivas* had learned from the mistakes of *Bridgestone/Firestone*, in which the defendants' expert witnesses had been discredited. One witness in *Bridgestone/Firestone* had formed his opinion of Venezuelan law based upon an "abrogated statute," and was unaware of the new *Statute on Private International Law*.[77] The other witness had been Ford's counsel in Venezuela and refused to answer questions about his involvement in the case.[78] The Venezuelan *Statute on Private International Law* is not a blocking statute designed to prevent forum non conveniens dismissals, however, so these cases may not be determinative of future forum non conveniens challenges coming from Latin America.

While decisions such as *Canales Martinez* have been receptive to claims by Latin American plaintiffs that their home courts do not provide available alternative fora, other courts continue to reject these claims, holding that the procedural nuances of Latin American law cannot trump the doctrine of forum non conveniens. This latter position was emphasized recently by the Federal District Court for the Southern District of Texas in *Morales v. Ford Motor Co.*:[79]

> Indeed, the Plaintiffs' argument turns the *forum non conveniens* inquiry on its head. The *forum non conveniens* doctrine exists to provide federal courts an opportunity to reconsider a foreign Plaintiff's choice of forum in light of convenience. As conceptualized by the Plaintiffs, no such reconsideration

---

[76] 2004 WL 1247018, *4 (M.D. Fla. 2004).

[77] *In re* Bridgestone/Firestone, 190 F. Supp. 2d 1125, 1130–31 (S.D. Ind. 2002).

[78] *Id.* at 1131–32.

[79] 313 F. Supp. 2d 672 (S.D. Tex. 2004).

may take place. Under the construction proposed by Plaintiffs, a Venezuelan plaintiff's choice of forum may never be reconsidered by the courts of this country, because Venezuelan plaintiffs have the option of rendering their home courts unavailable simply by bringing suits such as this one outside of their own country. Plaintiffs vociferously protest the Defendant's "unilateral submission to Venezuelan jurisdiction" as illegitimate, but evince no awareness that their own proposed construction of the *forum non conveniens* doctrine would empower themselves with unilateral authority regarding choice of forum. Nor do Plaintiffs indicate awareness that their own brand of unilateralism amounts to an utter abrogation of the *forum non conveniens* doctrine in cases of this nature where Venezuelan plaintiffs are concerned.[80]

Until resolution of this issue is found, the outcome of future challenges by Latin American plaintiffs to motions to dismiss based on the doctrine of forum non conveniens may depend not only on the legislation in their home fora, but also on the individual opinions of the judges before whom they argue their cases. The situation offers comparison to U.S. judicial responses to foreign blocking statutes in the area of discovery, where such statutes have often been considered inappropriate intrusions into the business of U.S. courts than appropriate legislation in a transnational setting.[81] In any event, the present tension between the U.S. doctrine of forum non conveniens and Latin American legal systems highlights a unique comparative quandary over what traditionally has been a rather easily resolved inquiry into whether an available alternative forum exists.

VI. Concluding thoughts

The German and Japanese examples demonstrate the very strict approach to declining jurisdiction taken in most civil law jurisdictions. Such an approach clearly conflicts with the application of the common law doctrine of forum non conveniens. Nonetheless, some openings for discretion in declining jurisdiction have surfaced in important civil law jurisdictions. Even so, however, the general approach remains one in which jurisdiction is exercised if it exists. Through a lis alibi pendens regime courts are considered not to have the ability to exercise

---

[80] 313 F. Supp. 2d 672, 676 (S.D. Tex. 2004).
[81] *See, e.g.*, RESTATEMENT (THIRD) OF FOREIGN RELATIONS LAW § 442 (1987); GARY B. BORN, INTERNATIONAL CIVIL LITIGATION IN UNITED STATES COURTS 847–55 (3d ed. 1996).

jurisdiction if another court is first seised of the same case, and courts are without discretionary authority to decide otherwise.

The Latin American experience indicates not only denial of any power to decline jurisdiction in national courts but legislative efforts to prevent U.S. courts from exercising such power under the forum non conveniens doctrine. The resulting legislation has met with mixed results in U.S. courts, with most courts finding that opportunity remains for application of the doctrine in such cases. In the larger context, the evident tensions between common law forum non conveniens and civil law jurisdictional regimes—highlighted in both theory and practice—inform the global perspective on jurisdiction, judicial discretion, and treaty making.

CHAPTER 8

The Global Search for a Convention on Jurisdiction and Judgments and Related Projects Addressing Lis Pendens and Declining Jurisdiction

I. Introduction

The very different approaches to parallel proceedings taken by common law and civil law jurisdictions create a conundrum for anyone attempting to deal with this issue on a global basis. Nonetheless, the matter was addressed at the Hague Conference on Private International Law beginning in the early 1990s in its project on jurisdiction and the recognition and enforcement of judgments in civil and commercial matters.[1] While the aim of that project narrowed in 2002 to a convention on choice of court agreements, much work was done on the parallel proceedings issue, and in particular on the relationship between common law doctrines of forum non conveniens and civil law rules of lis alibi pendens. The results of that work provide a useful starting point for any future effort to bring global (or even bilateral) harmonization to these issues.

---

[1] Information on the negotiations, including the resulting final text of the Convention on Choice of Court Agreements, is available on the website of the Hague Conference on Private International Law at http://www.hcch.net/index_en.php?act=conventions.text&cid=98.

The Hague negotiations demonstrate useful approaches to be considered in any discussion of the future of the doctrine of forum non conveniens. While the more comprehensive convention drafts of 1999 and 2001 were not adopted by the Hague Conference, they nonetheless include language that offers opportunities for future work on issues of declining jurisdiction and the evolution of the forum non conveniens doctrine. That is the focus of this chapter.[2]

II. The Hague Conference process

In May of 1992, Edwin Williamson, then Legal Adviser at the U.S. Department of State, wrote to the Secretary General of the Hague Conference on Private International Law proposing that the Conference take up the negotiation of a multilateral convention on the recognition and enforcement of judgments.[3] The matter was considered by a Working Group at The Hague in October of 1992, which "unanimously recognized the desirability of attempting to negotiate multi-laterally through the Hague Conference a convention on recognition and enforcement of judgments."[4] Such a convention would inevitably have to address the conflict between the common law doctrine of forum non conveniens and the strict civil law approach of lis alibi pendens.

A. The original mixed convention model

From the beginning of the discussions, the United States took the position that the product of the Hague Conference Special Commission should be a "mixed" convention;[5] a position supported by the original Hague Conference Working Group in 1992.[6] Single (sometimes referred to as "simple") conventions on the recognition of judgments deal only with indirect jurisdiction and apply only to

---

[2]   In Chapter 9 we focus on the Convention on Exclusive Choice of Court Agreements as it was adopted by the Hague Conference on Private International Law on June 30, 2005.

[3]   Letter of May 5, 1992 from Edwin D. Williamson, Legal Adviser, U.S. Department of State, to Georges Droz, Secretary General, The Hague Conference on Private International Law, *distributed with* Hague Conference document L.c. ON No. 15 (1992).

[4]   *Conclusions of the Working Group Meeting on Enforcement of Judgments*, Hague Conference on Private International Law, Doc. L.c. ON No. 2 (1993).

[5]   Arthur Taylor von Mehren, *Recognition Convention Study: Final Report.*

[6]   *Conclusions of the Working Group Meeting on Enforcement of Judgments*, Hague Conference on Private International Law, Doc. L.c. ON No. 2 (93), at 3 (4 Jan. 1993).

the decision of the court asked to enforce a foreign judgment.[7] Thus, the recognizing court considers the jurisdiction of the court issuing a judgment in deciding whether to recognize the judgment of the originating court. Double conventions, like the *Brussels Convention*[8] and the *Lugano Convention*,[9] not only deal with recognition, but also provided rules for direct jurisdiction applicable in the court in which the case is first brought—thus addressing the matter from the outset and preempting the need for substantial indirect consideration of the issuing court's jurisdiction by the court asked to recognize the resulting judgment. The mixed convention is a variation on the double convention, providing rules for both jurisdiction and the recognition of judgments, but not purporting to be exhaustive in its lists of required and prohibited bases of jurisdiction. It does not cover the entire field, but rather leaves some bases of jurisdiction available under national law, although these bases are not subject to the convention's rules on recognition and enforcement of any resulting judgment.

Under the mixed convention approach, there would exist a list of required bases of jurisdiction and a list of prohibited bases of jurisdiction. Judgments founded

---

[7]   Examples of simple conventions at the Hague Conference on Private International Law include the Convention on the Recognition and Enforcement of Foreign Judgments in Civil and Commercial Matters and Supplementary Protocol, *done* Feb. 1, 1971, *reprinted in* 15 Am. J. Comp. L. 362 (1967), and the Convention on the Recognition of Divorces and Legal Separations, opened for signature fall 1969, *printed in* 8 Int'l Legal Materials 31 (1969). The former came into force on February 1, 1971, but only Cyprus, The Netherlands, and Portugal are parties, and none of them ever deposited the bilateral agreements necessary to make the treaty operational. The divorce recognition convention came into force on June 1, 1970, with only fourteen countries (mostly European) having ever ratified or acceded. The United States has never ratified either convention.

[8]   The Brussels Convention is the most successful example of a regional approach to regulation of jurisdiction and enforcement of judgments. European Convention on Jurisdiction and Enforcement of Judgments in Civil and Commercial Matters, done at Brussels, Sept. 27, 1968, 41 O.J. Eur. Comm. (C 27/1) (Jan. 26, 1998) (consolidated and updated version of the 1968 Convention and the Protocol of 1971, following the 1996 accession of the Republic of Austria, the Republic of Finland and the Kingdom of Sweden) [hereinafter Brussels Convention]. On May 1, 1999, the Amsterdam Treaty became effective for the European Union Member States, and competence for coordination of internal rules on jurisdiction and recognition of judgments now lies with the Community institutions. The Council Regulation replacing the Brussels Convention was finalized on December 22, 2000, and became effective, except for Denmark, on Mar. 1 2002. Council Regulation (EC) No 44/2001 of Dec. 22, 2000 on Jurisdiction and the Recognition and Enforcement of Judgments in Civil and Commercial Matters, 2000 O.J. Eur. Comm. L 12 [hereinafter Brussels Regulation].

[9]   European Communities-European Free Trade Association: Convention on Jurisdiction and Enforcement of Judgments in Civil and Commercial Matters, done at Lugano, Sept. 16, 1988, O.J. Eur. Comm. (No. L 319) 9 (Nov. 25, 1988), *reprinted in* 28 Int'l Legal Materials 620 (1989) [hereafter, the Lugano Convention]. In addition to the Member States of the European Community, the Lugano Convention includes as Contracting States the Member States of the European Free Trade Association (EFTA).

on required bases of jurisdiction would be entitled to recognition under the convention. Courts could not exercise jurisdiction founded only on bases on the prohibited list. For a few other situations, some exceptions to recognition would apply. Any jurisdictional basis not included on one of the two lists would be permitted, but a resulting judgment would not be entitled to recognition under the convention. Instead, such judgments would be subject to review in the recognizing court in the manner applicable in the absence of a treaty.

A clear focus on a mixed convention would have allowed the Hague Conference to build up a convention from the existing status quo, and would not have required agreement on a comprehensive set of jurisdictional rules that cover and connect the entire field of possibilities. It also would have allowed the use of a consensus process likely to produce a convention acceptable to the largest number of states.[10] Such a convention would have allowed some areas of disagreement and experimentation to continue while at the same time locking in progress that could be achieved. A mixed convention also would have allowed certain issues that are unresolved in any single national legal system to remain outside the convention and subject to later conventions or protocols should an acceptable approach be developed.

B. Negotiation of a double convention text

In October of 1996, the Hague Conference decided to include the subject of a jurisdiction and judgments convention on the Agenda of its Nineteenth Session.[11] Special Commission meetings from 1997 to 1999 led to a Preliminary Draft Convention text.[12] The 1999 draft contained initial provisions on declining jurisdiction, dealing with both forum non conveniens and lis pendens.[13]

---

[10]   See Ronald A. Brand, *Jurisdictional Common Ground: In Search of A Global Convention, in* LAW AND JUSTICE IN A MULTI-STATE WORLD: ESSAYS IN HONOR OF ARTHUR T. VON MEHREN 11 (James A.R. Natziger and Simeon C. Symeonides eds., 2002).

[11]   *Final Act of the Eighteenth Session of the Hague Conference on Private International Law*, 19 Oct. 1996, at 21.

[12]   *Informational note on the work of the informal meetings held since October 1999 to consider and develop drafts on outstanding items, drawn up by the Permanent Bureau,* Hague Conference on Private International Law, Prel. Doc. No. 15 (May 2001) (containing the text of the Preliminary Draft Convention). This text is reproduced as Document A at the end of this volume.

[13]   *Working Document No 144 of the Special Commission on International Jurisdiction and the Effects of Foreign Judgments in Civil and Commercial Matters*, arts. 23 and 24, Hague Conference on Private International Law (20 Nov. 1998).

The first part of the Diplomatic Conference, held in June of 2001, produced a new Interim Text that followed the 1999 text, but contained many more bracketed provisions, footnotes, and explanations of various positions.[14] Those brackets, footnotes, and explanations made clearer some of the many remaining differences in legal, economic, and political systems. These differences stood between the 2001 draft and a successful convention.

While the negotiating process had begun with discussion of a mixed convention, it was not until June of 1999 that the Special Commission voted specifically to adopt the mixed convention model.[15] The intervening seven-year ambivalence of focus resulted in the primary development of double convention language. Thus, even in the *June 2001 Interim Text of the Proposed Hague Convention on Jurisdiction and Recognition of Judgments*, which purports to follow a mixed convention approach, the words generally are those of a double convention. Given that the negotiations prior to June 2001 were conducted by majority vote, and that (at that time) fifteen of the Hague Member States voting on specific articles during the process were also Member States of the European Union (and others were states planning and eager to become Member States of the EU), it is not surprising that the language of both the *October 1999 Preliminary Draft Hague Convention on Jurisdiction and the Enforcement of Civil Judgments* and the *2001 Hague Interim Text* resembled that of the *Brussels* and *Lugano Conventions* in force in the EU states. It also is not surprising that the EU states would prefer a convention that looks as much as possible like the sets of rules they customarily apply in similar cases within their regional system. That approach led to great difficulty in developing a convention that would work on a global basis. In particular, the resulting text led to many problems for the United States, which has a system of personal jurisdiction based on constitutional limitations that results in a different analysis than do the rules of the civil law-oriented Brussels system.[16]

---

[14] *Summary of the Outcome of the Discussion in Commission II of the First Part of the Diplomatic Conference 6–20 June 2001—Interim Text*, Hague Conference on Private International Law, Nineteenth Session (2001) [hereinafter Interim Text]. This text is reproduced as Document B at the end of this volume.

[15] *Preliminary Draft Convention on Jurisdiction and the Effects of Judgments in Civil and Commercial Matters*, adopted provisionally by the Special Commission, Hague Conference on Private International Law, Special Commission on International Jurisdiction and the Effects of Foreign Judgments in Civil and Commercial Matters, Working Document No. 241 (18 June 1999).

[16] *See, e.g.*, Ronald A. Brand, *Due Process, Jurisdiction and a Hague Judgments Convention*, 60 U. PITT. L. REV. 661 (1999).

C. Problems resulting from differing approaches to jurisdiction

This heavy influence of the EU states resulted in a general focus on distinctions between the *Brussels Convention* system and the approach to personal jurisdiction in the United States. The basic difference between the U.S. and European systems of jurisdiction is that the due process-oriented U.S. approach results in a principal focus on the relationship between the forum state and the defendant.[17] *International Shoe*,[18] *World-Wide Volkswagen*,[19] *Asahi*,[20] and related decisions of the U.S. Supreme Court require an analysis of the activity of the defendant within the forum state in order to determine whether the court has "jurisdiction over the defendant."[21]

The European approach begins with "general jurisdiction" at the domicile of the defendant,[22] thus containing a basic focus on a court/defendant connection. Virtually all other bases of jurisdiction, however, focus on the cause of action and its relation to the forum state. If a tort is committed in or has effects in the forum state, jurisdiction over the tort claim will exist in that state.[23] Similarly, if a contract is to be "performed" in the forum state, jurisdiction over the contract claim will exist in that state.[24] Thus, a "jurisdiction over the claim" approach focusing on the court/claim nexus is central to the *Brussels Regulation* approach.

The U.S. concept of "specific jurisdiction," on the other hand, takes account of both the court/defendant nexus and the court/claim nexus, by requiring that the

---

17   While Article 2 of the Brussels Convention and Regulation provides that a person may always be sued in the courts of that person's state of domicile, the difficult issues arise not in this element of general jurisdiction, which also exists in the United States, but in the "special" jurisdiction rules that follow, nearly all of which are based on a court-claim relationship rather than a court-defendant relationship. See Ronald A. Brand, *Jurisdictional Common Ground: In Search of A Global Convention*, LAW AND JUSTICE IN A MULTI-STATE WORLD: ESSAYS IN HONOR OF ARTHUR T. VON MEHREN 11 (James A.R. Nafziger and Simeon C. Symeonides eds., 2002).

18   International Shoe Co. v. Washington, 326 U.S. 310 (1945).

19   World-Wide Volkswagen Corp. v. Woodson, 444 U.S. 286 (1980).

20   Asahi Metal Industry Co. v. Superior Court, 480 U.S. 102 (1987).

21   For a more detailed discussion of the application of the U.S. Due Process Clauses to personal jurisdiction, *see* Ronald A. Brand, *Due Process, Jurisdiction and a Hague Judgments Convention*, 60 U. PITT. L. REV. 661, 664–89 (1999).

22   Brussels Regulation, 2000 O.J. Eur. Comm. L 12, art. 2.

23   Brussels Regulation, 2000 O.J. Eur. Comm. L 12, art. 5(3).

24   Brussels Regulation, 2000 O.J. Eur. Comm. L 12, art. 5(1).

cause of action arise out of the activity of the defendant in the forum state.[25] Thus, it brings in the court/claim connection that is important in the *Brussels Regulation* approach and provides common ground on which to build. The problems arise from the extent of differences in approach and the degree of willingness to allow those differences to exist outside the rules of a convention (*i.e.*, within the area of permitted jurisdictional bases). Under a mixed convention approach, this would not be a problem since not all such differences need to be specifically resolved. Because the Hague negotiations had been channeled into a double convention model, however, resolving such differences was fundamental to the question of how to proceed at the end of 2001. The more modest alternative of a mixed convention could have moved the law in all contracting states beyond the status quo in areas where that would be possible, while leaving the difficult areas for future evolution as legal developments permit. Such an approach was not taken, however, resulting in resort to an even more modest alternative: a *Hague Convention on Choice of Court Agreements*.

D. Conclusion of a *Convention on Choice of Court Agreements*

On April 24, 2002, Commission I of the Nineteenth Session of the Hague Conference acted to establish an informal working group to consider drafting a convention based on the jurisdictional provisions on which substantial consensus

---

[25] The U.S. distinction between general and specific jurisdiction was first suggested in Arthur Taylor von Mehren & Donald T. Trautman, *Jurisdiction to Adjudicate: A Suggested Analysis*, 79 HARV. L. REV. 1121, 1144–64 (1966). It was adopted by the U.S. Supreme Court in Helicopteros Nacionales de Colombia, SA v. Hall, 466 U.S. 408 (1984). In *Helicopteros* the Texas long-arm statute at issue was specifically written to bring within the jurisdiction of its courts those foreign corporations "doing business" in Texas. 466 U.S. 408, 412 n.7 (1984). The statute was TEX. REV. CIV. STAT. ANN., art. 2031(b) (Vernon 1964 and Supp.). On specific jurisdiction, Justice Blackmun's opinion noted the following implications of the minimum contacts test of *International Shoe*: "When a controversy is related to or 'arises out of' a defendant's contacts with the forum, the Court has said that a 'relationship among the defendant, the forum, and the litigation' is the essential foundation of in personam jurisdiction." 466 U.S. 408, 414 (1984). Therefore, specific jurisdiction requires that the cause of action in litigation "arise out of," and thus be directly related to, the activities of the defendant within the forum state. 466 U.S. 408, 414–15 (1984). The alternative is general jurisdiction: "Even when the cause of action does not arise out of or relate to the foreign corporation's activities in the forum State, due process is not offended by a State's subjecting the corporation to its in personam jurisdiction when there are sufficient contacts between the State and the foreign corporation." 466 U.S. 408, 414 (1984). Thus, so long as the contacts are "continuous and systematic," they may support jurisdiction even though the cause of action does not "arise out of" those contacts. 466 U.S. 408, 414–16 (1984) (discussing Perkins v. Benguet Consolidated Mining Co., 342 U.S. 437 (1952), and Keeton v. Hustler Magazine, Inc., 465 U.S. 770, 779–80 (1984)). The *Helicopteros* Court found the cause of action at issue not to have arisen out of the contacts with Texas, thereby avoiding a discussion of specific jurisdiction. It then ruled that general jurisdiction did not exist under the Due Process Clause. 466 U.S. 408, 418–19 (1984).

existed, beginning with jurisdiction based on agreement of the parties to the litiga-tion. The working group met three times,[26] and in March of 2003 produced a *Draft Text on Choice of Court Agreements*.[27] A Special Commission on Judgments was convoked in December of 2003 to work from the Draft Text toward a final conven-tion.[28] At that time, the goal of a more comprehensive jurisdiction and judgments convention was not completely off the table. Indeed, the April 2003 General Affairs meeting formally stated that any decision on the choice of court text "shall not pre-clude subsequent work on the remaining issues." Nonetheless, the process moved forward on a convention limited to exclusive, business-to-business choice of court agreements. A second Special Commission meeting was held in April of 2004, at which the draft was further developed. The final *Hague Convention on Choice of Court Agreements* was completed at a Diplomatic Conference in June of 2005.

III. Rules for declining jurisdiction in a global convention: a place for forum non conveniens?

As the discussion in previous chapters indicates, there are rather different approaches to questions of declining jurisdiction in common law and civil law systems. In the common law, the focus has come to be on the appropriate jurisdic-tion to hear a case, with an understanding that jurisdictional rules alone do not always place the case in the most appropriate forum. Thus, courts are assumed to have the discretion to decline to exercise jurisdiction even when it properly exists, under the doctrine of forum non conveniens.

In civil law systems the approach to the exercise of jurisdiction is more rigid. Courts are not assumed to have the discretion to decline to exercise valid jurisdiction. Once a court is properly seised of a case it is assumed that its jurisdiction will

---

[26]   The initial charge to the working group, and the reports on its first two meetings, are contained in *Reflection Paper to Assist in the Preparation of a Convention on Jurisdiction and Recognition and Enforcement of Foreign Judgments in Civil and Commercial Matters*, Hague Conference on Private International Law, Prel. Doc. No. 19 (August 2002); *Report on the First Meeting of the Informal Working Group on the Judgments Project—October 22–25, 2002*, Hague Conference on Private International Law, Prel. Doc. No. 20 of November 2002; and *Report on the Second Meeting of the Informal Working Group on the Judgments Project—January 6–9, 2003*, Hague Conference on Private International Law, Prel. Doc. No. 21 (January 2003).

[27]   *Preliminary Result of the Work of the Informal Working Group on the Judgments Project*, Hague Conference on Private International Law, Prel. Doc. No. 8 (March 2003) (corrected) for the attention of the Special Commission of April 2003 on General Affairs and Policy of the Conference.

[28]   *Convocation Special Commission on Judgments, 1–9 December 2003*, Hague Conference on Private International Law, Doc. L.c. ON No. 35(03) (19 Aug. 2003).

be exercised. The civil law doctrine of lis alibi pendens then requires a court second seised to decline to exercise jurisdiction in favor of the court first seised.[29] As the *Gasser* case in the European Court of Justice indicates, this policy in favor of the court first seised initially prevails over a policy favoring the enforcement of choice of court agreements, such that it will be up to the court first seised to determine the validity of a forum selection clause, even if that clause designates another court.[30] This provides incentives for a race to the courthouse in order to place the case in the most advantageous forum, and to obtain the deference of other courts through the lis pendens process.

This differs from the common law approach which generally allows parallel litigation until a judgment is rendered, and thus creates a race to judgment. While in civil law systems it is the act of seising a court that receives the deference of other courts, in a common law system it is the act of rendering a judgment that ultimately receives deference. This distinction implicates important policy choices. The common law approach generally is supported by arguments that it favors equitable results by getting the case to the most appropriate forum for resolution. The civil law approach is advanced as being more consistent with certainty and efficiency.[31]

Despite the rather different alternatives represented by common law forum non conveniens and civil law lis pendens approaches, this was one of the areas of early compromise in the Hague Conference negotiations.[32] This compromise combined elements of the lis pendens approach in Article 21 of the *2001 Hague Interim Text*

---

[29] For a more detailed discussion of the lis pendens rules of Germany and France, see Gregoire Andrieux, *Declining Jurisdiction in a Future International Convention on Jurisdiction and Judgments—How Can We Benefit from Past Experiences in Conciliating the Two Doctrines of Forum Non Conveniens and Lis Pendens?*, 27 LOY. L.A. INT'L & COMP. L. REV. 323, 332–36 (2005).

[30] Case C-116/02, Erich Gasser GmbH v. MISAT Srl., [2003] E.C.R. I–14693 (9 Dec. 2003).

[31] Note, however, that the doctrine resulting from the *Gasser* decision by the European Court of Justice can tend to frustrate efficiency where the court first seised is one in which proceedings generally take longer than in other countries, thus prolonging litigation and delaying results. *See* Chapter 2, Part IV, above.

[32] The Nygh-Pocar Report on the 1999 Preliminary Draft Convention explained this problem and compromise as follows:

> Both the civil law and the common law have developed mechanisms to deal with this problem. In the civil law the mechanism is that of *lis pendens* which is based on the priority of the first action commenced. It has the advantage of certainty, but the disadvantage of rigidity. It also can be abused by a defendant taking pre-emptive action in seeking a so-called "negative declaration" as to its liability. In the common law the mechanism is that of *forum non conveniens* which prefers the "natural" or "more appropriate" forum which need not be the forum which was seised first. It has the advantage of flexibility and adaptability to the circumstances of each case, but it lacks certainty and predictability. Needless to say, each side looked with some suspicion at a system with which it was unfamiliar.

with the inclusion of a modified forum non conveniens provision in Article 22. Article 21 begins with a basic lis pendens rule:

Article 21   Lis pendens

1. When the same parties are engaged in proceedings in courts of different Contracting States and when such proceedings are based on the same causes of action, irrespective of the relief sought, the court second seised shall suspend the proceedings if the court first seised has jurisdiction under Articles [white list of permitted bases of jurisdiction] [or under a rule of national law which is consistent with these articles] and is expected to render a judgment capable of being recognised under the Convention in the State of the court second seised, unless the latter has exclusive jurisdiction under Article 4 [, 11] or 12.

2. The court second seised shall decline jurisdiction as soon as it is presented with a judgment rendered by the court first seised that complies with the requirements for recognition or enforcement under the Convention.

3. Upon application of a party, the court second seised may proceed with the case if the plaintiff in the court first seised has failed to take the necessary steps to bring the proceedings to a decision on the merits or if that court has not rendered such a decision within a reasonable time.

4. The provisions of the preceding paragraphs apply to the court second seised even in a case where the jurisdiction of that court is based on the national law of that State in accordance with Article 17.

After long debate the Special Commission has adopted a compromise solution whereby provision is made for both *lis pendens* and for declining jurisdiction in certain circumstances. However, the *lis pendens* provision in Article 21 is made more flexible and priority is denied to the "negative declaration". In return the power to decline jurisdiction in Article 22 is subjected to stringent conditions which emphasise its exceptional character.

Hague Conference on Private International Law, *Preliminary Draft Convention on Jurisdiction and Foreign Judgments in Civil and Commercial Matters adopted by the Special Commission and Report by Peter Nygh and Fausto Pocar*, Prel. Doc. No. 11 of Aug. 2000, at 85.

5. For the purpose of this Article, a court shall be deemed to be seised—

   a) when the document instituting the proceedings or an equivalent document is lodged with the court; or

   b) if such document has to be served before being lodged with the court, when it is received by the authority responsible for service or served on the defendant.

   [As appropriate, universal time is applicable.]

6. If in the action before the court first seised the plaintiff seeks a determination that it has no obligation to the defendant, and if an action seeking substantive relief is brought in the court second seised—

   a) the provisions of paragraphs 1 to 5 above shall not apply to the court second seised; and

   b) the court first seised shall suspend the proceedings at the request of a party if the court second seised is expected to render a decision capable of being recognised under the Convention.

7. This Article shall not apply if the court first seised, on application by a party, determines that the court second seised is clearly more appropriate to resolve the dispute, under the conditions specified in Article 22.[33]

Thus, the civil law approach is the first element of the compromise. This is tempered, however, by several additional aspects of Article 21. The third and sixth paragraphs prevent an "Italian torpedo" strategy by which a party may take advantage of a strict lis pendens rule by rushing to file a negative declaratory judgment action against the natural plaintiff in a court in which proceedings will take so long as to frustrate the natural process of litigation. Thus, the third paragraph allows a court second seised to go ahead with the case if "the plaintiff in the court first seised has failed to take the necessary steps to bring the proceedings to a decision on the merits or if that court has not rendered such a decision within a

---

[33] *Summary of the Outcome of the Discussion in Commission II of the First Part of the Diplomatic Conference 6–20 June 2001—Interim Text*, Hague Conference on Private International Law, Nineteenth Session (2001), art. 21.

reasonable time."[34] The sixth paragraph goes on to provide that where the action in the court first seised is for a negative declaratory judgment, the normal lis pendens rules do not apply, and "the court first seised shall suspend the proceedings at the request of a party if the court second seised is expected to render a decision capable of being recognised under the convention."[35] Finally, paragraph (7) ties Article 21 to Article 22 by providing that the lis pendens rules shall not apply if the court first seised determines, under Article 22, that it should decline jurisdiction in favor of another court.[36] This indicates a clear compromise between the traditional civil law lis pendens approach and the common law forum non conveniens approach to declining jurisdiction.

Article 22 follows by incorporating a variation of the common law doctrine of forum non conveniens:

Article 22   Exceptional circumstances for declining jurisdiction

1. In exceptional circumstances, when the jurisdiction of the court seised is not founded on an exclusive choice of court agreement valid under Article 4, or on Article 7, 8 or 12, the court may, on application by a party, suspend its proceedings if in that case it is clearly inappropriate for that court to exercise jurisdiction and if a court of another State has jurisdiction and is clearly more appropriate to resolve the dispute. Such application must be made no later than at the time of the first defence on the merits.

2. The court shall take into account, in particular—

   a) any inconvenience to the parties in view of their habitual residence;

   b) the nature and location of the evidence, including documents and witnesses, and the procedures for obtaining such evidence;

   c) applicable limitation or prescription periods;

---

[34]   *Summary of the Outcome of the Discussion in Commission II of the First Part of the Diplomatic Conference 6–20 June 2001—Interim Text,* Hague Conference on Private International Law, Nineteenth Session (2001), art. 21(3).

[35]   *Id.,* art. 21(6).

[36]   *Id.,* art. 21(7).

d) the possibility of obtaining recognition and enforcement of any decision on the merits.

3. In deciding whether to suspend the proceedings, a court shall not discriminate on the basis of the nationality or habitual residence of the parties.

4. If the court decides to suspend its proceedings under paragraph 1, it may order the defendant to provide security sufficient to satisfy any decision of the other court on the merits. However, it shall make such an order if the other court has jurisdiction only under Article 17, or if it is in a non-Contracting State, unless the defendant establishes that [the plaintiff's ability to enforce the judgment will not be materially prejudiced if such an order is not made] [sufficient assets exist in the State of that other court or in another State where the court's decision could be enforced].

5. When the court has suspended its proceedings under paragraph 1,

a) it shall decline to exercise jurisdiction if the court of the other State exercises jurisdiction, or if the plaintiff does not bring the proceedings in that State within the time specified by the court; or

b) it shall proceed with the case if the court of the other State decides not to exercise jurisdiction.

6. This Article shall not apply where the court has jurisdiction only under Article 17 [which is not consistent with Articles [white list]]. In such a case, national law shall govern the question of declining jurisdiction.

[7. The court seised and having jurisdiction under Articles 3 to 15 shall not apply the doctrine of *forum non conveniens* or any similar rule for declining jurisdiction.][37]

The basic rule of Article 22 is that a court may "suspend its proceedings if in that case it is clearly inappropriate for that court to exercise jurisdiction and if a court of another state has jurisdiction and is clearly more appropriate to resolve

---

37   *Id.*, art. 22. Brackets in the text indicate proposed language on which agreement had not been reached.

the dispute."[38] As the language indicates, jurisdiction may be declined in this manner only in "exceptional circumstances." While that term does not itself place explicit limits on the court, the ability of a court to take such steps is subject to very specific conditions.

Paragraph (1) of Article 22 contains five separate and specific elements that must exist in order for the court to suspend proceedings and then later decline jurisdiction:

1) The court seised must not have jurisdiction under the *Convention* pursuant to:
    — Article 4, which allows the parties to select an exclusive judicial forum in a Contracting State;[39]
    — Articles 7 or 8, which create certain types of protective jurisdiction for consumers and employees;[40] or
    — Article 12, which sets out certain circumstances in which a court has exclusive jurisdiction.[41]

---

[38]   *Id.*, art. 22(1).

[39]   *Id.*, art. 4 (footnotes omitted):

   Article 4   Choice of court

   1. If the parties have agreed that [a court or] [the] courts of a Contracting State shall have jurisdiction to settle any dispute which has arisen or may arise in connection with a particular legal relationship, [that court or those] [the] courts [of that Contracting State] shall have jurisdiction, [provided the court has subject matter jurisdiction] and that jurisdiction shall be exclusive unless the parties have agreed otherwise. Where an agreement having exclusive effect designates [a court or][the] courts of a non-Contracting State, courts in Contracting States shall decline jurisdiction or suspend proceedings unless the [court or] courts chosen have themselves declined jurisdiction. [Whether such an agreement is invalid for lack of consent (for example, due to fraud or duress) or incapacity shall depend on national law including its rules of private international law.]

   . . . .

[40]   *Id.*, arts. 7 (Contracts concluded by consumers) and 8 (Individual contracts of employment).

[41]   Article 12 of the *Interim Text* sets forth exclusive jurisdiction for the following categories of case:

   1) proceedings involving rights *in rem* in immovable property,

   2) proceedings involving internal corporate governance issues,

   3) proceedings involving validity of entries in public registers, and

   4) proceedings involving registration and validity of intellectual property rights.

   Summary of the Outcome of the Discussion in Commission II of the First Part of the Diplomatic Conference 6–20 June 2001—Interim Text, Hague Conference on Private International Law, Nineteenth Session (2001), art. 12.

2) There must be an "application by a party" for such action. "The court cannot decline to exercise its jurisdiction on its own motion."[42]

3) It must be "clearly inappropriate for that [forum] court to exercise jurisdiction."

4) A "court of another state" (not necessarily a Contracting State) must have jurisdiction.

5) That other court must be a "clearly more appropriate" forum in which "to resolve the dispute."

The third of these requirements is an explicit adoption of the Australian "clearly inappropriate forum" test, but with the gloss of the "clearly more appropriate forum" overlay of the fifth requirement, which seems to build on the test applied in the United Kingdom, the United States, and Canada. The two are independent tests, however. "[T]he fact that another forum may be 'clearly more appropriate' does not necessarily mean that the forum seised is itself 'clearly inappropriate.'"[43] Thus, the result more closely approximates the current Australian approach to forum non conveniens, placing a greater burden on the defendant than is the case in the United Kingdom, the United States, and Canada under current doctrine.

A further important condition to declining jurisdiction under Article 22 is found in paragraph (5)(a). This provision allows the initial suspension of proceedings under paragraph (1) to mature fully to declining jurisdiction only if "the court of the other [more appropriate] State exercises jurisdiction, or if the plaintiff does not bring the proceedings in that State within the time specified by the court."[44]

---

[42] Hague Conference on Private International Law, *Preliminary Draft Convention on Jurisdiction and Foreign Judgments in Civil and Commercial Matters adopted by the Special Commission and Report by Peter Nygh and Fausto Pocar*, Prel. Doc. No. 11 of Aug. 2000, at 90. "Such application must be made no later than at the time of the first defence on the merits." *Summary of the Outcome of the Discussion in Commission II of the First Part of the Diplomatic Conference 6-20 June 2001—Interim Text*, Hague Conference on Private International Law, Nineteenth Session (2001), art. 22(1).

[43] Hague Conference on Private International Law, *Preliminary Draft Convention on Jurisdiction and Foreign Judgments in Civil and Commercial Matters adopted by the Special Commission and Report by Peter Nygh and Fausto Pocar*, Prel. Doc. No. 11 of Aug. 2000, at 90.

[44] *Summary of the Outcome of the Discussion in Commission II of the First Part of the Diplomatic Conference 6-20 June 2001—Interim Text*, Hague Conference on Private International Law, Nineteenth Session (2001), art. 22(5).

Thus, success on the declining jurisdiction motion cannot alone serve to terminate all proceedings in the case.[45] "[T]he court originally seised cannot decline jurisdiction unless and until the alternative forum actually commences to exercise jurisdiction with respect to the parties and the substance of the claim."[46]

The decision on whether the court seised is a "clearly inappropriate" forum, and on whether there exists a "clearly more appropriate forum," is committed to the discretion of the court. Thus, the court "may … suspend" proceedings under Article 22(1) and later decline jurisdiction under Article 22(5).[47] In the exercise of this discretion, Article 22(2) provides four non-exclusive factors to be weighed in determining what is an appropriate forum:

a) any inconvenience to the parties in view of their habitual residence;

b) the nature and location of the evidence, including documents and witnesses, and the procedures for obtaining such evidence;

c) applicable limitation or prescription periods;

d) the possibility of obtaining recognition and enforcement of any decision on the merits.[48]

This is a list of what would commonly be considered private interest factors in common law forum non conveniens analysis. Two results follow from the statement that "the court shall take into account, in particular" these factors. First, these are not the only private interest factors that may be considered; but these

---

[45] For a discussion of concerns that successful forum non conveniens motions in U.S. courts often end the case without action being brought in an alternative forum, *see* Jacqueline Duval-Major, *One-Way Ticket Home: The Federal Doctrine of Forum non conveniens and the International Plaintiff*, 77 CORNELL L. REV. 650 (1992).

[46] Hague Conference on Private International Law, *Preliminary Draft Convention on Jurisdiction and Foreign Judgments in Civil and Commercial Matters adopted by the Special Commission and Report by Peter Nygh and Fausto Pocar*, Prel. Doc. No. 11 of Aug. 2000, at 93.

[47] *Id.*, at 90.

[48] *Summary of the Outcome of the Discussion in Commission II of the First Part of the Diplomatic Conference 6–20 June 2001—Interim Text*, Hague Conference on Private International Law, Nineteenth Session (2001), art. 22(2).

must be considered.[49] Second, the Article neither specifically includes nor excludes the consideration of public interest factors.

Article 22(3) prohibits a protectionist approach to the application of the convention rule on forum non conveniens by stating that "[i]n deciding whether to suspend the proceedings, a court shall not discriminate on the basis of the nationality or habitual residence of the parties."[50] Thus, a court should not be able to give greater deference to the forum choice of a local plaintiff than to the forum choice of a foreign plaintiff. As noted earlier,[51] in *Iragorri v. United Technologies Corp.*,[52] the U.S. Second Circuit Court of Appeals ruled that favoring a domestic plaintiff's choice of forum is a natural result of a balancing of conveniences, and not necessarily the application of discrimination against foreign plaintiffs.[53] The *Nygh-Pocar Report* indicates that this type of balancing of conveniences is not prevented by Article 22(3):

> A decision which gives less deference to the choice of forum by a foreign plaintiff solely because that plaintiff is foreign, is prohibited by this provision. . . . This provision reinforces the basic rule that the plaintiff is entitled to choose a forum provided by the Convention. There is no conflict between this provision and the factor of inconvenience based on residence to be taken into account under Article 22(2)(a). Paragraph 3 prohibits discrimination against a party because that party is resident abroad.

---

[49] *See* Hague Conference on Private International Law, *Preliminary Draft Convention on Jurisdiction and Foreign Judgments in Civil and Commercial Matters adopted by the Special Commission and Report by Peter Nygh and Fausto Pocar*, Prel. Doc. No. 11 of Aug. 2000, at 91:

> The list is not exhaustive, as indicated by the words "in particular". Other factors, such as: the substantive law to be applied in resolving the dispute, the availability of legal aid or the extent of the relief which may be granted in each forum, may also be relevant. Nor should the list be read as indicating a hierarchy: which factor is the more important will depend on the circumstances of the case. None of the factors can be regarded as conclusive. . . .

[50] *Summary of the Outcome of the Discussion in Commission II of the First Part of the Diplomatic Conference 6–20 June 2001—Interim Text*, Hague Conference on Private International Law, Nineteenth Session (2001), art. 22(3).

[51] *See* Chapter 3, Part III.E., above.

[52] 274 F.3d 65 (2d Cir. 2001) (*en banc*).

[53] 274 F.3d 65, 73 (2d Cir. 2001) (*en banc*) ("It is not a correct understanding of the rule to accord deference only when the suit is brought in the plaintiff's home district. Rather, the court must consider a plaintiff's likely motivations in light of all the relevant indications. We thus understand the Supreme Court's teachings on the deference due to plaintiff's forum choice as instructing that we give greater deference to a plaintiff's forum choice to the extent that it was motivated by legitimate reasons, including the plaintiff's convenience and the ability of a U.S. resident plaintiff to obtain jurisdiction over the defendant, and diminishing deference to a plaintiff's forum choice to the extent that it was motivated by tactical advantage.").

Sub-paragraph a) of paragraph 2 raises for consideration any inconvenience which may result to a party because of its residence. As long as those inconveniences are properly balanced and one party is not preferred merely because that party resides within the forum in question, no issue of discrimination arises.[54]

Ultimately, how one views the application of the doctrine of forum non conveniens to a case brought by a foreign plaintiff probably depends on one's perspective. The foreign plaintiff will tend to see any consideration of its nationality as discrimination, while the local defendant will tend to consider the plaintiff's foreign nationality as a factor indicating inconvenience in the forum seised and weighing in favor of litigation in an alternative forum.

Article 22 makes no specific provision for placing conditions on the grant of a stay or dismissal based on forum non conveniens. It does, however, provide that a court may "order the defendant to provide security sufficient to satisfy any decision of the other court on the merits," and require such an order where jurisdiction in the "other court" is not a required basis under the Convention, unless the defendant establishes that the resulting judgment in the other court would clearly be enforceable in an appropriate jurisdiction.[55]

Article 27(3) of the *2001 Hague Interim Text* adds a wrinkle to the application of Article 22 by providing that "[r]ecognition or enforcement of a judgment may not be refused on the ground that the court addressed considers that the court of origin should have declined jurisdiction in accordance with Article 22."[56] Thus, a court asked to recognize a judgment from a court in another contracting state could not deny recognition or enforcement because it believed the court of origin should have exercised its right under Article 22 to decline to exercise its jurisdiction.

The work done in the Hague negotiations on Articles 21 and 22 of the 1999 and 2001 texts represent an important compromise between a strict civil law lis

---

[54] Hague Conference on Private International Law, *Preliminary Draft Convention on Jurisdiction and Foreign Judgments in Civil and Commercial Matters adopted by the Special Commission and Report by Peter Nygh and Fausto Pocar*, Prel. Doc. No. 11 of Aug. 2000, at 92.

[55] *Summary of the Outcome of the Discussion in Commission II of the First Part of the Diplomatic Conference 6–20 June 2001—Interim Text*, Hague Conference on Private International Law, Nineteenth Session (2001), art. 22(4).

[56] *Summary of the Outcome of the Discussion in Commission II of the First Part of the Diplomatic Conference 6–20 June 2001—Interim Text*, Hague Conference on Private International Law, Nineteenth Session (2001), art. 27(3).

pendens approach and the heavily discretionary common law forum non conveniens approach. It offers a level of predictability and avoidance of parallel litigation by beginning with a preference for litigation in the court first seised. At the same time, however, it recognizes that strict lis pendens is subject to abuse by parties rushing to courts less suited to deal with the case or which are likely to take an exorbitantly long time to reach a judgment. A court first seised may nonetheless decline to exercise jurisdiction, but under circumstances much more limited than those currently found in the forum non conveniens doctrine applied in most common law countries. The result seems to save the advantages of each doctrine, while limiting the excesses of both.

IV. The American Law Institute and UNIDROIT

The negotiations at The Hague Conference on Private International Law have not provided the only recent proposals for dealing with issues of declining jurisdiction. Two recent projects of the American Law Institute (one in cooperation with the International Institute for the Unification of Private Law—UNIDROIT) also contain relevant provisions.

A. The ALI/UNIDROIT Principles and Rules of Transnational Civil Procedure

The ALI/UNIDROIT *Principles of Transnational Civil Procedure* received the final approval of UNIDROIT in April of 2004 and were approved by the American Law Institute in May of 2004.[57] This project, begun in 1997 by Reporters Geoffrey Hazard and Michele Taruffo, represents an attempt to identify principles and rules that can be used to cut across the many differing procedural systems, primarily the common law and continental civil law models.[58] The document containing the Principles also includes "Rules" to accompany them.[59] The Rules are somewhat more specific than the Principles, and represent "The Reporters' model implementation of the Principles, suitable either for adoption or for further

---

[57]   *Transnational Civil Procedure Principles Receive Final Approval; Final Action Deferred on International Jurisdiction and Judgments*, 26 ALI REPORTER 1 (No. 4, 2004).

[58]   *See* Geoffrey C. Hazard, Jr., Michele Taruffo, Rolf Sturner & Antonio Gidi, *Introduction to the Principles and Rules of Transnational Civil Procedure*, 33 N.Y.U. J. INT'L L. & POL. 769 (2001).

[59]   American Law Institute, *ALI/UNIDROIT Principles and Rules of Transnational Civil Procedure* (2006) [hereinafter ALI/UNIDROIT Principles and Rules].

adaptation in particular jurisdictions."[60] Unlike the Principles, the Rules were not officially endorsed by either the ALI or UNIDROIT.[61]

While the ALI/UNIDROIT *Principles and Rules of Transnational Civil Procedure* do address issues of declining jurisdiction, the entire project is too broad to offer specific guidance for the future development of the doctrine of forum non conveniens on a global scale. Principle 2 addresses declining jurisdiction issues under the heading "Jurisdiction Over Parties," and includes the following provisions:

2.4 Exercise of jurisdiction must ordinarily be declined when the parties have previously agreed that some other tribunal has exclusive jurisdiction.

2.5 Jurisdiction may be declined or the proceeding suspended when the court is manifestly inappropriate relative to another more appropriate court that could exercise jurisdiction.

2.6 The court should decline jurisdiction or suspend the proceeding, when the dispute is previously pending in another court competent to exercise jurisdiction, unless it appears that the dispute will not be fairly, effectively, and expeditiously resolved in that forum.[62]

The Reporters' Comments note that Principle 2.5 "should be interpreted in connection with the Principle of Procedural Equality of the Parties, which prohibits any kind of discrimination on the basis of nationality or residence."[63]

The ALI/UNIDROIT Principles: (1) incorporate both a concept of forum non conveniens from common law systems and the basic civil law lis pendens concept that a court second seised should defer to a court first seised; (2) provide for deference to a court selected by the parties to have exclusive jurisdiction; (3) include a dual test requiring findings that the forum court is "manifestly inappropriate" and that another forum is "more appropriate" in the application of their forum

---

[60] American Law Institute, *ALI/UNIDROIT Principles and Rules of Transnational Civil Procedure*, Preface (2006).

[61] *Transnational Civil Procedure Principles Receive Final Approval; Final Action Deferred on International Jurisdiction and Judgments*, 26 ALI REPORTER 1 (No. 4, 2004).

[62] American Law Institute, *ALI/UNIDROIT Principles and Rules of Transnational Civil Procedure*, Principle 2 (2006).

[63] American Law Institute, *ALI/UNIDROIT Principles and Rules of Transnational Civil Procedure* (2006), at 20 (citing Principle 3.2 on the "right to equal treatment").

non conveniens element; (4) are to be applied in a non-discriminatory manner; and (5) lack clear guidelines for application when there might be a conflict between concepts of forum non conveniens and lis pendens (*e.g.*, when a court second seised finds that it is clearly the most appropriate forum, or when a court first seised declines jurisdiction under Principle 2.4 and a court second seised also declines jurisdiction under Principle 2.5).

The accompanying Rules essentially restate the basic elements of the Principles. In particular, Rule 4 includes the following provisions:

> 4.6 The forum should decline to exercise jurisdiction or suspend the proceeding, if:
> 4.6.1 Another forum was validly designated by the parties as exclusive;
> 4.6.2 The forum is manifestly inappropriate relative to another forum that could exercise jurisdiction; or
> 4.6.3 The dispute is previously pending in another court
> 4.7 The forum may nevertheless exercise its jurisdiction or reinstate the proceeding when it appears that the dispute cannot otherwise be effectively and expeditiously resolved or there are other compelling reasons for doing so.[64]

While Rule 4.6 does little more than succinctly restate the forum non conveniens and lis pendens rules of Principles 2.4 and 2.5, Rule 4.7 adds a gloss to the lis pendens element of Principle 2.5 by allowing a court second seised to exercise jurisdiction when it determines it appropriate to do so. This may allow resolution of some of the cases in which concepts of forum non conveniens and lis pendens can together create difficult situations.[65]

---

[64] American Law Institute, *ALI/UNIDROIT Principles and Rules of Transnational Civil Procedure*, Rule 4 (2006).

[65] Principle 28 provides some further elaboration of relationships in declining jurisdiction situations:

> 28.1 In applying the rules of lis pendens, the scope of the proceedings is determined by the claims in the parties' pleadings, including amendments.

> 28.2 In applying the rules of claim preclusion, the scope of the claim or claims decided is determined by reference to the claims and defenses in the parties' pleadings, including amendments, and the court's decision and reasoned explanation.

> 28.3 The concept of issue preclusion, as to an issue of fact or application of law to facts, should be applied only to prevent substantial injustice.

American Law Institute, *ALI/UNIDROIT Principles and Rules of Transnational Civil Procedure*, Principle 28 (2006).

The impact of the ALI/UNIDROIT project remains to be determined. It creates neither a treaty nor a model law for adoption, although the Rules could be adopted in some form by a state for application in cases involving transnational matters. The breadth and relative generality of the project—an effort to take on just about all of civil procedure in very disparate systems—both limits its value in discussion of specific issues and raises doubt about its ultimate effect in any one legal system.

Despite these limitations, the ALI/UNIDROIT project demonstrates consistency of approach with that taken in Articles 21 and 22 of the *2001 Hague Interim Text*. The "manifestly inappropriate" forum rule of Principle 2.4 leans toward the more strict Australian approach to forum non conveniens, as does the "clearly inappropriate" forum test of the *Interim Text*. In each case, the rule would serve to place limitations on common law discretion, thus moving some distance toward the more rigid approach of civil law courts. Nonetheless, each of the Hague and ALI/UNIDROIT rules would lead civil law courts to engage in *some* discretion in this area, moving beyond the existing stated rejection of any judicial discretion and even beyond the types of forays into declining jurisdiction suggested by Japanese and German developments in Chapter 7. In addition, both the Hague and ALI/UNIDROIT approaches would bring the lis pendens concept firmly into common law legal systems. The ALI/UNIDROIT project thus reinforces the approach taken in the *2001 Hague Interim Text* in terms of a global system for declining jurisdiction, without providing any significant accompanying contradictions to the Hague approach.

B. The ALI Recognition and Enforcement of Foreign Judgments Project

The other relevant ALI initiative of recent years began as the "International Jurisdiction and Judgments Project," and ended with the title "Recognition and Enforcement of Foreign Judgments: Analysis and Proposed Federal Statute."[66] This project originally began on two tracks: (1) preparation of proposed U.S. federal implementing legislation for the then proposed Hague jurisdiction and

---

[66] American Law Institute, *Recognition and Enforcement of Foreign Judgments: Analysis and Proposed Federal Statute* (2006). For more detailed information on the ALI International Jurisdiction and Judgments Project, *see* Linda J. Silberman & Andreas F. Lowenfeld, *The Hague Judgments Convention—and Perhaps Beyond*, in LAW AND JUSTICE IN A MULTISTATE WORLD: ESSAYS IN HONOR OF ARTHUR T. VON MEHREN 121, 130–35 (James A.R. Nafziger & Symeon C. Symeonides eds., 2002); Linda J. Silberman & Andreas F. Lowenfeld, *A Different Challenge for the ALI: Herein of Foreign Country Judgments, an International Treaty and an American Statute*, 75 IND. L.J. 635 (2000).

judgments convention, and (2) the preparation of proposed U.S. federal legislation to centralize foreign judgment recognition practice in the U.S. absent a treaty, which to date has been a matter of state law (even in the federal courts).[67] With delays and uncertainty in the Hague process, this turned to a singular focus on the second goal, with consideration of a draft text by the ALI at its 2003[68] and 2004[69] annual meetings. Final action on the project was deferred until the May 2005 Annual Meeting, in order to allow the Reporters to "return with a revision... taking into account the many suggestions received in the course of more than a day of full and stimulating discussion" at the May 2004 Meeting.[70]

The ALI Recognition and Enforcement of Foreign Judgments Project is intended to have direct impact only on U.S. law by proposing a federal statute. As a statute focused primarily on the recognition and enforcement of foreign judgments in U.S. courts, it could be structured without dealing with issues of forum non conveniens and lis pendens. The *Uniform Foreign Money-Judgments Recognition Act*,[71] promulgated by the National Conference of Commissioners on Uniform State Laws and adopted in 31 states, now serves this function, and contains no rules on declining jurisdiction. Nonetheless, the Reporters for the ALI Project determined it both appropriate and justified to include such provisions in their project:

> Declination of jurisdiction—whether via lis pendens or via forum non conveniens—is closely related to recognition and enforcement of foreign judgments. Both declination of jurisdiction and recognition of judgments depend on the conclusion that the exercise of jurisdiction by the foreign court is founded on an acceptable basis. Moreover, parallel litigation in different fora inevitably leads to the danger of inconsistent judgments.[72]

Interestingly, this concern for the relationship between enforcement of judgments and declining jurisdiction manifests itself in the ALI Project, not in a provision on

---

[67] For a discussion of U.S. law on the recognition and enforcement of foreign judgments, *see* ENFORCING FOREIGN JUDGMENTS IN THE UNITED STATES AND UNITED STATES JUDGMENTS ABROAD (Ronald A. Brand ed., 1992); Ronald A. Brand, *Enforcement of Foreign Money-Judgments in the United States: In Search of Uniformity and International Acceptance*, 67 NOTRE DAME L. REV. 253 (1991).

[68] American Law Institute, *International Jurisdiction and Judgments Project* (Tentative Draft, Apr. 14, 2003).

[69] American Law Institute, *International Jurisdiction and Judgments Project* (Tentative Draft, No. 2, Apr. 13, 2004).

[70] *Transnational Civil Procedure Principles Receive Final Approval; Final Action Deferred on International Jurisdiction and Judgments*, 26 ALI REPORTER 1, 6 (No. 4, 2004).

[71] UNIFORM FOREIGN MONEY-JUDGMENTS RECOGNITION ACT, 13-II UNI. L. ANN. 39 (2002).

[72] American Law Institute, *Recognition and Enforcement of Foreign Judgments: Analysis and Proposed Federal Statute* (2006), at 132.

forum non conveniens, as might be assumed would be the approach in a common law jurisdiction, but rather in a provision that would adopt as federal law a mandatory rule of lis pendens. Section 11 of the proposed statute is written to provide as follows:

§ 11. Declination of Jurisdiction When Prior Action Is Pending
    (a) Except as provided in subsection (b), when an action is brought in a court in the United States and it is shown that a proceeding concerning the same subject matter and including the same parties or related parties as adversaries has previously been brought and is pending in the courts of a foreign state, the court in the United States shall stay, or when appropriate, dismiss the action, if:
        (i) the foreign court has jurisdiction on a basis not unacceptable under § 6 [which lists the approved bases of jurisdiction for judgments from foreign courts]; and
        (ii) the foreign court is likely to render a timely judgment entitled to recognition under this Act.
    (b) A court in the United States may decline to stay or dismiss the action under subsection (a) if the party bringing the action shows
        (i) that the jurisdiction of the foreign court was invoked with a view to frustrating the exercise of jurisdiction of the court in the United States, when that court would be the more appropriate forum;
        (ii) that the proceedings in the foreign court are vexatious or frivolous; or
        (iii) that there are other persuasive reasons for accepting the costs of parallel litigation.[73]

The Reporters acknowledge that "[t]here is no general rule in the United States concerning lis pendens, either in domestic or in international litigation."[74]

The result of this section would be to adopt a first-in-time filing rule similar to that of the *Brussels Regulation* system in the European Union.[75] In one sense this rule would be less severe than the rule found in Article 27 of the *Brussels*

---

[73] *Id.* at 25–26.
[74] *Id.* at 133–34, Reporters' Note 1.
[75] Council Regulation 44/2001/EC of 22 December 2000 on Jurisdiction and the Recognition and Enforcement of Judgments in Civil and Commercial Matters, 2001 O.J. Eur. Comm. L 12, 1.

Regulation: rather than being mandatory, it would allow some discretion for the U.S. court that is second seised of the case. On the other hand, it is a rule much more expansive, and thus more severe, than that found in the *Brussels Regulation*. The lis pendens rule of the *Brussels Regulation* is part of a self-contained system that is applicable (1) only on a reciprocal basis within the Member States of the European Union, and (2) only in respect to cases subject to explicit lists of required bases of jurisdiction that are, in turn, further subject to challenge and interpretation before a single European Court of Justice. The ALI Project provision in § 11 would be applicable to cases filed in any country of the world (so long as the bases for non-recognition of § 5 and the jurisdictional standards of § 6 were met), and without coordinated review of jurisdiction in the foreign court by a court with authority to ensure consistent application throughout the world. Perhaps these are minor issues that U.S. courts can sort out upon application to recognize and enforce specific foreign judgment. But exclusive reliance on an after-the-fact method of review can be expensive and time consuming, and would be subject to fewer checks along the way than is the case with the *Brussels Regulation* lis pendens rule.

Adoption of the ALI lis pendens rule in a federal statute would mark a significant change in U.S. law. It would replace the traditional common law race-to-judgment approach with the civil law race-to-the-courthouse. This may be something American trial lawyers will welcome—with their reputation for being first on the scene of any potential litigation. Nonetheless, it would effect a dramatic change in the U.S. approach to issues of declining jurisdiction.

Interestingly, while the statute proposed in the ALI Project introduces a rule of lis pendens, it does not deal directly with the doctrine of forum non conveniens. One Reporters' Note suggests, however, that forum non conveniens would continue to operate in U.S. law, and that the "most appropriate forum" concept would play a role as well in the resulting lis pendens analysis:

> The reference to "other persuasive reasons" in subsection (b)(iii) applies the principle of looking for the most appropriate forum in the lis pendens context. Because of the substantial differences in the procedures and available remedies between litigation in the United States and in other countries, a strict lis pendens rule could work substantial hardship for parties seeking to litigate in a U.S. forum. Cf., e.g., Parex Bank v. Russian Savings Bank, 116 F. Supp. 2d 415 (S.D.N.Y. 2000), in which the court refused to dismiss on forum non conveniens grounds an action by a Latvian bank

against a Russian bank on the basis that Russian courts would not provide any avenue of relief for plaintiff's claims.[76]

This Reporters' Note goes on to acknowledge that U.S. courts have accomplished the same purpose as a lis pendens rule by "a sensitive application of forum non conveniens."[77] It is thus not entirely clear from either the text of the proposed rule, the Comments, or the Reporters' Notes, whether the proposed rule of lis pendens would be expected, or intended, to create results different from those available under current law. The statute would seem to affect existing approaches to the application of the doctrine of forum non conveniens only if the doctrine were raised as a supplemental path for deferring to a foreign jurisdiction previously seised of a case.

U.S. adoption of a civil law approach to lis pendens under the proposed ALI statute would be without any reciprocal changes in the law of other countries, on either lis pendens or forum non conveniens. Such a unilateral approach clearly is considered by the Reporters for the ALI Project to be advisable, but it would mean the United States would change its law without seeking reciprocal developments in the law of other countries on declining jurisdiction. This would limit the opportunity to bargain for compromise solutions in the context of future multilateral (or bilateral) negotiations.

V.   Lessons for the future

The work at the Hague Conference on Private International Law may not have led to a comprehensive jurisdiction and judgments convention to be adopted in the near term, but it has provided a focus for analyzing possible cooperative efforts to harmonize the law on issues related to declining jurisdiction. The *2001 Hague Interim Text* indicates both possible convergence among common law systems, and possible compromise between traditionally common law and civil law doctrines.

---

[76]   American Law Institute, *Recognition and Enforcement of Foreign Judgments: Analysis and Proposed Federal Statute* (2006), at 134, Reporters' Note 3.

[77]   *Id.* at 136, *citing* Hyatt Int'l Corp. v. Coco, 302 F.3d 707 (7th Cir. 2002).

A. Issues among common law states

Among common law states, there are lessons in the *2001 Hague Interim Text* relating to both the existing similarities among common law doctrines of forum non conveniens and the existing differences in those doctrines.

1. *Hague Interim Text Article 22 and common law similarities*

As we saw in Chapter 6, there are five common elements to the forum non conveniens doctrine in the four common law legal systems that have been considered here:

1. the requirement of an available, alternative forum;

2. allocation of the general burden of proof on the defendant;

3. consideration of private interest factors;

4. the trial court's discretion in applying forum non conveniens analysis; and

5. the ability to impose conditions on a stay or dismissal.

The first four of these are clearly represented in Article 22 of the *2001 Hague Interim Text*. By adopting a combination of the Australian "clearly inappropriate forum" test with a parallel focus on consideration of a forum that is "clearly more appropriate," Article 22(1) would require consideration of the appropriateness of both the forum in which the case is brought and the available alternative forum. Like the Australian test, it would create a higher burden for the defendant seeking the declination of jurisdiction in favor of another forum.

While it is not explicit in the language of Article 22(1), that provision does place the initial burden on the defendant by requiring that a court may decline jurisdiction only "upon application by a party." While it is possible that a plaintiff might file a forum non conveniens motion,[78] it is extremely unlikely. The "clearly

---

[78] This could occur, for example, if a plaintiff initially brought a case in a U.S. state court, but after removal to federal court, sought to avoid the federal forum.

inappropriate forum" test of Article 22 implies an obvious burden on the defendant.[79]

Article 22(2) provides a clear list of private interest factors, thus carrying forward the third element of similarity in the common law systems. The fourth common element—the trial court's broad discretion in the decision to decline jurisdiction—is found in the language of Article 22(1) that the court "may" suspend its proceedings.[80]

The common element that is not so clearly presented in Article 22 of the *2001 Hague Interim Text* is the ability to impose conditions upon the grant of a motion to suspend proceedings. In at least one way, however, Article 22 takes this element even further than does the traditional common law doctrine of forum non conveniens. Paragraph (4) addresses the concern that a judgment from the alternative forum might not be recoverable, by providing that the first court "may order the defendant to provide security sufficient to satisfy any decision of the other court on the merits."[81] This is similar to the condition granted in some cases that the defendant stipulate to enforcement of any resulting judgment from the alternative forum.[82]

Article 22 does not explicitly authorize a court to impose further conditions on suspension, such as a defendant's agreement to waive any time bar that may otherwise apply in the alternative forum—a condition often found at least in U.S. cases.[83] Thus, it is not clear whether such conditions would be within the

---

[79]   *See* Hague Conference on Private International Law, *Preliminary Draft Convention on Jurisdiction and Foreign Judgments in Civil and Commercial Matters adopted by the Special Commission and Report by Peter Nygh and Fausto Pocar*, Prel. Doc. No. 11 of Aug. 2000, at 90 ("The Convention does not address the question of onus, but it would be logical for the party requesting that the court decline jurisdiction to bring forward the facts and reasons for such a decision.").

[80]   *See* Hague Conference on Private International Law, *Preliminary Draft Convention on Jurisdiction and Foreign Judgments in Civil and Commercial Matters adopted by the Special Commission and Report by Peter Nygh and Fausto Pocar*, Prel. Doc. No. 11 of Aug. 2000, at 90 ("[A]s the words 'may' and 'peut' indicate, the power is discretionary. Even if the conditions are satisfied, the court originally seised is not obliged to decline jurisdiction.").

[81]   *Summary of the Outcome of the Discussion in Commission II of the First Part of the Diplomatic Conference 6–20 June 2001—Interim Text*, Hague Conference on Private International Law, Nineteenth Session (2001), art. 22(4).

[82]   *See* Chapter 6, Part II.E., above.

[83]   *See* Chapter 6, Part II.E., above.

discretion of the court.[84] At the same time, however, Article 22 actually goes further than the traditional common law doctrine of forum non conveniens in regard to conditional dismissal. The Hague Reporters believed that this characteristic actually set Article 22 apart from the common law doctrine:

> Article 22 is a provision whereby the forum may defer its jurisdiction in favour of that of a court of another State, but, with one exception, only if that other court actually assumes jurisdiction.[85]

Rather than setting Article 22 apart from the common law doctrine, this aspect of Article 22 actually has the effect of adopting a more extensive version of the fifth common element of the doctrine by conditioning deferral and ultimate dismissal on the actual exercise of jurisdiction by the foreign court that is the available alternative forum. This overriding condition would serve to make the more limited conditions found in many U.S. cases superfluous.

2. Hague Interim Text Article 22 and common law differences

In terms of the differences among common law approaches to the doctrine of forum non conveniens, the *2001 Hague Interim Text* leans quite far toward the stricter Australian test. This is clear in the "clearly inappropriate forum" test, which results in a stronger preference for upholding any juridical advantage of the plaintiff resulting in the original forum choice. While Article 22(2) allows consideration of such private interest factors as the convenience of the parties, the location of evidence, and procedures for obtaining evidence, it does not explicitly authorize consideration of factors like differences in the applicable law and potential differences in damage awards. It is not clear whether this represents a rejection of the English, U.S., and Canadian positions that a plaintiff's juridical advantage will not alone defeat a forum non conveniens motion. By stating that the court "shall take into account, in particular," the factors listed in paragraph

---

[84] It may be that any similar provision in a future treaty should include a clear indication of whether the condition explicitly provided for in Article 22 (the possibility of requiring security from the successful defendant) is exclusive or merely indicative.

[85] Hague Conference on Private International Law, *Preliminary Draft Convention on Jurisdiction and Foreign Judgments in Civil and Commercial Matters adopted by the Special Commission and Report by Peter Nygh and Fausto Pocar*, Prel. Doc. No. 11 of Aug. 2000, at 89.

(2), Article 22 does not prevent the consideration of other factors, but could be construed to require the existence of at least one of the stated factors in the analysis.

One element of the Article 22 rule would appear to represent movement toward the U.S. approach to forum non conveniens. The article's provisions seem to apply only when the court first seised has already determined that a valid jurisdictional basis exists—there is no language allowing application of its rules to questions of jurisdiction simpliciter. Thus, like the U.S. doctrine, this rule would apply only after a court has determined jurisdiction to exist, and would not apply to initial decisions of jurisdiction based, for example, on questions of service ex juris.[86] The *Interim Text* is drafted for the most part as if it were a double convention (with only a narrowly circumscribed category of permitted bases of jurisdiction in Article 17), and the discretionary right to decline jurisdiction is applicable under Article 22(1) only when jurisdiction is taken on a limited list of bases of jurisdiction. Moreover, jurisdiction by service upon a party temporarily present within the forum state is specifically prohibited under Article 18(2)(f). Thus, the application of an Article 22 forum non conveniens analysis in cases based on jurisdiction established in part through service of process is not likely to occur.

Article 22 does not explicitly prohibit the consideration of public interest factors like those considered in U.S. forum non conveniens cases.[87] While the list of factors in paragraph (2) that must be considered are limited to private interest elements, this is an indicative rather than an exclusive list.

Paragraph (3) of Article 22 specifically states that "[i]n deciding whether to suspend the proceedings, a court shall not discriminate on the basis of the nationality or habitual residence of the parties." Thus it rejects any approach that would allow preference for domestic plaintiffs over foreign plaintiffs. As noted in Chapter 6, while it has sometimes been suggested by commentators that U.S. forum non conveniens law incorporates such discrimination, careful analysis of the language of the major U.S. Supreme Court decisions by lower courts makes clear that overt

---

[86]   This is true despite the Reporters' comments that Article 22 could not be applied in a case of Article 5 jurisdiction (appearance by the defendant without contesting jurisdiction) because "by definition by the time the court gains jurisdiction under Article 5, the time for making a request to decline jurisdiction will have passed." Hague Conference on Private International Law, *Preliminary Draft Convention on Jurisdiction and Foreign Judgments in Civil and Commercial Matters adopted by the Special Commission and Report by Peter Nygh and Fausto Pocar*, Prel. Doc. No. 11 of Aug. 2000, at 89.

[87]   *See* Chapter 3, Part III.A., above.

discrimination is not a part of the analysis.[88] Like the U.S. case law that provides a coherent analysis of this issue,[89] the *Nygh-Pocar Report* notes that

> [t]here is no conflict between this provision and the factor of inconvenience based on residence to be taken into account under Article 22(2)(a). Paragraph 3 prohibits discrimination against a party because that party is resident abroad. Sub-paragraph a) of paragraph 2 raises for consideration any inconvenience which may result to a party because of its residence. As long as those inconveniences are properly balanced and one party is not preferred merely because that party resides within the forum in question, no issue of discrimination arises.[90]

The two final differences among common law applications of the forum non conveniens doctrine become only minimally relevant given the nature of the rule found in Article 22 of the *2001 Hague Interim Text*. First, concern with a shifting burden of proof in common law courts arises mostly in cases dealing with application of the doctrine to questions of service ex juris.[91] Since Article 22 appears to apply only when a determination has already been made that jurisdiction exists in the court seised of the matter, it should not require the same burden-shifting that arises at the initial stage of determining whether jurisdiction exists. As Professors Nygh and Pocar noted in their Report on the *Interim Text*, Article 22 "does not address the question of onus, but it would be logical for the party requesting that the court decline jurisdiction to bring forward the facts and reasons for such a decision."[92] This intuitive approach could be made more explicit in any future convention, but its conclusion serves to facilitate consistency and supports the absence of any shifting burden of proof.

The final difference—that the United Kingdom is subject to rules of the *Brussels Regulation* prohibiting application of the forum non conveniens doctrine in cases

---

[88] *See* Chapter 6, Part III.B.3, above.

[89] *See, e.g.,* Iragorri v. United Technologies, 274 F.3d 65 (2d Cir. 2001).

[90] Hague Conference on Private International Law, *Preliminary Draft Convention on Jurisdiction and Foreign Judgments in Civil and Commercial Matters adopted by the Special Commission and Report by Peter Nygh and Fausto Pocar*, Prel. Doc. No. 11 of Aug. 2000, at 92.

[91] *See* Chapter 6, Part II.B., above.

[92] Hague Conference on Private International Law, *Preliminary Draft Convention on Jurisdiction and Foreign Judgments in Civil and Commercial Matters adopted by the Special Commission and Report by Peter Nygh and Fausto Pocar*, Prel. Doc. No. 11 of Aug. 2000, at 90.

involving parties domiciled in European Union Member States[93]—will remain in any global convention. The regional application of the *Brussels Regulation* must be appropriately coordinated with any future multilateral convention that might address this issue.

B. Issues between civil law and common law states

Perhaps the most important lessons of the compromise approach found in the *2001 Hague Interim Text* deal with the manner in which its provisions address the differences between common law and civil law approaches to the issue of declining jurisdiction.

1. The general problem of the "homeward trend"

Articles 21 and 22 of the *2001 Hague Interim Text* demonstrate substantial progress toward a global approach to declining jurisdiction. They incorporate both the fundamental elements of the civil law lis pendens approach and the common law forum non conveniens approach to jurisdiction in the courts of multiple states. In doing so, Article 22 appears to deal reasonably with both similarities and differences in the major common law systems in the application of the forum non conveniens doctrine. Thus, while the *Interim Text* will not be adopted and made available for ratification by Hague Conference Member States, its provisions represent a substantial advance in the consideration of this area of law, and clearly should not be ignored in future efforts to find reasonable common ground.

When, and if, the matter is taken up again, it will be important to keep in mind that uniform words do not necessarily breed uniform interpretation and application. Doctrines relating to questions of declining jurisdiction are and will remain issues to be considered by national courts, beginning always at the trial level. While the *Brussels Regulation*, as internal legislation of the European Community, allows authoritative final interpretation by the European Court of Justice, no such single source of definitive interpretation is likely to exist for a global convention containing rules on issues of lis pendens and forum non conveniens.

---

[93]   *See* Chapter 2, Part II.D., above.

While other efforts at the harmonization or unification of law through international treaties have brought the world closer together, and have made commercial and legal relationships more predictable, even the most successful of such treaties is subject to what Professor Honnold has called the "homeward trend" in his discussion of the *United Nations Convention on Contracts for the International Sale of Goods (U.N. Sales Convention)*.[94] Thus, "tribunals, regardless of their merit, will be subject to a natural tendency to read the international rules in light of the legal ideas that have been imbedded at the core of their intellectual formation. The mind sees what the mind has means of seeing."[95] With any international agreement applied in national courts, the "process of building a common international framework for understanding . . . and thus escaping the pull of the 'homeward trend,' is . . . likely to be a long and difficult one."[96] This appears to have been the case with the otherwise enormously successful *U.N. Sales Convention*,[97] and would likely be so with any jurisdiction and judgments convention that included rules on declining jurisdiction.

2. *The civil law focus on jurisdiction based on the defendant's domicile*

Forum non conveniens is a doctrine focused on the exercise of jurisdiction. It thus is closely related to questions of jurisdiction and the relative status of the jurisdictional power of a court. When a legal system prioritizes different bases of jurisdiction in terms of status, that consideration may influence any decision to decline to exercise jurisdiction. Thus, differences in relative status of bases of jurisdiction may logically influence any decision of that court to decline jurisdiction when authorized to do so under a multilateral convention.

For purposes of determining judicial jurisdiction, the connection between the court and the defendant is the preferred nexus in just about every legal system. In the United States, the Due Process Clauses of the Fifth and Fourteenth Amendments to the *U.S Constitution* have been interpreted to mean that without such a nexus,

---

[94] United Nations Convention on Contracts for the International Sale of Goods, art. 31, U.N. Doc. A/CONF.97/18, Annex I, *English version reprinted in* 52 Fed. Reg. 6264 (1987) and in 19 I.L.M. 668 (1980).

[95] JOHN HONNOLD, DOCUMENTARY HISTORY OF THE UNIFORM LAW FOR INTERNATIONAL SALES 1 (1989).

[96] Harry Flechtner, *The Several Texts of the CISG in a Decentralized System: Observations on Translations, Reservations and Other Challenges to the Uniformity Principle in Article 7(1),* 17 J. L. & COM. 187, 204 (1998).

[97] *See* Harry Flechtner, *The Several Texts of the CISG in a Decentralized System: Observations on Translations, Reservations and Other Challenges to the Uniformity Principle in Article 7(1),* 17 J. L. & COM. 187, 204 (1998).

any basis of jurisdiction is unconstitutional.[98] The court-defendant nexus is enshrined as the preferred test in Article 2 of the *Brussels Regulation* of the European Union,[99] and in both the *1999 Hague Preliminary Draft* and the *2001 Hague Interim Text* of the Hague Conference.[100] Article 3 of the Hague texts provides for jurisdiction in the courts of the state in which the defendant is habitually resident.[101] Article 2 of the *Brussels Regulation* likewise provides for jurisdiction in the courts of the state in which the defendant is domiciled.[102]

In the Brussels context, Article 2 jurisdiction based on the defendant's domicile is referred to as the "general" rule of jurisdiction. The European Court of Justice made clear in *Kalfelis v. Schröder*[103] that other jurisdictional rules in the Convention and Regulation are "special" rules of jurisdiction, and thus more limited in their application:

> Pursuant to Article 2 of the Convention, persons domiciled in a Contracting State are, subject to the provisions of the Convention, "whatever their nationality, to be sued in the courts of that State". Section 2 of Title II of the Convention, however, provides for "special jurisdictions", by virtue of which a defendant domiciled in a Contracting State may be sued in another Contracting State. . . .[104]

> The principle laid down in the Convention is that jurisdiction is vested in the courts of the State of the defendant's domicile and that the jurisdiction provided for in [the "special jurisdiction" articles are] exception[s] to that principle.[105]

---

[98]   *See, e.g.*, Ronald A. Brand, *Due Process, Jurisdiction and a Hague Judgments Convention*, 60 U. PITT. L. REV. 661 (1999).

[99]   Council Regulation (EC) No. 44/2001 of Dec. 22, 2000 on Jurisdiction and the Recognition and Enforcement of Judgments in Civil and Commercial Matters, 2000 O.J. Eur. Comm. L 12, art. 2.

[100] Hague Conference on Private International Law, *Preliminary Draft Convention on Jurisdiction and Foreign Judgments in Civil and Commercial Matters adopted by the Special Commission and Report by Peter Nygh and Fausto Pocar*, Prel. Doc. No. 11 of Aug. 2000, art. 3; *Summary of the Outcome of the Discussion in Commission II of the First Part of the Diplomatic Conference 6–20 June 2001—Interim Text*, Hague Conference on Private International Law, Nineteenth Session (2001), art. 3.

[101] *Id.*

[102] Council Regulation (EC) No 44/2001 of Dec. 22, 2000 on Jurisdiction and the Recognition and Enforcement of Judgments in Civil and Commercial Matters, 2000 O.J. Eur. Comm. L 12, art. 2.

[103] Kalfelis v. Schröder, Case 189/87, [1988] E.C.R. 5565, 5583.

[104] [1988] E.C.R. 5565, 5583, ¶ 7.

[105] [1988] E.C.R. 5565, 5583, ¶ 8.

[T]he "special jurisdictions" enumerated in Articles 5 and 6 of the Convention constitute derogations from the principle that jurisdiction is vested in the courts of the State where the defendant is domiciled and as such must be interpreted restrictively.[106]

The restrictive interpretation of special jurisdiction provisions of the *Brussels Convention* was also a part of the decision in the *Shevill* case,[107] when the Court stated that the Article 5(3) tort rule of jurisdiction provides a two-pronged choice to the plaintiff:[108]

[It] is based on the existence of a particularly close connecting factor between the dispute and the courts other than those of the State of the defendant's domicile which justifies the attribution of jurisdiction to those courts for reasons relating to the sound administration of justice and the efficacious conduct of the proceedings.[109]

Hence, the Court emphasized the court/claim nexus that is the foundation of the "special" jurisdiction rules of the *Brussels Convention*.

---

[106] [1988] E.C.R. 5565, 5585, ¶ 19. Thus, in Kalfelis v. Schröder, the European Court of Justice held that, in an action in both tort (Article 5(3)), and contract (Article 5(1)), "a court which has jurisdiction under Article 5(3) over an action in so far as it is based on tort or delict does not have jurisdiction over that action in so far as it is not so based." [1988] E.C.R. 5565, ¶ 21. The existence of tort jurisdiction in the German courts over a Luxembourg defendant did not bring with it the existence of contract jurisdiction over the same defendant resulting from the same set of facts.

[107] Shevill v. Presse Alliance S.A., Case C-68/93, [1995] E.C.R. I-415. For a more detailed discussion of the *Shevill* case see Ronald A. Brand, *Current Problems, Common Ground, and First Principles: Restructuring the Preliminary Draft Convention Text, in* A GLOBAL LAW OF JURISDICTION AND JUDGMENTS: LESSONS FROM THE HAGUE CONVENTION 75 (John J. Barcelo III and Kevin M. Clermont eds., 2002).

[108] Paragraph (3) of Article 5 of the Brussels Convention reads as follows:

A person domiciled in a Contracting State may, in another Contracting State, be sued:

. . .

(3) in matters relating to tort, delict or quasi-delict, in the courts for the place where the harmful event occurred.

In Bier v. Mines de Potasse d'Alsace, Case 21/76, [1976] E.C.R. 1735, the European Court of Justice interpreted the words "place where the harmful event occurred" to include both the place where the damage occurred and the place of the event giving rise to the damage, allowing the plaintiff the choice of locations for bringing suit. Thus, where the defendant discharged saline into the Rhine River in France, resulting in injury to the plaintiff's horticultural interests in The Netherlands, the plaintiff could bring suit in either France or The Netherlands under Article 5(3).

[109] Shevill, [1995] E.C.R. I-415, I-459, ¶ 19.

Three rules of interpretation under the *Brussels Convention* are thus clearly established:

> (1) Article 2 jurisdiction is more "general" than the rules of special jurisdiction;

> (2) the special jurisdiction rules (Articles 5–16) are to be narrowly interpreted; and

> (3) the rules of special jurisdiction are based on a "close connecting factor between the dispute and the courts."

This means that, while the "special" jurisdiction articles are meant to provide the plaintiff with a choice of locations in which to bring a case, the principal focus remains on the domicile of the defendant as the preferred location for suit under Article 2.

This approach to jurisdictional rules raises interesting questions about how a court within the Brussels regime (or any similar civil law system of jurisdictional rules) would approach a motion brought under Article 22 of the *2001 Hague Interim Text* when the defendant is locally domiciled but seeks to have the case tried elsewhere. The homeward trend phenomenon would seem to generate a tendency in European civil law systems to favor the domicile of the defendant as the preferred jurisdictional rule, and give less weight to factors favoring the alternative forum. When suit is brought at the defendant's domicile, the civil law approach would magnify the very heavy burden on the defendant under the clearly inappropriate forum test. When suit is brought outside the state of the defendant's domicile, this conflict generates analytical tension between the application of a test that favors the plaintiff's choice of forum and a tendency to favor jurisdiction at the defendant's domicile. The *Owusu* decision of the European Court of Justice makes clear that for any case brought within an EU Member State on the basis of jurisdiction at the defendant's domicile, forum non conveniens analysis is not allowed.[110] The application of Article 22 of the *2001 Hague Interim Text* in a court subject to the *Brussels Regulation* would thus turn, at least in part, on the rules governing the relationship between two international instruments with conflicting rules—the *Brussels Regulation* and the *Hague Convention*.

---

[110] *See* Chapter 2, Part III.B., above.

In U.S. courts, some of the most important forum non conveniens cases have involved defendants locally domiciled but seeking to have the case tried elsewhere. Unlike the European approach in *Owusu*, however, in the United States the existence of local domicile of the defendant has not served as an impediment to a forum non conveniens dismissal. For example, in *Piper Aircraft v. Reyno*,[111] the Supreme Court ruled in favor of dismissal where the defendant was domiciled in the state of Pennsylvania, the state in which the federal district court hearing the case was located. Similarly, in the *Bhopal* case,[112] the court found it appropriate for the case to be dismissed in favor of litigation in India, even though one of the principal defendants was domiciled in the United States.

If one jurisdictional rule is considered paramount over all other jurisdictional rules—as appears to be the case with the "general" rule of jurisdiction at the domicile of the defendant under Article 2 of the *Brussels Regulation*—then it is not clear whether it would ever be possible to convince a court within that system to decline to exercise such jurisdiction through its discretionary power to find itself to be a "clearly inappropriate forum." Neither the language of Article 22 of the *2001 Hague Interim Text*, nor the discussion in the Report accompanying it indicates whether a court could give such weight to the underlying basis of jurisdiction so as to avoid declining jurisdiction in such a case. Whether there would be such a "homeward trend" in the interpretation of a future provision like Article 22 in a ratified and effective treaty thus remains a matter of speculation. Given the significant preferential status of the Article 2 general jurisdiction rule of the *Brussels Convention* and *Regulation*, however, this is a matter that will necessarily require consideration in any future efforts to complete a convention that would include global rules on declining jurisdiction.[113]

---

[111] 454 U.S. 235 (1981).

[112] *In re* Union Carbide Corp. Gas Plant Disaster at Bhopal, 809 F.2d 195 (2d Cir. 1986), *cert. denied*, 484 U.S. 871 (1987).

[113] The homeward trend phenomenon is, of course, not limited to civil law jurisdictions. With the U.N. Sales Convention, U.S. courts have tended to assume the Convention rules are much like those found in the Uniform Commercial Code, and then simply applied the U.C.C. without proper analysis of the Sales Convention. *See, e.g.*, Harry Flechtner, *The Several Texts of the CISG in a Decentralized System: Observations on Translations, Reservations and Other Challenges to the Uniformity Principle in Article 7(1)*, 17 J.L. & COM. 187, 204 (1998). The same could occur in the application of Article 22 of the 2001 Interim Text if a U.S. court would incorrectly assume that the "exceptional circumstances for declining jurisdiction" codified in that provision to be no more than a restatement of the U.S. common law doctrine of forum non conveniens.

3. Differing approaches to the concept of mandatory rules

The concept of mandatory rules is much stronger in civil law legal systems than in most common law states.[114] In the United States, a similar concept surfaced in the twentieth century in the rubric of public policy when requests to allow cases to be decided elsewhere than in the court first seised were met with arguments that to do so would violate the policy behind important regulatory laws.[115] In the forum non conveniens context, some early U.S. courts held that the presence of important regulatory issues meant that a case was not subject to forum non conveniens dismissal, and that such regulatory law required adjudication in U.S. courts.[116] More recent decisions have rejected this approach, however, holding that special venue rules of regulatory legislation do not prevent a forum non conveniens analysis.[117]

---

[114] For an example of the definition of mandatory rules in Europe, see Article 3 of the European Convention on the Law Applicable to Contractual Obligations, O.J. Eur. Comm. L 266/1 (1980) [Rome Convention]:

> 3. The fact that the parties have chosen a foreign law, whether or not accompanied by the choice of a foreign tribunal, shall not, where all the other elements relevant to the situation at the time of the choice are connected with one country only, prejudice the application of rules of the law of that country which cannot be derogated from by contract, hereinafter called "mandatory rules."

A similar approach for consumer contracts was taken by the National Conference of Commissioners on Uniform State Laws in the 2001 revision of Article 1 of the Uniform Commercial Code:

> (d) If one of the parties to a transaction is a consumer, the following rules apply:
>
> . . . .
>
> (2) Application of the law of the State or country determined pursuant to subsection (b) [choice of law clause] or (c) [conflict of laws principles] may not deprive the consumer of the protection of any rule of law, that both is protective of consumers and may not be varied by agreement. . . .

UNIFORM COMMERCIAL CODE, § 1–301(d)(2) (2001 revisions).

[115] This was one of the principal arguments in *Mitsubishi Motors Corp. v. Soler Chrysler-Plymouth*, 473 U.S. 614 (1985), where the Supreme Court determined that U.S. antitrust laws, though much different than the laws in effect in most of the world and expressing important U.S. public policy, could adequately be applied by a panel of Japanese arbitrators sitting in Japan, in a case arising from a contract governed by Swiss law.

[116] *See, e.g.,* U.S. v. Nat'l City Lines, Inc., 334 U.S. 573 (1948) (holding that Clayton Act venue rules prevented judicial discretion to dismiss antitrust actions on forum non conveniens grounds).

[117] *See, e.g.,* Howe v. Goldcorp. Investments Ltd., 946 F.2d 944 (1st Cir. 1991) (holding that securities law venue provisions did not preclude a forum non conveniens dismissal).

The interest of the state—in this case the United States—is a relevant consideration as a public interest factor in the U.S. balancing test applied in a forum non conveniens analysis. Some courts have considered regulatory laws relevant in this context in considering motions for dismissal on forum non conveniens grounds.[118] On the other hand, in *Capital Currency Exchange, N.V. v. Nat'l Westminster Bank plc*,[119] the Second Circuit noted decisions in which U.S. regulatory interests were not considered at all in forum non conveniens cases, and stated that "we have never held that the United States' interest in applying its laws is a determinative factor to be considered in weighing convenience."[120] Courts have likewise indicated that the availability of similar laws in the alternative foreign forum is sufficient to diffuse any concern about local regulatory policy.[121] Ultimately, according to at least one commentator, "the question is reduced to whether litigation in the foreign forum would afford the plaintiff virtually no remedy."[122] Unless this burden is met, forum non conveniens analysis is appropriate, and the regulatory policy may (at best) prove to be one public interest factor to be considered.

While this line of cases in the United States has reduced the potential role of regulatory laws in a forum non conveniens analysis, Professor Honnold's "homeward trend" might well come into play in the application of a provision similar to Article 22 of the *2001 Hague Interim Text* in a country with a strong history of the

---

[118]   *See, e.g.,* Lexington Insurance Co. v. Forrest, 263 F. Supp. 2d 986, 1002 (E.D. Pa. 2003) (denying forum non conveniens motion and stating that the availability of the Racketeer Influenced and Corrupt Organizations (RICO) Act "within this forum testifies to its commitment to providing legal redress for victims of racketeering conspiracies," and "the United States would have an interest in regulating such conduct and in indemnifying its citizens for their losses."). *See also* DiRienzo v. Philip Services Corp., 294 F.3d 21, 33 (2d Cir. 2002) (finding U.S. securities laws to indicate a "strong public interest" of the United States to be considered in a forum non conveniens analysis).

[119]   155 F.3d 603 (2d Cir. 1998).

[120]   155 F.3d 603, 611 (2d Cir. 1998).

[121]   *See* Hannah L. Buxbaum, *Regulatory policy in transnational litigation: the influence of judicial globalization, in* FESTSCHRIFT FÜR ERIK JAYME 73, 80 (Heinz-Peter Mansel et al. eds., 2004).

[122]   Hannah L. Buxbaum, *Regulatory policy in transnational litigation: the influence of judicial globalization, in* FESTSCHRIFT FÜR ERIK JAYME 73, 81 (Heinz-Peter Mansel et al. eds., 2004), *citing* Kempe v. Ocean Drilling & Exploration Co., 876 F.2d 1138, 1146 (5th Cir. 1989) ("a forum is inadequate only where it would afford a plaintiff no remedy at all").

application of mandatory rules. A principal example of the scope and effect of mandatory rules is found in Article 7 of the *Rome Convention*:[123]

Article 7

Mandatory rules

1. When applying under this Convention the law of a country, effect may be given to the mandatory rules of the law of another country with which the situation has a close connection, if and in so far as, under the law of the latter country, those rules must be applied whatever the law applicable to the contract. In considering whether to give effect to these mandatory rules, regard shall be had to their nature and purpose and to the consequences of their application or non-application.

2. Nothing in this Convention shall restrict the application of the rules of the law of the forum in a situation where they are mandatory irrespective of the law otherwise applicable to the contract.

The second paragraph of Article 7, in particular, sets forth the principle that each Contracting State may enforce its own mandatory rules, and no other state (or the other terms of the Convention) may intervene in or prevent such application. If this were the case in the application of mandatory rules in a case governed by the *2001 Hague Interim Text*, then it would seem that the right of a party to request that a court decline jurisdiction under Article 22 could be pre-empted, either through the peremptory application of the mandatory rule or through the exercise of discretion to favor the mandatory rule over Article 22.

VI. Looking ahead

Articles 21 and 22 of the *2001 Hague Interim Text* provide useful language for any future consideration of the possibility of coordinating the civil law concept of lis

---

[123] European Convention on the Law Applicable to Contractual Obligations, O.J. Eur. Comm. L 266/1 (1980). Like the Brussels Convention, the Rome Convention may soon be replaced by a Council Regulation. *See* Green Paper on the conversion of the Rome Convention of 1980 on the law applicable to contractual obligations into a Community instrument and its modernisation COM (2002) 654(01), and Proposal for a Regulation of the European Parliament and the Council on the Law Applicable to Non-Contractual Obligations ("Rome II"), COM (2003) 427(01).

pendens and the common law concept of forum non conveniens on a global basis. In particular, Article 22 retains the five common elements of forum non conveniens analysis found in the United Kingdom, the United States, Canada, and Australia. It also deals reasonably with the differences found in those legal systems in the application of the forum non conveniens doctrine.

While the ALI/UNIDROIT *Principles and Rules of Transnational Civil Procedure* and the ALI Recognition and Enforcement of Foreign Judgments Project both contain provisions that would affect application of the forum non conveniens doctrine, the former is unlikely to become effective in any state, and the latter would apply only in the United States without any requirement of reciprocal treatment in the courts of other countries. They thus provide little guidance in considering a multilateral approach to the forum non conveniens question (although the ALI Project may well result in a level of "unilateral disarmament" by the United States in a way that would substantially reduce any possibility of bargaining for equivalent terms from treaty partners in the future).

What is not clear is how national courts might receive and apply a provision such as Article 22 of the *2001 Hague Interim Text*. In particular, the homeward trend that already has emerged in the application of the *United Nations Convention on Contracts for the International Sale of Goods* is likely to surface also in the application of any treaty provision applicable to declining jurisdiction. This potential problem is particularly acute in cases in civil law systems where jurisdiction is based on the domicile of the defendant, and in cases involving the application of the type of mandatory rules so often found in civil law legal systems.

For the foreseeable future, there is little likelihood of a comprehensive global treaty on jurisdiction and the recognition and enforcement of judgments. Thus, there is no need for provisions on declining jurisdiction in such a treaty. The *2005 Hague Convention on Choice of Court Agreements* is likely to become effective in the near term, however, and its provisions will have an impact on the application of the doctrine of forum non conveniens when a choice of court agreement is present. That is the topic of the final chapter of this book.

CHAPTER 9

The Future for Now: Forum Non Conveniens and the 2005 Hague Convention on Choice of Court Agreements[1]

I. Introduction

A comprehensive convention on jurisdiction and the recognition and enforcement of judgments has been set aside for the current time at the Hague Conference on Private International Law. Nonetheless, the process has generated the *2005 Hague Convention on Choice of Court Agreements*.[2] This is an important text creating rules applicable to choice of court agreements between private business parties. It includes rules governing discretion to decline jurisdiction, and thus may affect the future application of the doctrine of forum non conveniens.

The intersection of party agreement on choice of court and forum non conveniens brings together rules that are not always consistent with one another. While previous chapters of this book have considered the common law doctrine of forum non conveniens, this chapter reviews how U.S. courts have dealt with choice of court agreements. In particular, it addresses those circumstances in which a court may be faced with both a party agreement on choice of court (and the

---

[1]   This chapter includes text previously published as Ronald A. Brand, *Forum Selection and Forum Rejection in US Courts: One Rationale for a Global Choice of Court Convention*, *in* Reform and Development of Private International Law: Festschrift for Sir Peter North 51, 58–64, 74–87 (James Fawcett ed., 2002). This material is used by permission of Oxford University Press, http://www.oup.com.

[2]   Hague Conference on Private International Law, Convention on Choice of Court Agreements, done at The Hague June 30, 2005, *available at*: http://www.hcch.net/index_ en.php?act=conventions.text&cid=98.

respect for party autonomy that results in the enforcement of those agreements), and a request for the exercise of judicial discretion to send the case to another court under the doctrine of forum non conveniens. The *2005 Hague Convention on Choice of Court Agreements* provides an opportunity to observe how analysis of these apparently conflicting doctrines demonstrates how treaty rules can be useful in providing greater predictability in commercial relationships at both the contract drafting and litigation stages.

Current U.S. case law demonstrates possibilities for confusion at the intersection of choice of court clauses and the application of the forum non conveniens doctrine. Nonetheless, the *2005 Hague Convention on Choice of Court Agreements* provides a rational approach to this confluence of legal doctrines. Its application to international transactions should provide a first step toward greater predictability in judicial consideration of private party agreements to take disputes to specific courts, as well as in the development of rules that may temper the application of the doctrine of forum non conveniens.

II. Forum non conveniens and choice of court agreements in the United States

The development of U.S. law on forum selection during the twentieth century witnessed concurrent evolution of two doctrines that do not necessarily bring consistent results, and which can bring to bear apparently inconsistent judicial policies.[3] One of these is the doctrine of forum non conveniens, for which a review of U.S. law is found in Chapter 3, above. The other is the law developing from the Supreme Court's 1972 decision in *Bremen v. Zapata*.[4] Following *Bremen*, U.S. courts have tended to honor forum selection clauses in freely negotiated contracts. With the Supreme Court's 1991 decision in *Carnival Cruise Lines*,[5] respect for choice of court clauses became, in the view of some commentators, almost unquestioning in allowing the imposition of forum selection on weaker parties to

---

[3]   While prior portions of this book have covered multiple countries, for purposes of discussion of choice of court agreements and forum non conveniens it seems both useful and sufficient to concentrate on a single country in order to consider the intersection of these two matters. Similar consideration of these issues in other countries is, of course, both possible and relevant, but not necessary in order to demonstrate the value of a convention on choice of court agreements to decisions in the forum non conveniens context.

[4]   M/S Bremen and Unterweser Reederei, GmbH v. Zapata Off-Shore Co., 407 U.S. 1 (1972).

[5]   Carnival Cruise Lines, Inc. v. Shute, 499 U.S. 972 (1991).

a contractual relationship.[6] At the same time, the forum non conveniens doctrine allows courts broad discretion to decline to hear a case even when it is filed in a court with proper jurisdiction and venue.

These doctrines come together when a motion is brought to stay or dismiss an action on grounds of forum non conveniens and there exists a choice of court clause in a contract between the parties. When the choice of court clause derogates from the forum court, that clause may be a factor weighing in favor of dismissal on grounds of forum non conveniens so that the case is tried in the chosen court. When the clause involves prorogation in favor of the forum court, however, its enforcement runs counter to an argument in favor of litigation in another court on the grounds of forum non conveniens. In this latter category of cases, respect for the chosen forum may come into conflict with the application of the doctrine of forum non conveniens in a manner that allows courts to produce results that can be difficult to reconcile.

A. Choice of court in U.S. law

As in most countries, courts in the United States now generally respect party autonomy in private commercial contracts and will uphold reasonable choice of forum clauses. This has not always been so, however. Prior to 1972, U.S. courts were reluctant to enforce clauses that would oust them of jurisdiction.[7] This changed when

---

[6] See, e.g., Patrick J. Borchers, *Forum Selection Agreements in the Federal Courts After* Carnival Cruise: *A Proposal for Congressional Reform*, 67 WASH. L. REV. 55 (1992); Walter W. Heiser, *Forum Selection Clauses in State Courts: Limitations on Enforcement After* Stewart *and* Carnival Cruise, 45 FLA. L. REV. 361 (1993); Jeffrey A. Liesemer, *Carnival's Got the Fun . . . and the Forum: A New Look at Choice-of-Forum Clauses and the Unconscionability Doctrine after* Carnival Cruise Lines, Inc. v. Shute, 53 U. PITT. L. REV. 1025 (1992).

[7] See, e.g., Carbon Black Export, Inc. v. The Monrose, 254 F.2d 297, 300–01 (5th Cir. 1958), *cert dismissed*, 359 U.S. 180 (1959) (stating that "agreements in advance of controversy whose object is to oust the jurisdiction of the courts are contrary to public policy and will not be enforced"). It has been said that this position rested on the rationale that "(1) the parties cannot by agreement in the contract alter the jurisdiction of the courts, and (2) such contractual stipulations are violative of public policy." VED NANDA, THE LAW OF TRANSNATIONAL BUSINESS TRANSACTIONS § 8.02[1][a] (1986). Some commentators consider significant the distinction between conferring and ousting jurisdiction ("prorogation" versus "derogation" in civil law terms). However, it has also been suggested that "[t]he real issue . . . is not whether the parties can by agreement 'confer' or 'oust' jurisdiction, but whether the selected or ousted court will exercise its own jurisdiction in such a way as to give effect to the intention of the parties." GEORGES DELAUME, TRANSNATIONAL CONTRACTS § 6.01 (1986). This latter approach is consistent with *Bremen*, 407 U.S. 1, 12 (1972) ("No one seriously contends in this case that the forum-selection clause 'ousted' the District Court of jurisdiction over [the plaintiff's] action. The threshold question is whether that court should have exercised its jurisdiction to do more than give effect to the legitimate expectations of the parties, manifested in their freely negotiated agreement, by specifically enforcing the forum clause.").

the Supreme Court ruled clearly in favor of upholding business-to-business choice of court clauses in a freely negotiated contract in *Bremen v. Zapata*.[8] A German firm had contracted to tow an American company's oil-drilling rig from Louisiana to a point in the Adriatic Sea off the coast of Italy. When the rig was damaged in an accident in international waters, it was brought to Tampa, Florida, where the rig's owner brought an admiralty action in Federal District Court against the owner of the tug, claiming both in personam jurisdiction over the owner and in rem jurisdiction over the tug.

Two contract clauses framed the analysis in the *Bremen* case. The first provided that the owner of the rig waived any right to hold the towing company liable for damage to the rig while at sea, even if such damage resulted from the negligence of the towing company or its employees.[9] Under the law at the time, this clause was likely to be enforced by a court in England,[10] but would be considered void as against public policy in the United States.[11] The second important clause provided that "[a]ny dispute arising must be treated before the London Court of Justice." If the latter clause were upheld, requiring the U.S. court to decline jurisdiction, then the waiver of liability clause would determine the outcome of the case.

The Supreme Court gave effect to the choice of court clause, stating that, "[t]he expansion of American business and industry will hardly be encouraged if, notwithstanding solemn contracts, we insist on a parochial concept that all disputes must be resolved under our laws and in our courts."[12] Confirming that parties to an international transaction could select a neutral forum for the settlement of their disputes,[13] the Court stated that forum selection clauses "are prima facie

---

[8] 407 U.S. 1 (1972). For a discussion of the pre-*Bremen* case law which often held choice of forum provisions void as against public policy, *see* Michael Gruson, *Forum-Selection Clauses in International and Interstate Commercial Agreements*, 1982 U. ILL. L. REV. 133, 138–47.

[9] Bremen, 407 U.S. 1, 3 n.2 (1972).

[10] Bremen, 407 U.S. 1, 8 n.8 (1972).

[11] Bremen, 407 U.S. 1, 9 n.10 (1972). *See, e.g.*, Dixilyn Drilling Corp. v. Crescent Towing & Salvage Co., 372 U.S. 697 (1963); Bisso v. Inland Waterways Corp., 349 U.S. 85 (1955).

[12] Bremen, 407 U.S. 1, 9 (1972).

[13] Bremen, 407 U.S. 1, 13 (1972). When the same dispute was litigated concurrently in the English courts, the English Court of Appeal sustained jurisdiction there under the choice of court clause despite the fact that the transaction had no connection with England, noting that, "in the absence of strong reason to the contrary," the discretion of the English court "will be exercised in favour of holding parties to their bargain." Unterweser Reederi GmbH v. Zapata Off-Shore Co., [1968] 2 Lloyd's L. Rep. 158, 163 (C.A.).

valid and should be enforced unless enforcement is shown by the resisting party to be unreasonable under the circumstances."[14]

While *Bremen* was a case in admiralty, both lower federal courts[15] and state courts[16] extended its rationale to non-admiralty cases. Deference to the parties' choice of forum was qualified only minimally when Chief Justice Burger noted that the agreement so enforced was "unaffected by fraud, undue influence, or overweening bargaining power."[17] Subsequent courts,[18] and the Restatement,[19] have interpreted *Bremen* to provide a presumption of validity for a choice of forum clause, with the party contesting the provision carrying the burden of proving grounds for an exception.

The *Bremen* analysis provides three exceptions to the enforcement of a choice of court clause. These can be summarily stated as: (1) where enforcement of the provision would result in substantial inconvenience, or denial of an effective remedy,[20] (2) where there has been fraud, overreaching, or unconscionable conduct in

---

[14]   Bremen, 407 U.S. 1, 10 (1972).

[15]   *See, e.g.,* Coastal Steel Corp. v. Tilgham Wheelabrator Ltd., 709 F.2d 190 (3d Cir.), *cert. denied,* 464 U.S. 938, 104 S. Ct. 349 (1983); Crown Beverage Co. v. Cerveceria Moctezuma, S.A., 663 F.2d 886, 888 (9th Cir. 1981); Staco Energy Prod. Co. v. Driver-Haris Co., 509 F. Supp. 1226, 1227 (S.D. Ohio 1981) (dictum); Republic Int'l Corp. v. Amco Eng'rs, Inc., 516 F.2d 161, 168 (9th Cir. 1975); Shepard Niles Crane & Hoist Corp. v. Fiat, S.p.A., 84 F.R.D. 299, 305 (W.D.N.Y. 1979) (dictum); Hoes of Am., Inc. v. Hoes, 493 F. Supp. 1205, 1209 (C.D. Ill. 1979); Cruise v. Castleton, Inc., 449 F. Supp. 564 (S.D.N.Y. 1978); Gaskin v. Stumm Handel GmbH, 390 F. Supp. 361 (S.D.N.Y. 1975).

[16]   *See, e.g.,* Abadou v. Trad, 624 P.2d 287 (Alaska 1981); Volkswagenwerk, A.G. v. Klippan, GmbH, 611 P.2d 498 (Alaska), *cert. denied,* 449 U.S. 974 (1980); Societe Jean Nicolas et Fils, J.B. v. Mousseux, 123 Ariz. 59, 597 P.2d 541 (1979); Smith, Valentino & Smith, Inc. v. Superior Court, 17 Cal. 3d 491, 551 P.2d 1206, 131 Cal. Rptr. 374 (1976); Elia Corp. v. Paul N. Howard Co., 391 A.2d 214 (Del. Super. Ct. 1978); Green v. Clinic Mawsters, Inc., 272 N.W.2d 813 (S.D. 1978); Hi Fashion Wigs Profit Sharing Trust v. Hamilton Inv. Trust, 579 S.W.2d 300 (Tex. Civ. App. 1979).

[17]   Bremen, 407 U.S. 1, 12 (1972).

[18]   *See, e.g.,* Santamauro v. Taito do Brasil Industria E Comercia, 587 F. Supp. 1312, 1314 (E.D. La. 1984) ("The burden is on the party resisting enforcement of the clause to prove that the choice was unreasonable, unfair or unjust, or to show that the clause is invalid by reason of fraud or overreaching or that enforcement would contravene a strong public policy of this forum."); City of New York v. Pullman, Inc., 477 F. Supp. 438, 441 n.10 (S.D.N.Y. 1979), *aff'd,* 662 F.2d 919 (2d Cir. 1981), *reh'g denied,* Sept. 28, 1981, *cert. denied,* 454 U.S. 1038, 102 S. Ct. 1038 (1982) ("Agreements entered into by knowledgeable parties in an arm's-length transaction that contain a forum selection provision are enforceable absent a showing of fraud, overreaching, unreasonableness or unfairness.").

[19]   Restatement (Second) of the Conflict of Laws § 80 (1971).

[20]   Bremen, 407 U.S. 1, 18 (1972).

contract relations,[21] or (3) where enforcement would result in a violation of public policy or the transaction is otherwise unfair, unjust or unreasonable.[22]

For the most part, success in the application of these exceptions is relatively rare.[23] The first—dealing with inconvenience or denial of an effective remedy—is worth further comment, however, since it can be seen as a modified forum non conveniens analysis. In the language of the *Bremen* decision:

> [W]here it can be said with reasonable assurance that at the time they entered the contract, the parties to a freely negotiated private international commercial agreement contemplated the claimed inconvenience, it is difficult to see why any such claim of inconvenience should be heard to render the forum clause unenforceable.[24]

---

[21] *Id.* at 15. The Supreme Court further developed the fraud exception in Scherk v. Alberto-Culver Co., 417 U.S. 506 (1974), when it stated:

This qualification does not mean that any time a dispute arising out of a transaction is based upon an allegation of fraud . . . the clause is unenforceable. Rather, it means that [a] . . . forum-selection clause in a contract is not enforceable if the *inclusion of that clause in the contract* was the product of fraud or coercion.

417 U.S. 506, 519 n.14 (1974) (emphasis in original).

[22] *Id.* The Court rejected Zapata's argument that the exculpatory clause contained in the agreement violated U.S. public policy.

[23] Commentators have divided these exceptions in different ways. *See, e.g.,* Anne E. Covey & Michael S. Morris, *The Enforceability of Agreements Providing for Forum and Choice of Law Selection*, 61 DENV. L.J. 837, 842 (1984) ("The primary limitations . . . are fraud, public policy, adhesion, statutory restrictions and inconvenience of the contractual forum."); Michael Gruson, *Forum-Selection Clauses in International and Interstate Commercial Agreements*, 1982 U. ILL. L. REV. 133, 163–85 (dividing the exceptions into the categories of (1) fraud, (2) bargaining relationship between the parties, (3) nature of the selected forum, (4) public policy of the forum, (5) statutory restrictions on forum-selection clauses, (6) inconvenience of the contractual forum, and (7) other instances of unreasonableness). *See also* The Model Choice of Forum Act, § 3, which lists the following exceptions to enforcement of choice of forum clauses:

(1) the court is required by statute to entertain the action;

(2) the plaintiff cannot secure effective relief in the other state, for reasons other than delay in bringing the action;

(3) the other state would be a substantially less convenient place for the trial of the action than this state;

(4) the agreement as to the place of the action was obtained by misrepresentation, duress, the abuse of economic power, or other unconscionable means; or

(5) it would for some other reason be unfair or unreasonable to enforce the agreement.

Willis L.M. Reese, *The Model Choice of Forum Act*, 17 AM. J. COMP. L. 292, 294 (1969).

[24] Bremen, 407 U.S. 1, 16 (1972).

The continued validity of some form of forum non conveniens analysis in the face of an otherwise valid choice of court agreement clearly is inconsistent with full respect for party autonomy in choosing a forum. Cases have most clearly faced this limitation on party choice when dealing with the related issues of transfer between federal courts under 28 U.S.C. § 1404(a). In such a case, the Third Circuit U.S. Court of Appeals stated:

> Congress set down in § 1404(a) the factors it thought should be decisive on a motion for transfer. Only one of these—the convenience of the parties— is properly within the power of the parties themselves to affect by a forum-selection clause. The other factors—the convenience of witnesses and the interest of justice—are third party or public interests that must be weighed by the district court; they cannot be automatically outweighed by the existence of a purely private agreement between the parties. Such an agreement does not obviate the need for an analysis of the factors set forth in § 1404(a) and does not necessarily preclude the granting of the motion to transfer.[25]

While the interpretation of a statute is a different matter than the application of a common law doctrine, the § 1404(a) analysis is very similar to that applied for a forum non conveniens decision.

The State of New York has taken a clear position on the intersection between choice of court and forum non conveniens, but in a rule that only applies in limited circumstances. When New York State recodified its doctrine of forum non conveniens in 1984, the legislature specifically provided that its courts cannot stay or dismiss an action on forum non conveniens grounds where the contract contains both a New York choice of forum clause and a New York choice of law clause and the transaction involved exceeds $1,000,000 in value.[26] This provision assures that New York State courts will accept jurisdiction in accordance with the parties' choice in large transnational contracts, and that a forum non conveniens challenge cannot be used to frustrate the agreement of the parties. It does not, however, provide a similar rule when the choice of court agreement leads away from New York courts.

In the European Union, Article 23 of the *Brussels Regulation* allows a useful comparison with U.S. case law on business-to-business choice of court issues.

---

[25]   Plum Tree, Inc. v. Stockment, 488 F.2d 754, 757–58 (3d Cir. 1973).

[26]   N.Y. C.P.L.R. § 327 (McKinney 2001) (1984 N.Y. Laws, Ch. 421, § 2).

Article 23 provides that where parties have agreed "that a court or the courts of a Member State are to have jurisdiction to settle any disputes which have arisen in connection with a particular legal relationship, that court or those courts shall have jurisdiction."[27] The same Article goes on to provide that "[s]uch jurisdiction shall be exclusive unless the parties have agreed otherwise."[28] Since the *Brussels Regulation* does not allow for declining such exclusive jurisdiction,[29] Article 23 ends the analysis when the alternative forum is another European Union Member State, and no forum non conveniens claim may be asserted.

There exist at least two important differences between the Brussels scheme for choice of court clauses and that existing under the common law in the United States. First, unlike the Brussels rule, U.S. courts have not been willing to consider the allocation of authority to the chosen court to be either absolute[30] or exclusive.[31] Thus, the existence of a choice of court clause does not guarantee that the dispute may be resolved only in that forum, unless the clause expressly creates such exclusivity. In this respect, under the Brussels system, European courts go further in their respect for the chosen court.

The other difference works the other way. U.S. courts will uphold choice of court clauses in consumer contracts where European courts will not do so. The Brussels rule honors a choice of court clause in a consumer contract only if the agreement: (1) is entered into after the dispute has arisen, (2) allows the consumer to bring proceedings in courts other than those otherwise available, or (3) provides for

---

[27]   Council Regulation 44/2001/EC of 22 December 2000 on Jurisdiction and the Recognition and Enforcement of Judgments in Civil and Commercial Matters, 2001 O.J. (L 12) 1, art. 23.

[28]   *Id.*

[29]   *See* Chapter 2, Part III.B., above.

[30]   *See, e.g.,* Sudduth v. Occidental Peruana, Inc., 70 F. Supp. 2d 691 (E.D. Tex. 1999) (denying defendant's motion to dismiss on forum non conveniens grounds in favor of the chosen court, holding that the mandatory choice of court clause was invalid under *Bremen*); Dentsply International, Inc. v. Benton, 965 F. Supp. 574 (M.D. Pa. 1997) (refusing to enforce the mandatory choice of court clause in an employment contract holding that it was the result of unequal bargaining power).

[31]   *See, e.g.,* Steve Weiss & Co., Inc. v. INALCO, 1999 WL 386653 (S.D.N.Y. 1999) (not reported in F. Supp. 2d) (stating that "where parties only specify in a contract clause where jurisdiction is proper" the clause generally will not be enforced unless other language clearly identifies "the parties intent to make jurisdiction exclusive"); Hull 753 Corp. v. Flugzeugwerke, 58 F. Supp. 2d 925 (N.D. Ill. 1999) (holding that a clause granting jurisdiction to German courts was not exclusive absent clear language that only German courts shall have jurisdiction).

jurisdiction in the courts of the state that is the habitual residence of both the consumer and the other party.[32]

U.S. law provides no such limitations on the enforcement of choice of court clauses for consumer contracts. In *Carnival Cruise Lines Inc. v. Shute*,[33] the Supreme Court upheld enforcement of a clause requiring that disputes be brought in the state courts of Florida. A Washington state consumer purchased a cruise ticket from a local travel agent for a trip off the coast of Mexico. The choice of court clause in fine print was on a cruise ticket that was not received until after the consumer had arranged and paid for the cruise. Justice Blackmun relied in part on an economic rationale to enforce the clause, stating that "passengers who purchase tickets containing a forum clause like that at issue in this case benefit in the form of reduced fares reflecting the savings that the cruise line enjoys by limiting the fora in which it may be sued."[34] Thus, the Supreme Court made clear the wide breadth of the *Bremen* policy favoring enforcement of choice of court clauses, encompassing even consumer contracts that contain no element of true negotiation.

In sum, in the United States, there is no simple resolution for a court faced with both a choice of court clause and a motion to stay or dismiss a case based on the doctrine of forum non conveniens. Both the forum non conveniens doctrine and the *Bremen* line of cases favoring the enforcement of choice of court agreements must be considered.

B. The convergence of choice of court clauses and the forum non conveniens doctrine

The U.S. common law doctrines on enforcement of choice of court clauses and forum non conveniens have, for the most part, developed separately. More recently, however, courts have addressed situations in which the two doctrines intersect.

---

[32] Council Regulation 44/2001/EC of 22 December 2000 on Jurisdiction and the Recognition and Enforcement of Judgments in Civil and Commercial Matters, 2001 O.J. (L 12) 1, art. 17.

[33] 499 U.S. 585 (1991).

[34] Carnival Cruise Lines, 499 U.S. 585, 594 (1991).

1. *Apparent resolution in* Bremen

Guidance regarding the manner in which the doctrines of forum selection and forum non conveniens intersect appears from the language of the *Bremen* decision of the U.S. Supreme Court, but has not always been consistently considered in subsequent lower court decisions. In *Bremen*, the Court of Appeals, in affirming denial of a motion to dismiss, had concluded that "a forum-selection clause 'will not be enforced unless the selected state would provide a more convenient forum than the state in which suit is brought.'"[35] The Court of Appeals had determined that "the District Court did not abuse its discretion in refusing to decline jurisdiction on the basis of *forum non conveniens*."[36] While the Supreme Court decided the case with a primary focus on the choice of court agreement, and not on a forum non conveniens analysis, it specifically remanded the case to the trial court in a manner that would seem to mix the choice of court and forum non conveniens analyses:

> [T]o allow Zapata opportunity to carry its heavy burden of showing not only that the balance of convenience is strongly in favor of trial in Tampa (that is, that it will be far more inconvenient for Zapata to litigate in London than it will be for Unterweser to litigate in Tampa), but also that a London trial will be so manifestly and gravely inconvenient to Zapata that it will be effectively deprived of a meaningful day in court, we remand for further proceedings.[37]

This approach seems to base the choice of court agreement analysis on a modified version of forum non conveniens, in which the burden is on the party seeking to avoid the chosen court to prove that court to be "manifestly and gravely inconvenient." Subsequent courts have not followed this balancing of conveniences approach in all regards.

2. *Separate doctrines, common issues*

Enforcement of choice of court clauses represents respect by the court for the autonomy of the parties in structuring their legal relationships, including their

---

[35] Bremen, 407 U.S. 1, 7 (1972) (quoting from the Court of Appeals).

[36] Bremen, 407 U.S. 1, 7 (1972).

[37] Bremen, 407 U.S. 1, 19 (1972).

choice to have a dispute settled in a specific forum. The doctrine of forum non conveniens, on the other hand, represents respect for justice in a particular case. It also requires respect for the ability of the trial court to exercise discretion in assessing conditions of convenience and justice in order to determine whether existing jurisdiction should in fact be exercised. Thus, the two doctrines may not always lead to consistent results.

This possible clash of doctrinal purposes is further complicated by the multiple conditions that may exist at the intersection of the two doctrines. This may be demonstrated by comparison with the *Brussels Regulation* rules addressing choice of court and alternative fora. The Brussels rules (at least in business-to-business cases) are rather simple:

Article 23

1. If the parties, one or more of whom is domiciled in a Member State, have agreed that a court or the courts of a Member State are to have jurisdiction to settle any disputes which have arisen or which may arise in connection with a particular legal relationship, that court or those courts shall have jurisdiction. Such jurisdiction shall be exclusive unless the parties have agreed otherwise. Such an agreement conferring jurisdiction shall be either:

   (a) in writing or evidenced in writing; or

   (b) in a form which accords with practices which the parties have established between themselves; or

   (c) in international trade or commerce, in a form which accords with a usage of which the parties are or ought to have been aware and which in such trade or commerce is widely known to, and regularly observed by, parties to contracts of the type involved in the particular trade or commerce concerned.[38]

Thus, parties not only may select one forum out of several in which jurisdiction otherwise exists, they may create jurisdiction in a forum that might not otherwise

---

[38] Council Regulation 44/2001/EC of 22 December 2000 on Jurisdiction and the Recognition and Enforcement of Judgments in Civil and Commercial Matters, 2001 O.J. (L 12) 1, art. 23(1).

have jurisdiction. Further, once that jurisdiction is established, it is exclusive and no other forum governed by the Regulation may exercise jurisdiction in the case. This rule has certain benefits in terms of predictability of application. It is simple and direct. The related doctrines in U.S. law have rather different, though equally legitimate, purposes.

3. Litigant problems at the intersection of choice of court and forum non conveniens

In the United States, respect for choice of court clauses extends to cases in which a pre-determined choice of court clause would not be possible under the *Brussels Regulation*.[39] At the same time, however, the nuances of the U.S. common law approach can complicate the analysis.

a. The possibilities

To begin with in the United States, courts have distinguished categories of choice of court clauses. An exclusive choice of court clause[40] may lead to the same results as under the *Brussels Regulation*, if, under the *Bremen* analysis, there is no substantial inconvenience, fraud, or public policy reason for a contrary result.[41] Because there is a presumption of non-exclusivity,[42] however, the certainty this analysis brings may be limited. Moreover, clauses may not be limited to exclusive and non-exclusive clauses. Courts have interpreted certain choice of court clauses to be non-exclusive, but accompanied by a waiver of the right to challenge jurisdiction and venue when an action is brought in the chosen court.[43] In these situations, the application of the clause may depend upon which party gets to the court first, and the court in which it files the case.

---

[39] Articles 13, 17 and 21 of the *Brussels Regulation* prevent pre-determined choice of court clauses in insurance contracts, consumer contracts and individual contracts of employment, respectively. Council Regulation 44/2001/EC of 22 December 2000 on Jurisdiction and the Recognition and Enforcement of Judgments in Civil and Commercial Matters, 2001 O.J. (L 12) 1, arts. 13, 17, 21.

[40] Courts often use the term "mandatory" clause to refer to an exclusive clause in U.S. courts.

[41] *See* Part II.A., above.

[42] *See* Part II.B.2.b., below.

[43] *See* Part III.B.1., below.

The existence of a choice of court clause may also affect the application of the *Gilbert-Koster-Piper* factors for purposes of the forum non conveniens doctrine.[44] A clause that derogates from the forum court will weigh in favor of dismissal, while a clause selecting the forum court will weigh against dismissal as part of the balancing of private interest factors.[45]

The combination of the choice of court and forum non conveniens doctrines creates the possibility of at least six different basic factual relationships, with conceivable further variations on each of them. This can be demonstrated in the following chart:

Choice of Court Clause	Forum Non Conveniens Status	
	chosen court	court not chosen
exclusive clause	1	2
non-exclusive clause (with waiver of right to consent	3	4
non-exclusive clause	5	6

While this chart demonstrates the multiple possibilities at the intersection between choice of court and forum non conveniens, it also begs the question of whether location of the case in a certain box within the chart provides an indication of the likely ruling on a motion to dismiss based on forum non conveniens. A purely

---

[44] *See* Chapter 3, Part III, above.

[45] While some courts consider the balancing of the *Gilbert* private and public interest factors a single step in the forum non conveniens analysis, others see them as two separate steps. In the latter group of courts, some have held that the existence of a choice of court clause makes unnecessary the private factor balancing, but does not prevent a public interest balancing that can result in denial of enforcement of the clause. *See, e.g., In re* Hilliard, 533 N.E.2d 543, 545 (Ill. App. Ct. 1989) (denying forum non conveniens motion based on choice of court clause, stating that "[i]f both parties freely entered into the agreement contemplating such inconvenience should there be a dispute, one party cannot successfully argue inconvenience as a reason for rendering the forum clause unenforceable." *See also* Walter W. Heiser, *Forum Selection Clauses in State Courts: Limitations on Enforcement After* Stewart *and* Carnival Cruise, 45 FLA. L. REV. 361, 397 (1993) ("The parties [to a choice of court clause] should be viewed as having given up their respective private interests for the most convenient forum in the event of litigation in exchange for whatever benefits each obtained in return for the concession.").

intuitive analysis is likely to lead to the following results depending on the box into which a case falls:

1) One would assume that a chosen court presented with an exclusive choice of court clause (box number 1) would focus on the *Bremen* analysis and uphold the clause, denying a motion for dismissal on the grounds of forum non conveniens.

2) It would seem likely that a court not chosen faced with an exclusive choice of court clause (box number 2) and a motion for dismissal, should grant that motion on either or both of (1) the *Bremen* factors (honoring the choice of court clause) or (2) the doctrine of forum non conveniens (considering the choice of court clause as a factor weighing heavily in favor of sending the case to the chosen court).

3) A non-exclusive choice of court clause combined with a waiver of a right to contest jurisdiction, venue, and appropriateness of the chosen court, when addressed by the chosen court (box number 3), should bring a result similar to that in box number 1: application of the *Bremen* analysis to uphold the clause, denying a motion for dismissal on the grounds of forum non conveniens.

4) A non-exclusive choice of court clause combined with a waiver of a right to contest jurisdiction, venue, and appropriateness of the chosen forum, when addressed by the court not chosen (box number 4) will not necessarily bring the same result as that in box number 2. The waiver of the right to contest having the suit brought in the chosen forum has no certain impact on the court not chosen; there is no suit in the chosen forum to contest because the right that has been waived has not been challenged. Thus, the existence of the non-exclusive choice of court clause is likely to be one of the factors (not necessarily a controlling factor) weighed by the court in the application of the doctrine of forum non conveniens.

5) A chosen court faced with a non-exclusive choice of court clause (box number 5) would seem less likely to decide to deny a motion for dismissal simply on a *Bremen* analysis. Here the case is more likely than a box number 1 case to proceed to a forum non conveniens analysis, with

the non-exclusive clause being a significant factor in the application of the private interest balancing test.

6) A court not chosen faced with a non-exclusive choice of court clause (box number 6) would similarly seem less likely to decide to grant a motion for dismissal simply on a *Bremen* analysis than would be the case in a box number 2 case. Here, as in a box number 5 case, it would seem logical to proceed to a forum non conveniens analysis, with the non-exclusive clause being a significant factor in the application of the private interest balancing test.

Recent cases provide examples of situations falling within some of these boxes. It is instructive to consider these decisions.

b. The case law

The chart above may oversimplify the analysis by indicating that it is always easy to determine whether a clause is exclusive or non-exclusive. This is often discussed in U.S. courts as the distinction between a mandatory and a permissive clause. The general U.S. rule is that all choice of court clauses are non-exclusive unless clearly stated otherwise.[46] The rationale for this position has been stated as follows:

> To be mandatory, a forum selection clause must contain language that clearly designates a forum as the exclusive one.
>
> A permissive clause merely grants jurisdiction to the named forum, and does not preclude a cause of action from being brought elsewhere. If the court determines that a forum selection clause is not mandatory, that does not mean that the clause is effectively written out of the contract. It simply means that the clause does not preclude a party from bringing suit in any jurisdiction where venue is proper.
>
> For a forum selection clause to be mandatory, the clause must clearly display the intent of the contracting parties to choose a particular forum to

---

[46] *See, e.g.,* Steve Weiss & Co., Inc. v. INALCO, S.P.A., 1999 WL 386653 (S.D.N.Y. 1999) (not reported in F. Supp. 2d) ("[i]n the absence of specific exclusionary language, this court will not assume an intent to confer exclusive jurisdiction on Italian courts").

the exclusion of all other fora. Despite containing forceful words like "shall," the clause will not be deemed mandatory unless it is clear that the clause mandates the exclusive use of a particular forum.[47]

This general preference for interpreting choice of court clauses as non-exclusive provides some guidance, but is not always conclusive in all courts. At least one court would appear to find all choice of court clauses to be exclusive.[48]

1) Exclusive (mandatory) clauses

The interplay of an exclusive choice of forum clause with the doctrine of forum non conveniens is not a clear matter in U.S. courts. A split in federal circuit courts demonstrates the positions on this issue. The Second Circuit has indicated that a federal district court should begin by applying the *Bremen* test to determine the enforceability of a forum selection clause, and that a defendant's motion to dismiss on forum non conveniens grounds should be considered only if the court first finds that the parties did *not* form a contract with a valid choice of court clause.[49] The Fifth Circuit has taken a similar approach, rejecting a forum non conveniens challenge to an exclusive choice of court clause on the grounds that "increased cost and inconvenience are insufficient reasons to invalidate foreign forum-selection or arbitration clauses."[50] The Seventh Circuit has interpreted the *Bremen* language to mean that a choice of court clause is to be enforced unless the "party challenging its enforcement can 'clearly show that enforcement would be unreasonable and unjust, or that the clause was invalid for such reasons as fraud or overreaching,' or that 'trial in the [chosen] forum will be so gravely difficult and

---

47 Arguss Communications Group, Inc. v. Teletron, Inc., 2000 WL 36936 at *6–7 (D.N.H. 1999) (not reported in F. Supp. 2d) (citations omitted).

48 Florida Polk County v. Prison Health Servs., Inc., 170 F.3d 1081, 1083–84 (11th Cir. 1999) ("It is a venerable principle of contract law that the provisions of a contract should be construed so as to give every provision meaning," and "[t]o read the forum-selection clause as permissive would render it surplusage, [but to] read the clause as mandatory—thus requiring all litigation arising out of the contract to take place in the [selected court]—gives the provision meaning.").

49 Evolution Online Sys., Inc. v. Koninklijke PTT Nederland N.V., 145 F.3d 505, 509–10 (2d Cir. 1998). *See also* Sudduth v. Occidental Peruana, Inc., 70 F. Supp. 2d 691 (E.D. Tex. 1999), where the district court denied the defendant's motion to dismiss on forum non conveniens grounds only after determining that a mandatory choice of court clause was invalid under the *Bremen* standards.

50 Mitsui & Co. (USA), Inc. v. Mira M/V, 111 F.3d 33, 37 (5th Cir. 1997).

inconvenient that he will for all practical purposes be deprived of his day in court."[51] Thus, the Seventh Circuit finds an exclusive choice of court clause

> ... presumptively valid and enforceable unless (1) "[its] incorporation into the contract was the result of fraud, undue influence, or overweening bargaining power; (2) the selected forum is so gravely difficult and inconvenient that [the complaining party] will for all practical purposes be deprived of its day in court; or (3) [its] enforcement ... would contravene a strong public policy of the forum in which the suit is brought, declared by statute or judicial decision."[52]

The First Circuit, on the other hand, has ruled that a choice of court clause does not control the decision on a forum non conveniens motion to dismiss, but is "simply one of the factors that should be considered and balanced" by the court in its forum non conveniens analysis.[53]

Despite this split in the Circuits (and recognizing that not all courts give clear consideration to whether the clause in question is exclusive or non-exclusive), the general approach to exclusive choice of court clauses is to enforce them, either under the *Bremen* test or under a forum non conveniens analysis.[54] Chosen courts have kept cases when faced with a forum non conveniens motion to dismiss,[55] and courts not chosen have dismissed cases in favor of the court selected in

---

[51] AAR International, Inc. v. Nimelias Enterprises S.A., 250 F.3d 510, 525 (7th Cir. 2001), quoting from Bremen v. Zapata Off-Shore Co., 407 U.S. 1, 15, 17 (1972). *See also* Northwestern Nat'l. Ins. Co. v. Donovan, 916 F.2d 372, 378 (7th Cir. 1990) (holding that agreement to an exclusive forum selection clause waives objections to venue on the basis of cost or inconvenience to the party).

[52] AAR International, 250 F.3d 510, 525 (7th Cir. 2001), quoting from Bonny v. Society of Lloyd's, 3 F.3d 156, 160 (7th Cir. 1993).

[53] Royal Bed & Spring Co., Inc. v. Famossul Industria e Comercio de Moveis Ltda., 906 F.2d 45, 51 (1st Cir. 1990).

[54] *See, e.g.*, Mercier v. Sheraton International, Inc., 981 F.2d 1345 (1st Cir. 1992) (applying forum non conveniens analysis despite apparent exclusive choice of court clause, but dismissing in favor of the Turkish court named in the clause). When New York recodified its doctrine of forum non conveniens in 1984, it specifically provided that its courts cannot stay or dismiss an action on forum non conveniens grounds where the contract contains both a New York choice of forum clause and a New York choice of law clause and the transaction involved exceeds $1,000,000. N.Y. C.P.L.R. § 327 (McKinney's 2001) (1984 N.Y. Laws, Ch. 421, § 2).

[55] *See, e.g.*, Heller Financial, Inc. v. Midwhey Powder Co., 883 F.3d 1286 (7th Cir. 1989) (denying motion for dismissal or transfer under 28 U.S.C. § 1404(a)); Poddar v. State Bank of India, 79 F. Supp. 2d 391, 393 (S.D.N.Y. 2000) (denying dismissal where clause created mandatory jurisdiction in courts in both India and the United States); Cambridge Nutrition A.G. v. Fotheringham, 840 F. Supp. 299 (S.D.N.Y. 1994) (enforcing New York choice of court clause despite motion to dismiss brought by Spanish defendant for whom trial in New York was inconvenient).

the clause.[56] Nonetheless, some courts have refused to enforce clauses choosing another court when considered in the context of a motion to dismiss based on forum non conveniens.[57]

2) Non-exclusive (permissive) clauses

While the Second Circuit relies strictly on a *Bremen* analysis when the choice of court clause is exclusive,[58] it applies a forum non conveniens analysis when addressing a non-exclusive choice of court clause. This is demonstrated in the case of *John Boutari & Son, Wines & Spirits, S.A. v. Attiki Importers & Distribs.*,[59]

---

[56]   *See, e.g.*, Royal Bed & Spring Co. v. Famoussul Industria E Comercio de Moveis Ltda., 906 F.2d 45 (1st Cir. 1990) (enforcing Brazilian choice of court clause in distributorship agreement under a *Bremen* analysis); Caribe BMW, Inc. v. Bayerische Motoren Werke Aktiengesellschaft, 821 F. Supp. 802, *set aside, vacated and remanded on other grounds*, 19 F.2d 745 (1st Cir. 1994) (finding German choice of court clause valid and enforceable on a multi-factor analysis); Bonny v. Society of Lloyd's, 3 F.3d 156 (7th Cir. 1993) (honoring English choice of court clause under *Bremen* analysis by dismissal of action under securities underwriting contract); General Elec. Co. v. G. Siempelkamp GmbH & Co., 29 F.3d 1095 (6th Cir. 1994) (dismissing case on forum non conveniens challenge in favor of German courts in accordance with choice of court clause in the sales contract); Omron Healthcare v. Maclaren Exports, 28 F.2d 600 (7th Cir. 1994) (applying forum non conveniens analysis to enforce English choice of court clause in distributorship contract); Aceequip, Ltd. v. Am. Eng'g Corp., 153 F. Supp. 2d 138 (D.C. Conn. 2001) (denying motion to dismiss in favor of Japanese court when mandatory clause selected Connecticut forum); Lawler v. Schumacher Filgters Am., 832 F. Supp. 1044 (E.D. Va. 1993) (enforcing choice of court clause in consultancy agreement naming German courts as the chosen forum); Hunter Distrib. Co. v. Pure Beverage Partners, 820 F. Supp. 284 (N.D. Miss. 1993) (granting motion to dismiss for improper venue when faced with choice of court clause naming Arizona courts); TUC Electronics, Inc. v. Eagle Telephonics, Inc., 698 F. Supp. 35 (D. Conn. 1988) (dismissing case brought in Connecticut in face of New York state court choice of court clause, applying combination of *Bremen* and forum non conveniens factors); Santamauro v. Taito do Brasil Industria E Comercia Ltda. 587 F. Supp. 1312 (E.D. La. 1984) (applying *Bremen* analysis to dismiss action on sales contract brought in Louisiana despite Brazilian choice of court clause); Skyline Steel Corp. v. RDI/Caesars Riverboat Casino, LLC, 44 F. Supp. 2d 1337, 1338 (N.D. Ala. 1999) (sending case to chosen forum under 28 U.S.C. § 1404(a) transfer statute, but stating, "the law of the Eleventh Circuit is that forum selection clauses are virtually impossible to overcome by an application of the general principles of forum non conveniens").

[57]   *See, e.g.*, Sudduth v. Occidental Peruana, Inc., 70 F. Supp. 2d 691 (E.D. Tex. 1999) (refusing enforcement of clause requiring disputes to be brought in Peruvian courts where both parties were in the United States); Pearcy Marine v. Seacor Marine, 847 F. Supp. 57 (S.D. Tex. 1993) (finding London choice of court clause to be unenforceable as a result of unequal bargaining power). Similarly, courts have found that the existence of a valid forum selection clause does not prevent a transfer for forum non conveniens purposes under 28 U.S.C. § 1404(a). Plum Tree, Inc. v. Stockment, 488 F.2d 754, 757–58 (3d Cir. 1973) ("Such an agreement does not obviate the need for an analysis of the factors set forth in § 1404(a) and does not necessarily preclude the granting of the motion to transfer.").

[58]   Evolution Online Sys., Inc. v. Koninklijke PTT Nederland N.V., 145 F.3d 505, 509–10 (2d Cir. 1998).

[59]   22 F.3d 51 (2d Cir. 1994). *See also* Blanco v. Banco Industrial de Venequela, S.A., 997 F.2d 974 (2d Cir. 1993) (affirming a dismissal on forum non conveniens grounds even though New York was one of three jurisdictions named in a non-exclusive choice of court clause).

where the Second Circuit held that dismissal of an action on a distributorship contract on forum non conveniens grounds was erroneous, and that the case should be tried in a U.S. Federal District Court despite a Greek choice of court clause. The result was based in part on a finding that the clause was permissive and not mandatory. The Ninth Circuit applied a similar analysis to a case involving a clause selecting the Hong Kong courts, but affirmed a dismissal on grounds of *forum non conveniens*.[60]

Federal district courts have gone both ways when faced with a non-exclusive choice of court clause and a motion for dismissal on forum non conveniens grounds. While courts in Illinois[61] and Georgia[62] have enforced permissive choice of court clauses favoring foreign courts in the face of a forum non conveniens motion for dismissal, federal district courts in North Carolina[63] and Arizona[64] have refused motions to dismiss even where the clause called for the actions to be brought in foreign countries. The decision often seems to hinge on the weight given to the choice of court clause in balancing the private and public interest factors applied in the forum non conveniens analysis.

3) Non-exclusive clauses with waiver of objections to venue

In *AAR Int'l, Inc. v. Nimelias Enterprises S.A.*,[65] the Seventh Circuit addressed the interplay of the *Bremen* analysis with the forum non conveniens doctrine when a case was brought in the court designated by a non-exclusive choice of court clause and that clause was accompanied by "unambiguous language providing that the [party] shall not object to venue in [the chosen] court on the ground that such a court is an inconvenient forum."[66] The court concluded that in such a case, "the stricter standards announced in *Bremen* should control the analysis of [the] forum

---

[60] FIL Leveraged US Gov't Bond Fund Ltd. v. TCW Funds Management, Inc., 156 F.3d 1236 (9th Cir. 1998).

[61] Hull, 753 Corp. v. Elbe Flugzeugwerke, 58 F. Supp. 2d 925, 926 (N.D. Ill. 1999) (enforcing non-exclusive clause favoring German courts).

[62] Amermed Corp. v. Disetronic Holding AG, 6 F. Supp. 2d 1371 (N.D. Ga. 1998) (granting dismissal in favor of Swiss court selected in non-exclusive clause).

[63] S & D Coffee, Inc. v. GEI Autowrappers, 995 F. Supp. 607 (M.D.N.C. 1997) (denying dismissal in favor of English court named in non-exclusive clause).

[64] Magellan Real Estate Inv. Trust v. Losch, 109 F. Supp. 2d 1144 (D.C. Ariz. 2000) (denying dismissal in favor of Ontario court named in non-exclusive clause).

[65] 250 F.3d 510, 525 (7th Cir. 2001).

[66] *Id.*, at 525–26.

non conveniens motion,"[67] and the traditional forum non conveniens analysis did not apply. Thus, the result was the same as if the clause had been exclusive.

4) The importance of the clause to the analysis

At least one commentator has stated that, in cases dealing with the convergence between choice of court clauses and the forum non conveniens doctrine, it makes "little difference" whether the *Bremen* factors are applied or the case is analyzed under the forum non conveniens analysis.[68] This does not seem to hold true in all circumstances, however. In U.S. courts, the designation of the type of choice of court clause helps determine whether the court will focus on a *Bremen* or a forum non conveniens analysis. This determination, in turn, has a substantial impact on the burden placed on each of the parties and the opportunity to challenge the trial court's decision on appeal.

Under a *Bremen* analysis, the party seeking to avoid the choice of court clause has the "heavy burden of showing not only that the balance of convenience is strongly in favor of trial in [the alternative forum] . . . but also that a . . . trial [in the chosen forum] will be so manifestly and gravely inconvenient to [that party] that it will be effectively deprived of a meaningful day in court."[69] This appears to be a much more substantial burden than what is necessary to meet the forum non conveniens test, which requires a showing of an adequate alternative forum and a balancing of private and public interest factors. Moreover, on appeal, the question of enforceability of a choice of court clause is a question of law subject to de novo review,[70] whereas "[t]he forum non conveniens determination is committed to the trial court's sound discretion and may be reversed only when there has been a clear abuse of discretion."[71]

5) Problems with categorization

Even if one can carefully catalogue each case to fit within the chart set forth above, that will not explain some U.S. cases, or the opinions of some commentators.

---

[67] *Id.*, at 526.

[68] Ryan Kelly McLemore, *Forum-Selection Clauses and Seaman Personal Injury*, 25 TUL. MAR. L.J. 327, 350 (2000) ("The issue is essentially one of fairness and justice.").

[69] Bremen, 470 U.S. 1, 19 (1972).

[70] AAR International, Inc. v. Nimelias Enterprises S.A., 250 F.3d 510, 527 (7th Cir. 2001).

[71] Piper Aircraft Co. v. Reyno, 454 U.S. 235, 237 (1981).

It has been suggested that "[u]sing forum non conveniens terminology, the parties lack the authority to contractually reallocate the various public interest factors, or those private ones of third parties not related to the contract."[72] This approach would mean that no court could stop with the *Bremen* factors, and that the balancing required under traditional forum non conveniens analysis would always be necessary, even in the face of a valid, exclusive choice of court clause. The same author suggests that, at a minimum, "the existence of a forum selection clause should remove the individual parties' convenience or inconvenience from the court's consideration of the various private and public interest factors."[73] Even the cases that take this approach, however, often end up enforcing the choice of court clause.[74]

Some courts tend to ignore the *Bremen* analysis entirely, holding choice of court clauses unenforceable where "enforcing the clause would 'seriously impair'" the plaintiff's law suit.[75] Others acknowledge *Bremen* and *Carnival Cruise Lines*, but then go on to refuse enforcement of choice of court clauses by finding distinctions considered to justify such results.[76]

---

[72]   Walter W. Heiser, *Forum Selection Clauses in State Courts: Limitations on Enforcement After* Stewart *and* Carnival Cruise, 45 FLA. L. REV. 361, 396 (1993).

[73]   *Id.* at 397. *See* Arthur Young & Co. v. Leong, 383 N.Y.S.2d 618, 619 (App. Div.), *appeal dismissed*, 390 N.Y.2d 927 (1976) (stating that the existence of a choice of court clause "obviated considerations of inconvenience to a party or a witness").

[74]   *See, e.g.*, Smith, Valentino & Smith, Inc. v. Superior Court, 131 Cal. Rptr. 374, 551 P.2d 1206, 1209–10 (Cal. 1976) (enforcing Pennsylvania choice of court clause despite residence of plaintiff's witnesses in California); Prudential Resources Corp. v. Plunkett, 583 S.W.2d 97, 99–100 (Ky. Ct. App. 1979) (enforcing choice of court clause even where one party's witnesses would have to be presented by deposition since they would be unable to appear in person); Hauenstein & Bermeister, Inc. v. Met-Fab Indus., 320 N.W.2d 886, 890 (Minn. 1982) (enforcing choice of court clause where inconvenienced witnesses could submit testimony by deposition).

[75]   *See, e.g.*, Morgan Trailer Mfg. Co. v. Hydraroll, Ltd., 759 A.2d 926, 931 (Pa. Super. 2000).

[76]   *See, e.g.*, Walker v. Carnival Cruise Lines, 107 F. Supp. 2d 1135, 1140 (N.D. Cal. 2000) (stating that the Supreme Court did not create a *per se* rule of enforcement of cruise line contract choice of court clauses, and holding that where the plaintiffs suffered severe physical disabilities, "it is hard to envision circumstances which, in their totality, more clearly demonstrate the fundamental unfairness of enforcing a forum selection clause."); Corna v. American Hawaii Cruises, Inc., 794 F. Supp. 1005, 1011 (D. Haw. 1992) (refusing to enforce choice of court clause where plaintiffs only received their tickets with the clause two or three days before departure, and therefore did not have time to consider the option to reject the cruise contract without forfeiting several thousand dollars).

III. The rationale for a Hague Convention on Choice of Court Agreements

The current status of U.S. law on both choice of court and forum non conveniens demonstrates the value of even a modest Hague convention on jurisdiction and judgments—not just for the United States, but for all of its potential treaty partners. The success of the *1958 New York Arbitration Convention* demonstrates the value of a convention that combines enforcement of choice of forum with enforcement of the resulting award.[77] The lack of any such global set of rules for litigation creates a relative disadvantage for persons with legitimate reasons for preferring litigation over arbitration. The *2005 Hague Convention on Choice of Court Agreements* is designed in part to fill this gap by providing increased predictability for the international commercial community. It also establishes a foundation upon which to build further judicial cooperation in the future.[78] Moreover, it would provide greater certainty for all parties to transnational cases litigated in the United States when a choice of court clause is involved.

U.S. law on choice of court differs from the mandatory and exclusive results of Article 23 of the *Brussels Regulation*, and does not contain the limitations on such clauses in insurance, consumer, and employment contracts that are found in Articles 13, 17 and 21 of the Regulation. U.S. common law presents a presumption of non-exclusivity of choice of court clauses, which, when combined with the *Bremen* analysis, allows courts to disregard even mandatory choice of court clauses in certain limited situations. The European approach focuses on efficiency, predictability, and minimal judicial discretion. The U.S. approach (and that of most other non-EU common law states) gives up some efficiency and predictability in exchange for discretion to accomplish equity and fairness in individual cases. While experts may debate whether one approach is better than the other, the answer to that debate may not matter so much as whether it is possible to bring the two systems closer together for the benefit of the global community.

Two parts of the *1999 Hague Convention Preliminary Draft Text* and the *2001 Hague Interim Text* demonstrate the manner in which this divergence of approaches initially was addressed at the Hague Conference on Private International Law.

---

[77] United Nations Convention on the Recognition and Enforcement of Foreign Arbitral Awards, done at New York, June 10, 1958, 21 U.S.T. 2517, T.I.A.S. No. 6997, 330 U.N.T.S. 38.

[78] See Ronald A. Brand, *Where To From Here? Prospects for a Hague Convention on Jurisdiction and the Enforcement of Judgments*, 16 INT'L ARB. RPT. 38 (Oct. 2001).

The first is the combination of articles dealing with choice of court. Like the *Brussels Regulation*, both Hague texts contain a general rule of exclusive jurisdiction for choice of court clauses.[79] Article 8 of the *Preliminary Draft Text* also contains a prohibition on pre-dispute choice of court clauses in employment contracts,[80] and Article 7 includes a prohibition on pre-dispute choice of court clauses in consumer contracts.[81] Article 7 of the *Interim Text* reflects the very substantial concerns with this prohibition in consumer contracts, with its numerous alternatives, variants, and bracketed text.[82] Much of the concern over the consumer contract rules related to jurisdiction in electronic commerce, which is a matter not clearly resolved in any legal system at the current time, and upon which there is not likely to be global consensus in the near future.[83]

The other part of the two initial Hague texts dealing with the divergence of approaches discussed here is found in Articles 21 and 22 in the *2001 Hague Interim Text*, representing a compromise on the application of rules of lis alibi pendens and forum non conveniens in various legal systems. As the discussion in Chapter 8 has indicated, while the Brussels approach includes a strict lis pendens rule that requires a court second seised to defer to the court first seised in any matter,[84] the U.S. approach is to allow parallel litigation and ultimately defer through principles of res judicata and issue preclusion in favor of the first judgment. Thus, the

---

[79] *Informational note on the work of the informal meetings held since October 1999 to consider and develop drafts on outstanding items, drawn up by the Permanent Bureau*, Hague Conference on Private International Law, art. 4, Prel. Doc. No. 15 (May 2001) (containing the text of the Preliminary Draft Convention). This text is reproduced as Document A at the end of this volume. *Summary of the Outcome of the Discussion in Commission II of the First Part of the Diplomatic Conference 6–20 June 2001—Interim Text*, Hague Conference on Private International Law, Nineteenth Session (2001) [hereinafter Interim Text], art. 4. This text is reproduced as Document C at the end of this volume.

[80] *Informational note on the work of the informal meetings held since October 1999 to consider and develop drafts on outstanding items, drawn up by the Permanent Bureau*, Hague Conference on Private International Law, Prel. Doc. No. 15 (May 2001), art. 8.

[81] *Informational note on the work of the informal meetings held since October 1999 to consider and develop drafts on outstanding items, drawn up by the Permanent Bureau*, Hague Conference on Private International Law, Prel. Doc. No. 15 (May 2001), art. 7; *Summary of the Outcome of the Discussion in Commission II of the First Part of the Diplomatic Conference 6–20 June 2001—Interim Text*, Hague Conference on Private International Law, Nineteenth Session (2001), art. 7.

[82] *Summary of the Outcome of the Discussion in Commission II of the First Part of the Diplomatic Conference 6–20 June 2001—Interim Text*, Hague Conference on Private International Law, Nineteenth Session (2001), art. 7.

[83] See Ronald A. Brand, *Intellectual Property, Electronic Commerce and the Preliminary Draft Hague Jurisdiction and Judgments Convention*, 62 U. PITT. L. REV. 581 (2001).

[84] Council Regulation 44/2001/EC of 22 December 2000 on Jurisdiction and the Recognition and Enforcement of Judgments in Civil and Commercial Matters, 2001 O.J. (L 12) 1, art. 23.

Brussels system promotes a race to the courthouse, and the U.S. common law system promotes a race to judgment. The U.S. approach is—like that in most common law countries—tempered by the doctrine of forum non conveniens, which places discretionary authority in a trial court to defer to a foreign court earlier seised of the matter, or even to dismiss in favor of filing the case in a foreign forum not yet seised of the matter.

The language of Articles 21 and 22 of the *2001 Hague Interim Text* indicates a compromise of approaches on issues of lis pendens and forum non conveniens. The many brackets and variations in the *Interim Text* articles dealing with choice of court demonstrate, however, that substantial differences remain before those systems might be brought together on very basic rules of jurisdiction. As long as the goal was a comprehensive convention, covering all aspects of jurisdiction in all civil matters not yet excluded from scope by the rules of Article 1 of the *Interim Text*, it was clear that those differences were unlikely to be narrowed sufficiently to have a successful convention.

This did not prevent a change in focus to a convention that nonetheless is likely to have significant practical effect. Current U.S. law demonstrates that the *2005 Hague Convention on Choice of Court Agreements* can add significant predictability in U.S. courts. It can also facilitate improved planning opportunities for parties entering into contracts with U.S. enterprises when those contracts contain choice of court agreements. Thus the adjustment in focus from a comprehensive treaty on all aspects of jurisdiction and recognition of foreign judgments was a very logical one.

IV. The 2005 Hague Convention on Choice of Court Agreements

The *2005 Hague Convention on Choice of Court Agreements* was concluded on June 30, 2005.[85] It consists of 34 articles, divided into five chapters. Chapter I (Articles 1–4) deals with scope and definitions; Chapter II (Articles 5–7) with jurisdiction; Chapter III (Articles 8–15) with recognition and enforcement; Chapter IV (Articles 16–26) with the general clauses of application and

---

[85] Convention on Choice of Court Agreements, Hague Conference on Private International Law, Final Act of the Twentieth Session 2 (2005). The Convention text is reproduced as an Appendix in this volume.

interpretation; and Chapter V (Articles 27–34) with the final clauses providing for ratification, acceptance, approval, and required notifications.

If successfully implemented, the *2005 Hague Convention* should have an effect on litigation similar to that of the *1958 New York Arbitration Convention*.[86] It will provide greater certainty that a choice of court clause will be honored and that any resulting judgment will be recognized and enforced. It does this through three basic rules:

1) Article 5 requires that the court chosen by the parties shall hear the dispute;[87]

2) Article 7 requires that any other court decline to hear the dispute;[88] and

3) Article 9 requires that other courts recognize and enforce the resulting judgment.[89]

Each of these articles contains limited grounds for avoiding the required response, but the structure is basically a simple one. Article 22 adds an optional fourth basic rule by allowing declaration into a regime in which states will also recognize and enforce judgments based on non-exclusive choice of court agreements.[90]

The doctrine of forum non conveniens will be affected by several provisions of the *2005 Hague Convention on Choice of Court Agreements*. It will arise in the context of the Convention only when there is a choice of court agreement between the parties, bringing the Article 3 definition of an exclusive choice of court agreement into the analysis. Paragraph (a) of this article sets out the basic definition, which states that,

---

[86] United Nations Convention on the Recognition and Enforcement of Foreign Arbitral Awards, done at New York, June 10, 1958, 21 U.S.T. 2517, T.I.A.S. No. 6997, 330 U.N.T.S. 38.

[87] Choice of Court Convention, art. 5 ("The court or courts of a Contracting State designated in an exclusive choice of court agreement shall have jurisdiction to decide a dispute to which the agreement applies").

[88] Choice of Court Convention, art. 7 ("If the parties have entered into an exclusive choice of court agreement, any court in a Contracting State other than that of the chosen court shall suspend or dismiss the proceedings").

[89] Choice of Court Convention, art. 9 ("A judgment given by a court of a Contracting State designated in an exclusive choice of court agreement shall be recognised and enforced in other Contracting States in accordance with this Chapter").

[90] For a concise introduction to the Choice of Court Convention, see Ronald A. Brand, *Introductory Note to the 2005 Hague Convention on Choice of Court Agreements*, 44 INT'L LEGAL MATERIALS 1291 (2005).

"[E]xclusive choice of court agreement" means an agreement concluded by two or more parties that meets the requirements of paragraph c) and designates, for the purpose of deciding disputes which have arisen or may arise in connection with a particular legal relationship, the courts of one Contracting State or one or more specific courts of one Contracting State to the exclusion of the jurisdiction of any other courts.

Greater predictability is provided in paragraph (b) of Article 3, which creates a presumption that a choice of court agreement is exclusive:

[A] choice of court agreement which designates the courts of one Contracting State or one or more specific courts of one Contracting State shall be deemed to be exclusive unless the parties have expressly provided otherwise.

Article 3 thus reverses the general common law rule in the United States that a choice of court agreement will be presumed to be non-exclusive.[91] The result will be greater predictability for the parties, and a clear allocation of the burden on the party seeking a non-exclusive choice to draft explicitly for that result. It will also make more likely a *Bremen* analysis focused on the choice of court, without reference to the doctrine of forum non conveniens to resolve a conflict between the choice of court agreement and a claim of forum non conveniens.[92]

The issue of conflict between a choice of court agreement and the doctrine of forum non conveniens generally will not arise, however, because of the additional rule contained in Article 5(2). That paragraph states that:

A court that has jurisdiction [by designation in a choice of court agreement] shall not decline to exercise jurisdiction on the ground that the dispute should be decided in a court of another State.

This provision is specifically intended to prevent the use of the forum non conveniens doctrine to frustrate litigation in the chosen court.

A court not chosen by the parties also generally will not be able to resort to the doctrine of forum non conveniens in dealing with a case involving an exclusive

---

91 *See* Part II.B.2., above.
92 *See* Part II.B., above.

choice of court agreement. Article 6 sets forth the general rule that such a court must defer to the chosen court by suspending or dismissing proceedings. The limited (and exclusive) exceptions do not include a forum non conveniens ground as that doctrine would generally be stated.[93]

Nor is a party allowed to bring forum non conveniens back into the analysis in a court faced with the question of recognition and enforcement of the resulting judgment. Article 9 provides the very limited bases for refusal of recognition and enforcement of a judgment based on a choice of court agreement. While these include recognition and enforcement that "would be manifestly incompatible with the public policy of the requested State," that is a threshold not likely to be met by application of a forum non conveniens analysis.

V. Conclusion

Any reasonable international litigation system should provide results that are predictable enough to allow parties to plan their relationships and to project likely outcomes when disputes arise. At the same time, that system should facilitate the resolution of disputes in a manner that is fair and equitable for all who are involved. Traditional civil law concepts of lis pendens favor a demand for certainty by giving priority to the court first seised. But this approach can result in a heightening of tensions between disputants by encouraging a race to the courthouse and allowing a case to proceed in a forum that is not the natural forum for the dispute. The common law development of the doctrine of forum non conveniens, on the other hand, seeks litigation in the proper forum, but at the risk of extra litigation over which forum is the most appropriate, and the possibility of displacement of the plaintiff's forum choice with another court—or even the failure of the plaintiff to pursue litigation in the second forum, resulting in the termination of the case on

---

[93] Under Article 6 the court not chosen must suspend or dismiss the proceedings "unless—

    a)   the agreement is null and void under the law of the State of the chosen court;

    b)   a party lacked the capacity to conclude the agreement under the law of the State of the court seised;

    c)   giving effect to the agreement would lead to a manifest injustice or would be manifestly contrary to fundamental principles of public policy of the State of the court seised;

    d)   for exceptional reasons beyond the control of the parties, the agreement cannot reasonably be performed; or

    e)   the chosen court has decided not to hear the case.

procedural grounds. Both systems pursue legitimate goals, but neither provides a perfect combination of predictability, efficiency, and equity in all circumstances.

The survey of common law approaches provided in this book demonstrates that, while variations exist in the way the forum non conveniens doctrine is applied, there is a common purpose behind the doctrine and general agreement on the need to prevent injustice by seeking the most appropriate forum in which to resolve a transnational dispute. While Australian cases demonstrate a tendency to stay with the traditional high threshold that requires a defendant to prove that the plaintiff's chosen forum is clearly inappropriate in order to obtain relief, the United Kingdom, the United States, and Canada all have moved to a lower threshold, with a focus on finding the most appropriate forum. Despite the continued use of the Latin term, in no country does the test focus simply on convenience for the parties or for the court. Rather, the focus most often is on a balancing of private interest factors, with the United States alone in its consideration of public interest factors in determining the most appropriate forum.

The negotiations at the Hague Conference on Private International Law did not result in a comprehensive global convention on jurisdiction and the recognition and enforcement of judgments. Nonetheless, those negotiations demonstrated common ground between the traditional civil law preference for a predictable "first to file" approach focused on the doctrine of lis alibi pendens and the common law predilection for discretionary equitable results found in the doctrine of forum non conveniens. Articles 21 and 22 of the 1999 and 2001 negotiating texts provide much that is worth revisiting whenever the attempt at common ground is resurrected.

In the meantime, the *2005 Hague Convention on Choice of Court Agreements* represents a valuable contribution to the development of the law regarding party autonomy in international commercial contracts. By creating rules favoring the enforcement of freely negotiated choice of court agreements and of the resulting judgments, the *2005 Hague Convention* offers a counterpart to the *1958 New York Arbitration Convention* that will make choice of forum in international contracts a more balanced process. Moreover, the *2005 Hague Convention* promises to clarify U.S. law on choice of court by providing a presumption of exclusivity that will reduce uncertainty in existing case law and by clarifying the intersection between the law on choice of court agreements and the law of forum non conveniens. This will result in greater predictability both for business parties entering a transaction and for those involved in litigating any resulting disputes. The result is a substantial step forward in global rules applicable to potential parallel proceedings.

Appendix A

1999 Hague Preliminary Draft Convention Text for a Convention on Jurisdiction and Enforcement of Judgments in Civil and Commercial Matters

HAGUE CONFERENCE ON PRIVATE
INTERNATIONAL LAW

PRELIMINARY DRAFT CONVENTION ON JURISDICTION
AND FOREIGN JUDGMENTS IN CIVIL AND COMMERCIAL MATTERS
adopted by the Special Commission on 30 October 1999
amended version (new numbering of articles)

Chapter I—Scope of the Convention

Article 1   Substantive scope

1. The Convention applies to civil and commercial matters. It shall not extend in particular to revenue, customs or administrative matters.

2. The Convention does not apply to—

    a) the status and legal capacity of natural persons;

    b) maintenance obligations;

    c) matrimonial property regimes and other rights and obligations arising out of marriage or similar relationships;

    d) wills and succession;

    e) insolvency, composition or analogous proceedings;

    f) social security;

    g) arbitration and proceedings related thereto;

    h) admiralty or maritime matters.

3.   A dispute is not excluded from the scope of the Convention by the mere fact that a government, a governmental agency or any other person acting for the State is a party thereto.

4.   Nothing in this Convention affects the privileges and immunities of sovereign States or of entities of sovereign States, or of international organisations.

Article 2   *Territorial scope*

1.   The provisions of Chapter II shall apply in the courts of a Contracting State unless all the parties are habitually resident in that State. However, even if all the parties are habitually resident in that State—

    a) Article 4 shall apply if they have agreed that a court or courts of another Contracting State have jurisdiction to determine the dispute;

    b) Article 12, regarding exclusive jurisdiction, shall apply;

    c) Articles 21 and 22 shall apply where the court is required to determine whether to decline jurisdiction or suspend its proceedings on the grounds that the dispute ought to be determined in the courts of another Contracting State.

2.   The provisions of Chapter III apply to the recognition and enforcement in a Contracting State of a judgment rendered in another Contracting State.

Chapter II—Jurisdiction

Article 3   Defendant's forum

1. Subject to the provisions of the Convention, a defendant may be sued in the courts of the State where that defendant is habitually resident.

2. For the purposes of the Convention, an entity or person other than a natural person shall be considered to be habitually resident in the State—

   a) where it has its statutory seat,

   b) under whose law it was incorporated or formed,

   c) where it has its central administration, or

   d) where it has its principal place of business.

Article 4   Choice of court

1. If the parties have agreed that a court or courts of a Contracting State shall have jurisdiction to settle any dispute which has arisen or may arise in connection with a particular legal relationship, that court or those courts shall have jurisdiction, and that jurisdiction shall be exclusive unless the parties have agreed otherwise. Where an agreement having exclusive effect designates a court or courts of a non-Contracting State, courts in Contracting States shall decline jurisdiction or suspend proceedings unless the court or courts chosen have themselves declined jurisdiction.

2. An agreement within the meaning of paragraph 1 shall be valid as to form, if it was entered into or confirmed—

   a) in writing;

   b) by any other means of communication which renders information accessible so as to be usable for subsequent reference;

c) in accordance with a usage which is regularly observed by the parties;

d) in accordance with a usage of which the parties were or ought to have been aware and which is regularly observed by parties to contracts of the same nature in the particular trade or commerce concerned.

3. Agreements conferring jurisdiction and similar clauses in trust instruments shall be without effect if they conflict with the provisions of Article 7, 8 or 12.

Article 5   *Appearance by the defendant*

1. Subject to Article 12, a court has jurisdiction if the defendant proceeds on the merits without contesting jurisdiction.

2. The defendant has the right to contest jurisdiction no later than at the time of the first defence on the merits.

Article 6   *Contracts*

A plaintiff may bring an action in contract in the courts of a State in which—

a) in matters relating to the supply of goods, the goods were supplied in whole or in part;

b) in matters relating to the provision of services, the services were provided in whole or in part;

c) in matters relating both to the supply of goods and the provision of services, performance of the principal obligation took place in whole or in part.

Article 7   *Contracts concluded by consumers*

1. A plaintiff who concluded a contract for a purpose which is outside its trade or profession, hereafter designated as the consumer, may bring a claim in the courts of the State in which it is habitually resident, if

a) the conclusion of the contract on which the claim is based is related to trade or professional activities that the defendant has engaged in or directed to that State, in particular in soliciting business through means of publicity, and

b) the consumer has taken the steps necessary for the conclusion of the contract in that State.

2. A claim against the consumer may only be brought by a person who entered into the contract in the course of its trade or profession before the courts of the State of the habitual residence of the consumer.

3. The parties to a contract within the meaning of paragraph 1 may, by an agreement which conforms with the requirements of Article 4, make a choice of court—

a) if such agreement is entered into after the dispute has arisen, or

b) to the extent only that it allows the consumer to bring proceedings in another court.

Article 8   *Individual contracts of employment*

1. In matters relating to individual contracts of employment—

a) an employee may bring an action against the employer,

   i) in the courts of the State in which the employee habitually carries out his work or in the courts of the last State in which he did so, or

   ii) if the employee does not or did not habitually carry out his work in any one State, in the courts of the State in which the business that engaged the employee is or was situated;

b) a claim against an employee may be brought by the employer only,

   i) in the courts of the State where the employee is habitually resident, or

ii) in the courts of the State in which the employee habitually carries out his work.

2.   The parties to a contract within the meaning of paragraph 1 may, by an agreement which conforms with the requirements of Article 4, make a choice of court—

a)   if such agreement is entered into after the dispute has arisen, or

b)   to the extent only that it allows the employee to bring proceedings in courts other than those indicated in this Article or in Article 3 of the Convention.

Article 9   Branches [and regular commercial activity]

A plaintiff may bring an action in the courts of a State in which a branch, agency or any other establishment of the defendant is situated, [or where the defendant has carried on regular commercial activity by other means,] provided that the dispute relates directly to the activity of that branch, agency or establishment [or to that regular commercial activity].

Article 10   Torts or delicts

1.   A plaintiff may bring an action in tort or delict in the courts of the State—

a)   in which the act or omission that caused injury occurred, or

b)   in which the injury arose, unless the defendant establishes that the person claimed to be responsible could not reasonably have foreseen that the act or omission could result in an injury of the same nature in that State.

2.   Paragraph 1 b) shall not apply to injury caused by anti-trust violations, in particular price-fixing or monopolisation, or conspiracy to inflict economic loss.

3.   A plaintiff may also bring an action in accordance with paragraph 1 when the act or omission, or the injury may occur.

4. If an action is brought in the courts of a State only on the basis that the injury arose or may occur there, those courts shall have jurisdiction only in respect of the injury that occurred or may occur in that State, unless the injured person has his or her habitual residence in that State.

Article 11   Trusts

1. In proceedings concerning the validity, construction, effects, administration or variation of a trust created voluntarily and evidenced in writing, the courts of a Contracting State designated in the trust instrument for this purpose shall have exclusive jurisdiction. Where the trust instrument designates a court or courts of a non-Contracting State, courts in Contracting States shall decline jurisdiction or suspend proceedings unless the court or courts chosen have themselves declined jurisdiction.

2. In the absence of such designation, proceedings may be brought before the courts of a State—

    a) in which is situated the principal place of administration of the trust;

    b) whose law is applicable to the trust;

    c) with which the trust has the closest connection for the purpose of the proceedings.

Article 12   Exclusive jurisdiction

1. In proceedings which have as their object rights *in rem* in immovable property or tenancies of immovable property, the courts of the Contracting State in which the property is situated have exclusive jurisdiction, unless in proceedings which have as their object tenancies of immovable property, the tenant is habitually resident in a different State.

2. In proceedings which have as their object the validity, nullity, or dissolution of a legal person, or the validity or nullity of the decisions of its organs, the courts of a Contracting State whose law governs the legal person have exclusive jurisdiction.

3. In proceedings which have as their object the validity or nullity of entries in public registers, the courts of the Contracting State in which the register is kept have exclusive jurisdiction.

4. In proceedings which have as their object the registration, validity, [or] nullity[, or revocation or infringement,] of patents, trade marks, designs or other similar rights required to be deposited or registered, the courts of the Contracting State in which the deposit or registration has been applied for, has taken place or, under the terms of an international convention, is deemed to have taken place, have exclusive jurisdiction. This shall not apply to copyright or any neighbouring rights, even though registration or deposit of such rights is possible.

[5. In relation to proceedings which have as their object the infringement of patents, the preceding paragraph does not exclude the jurisdiction of any other court under the Convention or under the national law of a Contracting State.]

[6. The previous paragraphs shall not apply when the matters referred to therein arise as incidental questions.]

Article 13   *Provisional and protective measures*

1. A court having jurisdiction under Articles 3 to 12 to determine the merits of the case has jurisdiction to order any provisional or protective measures.

2. The courts of a State in which property is located have jurisdiction to order any provisional or protective measures in respect of that property.

3. A court of a Contracting State not having jurisdiction under paragraphs 1 or 2 may order provisional or protective measures, provided that—

   a) their enforcement is limited to the territory of that State, and

   b) their purpose is to protect on an interim basis a claim on the merits which is pending or to be brought by the requesting party.

Article 14   Multiple defendants

1. A plaintiff bringing an action against a defendant in a court of the State in which that defendant is habitually resident may also proceed in that court against other defendants not habitually resident in that State if—

    a) the claims against the defendant habitually resident in that State and the other defendants are so closely connected that they should be adjudicated together to avoid a serious risk of inconsistent judgments, and

    b) as to each defendant not habitually resident in that State, there is a substantial connection between that State and the dispute involving that defendant.

2. Paragraph 1 shall not apply to a codefendant invoking an exclusive choice of court clause agreed with the plaintiff and conforming with Article 4.

Article 15   Counter-claims

A court which has jurisdiction to determine a claim under the provisions of the Convention shall also have jurisdiction to determine a counter-claim arising out of the transaction or occurrence on which the original claim is based.

Article 16   Third party claims

1. A court which has jurisdiction to determine a claim under the provisions of the Convention shall also have jurisdiction to determine a claim by a defendant against a third party for indemnity or contribution in respect of the claim against that defendant to the extent that such an action is permitted by national law, provided that there is a substantial connection between that State and the dispute involving that third party.

2. Paragraph 1 shall not apply to a third party invoking an exclusive choice of court clause agreed with the defendant and conforming with Article 4.

Article 17   *Jurisdiction based on national law*

Subject to Articles 4, 5, 7, 8, 12 and 13, the Convention does not prevent the application by Contracting States of rules of jurisdiction under national law, provided that this is not prohibited under Article 18.

Article 18   *Prohibited grounds of jurisdiction*

1. Where the defendant is habitually resident in a Contracting State, the application of a rule of jurisdiction provided for under the national law of a Contracting State is prohibited if there is no substantial connection between that State and the dispute.

2. In particular, jurisdiction shall not be exercised by the courts of a Contracting State on the basis solely of one or more of the following—

    a) the presence or the seizure in that State of property belonging to the defendant, except where the dispute is directly related to that property;

    b) the nationality of the plaintiff;

    c) the nationality of the defendant;

    d) the domicile, habitual or temporary residence, or presence of the plaintiff in that State;

    e) the carrying on of commercial or other activities by the defendant in that State, except where the dispute is directly related to those activities;

    f) the service of a writ upon the defendant in that State;

    g) the unilateral designation of the forum by the plaintiff;

    h) proceedings in that State for declaration of enforceability or registration or for the enforcement of a judgment, except where the dispute is directly related to such proceedings;

    i) the temporary residence or presence of the defendant in that State;

    j) the signing in that State of the contract from which the dispute arises.

3. Nothing in this Article shall prevent a court in a Contracting State from exercising jurisdiction under national law in an action [seeking relief] [claiming damages] in respect of conduct which constitutes—

[**Variant One:**

    [*a*) genocide, a crime against humanity or a war crime[, as defined in the Statute of the International Criminal Court]; or]

    [*b*) a serious crime against a natural person under international law; or]

    [*c*) a grave violation against a natural person of non-derogable fundamental rights established under international law, such as torture, slavery, forced labour and disappeared persons].

[Sub-paragraphs [*b*) and] *c*) above apply only if the party seeking relief is exposed to a risk of a denial of justice because proceedings in another State are not possible or cannot reasonably be required.]

Variant Two:

a serious crime under international law, provided that this State has established its criminal jurisdiction over that crime in accordance with an international treaty to which it is a party and that the claim is for civil compensatory damages for death or serious bodily injury arising from that crime.]

Article 19   Authority of the court seised

Where the defendant does not enter an appearance, the court shall verify whether Article 18 prohibits it from exercising jurisdiction if—

    a) national law so requires; or

    b) the plaintiff so requests; or

    [*c*) the defendant so requests, even after judgment is entered in accordance with procedures established under national law; or] [*d*) the document which instituted the proceedings or an equivalent document was served on the defendant in another Contracting State.] or

[*e*) it appears from the documents filed by the plaintiff that the defendant's address is in another Contracting State.]

Article 20

1. The court shall stay the proceedings so long as it is not established that the document which instituted the proceedings or an equivalent document, including the essential elements of the claim, was notified to the defendant in sufficient time and in such a way as to enable him to arrange for his defence, or that all necessary steps have been taken to that effect.

[2. Paragraph 1 shall not affect the use of international instruments concerning the service abroad of judicial and extrajudicial documents in civil or commercial matters, in accordance with the law of the forum.]

[3. Paragraph 1 shall not apply, in case of urgency, to any provisional or protective measures.]

Article 21   Lis pendens

1. When the same parties are engaged in proceedings in courts of different Contracting States and when such proceedings are based on the same causes of action, irrespective of the relief sought, the court second seised shall suspend the proceedings if the court first seised has jurisdiction and is expected to render a judgment capable of being recognised under the Convention in the State of the court second seised, unless the latter has exclusive jurisdiction under Article 4 or 12.

2. The court second seised shall decline jurisdiction as soon as it is presented with a judgment rendered by the court first seised that complies with the requirements for recognition or enforcement under the Convention.

3. Upon application of a party, the court second seised may proceed with the case if the plaintiff in the court first seised has failed to take the necessary

steps to bring the proceedings to a decision on the merits or if that court has not rendered such a decision within a reasonable time.

4. The provisions of the preceding paragraphs apply to the court second seised even in a case where the jurisdiction of that court is based on the national law of that State in accordance with Article 17.

5. For the purpose of this Article, a court shall be deemed to be seised—

    a) when the document instituting the proceedings or an equivalent document is lodged with the court, or

    b) if such document has to be served before being lodged with the court, when it is received by the authority responsible for service or served on the defendant.

[As appropriate, universal time is applicable.]

6. If in the action before the court first seised the plaintiff seeks a determination that it has no obligation to the defendant, and if an action seeking substantive relief is brought in the court second seised—

    a) the provisions of paragraphs 1 to 5 above shall not apply to the court second seised, and

    b) the court first seised shall suspend the proceedings at the request of a party if the court second seised is expected to render a decision capable of being recognised under the Convention.

7. This Article shall not apply if the court first seised, on application by a party, determines that the court second seised is clearly more appropriate to resolve the dispute, under the conditions specified in Article 22.

Article 22   Exceptional circumstances
for declining jurisdiction

1. In exceptional circumstances, when the jurisdiction of the court seised is not founded on an exclusive choice of court agreement valid under Article 4, or

on Article 7, 8 or 12, the court may, on application by a party, suspend its proceedings if in that case it is clearly inappropriate for that court to exercise jurisdiction and if a court of another State has jurisdiction and is clearly more appropriate to resolve the dispute. Such application must be made no later than at the time of the first defence on the merits.

2. The court shall take into account, in particular—

   a) any inconvenience to the parties in view of their habitual residence;

   b) the nature and location of the evidence, including documents and witnesses, and the procedures for obtaining such evidence;

   c) applicable limitation or prescription periods;

   d) the possibility of obtaining recognition and enforcement of any decision on the merits.

3. In deciding whether to suspend the proceedings, a court shall not discriminate on the basis of the nationality or habitual residence of the parties.

4. If the court decides to suspend its proceedings under paragraph 1, it may order the defendant to provide security sufficient to satisfy any decision of the other court on the merits. However, it shall make such an order if the other court has jurisdiction only under Article 17, unless the defendant establishes that sufficient assets exist in the State of that other court or in another State where the court's decision could be enforced.

5. When the court has suspended its proceedings under paragraph 1,

   a) it shall decline to exercise jurisdiction if the court of the other State exercises jurisdiction, or if the plaintiff does not bring the proceedings in that State within the time specified by the court, or

   b) it shall proceed with the case if the court of the other State decides not to exercise jurisdiction.

Chapter III—Recognition and Enforcement

Article 23   Definition of "judgment"

For the purposes of this Chapter, "judgment" means—

a) any decision given by a court, whatever it may be called, including a decree or order, as well as the determination of costs or expenses by an officer of the court, provided that it relates to a decision which may be recognised or enforced under the Convention;

b) decisions ordering provisional or protective measures in accordance with Article 13, paragraph 1.

Article 24   Judgments excluded from Chapter III

This Chapter shall not apply to judgments based on a ground of jurisdiction provided for by national law in accordance with Article 17.

Article 25   Judgments to be recognised or enforced

1. A judgment based on a ground of jurisdiction provided for in Articles 3 to 13, or which is consistent with any such ground, shall be recognised or enforced under this Chapter.

2. In order to be recognised, a judgment referred to in paragraph 1 must have the effect of res judicata in the State of origin.

3. In order to be enforceable, a judgment referred to in paragraph 1 must be enforceable in the State of origin.

4. However, recognition or enforcement may be postponed if the judgment is the subject of review in the State of origin or if the time limit for seeking a review has not expired.

Article 26 Judgments not to be recognised or enforced

A judgment based on a ground of jurisdiction which conflicts with Articles 4, 5, 7, 8 or 12, or whose application is prohibited by virtue of Article 18, shall not be recognised or enforced.

Article 27 Verification of jurisdiction

1. The court addressed shall verify the jurisdiction of the court of origin.

2. In verifying the jurisdiction of the court of origin, the court addressed shall be bound by the findings of fact on which the court of origin based its jurisdiction, unless the judgment was given by default.

3. Recognition or enforcement of a judgment may not be refused on the ground that the court addressed considers that the court of origin should have declined jurisdiction in accordance with Article 22.

Article 28 Grounds for refusal of recognition or enforcement

1. Recognition or enforcement of a judgment may be refused if—

    a) proceedings between the same parties and having the same subject matter are pending before a court of the State addressed, if first seised in accordance with Article 21;

    b) the judgment is inconsistent with a judgment rendered, either in the State addressed or in another State, provided that in the latter case the judgment is capable of being recognised or enforced in the State addressed;

    c) the judgment results from proceedings incompatible with fundamental principles of procedure of the State addressed, including the right of each party to be heard by an impartial and independent court;

    d) the document which instituted the proceedings or an equivalent document, including the essential elements of the claim, was not notified to the defendant in sufficient time and in such a way as to enable him to arrange for his defence;

e) the judgment was obtained by fraud in connection with a matter of procedure;

f) recognition or enforcement would be manifestly incompatible with the public policy of the State addressed.

2. Without prejudice to such review as is necessary for the purpose of application of the provisions of this Chapter, there shall be no review of the merits of the judgment rendered by the court of origin.

Article 29   Documents to be produced

1. The party seeking recognition or applying for enforcement shall produce—

   a) a complete and certified copy of the judgment;

   b) if the judgment was rendered by default, the original or a certified copy of a document establishing that the document which instituted the proceedings or an equivalent document was notified to the defaulting party;

   c) all documents required to establish that the judgment is *res judicata* in the State of origin or, as the case may be, is enforceable in that State;

   d) if the court addressed so requires, a translation of the documents referred to above, made by a person qualified to do so.

2. No legalisation or similar formality may be required.

3. If the terms of the judgment do not permit the court addressed to verify whether the conditions of this Chapter have been complied with, that court may require the production of any other necessary documents.

Article 30   Procedure

The procedure for recognition, declaration of enforceability or registration for enforcement, and the enforcement of the judgment, are governed by the law of the State addressed so far as the Convention does not provide otherwise. The court addressed shall act expeditiously.

Article 31   Costs of proceedings

No security, bond or deposit, however described, to guarantee the payment of costs or expenses shall be required by reason only that the applicant is a national of, or has its habitual residence in, another Contracting State.

Article 32   Legal aid

Natural persons habitually resident in a Contracting State shall be entitled, in proceedings for recognition or enforcement, to legal aid under the same conditions as apply to persons habitually resident in the requested State.

Article 33   Damages

1. In so far as a judgment awards non-compensatory, including exemplary or punitive, damages, it shall be recognised at least to the extent that similar or comparable damages could have been awarded in the State addressed.

2. *a)* Where the debtor, after proceedings in which the creditor has the opportunity to be heard, satisfies the court addressed that in the circumstances, including those existing in the State of origin, grossly excessive damages have been awarded, recognition may be limited to a lesser amount.

    b) In no event shall the court addressed recognise the judgment in an amount less than that which could have been awarded in the State addressed in the same circumstances, including those existing in the State of origin.

3. In applying paragraph 1 or 2, the court addressed shall take into account whether and to what extent the damages awarded by the court of origin serve to cover costs and expenses relating to the proceedings.

Article 34   Severability

If the judgment contains elements which are severable, one or more of them may be separately recognised, declared enforceable, registered for enforcement, or enforced.

Article 35   Authentic instruments

1. Each Contracting State may declare that it will enforce, subject to reciprocity, authentic instruments formally drawn up or registered and enforceable in another Contracting State.

2. The authentic instrument must have been authenticated by a public authority or a delegate of a public authority and the authentication must relate to both the signature and the content of the document.

[3. The provisions concerning recognition and enforcement provided for in this Chapter shall apply as appropriate.]

Article 36   Settlements

Settlements to which a court has given its authority shall be recognised, declared enforceable or registered for enforcement in the State addressed under the same conditions as judgments falling within the Convention, so far as those conditions apply to settlements.

Chapter IV—General Provisions

Article 37   Relationship with other conventions

[See annex]

Article 38   Uniform interpretation

1. In the interpretation of the Convention, regard is to be had to its international character and to the need to promote uniformity in its application.

2. The courts of each Contracting State shall, when applying and interpreting the Convention, take due account of the case law of other Contracting States.

[Article 39

1. Each Contracting State shall, at the request of the Secretary General of the Hague Conference on Private International Law, send to the Permanent Bureau at regular intervals copies of any significant decisions taken in applying the Convention and, as appropriate, other relevant information.

2. The Secretary General of the Hague Conference on Private International Law shall at regular intervals convene a Special Commission to review the operation of the Convention.

3. The Commission may make recommendations on the application or interpretation of the Convention and may propose modifications or revisions of the Convention or the addition of protocols.]

[Article 40

1. Upon a joint request of the parties to a dispute in which the interpretation of the Convention is at issue, or of a court of a Contracting State, the Permanent Bureau of the Hague Conference on Private International Law shall assist in the establishment of a committee of experts to make recommendations to such parties or such court.

[2. The Secretary General of the Hague Conference on Private International Law shall, as soon as possible, convene a Special Commission to draw up an optional protocol setting out rules governing the composition and procedures of the committee of experts.]]

Article 41   Federal clause

ANNEX

Article 37   Relationship with other conventions

Proposal 1

1. The Convention does not affect any international instrument to which Contracting States are or become Parties and which contains provisions on matters governed by the Convention, unless a contrary declaration is made by the States Parties to such instrument.

2. However, the Convention prevails over such instruments to the extent that they provide for fora not authorized under the provisions of Article 18 of the Convention.

3. The preceding paragraphs also apply to uniform laws based on special ties of a regional or other nature between the States concerned and to instruments adopted by a community of States.

Proposal 2

1. *a)* In this Article, the Brussels Convention [as amended], Regulation [. . .] of the European Union, and the Lugano Convention [as amended] shall be collectively referred to as "the European instruments".

    b) A State party to either of the above Conventions or a Member State of the European Union to which the above Regulation applies shall be collectively referred to as "European instrument States".

2. Subject to the following provisions [of this Article], a European instrument State shall apply the European instruments, and not the Convention, whenever the European instruments are applicable according to their terms.

3. Except where the provisions of the European instruments on—

 a) exclusive jurisdiction;

 b) prorogation of jurisdiction;

 c) *lis pendens* and related actions;

 d) protective jurisdiction for consumers or employees;

are applicable, a European instrument State shall apply Articles 3, 5 to 11, 14 to 16 and 18 of the Convention whenever the defendant is not domiciled in a European instrument State.

4. Even if the defendant is domiciled in a European instrument State, a court of such a State shall apply—

 a) Article 4 of the Convention whenever the court chosen is not in a European instrument State;

 b) Article 12 of the Convention whenever the court with exclusive jurisdiction under that provision is not in a European instrument State; and

 c) Articles 21 and 22 of this Convention whenever the court in whose favour the proceedings are stayed or jurisdiction is declined is not a court of a European instrument State.

<u>Note</u>: Another provision will be needed for other conventions and instruments.

Proposal 3

5. Judgments of courts of a Contracting State to this Convention based on jurisdiction granted under the terms of a different international convention ("other Convention") shall be recognised and enforced in courts of Contracting States to this Convention which are also Contracting States to the other Convention. This provision shall not apply if, by reservation under Article . . ., a Contracting State chooses—

 a) not to be governed by this provision, or

 b) not to be governed by this provision as to certain designated other conventions.

Appendix B

Relevant provisions of the Nygh/Pocar Report

REPORT OF THE SPECIAL COMMISSION
drawn up by Peter Nygh and Fausto Pocar

PRELIMINARY DOCUMENT No. 11

INTRODUCTION

On 19 October 1996, the States represented at the Eighteenth Session of the Hague Conference on Private International Law decided:

"... to include in the Agenda of the Nineteenth Session the question of jurisdiction, and recognition and enforcement of foreign judgments in civil and commercial matters".[1]

This decision was preceded by work done in the Conference in previous years, subsequent to a Decision by its Seventeenth Session to request the Secretary General to convene a Special Commission to study the problems raised by the preparation of a new Convention on the recognition and enforcement of judgments in civil and commercial matters, to replace the Convention of 1 February 1971 which had not been entirely successful.[2] The Special Commission held two meetings, on 20-24 June 1994 and 4-7 June 1996, at which it considered several

---

[1] *Final Act of the Eighteenth Session*, Part B, No. 1.

[2] The reasons are explained by KESSEDJIAN C., in International Jurisdiction and Foreign Judgments in Civil and Commercial Matters, *Prel. Doc. No. 7*, April 1997.

aspects of the subject[3] and proposed including it in the future programme of work of the Conference.

In accordance with the Decision of the Eighteenth Session of the Conference, the Permanent Bureau established a Special Commission which held five meetings: 17-27 June 1997, 3-13 March 1998, 10-20 November 1998, 7-18 June 1999 and 25-30 October 1999.

The Special Commission appointed as Chairman M.T. Bradbrooke Smith, Expert from Canada, as Vice-Chairmen Andreas Bucher, Expert from Switzerland, Masato Dogauchi, Expert from Japan, Jeffrey D. Kovar, Expert from the United States, José-Luis Siqueiros, Expert from Mexico; and as Co-Reporters Peter Nygh, Expert from Australia, and Fausto Pocar, Expert from Italy.

The work of the Special Commission was greatly facilitated by the following excellent Preliminary Documents, drawn up by Madame Catherine Kessedjian, Deputy Secretary General:

- International jurisdiction and foreign judgments in civil and commercial matters (*Prel. Doc. No. 7 of April 1997*)

- Synthesis of the work of the Special Commission of June 1997 on international jurisdiction and the effects of foreign judgments in civil and commercial matters (*Prel. Doc. No. 8 of November 1997*)

- Synthesis of the work of the Special Commission of March 1998 on international jurisdiction and the effects of foreign judgments in civil and commercial matters (*Prel. Doc. No. 9 of July 1998*)

- Note on provisional and protective measures in private international law and comparative law (*Prel. Doc. No. 10 of October 1998*).

---

[3] Conclusions of the Special Commission of June 1994 on the question of the recognition and enforcement of foreign judgments in civil and commercial matters, drawn up by the Permanent Bureau, *Prel. Doc. No. 1*, August 1994, *Proceedings of the Eighteenth Session (1996)*, Tome I, *Miscellaneous matters*, p. 62; Conclusions of the second meeting of the Special Commission on the question of the recognition and enforcement of foreign judgments in civil and commercial matters, drawn up by the Permanent Bureau, *Prel. Doc. No. 12*, August 1996, *Proceedings of the Eighteenth Session (1996)*, Tome I, *Miscellaneous matters*, p. 184.

This Report deals with the *preliminary draft Convention on Jurisdiction and Foreign Judgments in Civil and Commercial Matters*, which was adopted by the Special Commission at the end of its fifth meeting on 30 October 1999, and is to be submitted to the Diplomatic Conference (Nineteenth Session).

GENERAL FRAMEWORK AND NATURE OF THE CONVENTION

Traditionally, in drafting a Convention on the recognition and enforcement of judgments a decision has to be made whether the Convention should be framed as a "double Convention" or as a "single Convention". In a "double Convention" both the jurisdiction which the courts of Contracting States are permitted to exercise is regulated as well as the conditions upon which such judgments are to be recognised. If the list of required jurisdictions[4] is "closed", that is to say, exhaustive, parties can be assured that not only will all judgments rendered in the exercise of the required list of jurisdictions be recognised, subject to reservations based on public policy, due process and inconsistency of judgments, but that the exercise of jurisdiction on any other basis will not be recognised in other Contracting States. Such a Convention has the advantage of predictability and relative simplicity, but it requires a high degree of consensus on what the required grounds of jurisdiction ought to be. It also requires Contracting States to change their national laws relating to international jurisdiction in accordance with the provisions of the Convention. The obligations facing Contracting States can therefore be substantial.

For that reason, most international agreements and Conventions in this area are framed as "single Conventions". In a "single Convention" the jurisdiction of Contracting States is only dealt with indirectly, that is to say, as a condition for the recognition of judgments. Contracting States remain free to exercise jurisdiction on other grounds in accordance with their national laws which do not require any change. Such a Convention is rightly described as "imperfect", because it does not prevent the exercise of exorbitant grounds of jurisdiction which are as much a hindrance to international commerce as the uncertainty about recognition and enforcement of judgments. The *Hague Convention of 1 February 1971 on the*

---

[4] By "required jurisdiction", we mean jurisdictional grounds which Contracting States are obliged to provide to potential litigants.

Recognition and Enforcement of Foreign Judgments in Civil and Commercial Matters (the "1971 Judgments Convention") is essentially a "single Convention", even if in the Protocol attached thereto, recognition of judgments based on the exercise of certain listed "exorbitant jurisdictions" is prohibited.[5]

As between the Member States of the European Union the *Convention of 27 September 1968 on Jurisdiction and the Enforcement of Judgments in Civil and Commercial Matters* (the "Brussels Convention") is applicable. It is accompanied by the largely identical *Convention of 16 September 1988 on Jurisdiction and the Enforcement of Judgments in Civil and Commercial Matters* (the "Lugano Convention") which applies to the relationship between Member States of the European Union and certain contiguous States. Both Conventions are "double Conventions" which are "closed", at least in relation to persons domiciled in Contracting States.[6] Whatever jurisdiction is not on the required list is prohibited. The express prohibition of the exercise of certain jurisdictions in Article 3 of the Conventions serve an educational function only.

Another "double Convention", albeit one limited to a specialised area, is the Hague Convention on Jurisdiction, Applicable Law, Recognition, Enforcement and Co-operation in Respect of Parental Responsibility. Since it defines exhaustively the jurisdiction which authorities of Contracting States can exercise even as regards children habitually resident in non-Contracting States, it can be seen as a "closed Convention", without any margin of manoeuvre for States Parties.

The Working Group which met in October 1992 acknowledged that a "single" Convention on the pattern of the 1971 Judgments Convention would fall short of present day needs. It expressed a preference for "an approach in the direction of a 'double Convention' like the Brussels Convention of 1968". However, the Group felt that "a complete double Convention" of the Brussels type would be "overly ambitious". It therefore favoured a Convention "which would offer some of the advantages of a double Convention, while at the same time having a greater degree of flexibility than that available with a Convention of the Brussels/Lugano type".[7]

---

[5] See, Rapport explicatif de M. CH.N. FRAGISTAS, in *Acts and documents of the Extraordinary Session (1966)*, § 3 at p. 365.

[6] Since under Article 4 of both Conventions jurisdiction under national law (including "exorbitant jurisdiction") can be exercised in respect of persons domiciled outside Contracting States, the Conventions are not totally "closed".

[7] See, Conclusions of the Working Group meeting on enforcement of judgments, *Proceedings of the Seventeenth Session (1993)*, Tome I, *Miscellaneous matters—Centenary*, para. 4 at pp. 257–8.

Thus, a third possibility was created: the so-called "mixed Convention". This type of Convention follows the pattern of a "double Convention" in regulating the jurisdiction of the courts of Contracting States directly and not merely for the purposes of recognition. Any basis of jurisdiction which is on the list of required jurisdictions will suffice for recognition. But, unlike the "double Convention" it does not do so exhaustively: it allows the use of jurisdictions based on national law within certain limits. Any judgment based on a jurisdiction within this "grey zone" will not be entitled to recognition under the Convention, although it may be recognised under the national law of the State addressed. The limits of the "grey zone" are defined by a list of prohibited jurisdictions which may not be exercised by the courts of a contracting State, except possibly against those who are habitually resident outside the Contracting States, and on no account may judgments based on the exercise of prohibited jurisdiction in a contracting State be recognised in another contracting State. The list of prohibited jurisdictions is therefore an important part of a "mixed Convention".

The Special Commission has accepted the Working Group's conclusion that a "single Convention" would not be useful. At first, the Special Commission proceeded on the basis that a closed "double Convention" should be its goal, if that were possible. However, at its session in June 1999 the Commission decided that there should be some degree of flexibility permitted in the use of national law within limits. In consequence, Article 17 of the preliminary draft Convention completed by the Special Commission on 30 October 1999 permits the application of rules of jurisdiction under national law, subject to the rules relating to choice of court, protective jurisdiction, exclusive jurisdiction and the restrictions imposed on the exercise of jurisdiction to order protective and provisional measures, and provided that the exercise of jurisdiction is not prohibited by Article 18. Article 18(1) prohibits the exercise of jurisdiction in respect of a defendant who is habitually resident in a Contracting State if there is no substantial connection between that State and the dispute. Article 18(2) lists in a non-exhaustive manner certain bases for jurisdiction the exercise of which is prohibited. Article 24 excludes from recognition under Chapter III of the preliminary draft Convention judgments based on a ground of jurisdiction within the area of permitted national law, but does not exclude the possibility of recognition of such judgments under national law. Article 26 prohibits the recognition of judgments based on a ground of jurisdiction whose application is prohibited by Article 18 both pursuant to Chapter III and under national law.

There are therefore three kinds of jurisdiction under the preliminary draft Convention:

1   a list of required jurisdictions whose judgments are entitled to recognition and enforcement in other Contracting States subject to conditions of due process, public policy and the need to avoid inconsistent judgments;

2   a list of prohibited jurisdictions which may not be exercised and, if by any ill chance, a judgment is based upon any of them, such judgment shall not be recognised; and

3   an undefined area, not falling within 1 and 2 above, where jurisdiction pursuant to national law may be exercised and where recognition likewise depends on the national law of the State addressed.

It will be obvious from a reading of the provisions that to some extent the preliminary draft Convention has borrowed from the Brussels and Lugano Conventions, including the recent amendments made to those Conventions. In its turn the preparation of the Brussels Convention was greatly influenced by the work of the Hague Conference on Private International Law in drafting the 1971 Judgments Convention which was completed in 1966. The use of a list of prohibited jurisdictions which first appeared in Article 4 of the Protocol to what later became the 1971 Judgments Convention is a very good example of this useful process of cross-fertilisation. In some instances the Special Commission was mindful of the jurisprudence of the European Court of Justice in the interpretation of the Brussels Convention, either as indicating what the Commission wished to achieve or as indicating what the Commission wished to avoid. In like manner, consideration was paid to the jurisprudence of national courts both within and outside the European Union.

However, the preliminary draft Convention differs in several fundamental aspects from the Brussels and Lugano Conventions:

In the first place, as indicated earlier, the preliminary draft Convention is not a "closed double Convention", but leaves room for the application of jurisdictions under national law, even as between Contracting States.

Secondly, and this flows logically from the first point, there is provision made in respect of prohibited jurisdictions which is not merely educational in purpose, but represents a real restraint on the exercise of jurisdiction under national law.

Thirdly, as more fully explained in relation to Article 3 below, jurisdiction under the preliminary draft Convention does not proceed on the assumption that there exists a fundamental jurisdiction based on the domicile of the defendant with the result that all other jurisdictions must be seen as exceptions which must be narrowly interpreted. Instead the preliminary draft Convention proceeds on the basis that there is no hierarchy of jurisdictions.

Fourthly, it should be remembered throughout that the preliminary draft Convention is not designed for a group of contiguous States sharing similar social, economic and political objectives. It is intended as a worldwide Convention. This is reflected in important differences such as the need for a greater control by the court addressed over the exercise of jurisdiction in the court of origin. But it permeates the preliminary draft Convention in a general sense leading to a difference not only in terminology, but also in a more flexible approach. This is, for instance, illustrated in the greater flexibility permitted in Article 21 relating to *lis pendens* and the existence of a provision for declining jurisdiction in Article 22 which is lacking in the Brussels Convention even after its revision.

Finally, the preliminary draft Convention will not have the benefit of a uniform interpretation by a common court. Although it will contain provisions encouraging a uniform application, in the ultimate the highest national courts will be the arbiters of the Convention. Nor will the jurisprudence of the European Court of Justice be necessarily relevant, even where the provisions are similar. Reference will from time to time be made in this Report to decisions by the European Court of Justice and of other courts in order to illustrate the issues and problems the Special Commission had in mind. In that respect only may it sometimes be helpful to refer to those decisions as a matter of historical development of the preliminary draft Convention.

ARTICLE BY ARTICLE COMMENTARY ON THE CONVENTION

* * *

Article 21—Lis pendens

The preliminary draft Convention will offer the plaintiff a choice of fora. For instance, as an alternative to the specific jurisdictions in Articles 6 (contract) and 10 (tort), there will be a general jurisdiction based on Article 3. As regards corporate defendants, there may be four alternative fora available under the definition given in Article 3(2). It is obvious that this may lead in some cases to a conflict of jurisdictions and in others to situations where a defendant may be sued in an inappropriate forum. Both the civil law and the common law have developed mechanisms to deal with this problem. In the civil law the mechanism is that of *lis pendens* which is based on the priority of the first action commenced.[132] It has the advantage of certainty, but the disadvantage of rigidity. It also can be abused by a defendant taking pre-emptive action in seeking a so-called "negative declaration" as to its liability. In the common law the mechanism is that of *forum non conveniens* which prefers the "natural" or "more appropriate" forum which need not be the forum which was seised first. It has the advantage of flexibility and adaptability to the circumstances of each case, but it lacks certainty and predictability. Needless to say, each side looked with some suspicion at a system with which it was unfamiliar.

After long debate the Special Commission has adopted a compromise solution whereby provision is made for both *lis pendens* and for declining jurisdiction in certain circumstances. However, the *lis pendens* provision in Article 21 is made more flexible and priority is denied to the "negative declaration". In return the power to decline jurisdiction in Article 22 is subjected to stringent conditions which emphasise its exceptional character.

---

[132] For its history in French law, see GAUDEMET-TALLON H., La litispendence internationale dans la jurisprudence francaise, *Melanges D. Holleaux*, 1990, 121.

Paragraph 1

For a situation of *lis pendens* to arise, the following conditions must exist:

- There must be an identity of parties and of cause of action. The English term "cause of action" can be interpreted narrowly as referring to a particular cause of action such as trespass or negligence. The French version, however, is broader and speaks of "*la même cause et le même objet*" which does not refer to the procedural peculiarities of the common law, but to the underlying cause and object of the litigation. This is further clarified by the use of the words "irrespective of the relief sought". The result is that the words "cause of action" in the English text should be broadly interpreted as referring to the subject matter of the litigation, such a dispute arising out of a particular contract or incident, rather than to the particular form in which relief is sought. Thus, a claim by one party against the other for damages for breach of contract and a claim by the other party against the firstnamed that the contract in question was avoided for misrepresentation are based on the same cause of action.[133]

- The competing proceedings must lie in courts of different Contracting States. Obviously, a conflict of litigation in the same State will be dealt with by the internal law of that State. Similarly, a conflict of litigation between a Contracting and a non-Contracting State is a matter for the national law of the State concerned to resolve.

- The court first seised in order to gain priority must have a required jurisdiction under Chapter II. It need not specifically exercise that jurisdiction as such: it is possible that the action in the court first seised is between persons habitually resident there and thus outside Chapter II, but the jurisdiction it exercises must be consistent with a required ground under Chapter II which will obviously be the case when the defendant is habitually resident there.

- The court first seised must be expected to render a judgment which is capable of being recognised under Chapter III of the Convention.

---

[133]   Compare *Gubisch Maschinenfabrik v. Palumbo* (C 144/86) [1987] *ECR* 4861.

The decision must therefore fall within the definition of "judgment" in Article 23. A judgment given in the exercise of jurisdiction based on a required ground set out in Chapter II has that capacity by virtue of Article 25, provided it is capable of gaining the quality of *res judicata*. Thus no *lis pendens* can arise as between proceedings for provisional and protective measures brought in different States under Article 13. Judgments rendered in pursuance of Article 17 do not have the capacity of being recognised under Chapter III and hence proceedings based on a jurisdiction authorised by Article 17 do not have priority. But, by reason of Article 21(4), proceedings based on a jurisdiction authorised by Article 17 must give way to earlier proceedings based on a required jurisdiction. If both proceedings arise under Article 17 jurisdiction, the national law of the relevant court will be applied to resolve the issue.

- Finally, the court second seised must not have exclusive jurisdiction under Articles 4 or 12. If the court second seised has exclusive jurisdiction, the court first seised lacks jurisdiction and this is likely to be the case in relation to Article 11(1) even though that article is not specifically mentioned.

Once those conditions exist, the obligation on the court second seised to suspend proceedings arises even though no application is made to it to do so. In other words, the court second seised shall act, if need be, on its own motion.

Paragraph 2

If a situation of *lis pendens* is established, the court second seised is obliged to suspend proceedings in the first instance. It does not decline jurisdiction until it is presented with a judgment rendered by the court first seised that complies with the requirements for recognition or enforcement under Chapter III. It must therefore be a "judgment" as defined in Article 23 which meets the requirements set out in Article 25. These have been discussed in the preceding section. It is obvious that the judgment must be one on the merits of the dispute between the same parties as in the court second seised.

If the plaintiff fails to bring the proceedings in the court first seised to a conclusion on the merits or that court does not render a decision within a reasonable time, the court second seised may pursuant to Article 21(3) on the application of a party, decide to proceed with the case. What amounts to a reasonable time is not defined and will depend on the assessment of the court second seised.

Paragraph 3

The mere fact that another court was seised first does not deprive the court second seised of jurisdiction. The court second seised is only obliged to decline jurisdiction when it is presented with a judgment rendered by the court first seised that complies with the requirements for recognition or enforcement under Chapter III. In the meanwhile the exercise of its jurisdiction is merely suspended. Should the plaintiff fail to take the necessary steps to bring the proceedings to a decision in the court first seised or should that court fail to render a decision within a reasonable time, the court second seised may terminate the stay and proceed with the case.

Paragraph 4

As mentioned before, by reason of Article 21(4), proceedings based on a jurisdiction authorised by Article 17 must give way to earlier proceedings based on a required jurisdiction.

Paragraph 5

Paragraph 5 provides a common definition of the moment when a court shall be deemed to be seised. The absence of such a provision in Article 21 of the Brussels Convention, as originally drafted, led to the matter being referred to the national law of each court seised.[134] Unfortunately, even within the European Union, those laws differ: some regard a court to be seised only after the defendant has been served or after the necessary steps have been taken to notify the defendant; others regard a court as seised of a matter as soon as the initiating document has been filed in the court registry, or, where notification is required before filing, as soon as the documents are delivered to the person or authority responsible for service.[135] The former test favours the defendant in the first action who may be

---

[134] See, *Zelger v. Salanitri* [1984] *ECR* 2397.

[135] See, MØLLER G., The Date upon which a Finnish and a Swedish Court Becomes Seised for the Purposes of the European Judgments Convention, in *E Pluribus Unum: Liber Amicorum Georges A.L. Droz* (1996) at pp. 219–233.

able to take pre-emptive action as soon as it becomes aware of the filing of the writ. The second test favours the plaintiff in the first action who may be able to take the defendant by surprise.

The Special Commission has decided to adopt the second option: a court is to be regarded as seised once the initiating document is lodged with the court or, if it is required to be served before lodgment under the law applicable in that court at the time when that document is received by the authority responsible for service (such as the "*huissier*" or "court bailiff") or when it is actually served on the defendant.

The provision referring to "universal time" as the ultimate measure of priority remains in brackets for decision by the Diplomatic Conference. This is a system of time measurement based on Greenwich Mean Time but counted from 0 hour which is equivalent to midnight Greenwich Mean Time.

Paragraph 6

Paragraph 6 deals with the problem of the so-called "negative declaration" whereby a party to a dispute seeks a declaration that it has no obligation to the other party to the dispute. Although such a procedure is known to both the common law and the civil law and often serves a legitimate purpose, there is no doubt that the procedure has at times been used by a prospective defendant to pre-empt the choice of forum by a prospective plaintiff. As paragraph 1 is framed, a proceeding seeking a negative declaration if first instituted in time would prevail over a subsequent action commenced in another Contracting State seeking to enforce the substantive obligation.[136] The Special Commission wanted to avoid such an effect.

In the case of the first action being an action for a negative declaration and the action subsequent in time being one seeking substantive relief, the position provided for in paragraphs 1 to 5 is effectively reversed. It is the court first seised that must suspend the proceedings, if a party so requests, provided the court second seised is expected to render a decision capable of being recognised under Chapter III of the Convention. If no application to suspend proceedings is made to the court first seised or the court second seised is exercising jurisdiction under

---

[136] See, *The Tatry* [1994] *ECR* I–5431.

national law pursuant to Article 17, both actions can proceed since the obligation on the court second seised to suspend proceedings has been rendered inapplicable by sub-paragraph *a)*.

Paragraph 7

Paragraph 7 provides that the court first seised may, on the application of a party, decline jurisdiction in favour of the court second seised, if it determines that the latter court is clearly more appropriate to resolve the dispute. Although the paragraph starts with the words "This article shall not apply", it is in fact by virtue of this paragraph and not by virtue of Article 22 that the jurisdiction is declined in such a case. For that purpose the concluding words of paragraph 7 import the conditions specified in Article 22, in so far as they are relevant, in particular paragraphs 2 and 3 of Article 22. There is, however, one omission which may not have been intended. Article 22 does not contain a provision similar to Article 21(3) dealing with the situation where the plaintiff fails to proceed in the transferee court or that court delays proceedings unreasonably. Paragraph 7 excludes the application of any paragraph of Article 21, except presumably itself.

There are, however, some differences between the scope of Article 21(7) and Article 22. In the first place, the court first seised can only decline in favour of the court second seised and not in favour of a third court, even though that court might be even more appropriate. Secondly, since a *lis pendens* can only arise between courts of Contracting States, the second court must be that of a Contracting State. Thirdly, since there is no *lis pendens* situation to which Article 21 applies, if the court first seised is exercising jurisdiction pursuant to Article 17, paragraph 7 is inapplicable, although it may be open to the court first seised to decline jurisdiction under its national law. However, since Article 21 does apply to the reverse situation, a court first seised exercising a required jurisdiction could decline jurisdiction in favour of a court exercising jurisdiction under Article 17.

Article 22—Exceptional circumstances for declining jurisdiction

Under several legal systems it is possible for a court to decline a jurisdiction it might otherwise possess. This happens in common law countries under the doctrine of *forum non conveniens*, which term, however, does not have a uniform meaning in those countries.[137] Civil law systems, generally, do not know of the doctrine of *forum non conveniens*. But there are situations where a civil law court will, and sometimes must, decline jurisdiction by reason of an insufficient connection between the dispute and the forum.[138]

Article 22 provides that a court in a Contracting State may, in exceptional circumstances, decline required jurisdiction under Chapter II which it otherwise possesses. It cannot, however, decline jurisdiction if it arises under Articles 4, 7, 8 or 12. No mention is made of jurisdiction under national law which can be invoked under Article 17. On a literal interpretation, Article 17 by referring to "rules of jurisdiction under national law" does not include rules for declining jurisdiction under national law. On that approach a court exercising jurisdiction under Article 17 can only decline that jurisdiction if the conditions laid down in Article 22 apply. However, it could be argued to the contrary that the scheme of Chapter II, as indicated by Article 21(4), indicates that, unless national jurisdiction under Article 17 is specifically included, it stands outside the provisions of Articles 21 and 22. This point will require clarification at the Diplomatic Conference.

The provisions of Article 22 must not be confused, however, with the doctrine of *forum non conveniens* as it has operated in common law countries. Article 22 is a provision whereby the forum may defer its jurisdiction in favour of that of a court of another State, but, with one exception, only if that other court actually assumes jurisdiction. It must also be noted that Article 22 applies to all Contracting States. Earlier proposals whereby acceptance of the provision for declining jurisdiction would be optional were not accepted by the Special Commission.

However, the Special Commission accepted the proposition that jurisdiction can be declined in favour of a court of a non-Contracting State under the same conditions as apply to a Contracting State.

Paragraph 1

The paragraph commences by making it clear that the power to decline jurisdiction can only be exercised in exceptional circumstances. The normal rule is that the plaintiff is entitled to be heard in the forum which the plaintiff has selected

---

[137]   See, FAWCETT J.J., Declining Jurisdiction in Private International Law, *OUP* 1995, at pp. 14–16.

[138]   For a general overview, see FAWCETT, *op. cit.*, especially at pp. 24–27.

and which has required jurisdiction under Chapter II of the Convention. Before that basic rule can be departed from a number of conditions must be satisfied.

Firstly, the jurisdiction of the court must not be based on certain grounds. If the forum has been selected as the exclusive forum under a valid choice of jurisdiction clause pursuant to Article 4, it cannot decline to accept that jurisdiction as is currently possible under the laws of certain States.[139] Nor can a court which is asked to exercise jurisdiction by a plaintiff under the protective provisions of Articles 7 or 8 decline to do so. Finally, the exclusive jurisdictions under Article 12 by reason of the issues of public interest they seek to protect, cannot be declined. Although Article 5 is not specifically referred to, as a practical matter, a court which has jurisdiction by virtue of Article 5 based on the appearance of the defendant without contesting the jurisdiction must also accept that jurisdiction since by definition by the time the court gains jurisdiction under Article 5, the time for making a request to decline jurisdiction will have passed. No mention is made of the exclusive jurisdiction under Article 11(1) in relation to trusts and it may be possible for the selected court to decline jurisdiction in favour of a court of the State where the trusts are administered.

Secondly, the application that the court seised decline jurisdiction must be made by a party to the proceedings, almost always the defendant. The court cannot decline to exercise its jurisdiction on its own motion. The application must be made timely: not later than the time of the first defence on the merits. As to what is meant by that term, see the discussion in relation to Article 5, paragraph 2.

Thirdly the court must be satisfied that in the circumstances of that particular case:

1   it is clearly inappropriate for that court to exercise jurisdiction;

2   a court of another State has jurisdiction; and

3   that court is clearly more appropriate to resolve the dispute.

Each of these three conditions must be fulfilled. The Convention does not address the question of onus, but it would be logical for the party requesting that the court

---

[139]   See, FAWCETT, *op. cit.* at pp. 57–58.

decline jurisdiction to bring forward the facts and reasons for such a decision. The three conditions must also be looked at separately. Thus, the fact that another forum may be "clearly more appropriate" does not necessarily mean that the forum seised is itself "clearly inappropriate". For example, a plaintiff may bring suit against a corporate defendant at its principal place of business in respect of injuries the plaintiff received while employed by that corporation in another country where the plaintiff was resident and was hired. It may be that the second country is the "clearly more appropriate" forum, but, if the major decisions, including those affecting safety of employees throughout its operations, were made at the principal place of business, it cannot be said that this place is a "clearly inappropriate" forum.[140] On the other hand, if the only connection with the forum seised is the incorporation of the company within the jurisdiction, but the principal place of business as well as the residence of the plaintiffs and the subject matter of the dispute are all more closely connected with another country, it could be said that the forum seised is clearly inappropriate and the other forum clearly more appropriate.[141] In each case it will depend on the facts and circumstances of the case. Finally, as the words "may" and "peut" indicate, the power is discretionary. Even if the conditions are satisfied, the court originally seised is not obliged to decline jurisdiction.

The court seised must also be satisfied that a court of another State has jurisdiction. That jurisdiction must exist not only as regards the parties but also with respect to the subject matter of the dispute. It cannot be said that the alternative court has jurisdiction if the claim raised by the plaintiff is unknown to its law and it cannot grant relief in respect of it. Since the other State need not be a Contracting State, it follows, a fortiori, that the other court may be a court of another Contracting State having jurisdiction by reference to its national law pursuant to Article 17. This conclusion is re-enforced by the second sentence in Article 22(4) which requires the defendant to lodge security if the alternative court's jurisdiction arises from Article 17. However, as indicated by Article 22(2)(d), the question of obtaining recognition and enforcement of any decision on the merits is an important factor. This makes it at least desirable that the alternative court have required jurisdiction under Chapter II, unless adequate security can be obtained under Article 22(4). It is, of course, open to a defendant voluntarily to confer

---

[140] The example is based on the facts of the United Kingdom case of *Connelly v. RTZ Corp. Plc* [1997] 3 *WLR* 373.

[141] The example is based on the facts of the United Kingdom case of *Re Harrods (Buenos Aires) Ltd.* [1992] Ch. 72.

jurisdiction on the alternative forum either through Article 4 or through Article 5. That alternative jurisdiction must not only be available in the abstract sense, but, as paragraph 5 indicates, the alternative court, if approached by the plaintiff, must actually commence to exercise jurisdiction before the original court seised can decline jurisdiction. Until then, the original court seised can only suspend the exercise of jurisdiction.

Paragraph 2

This paragraph sets out the matters which the court shall take into account in determining whether the forum seised is clearly inappropriate and the alternative forum clearly more appropriate. The list is not exhaustive, as indicated by the words "in particular". Other factors, such as: the substantive law to be applied in resolving the dispute, the availability of legal aid or the extent of the relief which may be granted in each forum, may also be relevant. Nor should the list be read as indicating a hierarchy: which factor is the more important will depend on the circumstances of the case. None of the factors can be regarded as conclusive: although a court may hesitate to decline jurisdiction in favour of a court whose judgment on the merits is unlikely to be recognised, other factors may outweigh this consideration.

Sub-paragraph a)

This directs the court's attention to the relative inconvenience of the parties. This refers not merely to the distance to be travelled, but also to the inconvenience a party may suffer because of lack of familiarity with the law, procedure, access to lawyers and the language of the other forum.

Sub-paragraph b)

This directs the court's attention to the nature and location of the evidence, including documents and witnesses, and the procedure for obtaining such evidence. As regards the latter, there are notable differences under various legal systems about the collection of evidence. Frequently a plaintiff seeks out a particular forum for that reason.

Sub-paragraph c)

This directs the court's attention to the applicable limitation periods. In most common law countries limitation periods are characterised as procedural and hence governed by the law of the forum.[142] It has been said by the Supreme Court of the United States that a plaintiff is entitled to seek out the forum with the longest limitation period.[143] In most common law countries it is possible for a defendant to waive the benefit of a limitation period by agreeing not to plead it. Such an agreement may counteract consideration set out in sub-paragraph *c*).

Sub-paragraph d)

This factor directs the court's attention to the possibility of obtaining recognition and enforcement of any decision on the merits given either by itself or by the alternative forum. In most cases this will involve an inquiry whether the forum will recognise any decision given by the alternative forum and vice versa. Clearly, the question of whether the relevant courts will be able to exercise a jurisdiction which will be entitled to recognition and enforcement under Part III of the Convention will be most relevant. But there may be cases where the likelihood of recognition or enforcement in third States may have to be considered, for instance, a third State where the defendant has substantial assets out of which the judgment can be recovered.[144] The court may by making an order for security under Article 22(4) overcome possible problems of recognition.

Paragraph 3

This paragraph prohibits discrimination in making the decision to suspend the proceedings either on the basis of favouring a locally resident party or on the basis of giving less weight to the position of a party because it is foreign. A decision which gives less deference to the choice of forum by a foreign plaintiff solely because that plaintiff is foreign, is prohibited by this provision.[145] It makes no difference whether the plaintiff is habitually resident or has its seat in another Contracting State or in a non-Contracting State. This provision reinforces the basic rule that the plaintiff is entitled to choose a forum provided by the Convention. There is no conflict between this provision and the factor of inconvenience based on residence to be taken into account under Article 22(2)(a). Paragraph 3 prohibits discrimination against a party because that party is resident abroad.

---

[142] But see, *Foreign Limitation Periods Act* 1984 (UK).

[143] *Keeton v. Hustler Magazine Inc.* 465 US 770 (1984).

[144] See, for instance, the Australian case of *Henry v. Henry* (1996) 185 CLR 571, a family property dispute where the alternative fora were Australia and Monaco, but most of the assets were in Switzerland.

[145] Contrast: *Piper Aircraft Co. v. Reyno* 454 US 235 (1981).

Sub-paragraph *a)* of paragraph 2 raises for consideration any inconvenience which may result to a party because of its residence. As long as those inconveniences are properly balanced and one party is not preferred merely because that party resides within the forum in question, no issue of discrimination arises.

Paragraph 4

This paragraph allows the court originally seised to order the defendant to lodge security sufficient to satisfy any decision on the merits which may be made by the alternative forum. Where the alternative court is a court of a Contracting State exercising required jurisdiction under Chapter II, the provision is discretionary; there is no obligation on the original court to make such an order. As remarked before, such an order may be appropriate where doubts exist as to the recognition and enforcement of any judgment to be made by the alternative court or there are fears that the defendant may use the delay caused by the suspension of proceedings pending the institution of fresh proceedings to dissipate its assets.

Where the jurisdiction of the alternative court arises under Article 17 the court is obliged to make an order for security if it decides to suspend proceedings under paragraph 1, unless the defendant establishes that sufficient assets exist in the State of the other court or in another State where the court's decision could be enforced. This latter provision raises some questions.

In the first place, no provision is made for the case of the alternative court being in a non-Contracting State. Jurisdiction under Article 17 can only arise in a Contracting State. Presumably, in the case of a non-Contracting State the power to order security is discretionary which does not seem logical.

Secondly, the existence of sufficient assets in the State of the other court at the time of the suspension of proceedings is hardly a guarantee that they will still be there when judgment is given. Presumably, even if such assets are shown to exist the original court will still have a discretion to order security; only the obligation to do so has gone.

Finally, the question of enforceability in another State which could be either a Contracting or non-Contracting State, will depend on the national law of that third State and not on the Convention. Such a possibility may be hard to assess.

Paragraph 5

As remarked earlier, the court originally seised cannot decline jurisdiction unless and until the alternative forum actually commences to exercise jurisdiction with respect to the parties and the substance of the claim. The only exception exists in the case where the plaintiff neglects to bring the proceedings afresh in the alternative forum within the time specified by the original court. Only in that case, by way of sanction against possible sabotage by the plaintiff, can the original court dismiss the proceedings without the proceedings in the alternative forum having commenced.

It is for the plaintiff to take action in the other court. There is no obligation under the Convention for the courts themselves to communicate with each other, although, if national law or practice permits this, it is not precluded either. Filing a document instituting proceedings would not be sufficient; the original court must be in a position to determine whether or not the other court has decided to exercise jurisdiction, before it can dismiss the proceedings before it.

If the other court decides not to exercise jurisdiction, the original court is under an obligation to terminate the suspension and proceed to adjudicate the case. The word "decides" implies a conscious decision. If the other court simply fails to take action or to proceed, a decision not to exercise jurisdiction may presumably be inferred from a long period of inaction.

Appendix C

2001 Hague Interim Text for a Convention on Jurisdiction and Enforcement of Judgments in Civil and Commercial Matters

HAGUE CONFERENCE ON PRIVATE INTERNATIONAL LAW

COMMISSION II

**Jurisdiction and Foreign Judgments
in Civil and Commercial Matters**

DIX-NEUVIÈME SESSION
NINETEENTH SESSION

Distribution:

**Summary of the Outcome of the Discussion in Commission II of the
First Part of the Diplomatic Conference 6-20 June 2001**

Interim Text

Prepared by the Permanent Bureau and the Co-reporters

For the sake of clarity this summary follows the order of the articles as set out in the preliminary draft Convention of October 1999. It is understood that the structure and form of the Convention awaits final discussion.[*]

---

[*]   Note: proposals have only been included if endorsed by Member State delegations.

CHAPTER *—SUBSTANTIVE SCOPE

Article 1   Substantive scope

1. The Convention applies to civil and commercial matters.[1] It shall not extend in particular to revenue, customs or other[2] administrative matters.[3]

2. The Convention does not apply to—

    a) the status and legal capacity of natural persons;

    b) maintenance obligations;

    c) matrimonial property regimes and other rights and obligations arising out of marriage or similar relationships;

    d) wills and succession;

    e) insolvency, composition or analogous proceedings;

    f) social security;

    g)[4] arbitration and proceedings related thereto;[5]

---

[1] It has been proposed to add the words 'before courts of Contracting States' at the end of the first sentence. This proposal has not been discussed. Note the statement in Preliminary Document No. 11 (the Nygh/Pocar Report) at p. 31 that there was a consensus in the Special Commission that the application of the Convention should be confined to proceedings before courts. There was no suggestion in the Diplomatic Conference that this consensus should be departed from with the possible exception of authentic instruments (see Art. 35 below). It should be noted, however, that there were proposals to include decisions of certain administrative organs in the scope of Article 12. See footnote 88 below.

[2] It was agreed to add the word 'other' in order to indicate that revenue and customs matters are also of an administrative nature.

[3] A desire was expressed for further clarification of the meaning and scope of 'administrative matters'. An attempt to provide further clarification was made, but this did not achieve consensus. That clarification would also have merged paragraph 3 with paragraph 1.

[4] There was general agreement that alternative dispute resolution was also outside the scope of the Convention, except to the extent that it has resulted in a consent judgment or settlement to which the court has given its authority under Article 36, below.

[5] If paragraph 3 (see below) was accepted, this sub-paragraph should be deleted.

h) admiralty or maritime matters;

[*i)* anti-trust or competition claims;][6]

[*j)* nuclear liability;][7]

k)[8] Alternative A

[provisional and protective measures other than interim payment orders;][9]

Alternative B

[provisional or protective measures [other than those mentioned in Articles 13 and 23A];][10]

[*l)* rights *in rem* in immovable property;][11]

[*m)* validity, nullity, or dissolution of a legal person and decisions related thereto].[12]

---

[6] There was general agreement towards the proposal's approach, subject to further study, that certain aspects of what is covered in the United States (including the Sherman Act, the Clayton Act and the antitrust portions of the Federal Trade Commission Act) by the term 'anti-trust claims' such as actions against cartels, monopolisation, abuse of market dominance, horizontal or vertical restraints, mergers and acquisitions, price fixing or price discrimination be excluded from the Convention. On the other hand, it was acknowledged that words such as 'unfair competition' (*concurrence déloyale*) went too far since in certain systems it might include matters such as misleading or deceptive practices, passing off and infringement of marks, copyrights and patents. The problem remains of finding the appropriate terminology to define the area to be excluded and which can be understood at the international level.

[7] There is no consensus on this proposed exclusion.

[8] This paragraph would be deleted if Article 13 (Alternative A) was adopted.

[9] The intention of this Alternative (see the discussion of Article 13 below) is to exclude provisional and protective measures from the scope of the Convention but to ensure that jurisdiction to make interim payment orders remains subject to the list of prohibited jurisdictions. The proponents of this version favour the inclusion of a provision in the chapter on recognition and enforcement to clarify that interim payment orders will not be recognised or enforced under the Convention. No consensus exists on this proposal.

[10] This second Alternative is primarily inspired by a wish to exclude provisional and protective measures from the scope of the Convention. It differs from the first Alternative in specifically excluding each of the categories of provisional measures and protective measures by using the word 'or' and by omitting any reference to interim payments. However, the words within the final brackets 'other than those mentioned in Articles 13 and 23A' are put forward as a further option for those who favour a restricted provision for jurisdiction and recognition and enforcement in respect of provisional and protective measures. There is no consensus in respect of any of these options.

[11] The exclusion of this matter from the scope of the Convention has been proposed. See Article 12(1) below.

[12] The exclusion of this matter from the scope of the Convention has been proposed. See Article 12(2) below.

[3. This Convention shall not apply to arbitration and proceedings related thereto, nor shall it require a Contracting State to recognise and enforce a judgment if the exercise of jurisdiction by the court of origin was contrary to an arbitration agreement.][13]

4. A dispute is not excluded from the scope of the Convention by the mere fact that a government, a governmental agency or any person acting for the State is a party thereto.

5. Nothing in this Convention affects the privileges and immunities of sovereign States or of entities of sovereign States, or of international organisations.

Article 2   Territorial scope[14]

1. The provisions of Chapter II shall apply in the courts of a Contracting State unless all the parties are habitually resident in that State. However, even if all the parties are habitually resident in that State—

    a) Article 4 shall apply if they have agreed that a court or courts of another Contracting State have jurisdiction to determine the dispute [provided that dispute is of an international character];[15]

    b) Article 12, regarding exclusive jurisdiction shall apply;

---

[13]   This proposal is designed to meet the desire expressed that a judgment given in breach of an arbitration agreement or contrary to an arbitration award not be recognised or enforced. No consensus exists on this proposal.

[14]   Another proposal for the amendment of paragraph 1 of this Article has been reproduced as part of Proposal 4 in Annex I.

[15]   Concern has been expressed that sub-paragraph a) as it stands, will have the effect of making the Convention applicable to purely domestic situations involving not only parties who were habitually resident within the same State but also involving a legal relationship and a subject matter entirely confined to that State: see the Report of the co-reporters Prel. Doc. 11 at p. 41, note 40. The words in brackets were proposed to require an international connection. This proposal was opposed, and it was pointed out that it was difficult to define when a dispute was of an international nature and that this might lead to divergent interpretations. The view was also expressed that this issue should be determined only by the selected court. Other suggestions made were: that paragraph a) be deleted with the result that the Convention, including Article 4, would not apply if all the parties to the choice of forum agreement were habitually resident in the same State, or extending Article 22 in order to allow the selected court in such a situation to decline jurisdiction.

c) Articles 21 and 22 shall apply where the court is required to determine whether to decline jurisdiction or suspend its proceedings on the grounds that the dispute ought to be determined in the courts of another Contracting State.

2. The provisions of Chapter III apply to the recognition and enforcement in a Contracting State of a judgment rendered in another Contracting State.

Chapter **—Jurisdiction

Article 3   Defendant's forum[16]

1. Subject to the provisions of the Convention, a defendant may be sued in the courts of [a] [the] State [in which] [where] that defendant is [habitually] resident.

[2. For the purposes of the Convention, a natural person shall be considered to be resident—

   a) if that person is resident in only one State, in that State;

   b) if that person is resident in more than one State,

      i) in the State in which that person has his or her principal residence; or

      ii) if that person does not have a principal residence in any one State, in each State in which that person is resident.][17]

---

[16] There is agreement on the defendant's forum as a forum of general jurisdiction.

[17] The view has been expressed that 'habitual residence' has acquired a too technical meaning in the interpretation of earlier Hague Conventions, particularly the *Convention of 1980 on the Civil Aspects of International Child Abduction*. Another view favoured continuity of the established concept of 'habitual residence' and feared that 'residence' provided too slight a connection. Reference was made to the appearance of 'the temporary residence [. . .] of the defendant' in Article 18(2)(i), as it now stands, as one of the prohibited grounds of jurisdiction. If the proposed paragraph 2 were accepted, consequential amendments to other articles would be necessary. It was also suggested that a separate definitions article be drafted. There is no consensus on these points.

3. For the purposes of the Convention, an entity or person other than a natural person shall be considered to be [habitually] resident in the State—

    a) where it has its statutory seat;

    b) under whose law it was incorporated or formed;

    c) where it has its central administration; or

    d) where it has its principal place of business.[18]

Article 4   Choice of court

1. If the parties have agreed that [a court or] [the][19] courts of a Contracting State shall have jurisdiction to settle any dispute which has arisen or may arise in connection with a particular legal relationship, [that court or those] [the][20] courts [of that Contracting State][21] shall have jurisdiction[, provided the court has subject matter jurisdiction][22] and that jurisdiction shall be exclusive unless the parties have agreed otherwise. Where an agreement having exclusive effect designates [a court or] [the] courts of a non-Contracting State, courts in Contracting States shall decline jurisdiction or suspend proceedings unless the [court or][23] courts chosen have themselves declined jurisdiction. [Whether such an agreement is invalid for lack of consent (for example, due

---

18 There appears to be agreement on this paragraph, except for the inclusion of the word 'habitual', see note 17 above. A re-numbering would be required if paragraph 2 were inserted.

19 It has been proposed to delete the reference in paragraph 1 to 'a court' and refer to 'the courts' of the chosen country, to meet the concern that paragraph 1 could allow a court to interpret a choice of forum clause in a contract as conferring jurisdiction on a specific court that it would not otherwise be authorised to exercise under national law. There was a general agreement that a choice of forum clause could only confer jurisdiction over the person of the defendant and not in respect of subject matter outside the competence of the chosen court; see the comments of the Co-reporters in Preliminary Document No. 11, at p. 44. However, doubts were expressed whether this proposal was either necessary or appropriate.

20 See note 19, above.

21 See note 19, above.

22 This is an alternative proposal to address the problem referred to in note 19, above.

23 See note 19, above.

to fraud or duress) or incapacity shall depend on national law including its rules of private international law.][24]

2. An agreement within the meaning of paragraph 1 shall be valid as to form, if it was entered into—

    a) in writing or by any other means of communication which renders information accessible so as to be usable for subsequent reference;

    b) orally and confirmed in writing or by any other means of communication which renders information accessible so as to be usable for subsequent reference;

    c) in accordance with a usage which is regularly observed by the parties;

    d) in accordance with a usage of which the parties were or ought to have been aware and which is regularly observed by parties to contracts of the same nature in the particular trade or commerce concerned.[25]

3. Where a defendant expressly accepts jurisdiction before a court of a Contracting State, and that acceptance is [in writing or evidenced in writing], that court shall have jurisdiction.[26]

[4. The substantive validity of an agreement conferring jurisdiction shall be determined in accordance with the applicable law as designated by the choice of law rules of the forum.][27]

---

[24] This proposal seeks to confirm that the substantive validity of the choice of forum agreement is governed by the national law of the forum seised, including its choice of law rules. It also seeks to confine substantive validity to questions affecting the consent or capacity of the parties as opposed to questions of reasonableness and public policy. Objections were raised, however, that reasonableness could be an element of consent or capacity. It was also pointed out that general rules of contract validity should apply without limitation to consent or capacity. See also paragraphs 4 and 5 and footnotes 27 and 28. There was no consensus in respect of this proposal.

[25] This paragraph as redrafted was accepted by agreement. The redraft removes the words 'or confirmed' from the chapeau to sub-paragraph b) where it is more appropriate.

[26] This paragraph is intended to deal with the situation where a defendant consents to appear and defend in a jurisdiction other than the chosen one. There was agreement as regards the purpose of this provision, but the view was expressed that the reference to 'writing' should be aligned with paragraph 2.

[27] This is an alternative proposal to that discussed in note 24, above. There was no consensus on this proposal.

5.   [The parties cannot be deprived of the right to enter into agreements confer-
     ring jurisdiction.][28] [However,] [such agreements and similar clauses in trust
     instruments shall be without effect, if they conflict with the provisions of
     Article 7, 8 or 12.][29]

Article 5   *Defendant's right to contest jurisdiction*[30]

[The defendant shall have the right to contest jurisdiction under Articles [white
list] [at least until] [no later than at][31] the time of the first defence on the merits.][32]

Article 6   *Contracts*[33]

[Alternative A

1.   [Subject to the provisions of Articles 7 and 8,][34] a plaintiff may bring an action
     in contract in the courts of the State—

     a)   in which the defendant has conducted frequent [and] [or][35] significant
          activity; [or

---

28   This proposal seeks to make it clear that national law may not prohibit the entry into choice of forum
     clauses by express prohibition or the use of public policy, except in the cases which may be provided for
     in the Convention, such as consumer transactions or employment contracts; see the views expressed by
     the co-reporters in Preliminary Document No. 11, at p. 42. This proposal did not receive consensus.

29   This is the text as it appeared in the preliminary draft Convention of October 1999. The relationship
     between the choice of forum provisions and consumer transactions and employment contracts still has to
     be resolved.

30   See also Article 27A below.

31   It has been proposed to delete the words 'no later than at' and substitute the words 'at least until' the
     time of. The purpose of this proposal is to make clear it was a minimum condition. It did not receive
     consensus.

32   It has been proposed that this provision be deleted in its entirety as an intrusion into the proper role of
     national law. No consensus was reached on this issue.

33   There was no consensus on the basis for jurisdiction in contractual matters. In the material that follows,
     two basic options are put forward: one alternative refers to activity (with several sub-options) and the
     other alternative focuses on the place of performance.

34   This refers to the provisions on consumer transactions and employment contracts on which no decisions
     have been taken as yet.

35   This leaves open the question of whether the requirements of frequency and significance should be
     cumulative or alternative.

b) into which the defendant has directed frequent [and] [or] significant activity;][36]

provided that the claim is based on a contract directly related to that activity [and the overall connection of the defendant to that State makes it reasonable that the defendant be subject to suit in that State].[37]

[*Variant 1*[38]

2. For the purposes of the preceding paragraph, 'activity' means one or more of the following—

 a) [regular and substantial] promotion of the commercial or professional ventures of the defendant for the conclusion of contracts of this kind;

 b) the defendant's regular or extended presence for the purpose of negotiating contracts of this kind, provided that the contract in question was performed at least in part in that State. [Performance in this sub-paragraph refers [only] to non-monetary performance, except in case of loans or of contracts for the purchase and sale of currency];[39]

 c) the performance of a contract by supplying goods or services, as a whole or to a significant part.]

[*Variant 2*[40]

2. For the purpose of the preceding paragraph, 'activity' includes, *inter alia*, the promotion, negotiation, and performance of a contract.

---

[36] This leaves open the question of whether the activity of the defendant should take place within the State of the forum or could be directed from outside that State into the State of the forum.

[37] If the words within brackets are accepted, this would be a condition to be satisfied in addition to that of frequent and/or significant activity.

[38] In this variant the scope of 'activity' would be confined to the activities of promotion, negotiation and performance which are further defined in the following sub-paragraphs.

[39] The words in brackets, if accepted, would exclude the payment of the purchase price or fee for services rendered from the scope of 'performance'.

[40] Under this variant the activities of promotion, negotiation and performance would be within the scope of 'activity' but would not define its parameters.

[3. The preceding paragraphs do not apply to situations where the defendant has taken reasonable steps to avoid entering into or performing an obligation in that State.][41]]]

[Alternative B[42]

A plaintiff may bring an action in contract in the courts of a State in which—

  a) in matters relating to the supply of goods, the goods were supplied in whole or in part;

  b) in matters relating to the provision of services, the services were provided in whole or in part;

  c) in matters relating both to the supply of goods and the provision of services, performance of the principal obligation took place in whole or in part.]

[*Article 7   Contracts concluded by consumers*[43]

1. This Article applies to contracts between a natural person acting primarily for personal, family or household purposes, the consumer, and another party acting for the purposes of its trade or profession, [unless the other party demonstrates that it neither knew nor had reason to know that the consumer was

---

[41] This proposal that would have to be considered whether Variant 1 or 2 was adopted, seeks to protect business parties, including those using electronic commerce, who take measures to avoid entering into obligations in a particular State and thereby avoid becoming subject to the jurisdiction of the courts of that State.

[42] This alternative option consists of the text as it appeared in the preliminary draft Convention of October 1999.

[43] This Article consists of the first four common paragraphs with three different alternative solutions (including two variants of the second alternative) to meet the desire of some delegations to allow a choice of forum clause in consumer contracts in cases where the relevant law permits this, the agreement complies with the requirements of Article 4, paragraphs (1) and (2), and provided the agreement is valid as to substance under the applicable law. A fourth alternative solution has also been suggested: to exclude business to consumer contracts from the scope of the Convention. For that reason the whole of the Article is placed in square brackets. There is no consensus in respect of any of them either that one or more should be omitted or that any one of them should be preferred.

concluding the contract primarily for personal, family or household purposes, and would not have entered into the contract if it had known otherwise].[44]

2. Subject to paragraphs [5-7], a consumer may bring [proceedings][an action in contract][45] in the courts of the State in which the consumer is habitually resident if the claim relates to a contract which arises out of activities, including promotion or negotiation of contracts, which the other party conducted in that State, or directed to that State, [unless[46] [that party establishes that][47]—

   a) the consumer took the steps necessary for the conclusion of the contract in another State; [and

   b) the goods or services were supplied to the consumer while the consumer was present in the other State.][48]]

[3. For the purposes of paragraph 2, activity shall not be regarded as being directed to a State if the other party demonstrates that it took reasonable steps to avoid concluding contracts with consumers habitually resident in the State.][49]

---

[44] The purpose of this provision within brackets is to give some protection to the business party, especially in a long distance transaction such as in electronic commerce, where the business party cannot easily ascertain with whom it is dealing or the truthfulness of that person's representations. There was opposition to the insertion of this provision on the ground that it would be very difficult for a consumer to rebut an allegation that the business was unaware that the buyer was a consumer.

[45] Not all proceedings brought by consumers are actions in contract. They may be actions for a common law tort or delict, or a civil claim on a ground provided for by a statute enacted for the protection of consumers. Some delegations wanted to confine paragraph 2 to actions in contract. There was no consensus on this point.

[46] This is the so-called 'small shop' exception that seeks to protect a business party who has dealt with a foreign consumer, such as a tourist, entirely in its State of habitual residence. The question was raised whether there was a need to make such a provision that could only be of relevance to small transactions that are unlikely to become the subject of proceedings under the Convention.

[47] This provision would place the burden of establishing that the two conditions in sub-paragraphs (a) and (b) were fulfilled on the business party. The fear was expressed that the burden would be too high for many small businesses. If this issue was not resolved one way or the other, the question of on whom the burden lies, will remain uncertain and would lead to divergent interpretations. There was no consensus on this point.

[48] There was no consensus on whether this condition should be added to that set out in sub-paragraph (a).

[49] This proposal seeks to protect business parties, including those using electronic commerce, who take measures to avoid entering into obligations in a particular State and thereby avoid becoming subject to the jurisdiction of the courts of that State. There is no consensus on this provision.

4. Subject to paragraphs [5-7], the other party to the contract may bring pro-ceedings against a consumer under this Convention only in the courts of the State in which the consumer is habitually resident.[50]

[Alternative A[51]

5. Article 4 applies to a jurisdiction agreement between a consumer and the other party if the agreement is entered into after the dispute has arisen.[52]

6. Where a consumer and the other party have entered into an agreement which conforms with the requirements of Article 4(1) and (2) before the dispute has arisen, the consumer may bring proceedings against the other party in the courts of the State designated in that agreement.[53]

7. Where a consumer and the other party have entered into an agreement which conforms with the requirements of Article 4(1) and (2) before the dispute has arisen, Article 4 applies to the agreement to the extent that it is binding on both parties under the law of the State in which the consumer is habitually resident at the time the agreement is entered into.[54]

Add at the beginning of Article 25 the words:

'Subject to Article 25 *bis*'

---

[50] This is proposed as the general rule to which Alternatives A to C are exceptions.

[51] This Alternative is a revised version of the solution that was presented to the informal discussions held in Edinburgh in April 2001: see Prel. Doc. 15, Annex III-A. It provides that a choice of forum clause in a consumer contract will be effective if valid under the law of the habitual residence of the consumer and the Contracting State in which recognition and enforcement is sought has made the declaration provided for in the proposed Article 25 *bis*. For the sake of convenience that proposed Article is reproduced here as part of Alternative A. Several delegations objected to this proposal on the ground of its complexity, but there was no agreement that it should be omitted from the list of alternatives.

[52] This is the provision that appeared as Article 7(3)(a) in the preliminary draft Convention of October 1999. It is not controversial.

[53] This repeats the provision that appeared as Article 7(3)(b) in the preliminary draft Convention of October 1999. It is not controversial in so far as it allows the consumer to bring proceedings in the chosen forum in addition to other fora, including the forum under Article 7(2). The controversial issue is whether the proceedings brought by the consumer could be confined to the chosen forum.

[54] This provision contains a choice of law provision referring to the law of the consumer's habitual residence, and the issues of whether the choice of forum clause is lawful as regards each party and whether it is substantially valid (including issues of public policy and reasonableness): see Report of the co-reporters, Prel. Doc. No. 11 at p. 42.

Insert [*Article 25 bis*[55]

1. A Contracting State may make a declaration that it will not recognise or enforce a judgment under this Chapter, or a declaration specifying the conditions under which it will recognise or enforce a judgment under this Chapter, where—

    a) the judgment was rendered by the court of origin under Article 7(2) [or Article 8(2)][56]; and

    b) the parties had entered into an agreement which conforms with the requirements of Article 4 designating a court other than the court of origin.[57]

[2. A declaration under this Article may not deny recognition and enforcement of a judgment given under Article 7(2) [or Article 8(2)] if the Contracting State making the declaration would exercise jurisdiction under the relevant Article in a corresponding case.][58]

3. Recognition or enforcement of a judgment may be refused by a Contracting State that has made a declaration contemplated by paragraph 1 in accordance with the terms of that declaration.]]

---

[55] If accepted, this Article should be placed among the articles dealing with recognition and enforcement.

[56] The reference to Article 8(2) will be relevant if this solution is extended to individual contracts of employment.

[57] Under this provision a State may declare that it will only recognise or enforce judgments under the Convention that are consistent with a choice of court clause. A State making the declaration would not be bound to recognise or enforce a judgment given in accordance with Article 7(2) if this jurisdiction was incompatible with the choice of court clause. On the other hand, a State not making the declaration would be bound to recognise or enforce a judgment rendered in accordance with Article 7(2) in other Contracting States, including a State that had made the declaration. But a non-declaring State would not be bound to recognise or enforce a judgment rendered by the chosen court, including one of a State that had made the declaration. A concern was expressed at this lack of reciprocity and fear of possible complexities that might be introduced if the declaration also specified conditions.

[58] This provision is intended to prevent States that make a declaration under Article 25 *bis* (1) from denying recognition or enforcement of a judgment when that State does not treat such choice of court provisions as binding on its own consumers.

[Alternative B[59]

[*Variant 1*[60]

5. This provision may be departed from by a jurisdiction agreement provided that it conforms with the requirements of Article 4.

6. A Contracting State may declare that—

    a) it will only respect a jurisdiction agreement if it is entered into after the dispute has arisen or to the extent that it allows the consumer to bring proceedings in a court other than a court indicated in this Article or in Article 3; and

    b) it will not recognise and enforce a judgment where jurisdiction has been taken in accordance with a jurisdiction agreement that does not fulfil the requirements in sub-paragraph *a)*.]

[*Variant 2*[61]

5. Article 4 applies to an agreement between a consumer and the other party if the agreement is entered into after the dispute has arisen; or to the extent that the agreement permits the consumer to bring proceedings in a court other than the consumer's habitual residence.

---

[59] There are two variants in this Alternative. The basic rule is that stated in paragraph 4 above which limits the business party to the forum of the consumer's habitual residence. Both Variants allow a departure from this rule, but differ in whether departure is allowed unless a declaration is made to the contrary (Variant 1) or whether a departure is not allowed unless a State makes a declaration to the opposite effect (Variant 2).

[60] Variant 1 allows the parties to depart from the basic rule by an agreement that complies with the requirements of Article 4, but this choice of forum will not be regarded as excluding the forum provided for in paragraph 2 nor will a judgment rendered by the chosen forum (unless the consumer commenced the proceedings there or it coincided with the habitual residence of the consumer) be recognised or enforced in a State that makes a declaration to that effect. That State thereby 'opts-in' into the system of restricted jurisdiction over proceedings brought by the business party against the consumer.

[61] Under Variant 2 pre-dispute choice of forum clauses are not binding on consumers except in States that have made a declaration that they will respect such an agreement and that they will recognise and enforce judgments given in pursuance of such agreements. Such States will not recognise and enforce judgments given in breach of choice of forum clauses. Whatever system of declaration is adopted, problems of reciprocity remain.

6. A Contracting State may declare that in the circumstances specified in that declaration—

    a) it will respect a jurisdiction agreement entered into before the dispute has arisen;

    b) it will recognise and enforce a judgment in proceedings brought by the other party given by a court under a jurisdiction agreement entered into before the dispute has arisen;

    c) it will not recognise and enforce a judgment given by a court in which proceedings could not be brought consistently with a jurisdiction agreement entered into before the dispute has arisen.]]

[Alternative C[62]

5. Article 4 applies to a jurisdiction agreement between a consumer and the other party if the agreement is entered into after the dispute has arisen.

6. Where a consumer and the other party have entered into an agreement which conforms with the requirements of Article 4(1) and (2) before the dispute has arisen—

    a) the consumer may bring proceedings against the other party under the Convention in the courts of the State designated in that agreement;

    b) the consumer may not bring proceedings against the other party under this Convention in any other court, unless the agreement permits the proceedings to be brought in that court;

---

[62] This Alternative limits the 'white list' jurisdiction that may be invoked by each of the parties in cases where a choice of forum agreement has been concluded between the parties. In essence there will only be 'white list' jurisdiction if the consumer brings proceedings in the chosen forum. Conversely, there will only be 'white list' jurisdiction in the chosen forum in relation to an action brought by the business party if the chosen forum coincides with the habitual residence of the consumer. If the consumer brings proceedings in the forum provided for under paragraph 2 or in any other 'white list' forum contrary to a choice of forum clause, that forum will be deprived of its 'white list' status. It will then depend on the national law of the forum to determine whether the consumer will be permitted to rely on that jurisdiction and it will also depend on the national law of the State addressed to determine whether a judgment rendered in a State other than that of the chosen forum will be recognised or enforced, even if, in the absence of a choice of forum clause, the court in the State of origin would have exercised a 'white list' jurisdiction, such as a jurisdiction under paragraph 2.

c) the other party may bring proceedings against the consumer under this Convention only if the agreement permits the proceedings to be brought in the courts of the State in which the consumer is habitually resident.]]

Article 8   Individual contracts of employment

This matter was not discussed by Commission II. The Commission agreed that the Working Documents put forward in relation to this subject as well as the draft prepared at the informal discussions in Edinburgh in April 2001 should be reproduced in Annex II to facilitate further discussion. The proposals in Annex II should be viewed in the light of the Alternatives proposed in relation to Article 7 above.

Article 9   Branches [and regular commercial activity][63]

1. A plaintiff may bring an action in the courts of a State in which a branch, agency or any other establishment of the defendant is situated, [, or where the defendant has carried on regular commercial activity by other means,] provided that the dispute relates directly to the activity of that branch, agency or other establishment [or to that regular commercial activity].

[2. For purposes of applying paragraph 1, a legal entity shall not be considered a 'branch, agency or other establishment' by the mere fact that the legal entity is a subsidiary of the defendant.][64]

---

[63] The matter placed between the brackets has not been discussed pending general discussion of the 'activity jurisdiction' elsewhere. There appears to be general agreement, subject to further clarification (see note 64 below), on the remainder of the paragraph.

[64] It was proposed to delete the term 'nécessairement' in the French text. It was also proposed to replace the term 'simple' by the term 'seul' in the French text. There does not appear to be any objection with the interpretation given by the Co-Reporters in Preliminary Document No. 11 at p. 56 that a subsidiary, even one that is wholly owned by a parent, will not by that fact alone be regarded as falling within the definition of 'a branch, agency or other establishment'. However, some delegations expressed a fear that the formal incorporation of those comments into the body of the text might be misinterpreted. There is no consensus on this provision.

Article 10   Torts [or delicts][65]

1. A plaintiff may bring an action in tort [or delict] in the courts of the State—

    a) in which the act or omission that caused injury occurred, or

    b) in which the injury arose, unless the defendant establishes that the person claimed to be responsible could not reasonably foresee that the act or omission could result in an injury of the same nature in that State.[66]

[2. A plaintiff may bring an action in tort in the courts of the State in which the defendant has engaged in frequent or significant activity, or has directed such activity into that State, provided that the claim arises out of that activity and the overall connection of the defendant to that State makes it reasonable that the defendant be subject to suit in that State.][67]

[3. The preceding paragraphs do not apply to situations where the defendant has taken reasonable steps to avoid acting in or directing activity into that State.][68]

[4. A plaintiff may also bring an action in accordance with paragraph 1 when the act or omission, or the injury may occur.][69]

---

[65] The deletion of the words 'or delicts' in the title and in the first paragraph has been proposed. The concern was raised that the term includes both civil and criminal offences in some legal systems and may extend the reach of Article 10 or result in other unintended consequences in those systems. There is no consensus on this proposal.

[66] This is the text of the preliminary draft Convention of October 1999. No specific proposals were made to modify this text. However, it was noted that the paragraph would have to remain under consideration in light of e-commerce and intellectual property issues, its relation to activity jurisdiction proposals, and constitutional issues in one State. There was agreement that the material appearing as paragraph 2 in the preliminary draft Convention of October 1999 should be deleted.

[67] This proposal seeks to insert an activity based jurisdiction similar to that proposed in relation to Article 6 Contracts, Alternative A, paragraph 1. There is no consensus on this proposal.

[68] This proposal seeks to protect business parties, including those using electronic commerce, who take measures to avoid entering into obligations in a particular State and thereby avoid becoming subject to the jurisdiction of the courts of that State. There is no consensus on this proposal.

[69] The deletion of this paragraph that appeared as Article 10, paragraph 3 of the preliminary draft Convention of October 1999 has been proposed. There is no consensus on its deletion.

[5. If an action is brought in the courts of a State only on the basis that the injury arose or may occur there, those courts shall have jurisdiction only in respect of the injury that occurred or may occur in that State, unless the injured person has his or her habitual residence in that State.][70]

Article 11   Trusts

1. In proceedings concerning the validity, construction, effects, administration or variation of a trust created voluntarily and evidenced in writing, the courts of a Contracting State designated in the trust instrument for this purpose shall have jurisdiction, and that jurisdiction shall be exclusive unless the instrument provides otherwise.[71] Where the trust instrument designates a court or courts of a non-Contracting State, courts in Contracting States shall decline jurisdiction or suspend proceedings unless the court or courts chosen have themselves declined jurisdiction. [The validity of such a designation shall be governed by the law[72] applicable to the validity of the trust.][73]

2. In the absence of such [valid][74] designation, proceedings may be brought before the courts of a State—

   a) in which is situated the principal place of administration of the trust; or

   b) whose law is applicable to the trust; or

   c) with which the trust has the closest connection for the purpose of the proceedings, taking into account in particular the principal place where the trust is administered, the place of residence or business of the trustee,

---

[70] The deletion of this paragraph that appeared as Article 10, paragraph 4 of the preliminary draft Convention of October 1999 has been proposed. There is no consensus on its deletion.

[71] There was agreement on the insertion of the last sub-sentence in order to bring the provision in conformity with the similar provision found in Article 4, paragraph 1.

[72] It was noted that the phrase 'national law' should replace the word 'law' if the Convention consistently uses 'national law' in such cases.

[73] The words within brackets were proposed to ensure that the question of the existence and validity of the choice of forum clause would be determined by the law applicable under the choice of law rules of the court seised and not necessarily by any law nominated as the applicable law by the settlor. No consensus was reached on this provision.

[74] See note 73 above.

the situation of the assets of the trust, and the objects of the trust and the places where they are to be fulfilled; or

d) in which the settlor (if living) and all living beneficiaries are habitually resident, if all such persons are habitually resident in the same State.[75]

[3. This Article shall only apply to disputes among the trustee, settlor and beneficiaries of the trust.][76]

Article 12   Exclusive jurisdiction

[1. In proceedings which have as their object rights *in rem* in immovable property or tenancies of immovable property, the courts of the Contracting State in which the property is situated have exclusive jurisdiction, unless in proceedings which have as their object tenancies of immovable property [concluded for a maximum period of six months][77], the tenant is habitually resident in a different State.][78]

[2. In proceedings which have as their object the validity, nullity, or dissolution of a legal person, or the validity or nullity of the decisions of its organs, the courts of a Contracting State whose law governs the legal person have exclusive jurisdiction.][79]

3. In proceedings concerning the validity of entries in public registers other than those dealing with intellectual property rights, the courts of the Contracting State in which the register is kept shall have exclusive jurisdiction.

---

[75] Subject to the use of the word 'valid' in the chapeau, this paragraph was approved by consensus.

[76] This paragraph did not achieve consensus. It has been proposed that this matter should be left to national law: see the comment of the co-reporters in Preliminary Document No. 11, at p. 62 that the disputes covered by this Article are disputes that are internal to the trust.

[77] It has been proposed to limit the exclusion of tenancies of immovable property from the exclusive jurisdiction of the State of situation to a lease for a single period not exceeding 6 months. There was no consensus on this proposal.

[78] It has been proposed to exclude rights *in rem* in immovable property and tenancies of movable property from the scope of the Convention. There was no consensus on this proposal.

[79] It has been proposed to exclude the validity, nullity, or dissolution of a legal person and decisions related thereto from the scope of the Convention. There was no consensus on this proposal.

Intellectual property[80]

[Alternative A[81]

4. In proceedings in which the relief sought is a judgment on the grant, registration, validity, abandonment, revocation or infringement[82] of a patent or a mark, the courts of the Contracting State of grant or registration shall have exclusive jurisdiction.[83]

5. In proceedings in which the relief sought is a judgment on the validity, abandonment, or infringement of an unregistered mark [or design], the courts of the Contracting State in which rights in the mark [or design] arose shall have exclusive jurisdiction.]

[Alternative B[84]

5A. In relation to proceedings which have as their object the infringement of patents, trademarks, designs or other similar rights, the courts of the Contracting

---

[80] Three proposals have been made with respect to the treatment of intellectual property in the Convention. The first two appear within general brackets and are each bracketed also (Alternatives A and B). That indicates that there is no consensus on the inclusion of intellectual property within the scope of the Convention or in respect of each of the proposals themselves. For the third proposal, see note 88 below.

[81] The main difference between Alternatives A and B is whether proceedings for the infringement of patents and marks and such other rights as may be covered by this provision should fall within the exclusive jurisdiction or not. In addition, for a number of the delegations that favour an exclusive jurisdiction also for infringement under this provision, a satisfactory final or disconnection clause with respect to existing and future instruments regulating jurisdiction, recognition and enforcement for specific areas such as intellectual property is a precondition for including infringement in this Article on exclusive jurisdiction.

[82] It was pointed out that, when deciding which proceedings (e.g. infringement proceedings based on provisions of an Unfair Competition Act or of a Patent or Trademark Act, or proceedings concerning certain common law torts such as passing off) were to be covered by 'infringement', the solution should be consistent with the possible exclusion of 'antitrust or competition claims' from the scope of the Convention.

[83] This paragraph also covers situations where an application for the grant or registration of a patent or mark has been filed.

[84] This Alternative does not dispute the proposition in Alternative A that there should be exclusive jurisdiction in respect of proceedings that have as their object the registration, validity, nullity or revocation of patents, trade marks, designs or other similar rights. To that extent paragraphs 4 and 5 would remain if paragraph 5A was accepted. Alternative B refers only to proposed paragraph 5A. Paragraphs 6, 7 and 8 are common to both Alternatives.

State referred to in the preceding paragraph [or in the provisions of Articles [3 to 16]] have jurisdiction.[85]]

Alternatives A and B

[6. Paragraphs 4 and 5 shall not apply where one of the above matters arises as an incidental question in proceedings before a court not having exclusive jurisdiction under those paragraphs. However, the ruling in that matter shall have no binding effect in subsequent proceedings, even if they are between the same parties. A matter arises as an incidental question if the court is not requested to give a judgment on that matter, even if a ruling on it is necessary in arriving at a decision.][86]

7. [In this Article, other registered industrial property rights [(but not copyright or neighbouring rights, even when registration or deposit is possible)][87] shall be treated in the same way as patents and marks]

[8. For the purpose of this Article, 'court' shall include a Patent Office or similar agency.][88]

---

85 This provision will have to be excluded from the exceptions stated in Article 17.

86 The purpose of this paragraph is to maintain non-exclusive jurisdiction where a matter otherwise falling within the scope of paragraphs 4 and 5 arises as an incidental question in proceedings which do not have as their object one or more of the matters described in that paragraph. The intention is that any decision made between the parties on such an incidental question will not have a preclusory effect in another State, in other cases when produced by one of the parties. There is no consensus on this paragraph.

87 There is no consensus on the words included within the brackets. Other suggestions are to exclude copyright from the scope of the Convention either in whole or only copyright infringement on-line. Furthermore, the following text was proposed as an alternative: ["*In proceedings concerning the infringement of a copyright or any neighbouring right, the courts of the Contracting State under whose laws the copyright or the neighbouring right is claimed to be infringed shall have exclusive jurisdiction*"]. This proposal seeks to include copyright within the exclusive jurisdiction of the courts of the Contracting State under whose law a copyright is claimed to have been infringed. This is an alternative to the exclusion of proceedings for the infringement of copyright proposed in paragraph 7 above.

88 This paragraph might be necessary to ensure that decisions of these organs are covered by the chapter on recognition: see the definition of 'judgment' in Article 23.

Article 13 Provisional and protective measures[89]

[Alternative A[90]

1. A court seised[91] and having jurisdiction under Articles [in the white list] to determine the merits of the case has jurisdiction to order provisional and protective[92] measures.

2. A court of a Contracting State [may] [has jurisdiction to],[93] even where it does not have jurisdiction to determine the merits of a claim, order a provisional and protective measure in respect of property in that State or the enforcement of which is limited to the territory of that State, to protect on an interim basis a claim on the merits which is pending or to be brought by the requesting party in a Contracting State which has jurisdiction to determine that claim under Articles [in the white list].[94]

3. Nothing in this Convention shall prevent a court in a Contracting State from ordering a provisional and protective measure for the purpose of protecting on an interim basis a claim on the merits which is pending or to brought by the requesting party in another State.[95]

---

[89] This Article would be deleted if Alternative A of Article 1(2)(k) was adopted. It would also be deleted if the Alternative B of Article 1(2)(k) was adopted without the reference to Articles 13 and 23A. Some delegations have also suggested that provisional and protective measures should be dealt with in a separate Chapter in the Convention. This would certainly be necessary if no provision were made for the recognition and enforcement of provisional and protective measures.

[90] For another proposal in relation to Article 13, see Article 1(2)(k) which proposes that provisional and protective measures be excluded from the scope of the Convention with certain qualifications.

[91] It has been suggested that it would be sufficient if a court is seised after a provisional and protective measure is made. This would require the addition of the words 'or about to be seised' or similar.

[92] The description 'provisional and protective' is intended to be cumulative, that is to say, the measures must meet with both criteria.

[93] A form of words has also been suggested that would make it clear that Contracting States are obliged to provide this jurisdiction, although it was also stressed that this would not interfere with the discretion of the courts of such States either to make or to refuse to make such orders.

[94] It was noted that some States, especially those in the Commonwealth other than the United Kingdom, did not provide for jurisdiction to make provisional and protective orders unless the court was seised of jurisdiction to determine the merits of the case. This could operate to the detriment of foreign plaintiffs who sought to 'freeze' assets within the jurisdiction in aid of litigation pending elsewhere. The provision is intended to provide such States with jurisdiction to make such orders based on the existence of property in the forum and limited to the territory of the forum. There was no consensus on this provision.

[95] This provision is intended to overcome any restrictions imposed on the exercise of jurisdiction by the courts of Contracting States by the list of prohibited jurisdictions (at present found in Article 18).

4. In paragraph 3[96] a reference to a provisional and protective measure means

    a) a measure to maintain the status quo pending determination of the issues at trial; or

    b) a measure providing a preliminary means of securing assets out of which an ultimate judgment may be satisfied; or

    c) a measure to restrain conduct by a defendant to prevent current or imminent future harm.]

[Alternative B[97]

A court which is or is about to be seised of a claim and which has jurisdiction under Articles [3 to 15] to determine the merits thereof may order provisional and protective measures, intended to preserve the subject-matter of the claim.]

Article 14   Multiple defendants

It was agreed to delete this Article.

Article 15   Counter-claims[98]

[Subject to Article 12,][99] a court which has jurisdiction to determine a claim under the provisions of the Convention shall also have jurisdiction to determine a

---

The provision would also allow the exercise of jurisdiction to make provisional and protective orders under national law without the restrictions imposed by the list of prohibited jurisdictions. It is proposed to remove the reference to Article 13 in Article 17 in order to allow the exercise of such jurisdiction under national law. Some delegations took the view that this paragraph was the only provision on provisional and protective measures that should be included in the Convention.

96 It has been proposed that this definition apply also to paragraphs 1 and 2.

97 This proposal is linked with the second alternative in Article 1(2)(k) which in itself contains the options either to exclude provisional or protective measures entirely from the scope of the Convention or to permit a limited jurisdiction to make such orders. Alternative B provides for such a limited jurisdiction, if so desired.

98 There was agreement that there should be provision for a jurisdiction based on a counter-claim and that this jurisdiction should be one that is entitled to recognition and enforcement under Article 25(1). There was some debate on whether this was already obvious or should be further clarified: see the remarks of the co-reporters in Preliminary Document No. 11, at p. 95. The language not within brackets was also approved by consensus.

99 It was agreed that the proposal to add this qualification should remain within brackets pending resolution of the status of Article 12.

counter-claim arising out of the transaction or occurrence on which the original claim is based [unless the court would be unable to adjudicate such a counter-claim against a local plaintiff under national law].[100]

Article 16   Third party claims

It was agreed to delete this Article.

Article 17   Jurisdiction based on national law[101]

[Subject to Articles 4, 7, 8, 11(1), 12 and 13[102],][103] the Convention does not prevent the application by Contracting States of rules of jurisdiction under national law, provided that this is not prohibited under Article 18.

[Article 18   Prohibited grounds of jurisdiction[104]

[1. Where the defendant is habitually resident in a Contracting State, the application of a rule of jurisdiction provided for under the national law of a Contracting

---

[100] It was proposed to add the language within brackets to provide for the situation where the counter-claim is outside the subject matter jurisdiction of the court. There was general agreement that a counter-claim could only confer jurisdiction over the person of the defendant and not subject matter jurisdiction (including excess of any monetary limits) which it did not possess under national law. There was some discussion as to whether this was already obvious, or whether the issue which also arises in relation to forum selection clauses, should be dealt with in a general provision, and whether the language proposed within the brackets was adequate for the intended purpose. In relation to the last issue, the following alternative words have been proposed: "[. . .], unless the court seised does not have subject matter jurisdiction to adjudicate the counter-claim".

[101] Subject to the determination of the material in brackets, this Article was approved by agreement.

[102] It has been proposed that the reference to Article 13 be deleted. This will allow the making of provisional and/or protective orders under national law.

[103] The question of the existence or exclusivity of Articles 7, 8, 12 and 13 still remain to be resolved.

[104] There was no consensus on this provision.

State is prohibited if there is no substantial connection between that State and [either] the dispute [or the defendant].[105]][106]

2.   [In particular,][107] [Where the defendant is habitually resident in a Contracting State,][108] jurisdiction shall not be exercised by the courts of a Contracting State on the basis [solely of one or more][109] of the following—

   [a) the presence or the seizure in that State of property belonging to the defendant, except where the dispute is directly related to that property;][110]

   b) the nationality of the plaintiff;

   c) the nationality of the defendant;

   d) the domicile, habitual or temporary residence, or presence of the plaintiff in that State;

   [e) the carrying on of commercial or other activities by the defendant in that State, [whether or not through a branch, agency or any other establishment of the defendant,][111] except where the dispute is directly related to those activities;][112]

---

[105] It has been proposed to add the words 'either' and 'or the defendant' in order to meet the difficulties in national legal systems where the main emphasis for jurisdictional competence lies on the link between the forum and the defendant, rather than the subject matter of the dispute. There is no consensus on this point.

[106] The deletion of the whole of paragraph 1 has been proposed in order to emphasise the basic concept of the Convention that there be a limited number of required bases of jurisdictions that are generally accepted, a limited number of jurisdictional bases so universally disapproved as exorbitant that they should be listed as prohibited jurisdictions, and that any other jurisdiction not listed in either category should remain open for the exercise of jurisdiction under national law (the 'grey zone'). There was no consensus on the deletion of paragraph 1.

[107] If paragraph 1 is to be deleted, the words in brackets should also be deleted.

[108] If paragraph 1 is to be deleted, the words in brackets should be placed in what is now paragraph 2.

[109] It has been proposed to delete the words within the brackets. No consensus exists on this point.

[110] It has been proposed to delete sub-paragraph a) entirely. There is no consensus on this issue.

[111] The addition of the words within the brackets is proposed to make it clear that the presence of a branch, agency or other establishment within the forum should not be a basis for the exercise of general jurisdiction under national law: see the view expressed by the co-reporters in Preliminary Document No. 11 at p. 57 that 'such a general jurisdiction is inconsistent with the Convention' (the preliminary draft Convention of October 1999). No consensus was reached on this proposal.

[112] It has been proposed to delete sub-paragraph e) entirely. There is no consensus on this issue.

f) the service of a writ upon the defendant in that State;

[*g)* the unilateral designation of the forum by the plaintiff;][113]

h) [proceedings in that State for declaration of enforceability or registration or for the enforcement of a judgment, except where the dispute is directly related to such proceedings][114] [initiation of proceedings in that State by the party against whom jurisdiction is claimed, for the purpose of recognising or enforcing a judgment from another State][115];

[*i)* the temporary residence or presence of the defendant in that State;][116]

[*j)* the signing in that State of the contract from which the dispute arises;][117]

[*k)* the location of a subsidiary or other related entity of the defendant in that State;][118]

[*l)* the existence of a related criminal action in that State].[119]

[3. Nothing in this article shall prevent a court in a Contracting State from exercising jurisdiction under national law in an action claiming damages in respect of conduct which constitutes—

[*a)* genocide, a crime against humanity or a war crime];[120] or][121]

---

[113] It has been proposed to delete sub-paragraph g) entirely. There is no consensus on this point.

[114] This was the text as it appeared in the preliminary draft Convention of October 1999.

[115] The language within the brackets was proposed as an alternative to the October 1999 text by way of clarification only. However, it was objected that the omission of the words 'except where the dispute is directly limited to such proceedings' had a substantive effect and would deprive the judgment debtor of the opportunity to raise objections directly related to the enforcement, such as part payment of the debt.

[116] It has been proposed to delete this sub-paragraph entirely. There is no consensus on this point.

[117] It has been proposed to delete this sub-paragraph entirely. There is no consensus on this point.

[118] The addition of this item to the list of prohibited jurisdiction has been proposed. There is no consensus on this point.

[119] The addition of this item to the list of prohibited jurisdictions has been proposed. There is no consensus on this point: see the comments of the co-reporters in Preliminary Document No. 11, at p. 31, footnote 14 and accompanying text.

[120] It was proposed to include a reference to the definitions contained in the Statute of the International Criminal Court. However, it was pointed out that this Statute had not as yet entered into force.

[121] There was agreement that the material in sub-paragraph a) be placed in separate brackets, because sub-paragraphs a) and b) raised different issues.

b) a serious crime under international law, provided that this State has exercised its criminal jurisdiction over that crime in accordance with an international treaty to which it is a Party and that claim is for civil compensatory damages for death or serious bodily injuries arising from that crime.[122]

Sub-paragraph b) only applies if the party seeking relief is exposed to a risk of a denial of justice[123] because proceedings in another State are not possible or cannot reasonably be required.][124]]

Article 19   Authority of the court seised

1. Where the defendant does not enter an appearance, the court shall verify whether Article 18 prohibits it from exercising jurisdiction if—

   a) national law so requires; or

   b) the plaintiff so requests; or

   [*c)* the defendant so requests, even after judgment is entered in accordance with procedures established under national law; or]

   d) [the document which instituted the proceedings or an equivalent document was served on the defendant in another Contracting State]

   or

   [it appears from the documents filed by the plaintiff that the defendant's address is in another Contracting State].[125]

---

[122] The original proposal had translated the French 'exerce' as 'established'. Some favourable comments on the proposal were withdrawn when it was pointed out that the intention was not to say 'established' in English but to restrict the article to situations where criminal jurisdiction is 'exercised'.

[123] It was pointed out that the concept of 'denial of justice' was unknown under certain legal systems.

[124] There was no consensus on the proposed paragraph 3. It is included in the text within square brackets to facilitate future discussion.

[125] It was agreed to place the text of Article 19, paragraph 1, as it appeared in the preliminary draft Convention of October 1999 (including any bracketed material) in the present document.

[2. When the jurisdiction of the court seised in a Contracting State is based on or is consistent with a ground of jurisdiction provided for in Articles 3 to 16, a party may request the court to declare so in the judgment.][126]

Article 20[127]

1. The court shall stay the proceedings so long as it is not established that the document which instituted the proceedings or an equivalent document, including the essential elements of the claim, was notified to the defendant in sufficient time and in such a way as to enable him to arrange for his defence, or that all necessary steps have been taken to that effect.

[2. Paragraph 1 shall not affect the use of international instruments concerning the service abroad of judicial and extrajudicial documents in civil or commercial matters, in accordance with the law of the forum.]

[3. Paragraph 1 shall not apply, in case of urgency, to any provisional or protective measures.]

Article 21   Lis pendens

1. When the same parties are engaged in proceedings in courts of different Contracting States and when such proceedings are based on the same causes of action, irrespective of the relief sought, the court second seised shall suspend the proceedings if the court first seised has jurisdiction under Articles [white list][128] [or under a rule of national law which is consistent with these articles][129] and is expected to render a judgment capable of being recognised

---

126   There was no consensus on this proposal.

127   It was agreed to place the text of Article 20, as it appeared in the preliminary draft Convention of October 1999 (including any bracketed material) in the present document.

128   It was agreed to add the words within brackets in order to make it clear that the *lis pendens* rule only applies when the court first seised exercises jurisdiction under the Convention: see the Report of the co-reporters, Preliminary Document 11, at p. 86.

129   This proposal sought to make it clear that the *lis pendens* rule will not only apply where the court first seised is exercising 'white list' jurisdiction as such, but also in the case where that court exercises a jurisdiction under national law in a situation that is consistent with 'white list' jurisdiction, such as proceedings against a defendant who is habitually resident in that State: see Report of co-reporters, Preliminary Document 11, at p. 86. There was no consensus on this point.

under the Convention in the State of the court second seised, unless the latter has exclusive jurisdiction under Article 4 [, 11][130] or 12.

2. The court second seised shall decline jurisdiction as soon as it is presented with a judgment rendered by the court first seised that complies with the requirements for recognition or enforcement under the Convention.

3. Upon application of a party, the court second seised may proceed with the case if the plaintiff in the court first seised has failed to take the necessary steps to bring the proceedings to a decision on the merits or if that court has not rendered such a decision within a reasonable time.

4. The provisions of the preceding paragraphs apply to the court second seised even in a case where the jurisdiction of that court is based on the national law of that State in accordance with Article 17.

5. For the purpose of this Article, a court shall be deemed to be seised—

    a) when the document instituting the proceedings or an equivalent document is lodged with the court; or

    b) if such document has to be served before being lodged with the court, when it is received by the authority responsible for service or served on the defendant.

    [As appropriate, universal time is applicable.]

6. If in the action before the court first seised the plaintiff seeks a determination that it has no obligation to the defendant, and if an action seeking substantive relief is brought in the court second seised—

    a) the provisions of paragraphs 1 to 5 above shall not apply to the court second seised; and

---

[130] There was no consensus on the insertion of a reference to Article 11 (trusts).

b) the court first seised shall suspend the proceedings at the request of a party if the court second seised is expected to render a decision capable of being recognised under the Convention.

7. This Article shall not apply if the court first seised, on application by a party, determines that the court second seised is clearly more appropriate to resolve the dispute, under the conditions specified in Article 22.

Article 22   *Exceptional circumstances for declining jurisdiction*

1. In exceptional circumstances, when the jurisdiction of the court seised is not founded on an exclusive choice of court agreement valid under Article 4, or on Article 7, 8 or 12, the court may, on application by a party, suspend its proceedings if in that case it is clearly inappropriate for that court to exercise jurisdiction and if a court of another State has jurisdiction and is clearly more appropriate to resolve the dispute. Such application must be made no later than at the time of the first defence on the merits.

2. The court shall take into account, in particular—

    a) any inconvenience to the parties in view of their habitual residence;

    b) the nature and location of the evidence, including documents and witnesses, and the procedures for obtaining such evidence;

    c) applicable limitation or prescription periods;

    d) the possibility of obtaining recognition and enforcement of any decision on the merits.

3. In deciding whether to suspend the proceedings, a court shall not discriminate on the basis of the nationality or habitual residence of the parties.

4. If the court decides to suspend its proceedings under paragraph 1, it may order the defendant to provide security sufficient to satisfy any decision of the other court on the merits. However, it shall make such an order if the other court has jurisdiction only under Article 17, or if it is in a non-Contracting

State,[131] unless the defendant establishes that [the plaintiff's ability to enforce the judgment will not be materially prejudiced if such an order is not made][132] [sufficient assets exist in the State of that other court or in another State where the court's decision could be enforced].[133]

5. When the court has suspended its proceedings under paragraph 1,

    a) it shall decline to exercise jurisdiction if the court of the other State exercises jurisdiction, or if the plaintiff does not bring the proceedings in that State within the time specified by the court; or

    b) it shall proceed with the case if the court of the other State decides not to exercise jurisdiction.

6. This Article shall not apply where the court has jurisdiction only under Article 17 [which is not consistent with Articles [white list]].[134] In such a case, national law shall govern the question of declining jurisdiction.[135]

[7. The court seised and having jurisdiction under Articles 3 to 15 shall not apply the doctrine of forum non conveniens or any similar rule for declining jurisdiction.][136]

---

[131] It was agreed to insert the words "or if it is in a non-Contracting State" in order to fill a gap in the provision, see the Report of the co-reporters, Preliminary Document 11, at pp. 92-93.

[132] The words in the preceding brackets were proposed in substitution of the existing text which were thought to set too high a standard for the defendant to be able to meet on the one hand and still not give the plaintiff the security needed on the other: see the Report of the co-reporters, Preliminary Document 11 at p. 93. There was no consensus on this point.

[133] This is the text of the preliminary draft Convention of October 1999.

[134] This proposal sought to ensure that the preservation of national rules of *forum non conveniens* will not apply both where the court seised is exercising 'white list' jurisdiction as such, and also in the case where that court exercises a jurisdiction under national law in a situation that is consistent with 'white list' jurisdiction, such as proceedings against a defendant who is habitually resident in that State. There was no consensus on this point.

[135] This paragraph makes it clear that Article 22 does not apply where the court is only exercising jurisdiction under national law. In that case, the court can apply its own rules of *forum non conveniens* or similar (if any). This resolves the question raised by the co-reporters in Preliminary Document 11, at p. 89. It was agreed to insert this paragraph.

[136] This paragraph was proposed to ensure that national rules of *forum non conveniens* or similar rules would not be used in relation to 'white list' jurisdiction as a means of declining jurisdiction. There was no consensus on this point.

Chapter ***—Recognition and Enforcement

Article 23   Definition of 'judgment'

For the purposes of this Chapter, 'judgment' means any decision given by a court, whatever it may be called, including a decree or order, as well as the determination of costs or expenses by an officer of the court, provided that it relates to a decision which may be recognised or enforced under the Convention.[137]

[Article 23A   Recognition and enforcement of provisional and protective measures[138]

[Alternative A

1.   A decision ordering a provisional and protective[139] measure, which has been taken by a court seised[140] with the claim on the merits, shall be recognised and enforced in Contracting States in accordance with Articles [25, 27-34].

2.   In this article a reference to a provisional or protective measure means—

---

[137]   For those delegations that support the complete exclusion of provisional and protective measures from the Convention, no reference to such measures will be necessary in this Article. It has been proposed to include in the Convention provisions both for jurisdiction to take provisional and protective measures and for their recognition and enforcement. As for jurisdiction, it was pointed out that the definition of 'judgment' in Article 23 could be read to include provisional and protective measures. As for recognition and enforcement, proposals are made in Article 23A below.

[138]   The two alternatives which do not appear to differ much in substance, provide for the recognition and enforcement of provisional and protective orders made by a court that is seised (or about to be seised) of the substantive dispute. Such a provision is opposed naturally by those delegations that favour exclusion of such measures from the scope of the Convention. But several delegations that favoured the inclusion of a provision relating to such measures in the jurisdictional or procedural part of the Convention, opposed making provision for the recognition and enforcement of provisional and protective orders. Note also that there may be a need to address: the extent to which similar relief is known in the State of the court addressed; and, procedures to safeguard the interests of third parties or of the defendant (e.g. an undertaking to pay damages).

[139]   The two descriptions 'provisional' and 'protective' are intended to be cumulative.

[140]   It was suggested that it would be sufficient if a court is seised after a provisional and protective measure is made as long as it is already seised by the time of recognition and enforcement of the provisional and protective measure is sought abroad.

a) a measure to maintain the status quo pending determination of the issues at trial; or

b) a measure providing a preliminary means of securing assets out of which an ultimate judgment may be satisfied; or

c) a measure to restrain conduct by a defendant to prevent current or imminent future harm.]

[Alternative B

Orders for provisional and protective measures issued in accordance with Article 13[141] shall be recognised and enforced in the other Contracting States in accordance with Articles [25, 27-34].]]

Article 24   Judgments excluded from Chapter III

This Chapter shall not apply to judgments based solely on a ground of jurisdiction provided for by national law in accordance with Article 17, and which is not consistent with any basis of jurisdiction provided for in Articles [white list].[142]

Article 25   Judgments to be recognised or enforced

1. A judgment based on a ground of jurisdiction provided for in Articles 3 to 13, or which is consistent with any such ground, shall be recognised or enforced under this Chapter.

---

[141] This refers back to the proposal made as Alternative B in Article 13, above. The order must have been made by a court which is seised or about to be seised of a claim and which has white list jurisdiction to determine the merits thereof.

[142] The addition of the second part of the sentence was accepted by consensus. The additional words make it clear that Chapter III will apply to any judgment based on one or more grounds of jurisdiction, so long as any one of those grounds is consistent with a required basis for jurisdiction under the Convention. For recognition purposes, the application of Article 24 is confined to judgments that can only be based on jurisdiction provided for by national law.

2. [In order to be recognised, a judgment referred to in paragraph 1 must have the effect of res judicata in the State of origin.][143]

or

[A judgment referred to in paragraph 1 shall be recognised from the time, and for as long as, it produces its effects in the State of origin.][144]

3. [In order to be enforceable, a judgment referred to in paragraph 1 must be enforceable in the State of origin.][145]

or

[A judgment referred to in the preceding paragraphs shall be enforceable from the time, and for as long as, it is enforceable in the State of origin.][146]

4. However, recognition or enforcement may be postponed [or refused][147] if the judgment is the subject of review in the State of origin or if the time limit for seeking a review has not expired.

Article 26   Judgments not to be recognised or enforced[148]

A judgment based on a ground of jurisdiction which conflicts with Article 4, 5, 7, 8 or 12, or whose application is prohibited by virtue of Article 18, shall not be recognised or enforced.[149]

---

[143] This is the text of paragraph 2 as it appeared in the preliminary draft Convention of October 1999. It was suggested to avoid the use of technical terms such as 'res judicata' or 'autorité de la chose jugée' which may not have a uniform meaning in all legal systems.

[144] This text was proposed as an alternative text to paragraph 2 by the Informal Working Group on Article 25. It has been agreed to insert it in the text to facilitate future discussion.

[145] This is the text of paragraph 3 as it appeared in the preliminary draft Convention of October 1999.

[146] This text was proposed as an alternative text to paragraph 3 by the Informal Working Group on Article 25. It has been agreed to insert it in the text for future discussion.

[147] The addition of the words in brackets is proposed in order to ensure that Contracting States are not obliged to recognise or enforce judgments under the circumstances described in this paragraph. The decision whether to postpone or refuse recognition should be left to national law. The proposal has not as yet been discussed.

[148] Agreement was reached on this Article subject to further identification of the Articles to which it will apply.

[149] Agreement was reached on this paragraph subject to further identification of the Articles to which it will apply.

Article 27   Verification of jurisdiction[150]

1. The court addressed shall verify the jurisdiction of the court of origin.

2. In verifying the jurisdiction of the court of origin, the court addressed shall be bound by the findings of fact on which the court of origin based its jurisdiction, unless the judgment was given by default.

3. Recognition or enforcement of a judgment may not be refused on the ground that the court addressed considers that the court of origin should have declined jurisdiction in accordance with Article 22.

Article 27A   Appearance without protest

1. If, in the proceedings before the court of origin,—

   a) the plaintiff claimed that the court had jurisdiction on one of the grounds specified in Articles [white list]; and

   b) the plaintiff did not claim that the court had jurisdiction on any other ground under national law; and

   c) the court did not determine that it had jurisdiction under any other ground under national law; and

   d) the defendant proceeded on the merits without contesting jurisdiction,[151]

   the defendant shall, in the court addressed, be precluded from contesting the jurisdiction of the court of origin.

2. This Article shall not apply if the courts of a Contracting State other than the State of the court of origin had exclusive jurisdiction under Article 12.[152]

---

150 This Article was agreed to.

151 The view was expressed that the time limits presently specified in Article 5, above, should be incorporated in sub-paragraph d). There was no consensus on this point.

152 Apart from the matter noted in note 151, above, there was consensus on this proposed new article. Its purpose is to overcome the difficulty referred to by the co-reporters in relation to the text of Article 5 as

Article 28   Grounds for refusal of recognition or enforcement

1. Recognition or enforcement of a judgment may be refused [only][153] if—

    a) proceedings between the same parties and having the same subject matter are pending before a court of the State addressed, if first seised in accordance with Article 21;[154]

    b) the judgment is inconsistent with a judgment rendered, either in the State addressed or in another State, provided that in the latter case the judgment is capable of being recognised or enforced in the State addressed;[155]

    [c) the [judgment results from] proceedings [in the State of origin were][156] incompatible with fundamental principles of procedure of the State addressed, [including the right of each party to be heard by an impartial and independent court];][157]

    d) the document which instituted the proceedings or an equivalent document, including the essential elements of the claim, was not notified to

---

it appeared in the preliminary draft Convention of October 1999 (see Preliminary Document No. 11, at p. 46) that under the text as it then stood appearance without protest to a jurisdiction exercised pursuant to national law (the 'grey zone') would convert that jurisdiction into required jurisdiction. There was a consensus that this would be an undesirable effect of the previous provision. The effect of the new provision would remove appearance by the defendant from the list of required jurisdictions (the 'white list'), but appearance of the defendant without protest will, if the conditions set out in paragraph 1 are fulfilled, preclude the defendant from contesting the jurisdiction of the court of origin upon the verification of the jurisdiction of that court by the court addressed.

[153]   The insertion of the word 'only' has been proposed to make clear that the following list is an exclusive list of grounds for refusal or enforcement, see Preliminary Document No. 11, at p. 102. No consensus was reached on the inclusion of this word in the text.

[154]   This sub-paragraph was agreed to.

[155]   This sub-paragraph was agreed to.

[156]   The deletion of the words 'judgment results from' and the insertion of the words 'in the State of origin' has been proposed. This is intended to clarify the provision. Further discussion depends on the decision of the issue raised in footnote 157.

[157]   The deletion of this sub-paragraph has been proposed because it would encourage attacks on the impartiality and independence of the court by the losing party in an attempt to delay enforcement. It would also be contrary to the need for mutual trust and confidence among the courts of Contracting States. It may be that, subject to revision, the first part of the sub-paragraph could be acceptable. No consensus was reached on the continued inclusion of the sub-paragraph in its present form.

the defendant in sufficient time and in such a way as to enable him to arrange for his defence [, or was not notified in accordance with [an applicable international convention] [the domestic rules of law of the State where such notification took place]],[158] unless the defendant entered an appearance and presented his case without contesting the matter of notification in the court of origin, provided that the law of that court permits objection to the matter of notification and the defendant did not object.[159]

e) the judgment was obtained by fraud in connection with a matter of procedure;[160]

f) recognition or enforcement would be manifestly incompatible with the public policy of the State addressed.[161]

2. Without prejudice to such review as is necessary for the purpose of application of the provisions of this Chapter, there shall be no review of the merits of the judgment rendered by the court of origin.[162]

Article 29   Documents to be produced[163]

1. The party seeking recognition or applying for enforcement shall produce—

a) a complete and certified copy of the judgment;

---

[158] No difficulties were raised about the portion of the sub-paragraph not in brackets. The material within the brackets was put forward as containing two options. The option contained within the first set of brackets would permit the requested court to deny recognition in cases where the applicable international convention was violated, such as the *Hague Convention of 1965 on the Service Abroad of Judicial and Extrajudicial Documents in Civil or Commercial Matters*. The second option would permit the requested court to deny recognition where service was not effected in accordance with the requirements of the law of the State where notification took place. In most cases, but not all, this would coincide with the State addressed. There was no consensus on the acceptance of either option.

[159] The addition of the words after the last comma was agreed to, subject to drafting.

[160] Agreement was reached on this sub-paragraph.

[161] Agreement was reached on this sub-paragraph.

[162] Agreement was reached on this paragraph.

[163] This Article was approved by consensus as it appeared in the preliminary draft Convention of October 1999. It was noted that drafting changes would have to be made if the proposed amendments to Article 25 were accepted.

> b) if the judgment was rendered by default, the original or a certified copy of a document establishing that the document which instituted the proceedings or an equivalent document was notified to the defaulting party;
>
> c) all documents required to establish that the judgment is res judicata in the State of origin or, as the case may be, is enforceable in that State;
>
> d) if the court addressed so requires, a translation of the documents referred to above, made by a person [legally][164] qualified to do so.

[2. An application for recognition or enforcement may be accompanied by the form annexed to this Convention[165] and, if the court addressed so requires, a translation of the form made by a person [legally][166] qualified to do so.][167]

3. No legalisation or other formality may be required.

4. If the terms of the judgment do not permit the court addressed to verify whether the conditions of this Chapter have been complied with, that court may require the production of any other necessary documents.

Article 30   Procedure

The procedure for recognition, declaration of enforceability or registration for enforcement, and the enforcement of the judgment, are governed by the law of the State addressed so far as the Convention does not provide otherwise. [The law of the State addressed must provide for the possibility to appeal against the declaration of enforceability or registration for enforcement.][168] The court addressed

---

[164]   It was proposed to add the words 'legally'. There was no consensus.

[165]   A draft of such a form is attached in Annex III as a basis for further discussion.

[166]   It was proposed to add the words 'legally'. There was no consensus.

[167]   It was agreed that the nature of the form and whether it should be mandatory, available upon request, or discretionary on the part of the rendering court, required further discussion.

[168]   This proposal was put forward in order to ensure that there be at least one possibility of an appeal against a decision either to grant or to refuse *exequatur* or registration. This proposal was opposed on the ground that the provision of a method of challenging or reviewing such a decision should be left to national law. The matter remains unresolved.

shall act [in accordance with the most rapid procedure available under local law][169] [expeditiously].

Article 31   Costs of proceedings

1. No security, bond or deposit, however described, to guarantee the payment of costs or expenses [for the procedure of Article 30][170] shall be required by reason only that the applicant is a national of, or has its habitual residence in, another Contracting State.

[2. An order for payment of costs and expenses of proceedings, made in one of the Contracting States against any person exempt from requirements as to security, bond, or deposit by virtue of paragraph 1 shall, on the application of the person entitled to the benefit of the order, be rendered enforceable without charge in any other Contracting State.][171]

---

[169] The language within the brackets was proposed to replace the word 'expeditiously' in the existing text. Its intention was to give expression in the text of the Convention to the comment of the Reporters in Preliminary Document No. 11 at p. 110 that Article 30 'obliges Contracting States to use . . . the most rapid procedure they possess in their national law'. Concerns were expressed that the proposal would constitute too great an intrusion into national law and that certain rapid procedures that are provided for, for example, in the context of regional arrangements, are not necessarily appropriate in a world wide convention. In a further clarification the Reporters pointed out that such a provision would not oblige a State to use a procedure made available specifically for the purposes of a treaty or arrangement to which that State was a party, but referred to its non-treaty law (*droit commun*). No consensus was reached on this provision.

[170] This addition was proposed with the intention of clarifying the scope of the Article without changing the substance. The necessity for this provision was questioned and fears were expressed about unintended consequences. Reference was also made to Article 16 of the *Hague Convention of 1973 on the Recognition and Enforcement of Decisions relating to Maintenance Obligations*. Consensus was reached on the substance of this paragraph.

[171] The proposal for this paragraph is based on Article 15 of the Hague Convention of 1980 on International Access to Justice and Article 18 of the Hague Convention of 1954 on Civil Procedure. Its purpose is to secure enforcement of an order made by the requested court for the payment of the costs and expenses borne by the judgment debtor in a case where the requested court has rejected enforcement of the judgment on a ground such as the fraud of the judgment creditor upon the court of origin. There was no consensus on this point.

Article 32   Legal aid[172]

[Natural persons habitually resident in a Contracting State shall be entitled, in proceedings for recognition and enforcement, to legal aid under the same conditions as apply to persons habitually resident in the requested State.]

Article 33   Damages

1. A judgment which awards non-compensatory damages, including exemplary or punitive damages, shall be recognised and enforced to the extent that a court in the State addressed could have awarded similar or comparable damages. Nothing in this paragraph shall preclude the court addressed from recognising and enforcing the judgment under its law for an amount up to the full amount of the damages awarded by the court of origin.[173]

2. *a)* Where the debtor, after proceedings in which the creditor has the opportunity to be heard, satisfies the court addressed that in the circumstances, including those existing in the State of origin, grossly excessive damages[174] have been awarded, recognition and enforcement may be limited to a lesser amount.

   b) In no event shall the court addressed recognise or enforce[175] the judgment in an amount less than that which could have been awarded in the State

---

[172] It was proposed that this provision be deleted from the Convention because it raised constitutional concerns. Some delegations did not consider the provision essential and it could therefore be deleted. But for yet other delegations it was of great importance. It was suggested that the issue could be resolved through an 'opt-in' provision. There was no consensus on these proposals.

[173] The text of paragraph 1 has been approved by consensus and replaces the text of the preliminary draft Convention of October 1999. The working group that produced this text also recommended consideration of reversing the order of paragraphs 1 and 2.

[174] The Reporters explained that the statement at p. 114 of Preliminary Document No. 11 to the effect that as a general principle 'grossly excessive' was likely to mean 'grossly excessive by the standards of the court of origin', did not mean that the question of whether the damages were grossly excessive should be judged only by the standards of the court of origin. This would depend on the circumstances of each case, especially on whether the judgment creditor was a resident of the State of origin or of the requested State. In the latter case, obviously the standards of the requested State would assume greater importance.

[175] The addition of the reference to enforcement here and in other parts of the Article was proposed in order to make clear that the Article applies to both recognition and enforcement, see the comments of the Reporters in Preliminary Document No. 11, at p. 113. The proposal was accepted by consensus.

addressed in the same circumstances, including those existing in the State of origin.[176]

3. In applying paragraph 1 or 2, the court addressed shall take into account whether and to what extent the damages awarded by the court of origin serve to cover costs and expenses relating to the proceedings.

Article 34   Severability

[Alternative A

If the judgment contains elements which are severable, one or more of them may be separately recognised, declared enforceable, registered for enforcement, or enforced.][177]

[Alternative B

Partial recognition or enforcement

Partial recognition or enforcement of a judgment shall be granted where:

a) partial recognition or enforcement is applied for; or

b) only part of the judgment is capable of being recognised or enforced under this Convention; or

c) the judgment has been satisfied in part.][178]

---

[176] It was inquired whether statutory damages (where a statute has determined the amount to be awarded in case of breach), liquidated damages (where a contract has determined the amount to be paid in case of breach) and fixed interest on damages awards would fall within the scope of Article 33 and, if so, whether their character would be compensatory or non-compensatory. The co-reporters indicated that Article 33 would be applicable in such cases and that the classification of such damages as compensatory or punitive would be determined by the requested court. That court would take into account whether the statutory provision in question of the originating forum, or the contractual provision as interpreted according to its governing law, merely sought to estimate what was required to compensate the plaintiff or sought to impose a penalty.

[177] This is the text as it appeared in the preliminary draft Convention of October 1999. It was noted by the co-reporters in Preliminary Document No. 11, at p. 115 that this text made no express provision for partial enforcement. Such a provision would allow the court addressed to sever the portion of the judgment which had already been paid or otherwise satisfied.

[178] This is an alternative text which has been included in this document to facilitate future discussion.

Article 35 *Authentic instruments*

[Alternative A

1. Each Contracting State may declare that it will enforce, subject to reciprocity, authentic instruments formally drawn up or registered and enforceable in another Contracting State.][179]

[Alternative B

1. Authentic instruments formally drawn up or registered and enforceable in a Contracting State shall, upon request,[180] be declared enforceable in another Contracting State.][181]

2. The authentic instrument must have been authenticated by a public authority or a delegate of a public authority and the authentication must relate to both the signature and the content of the document.[182]

[3. The provisions concerning recognition and enforcement provided for in this Chapter shall apply as appropriate.][183]

[*Article X*[184]

Any Contracting State may, at the time of ratification, acceptance, approval of, or accession to, this Convention, or at any time thereafter, make a declaration

---

[179] This is the text as it appeared in the preliminary draft Convention of October 1999. According to that text States wishing to take advantage of Article 35 should specifically elect to adopt it on the basis of reciprocity with other States making a similar declaration.

[180] Further discussion will be necessary to clarify what is meant by the words 'upon request' or whether the method and form of making the request (in writing, to a court or other instance) should be left to national law.

[181] According to this alternative text, Article 35 will apply to all Contracting States in the absence of a declaration as envisaged in the proposed Article X below. No consensus was reached on the version of paragraph 1 to be preferred.

[182] This was the text as it appeared in the preliminary draft Convention of October 1999.

[183] It was decided that this paragraph should remain within square brackets.

[184] This provision is part of Alternative 2 to paragraph 1, above. If accepted, it will probably be placed among the General Provisions of the Convention. If accepted, it will give Contracting States the following options:
—not to apply Article 35 under any circumstances;

that it will not apply Article 35, or that it will apply that Article subject to reciprocity.[185]][186]

Article 36   Settlements[187]

Settlements to which a court has given its authority shall be recognised, declared enforceable, registered for enforcement, or enforced in the State addressed under the same conditions as judgments falling within the Convention, so far as those conditions apply to settlements.

Chapter ****—General Provisions

Article 37   Relationship with other Conventions

It was agreed that the proposals made in the Annex to the preliminary draft Convention as well as the Working Documents produced for the purposes of the present Session be reproduced in Annex 1 of this Summary.

Articles 38 to 40 inclusive Uniform interpretation

This matter has not yet been discussed.

Article 41   Federal clause

This matter has not yet been discussed.

—to apply Article 35 on condition of reciprocity; or

—to apply Article 35 without requiring reciprocity, that is, where a Contracting State is prepared to give effect to authentic instruments, although it does not provide for that institution under its domestic law.

[185] It remains to be decided whether reciprocity should be required in this proposal.

[186] There is no consensus as regards this provision.

[187] This Article was approved by consensus.

[*Article 42   Ratification of and accession to the Convention*[188]

[Alternative A

1. This Convention shall become effective between any two Contracting States on the date of entry into force provided that the two States have each deposited a declaration confirming the entry into force between the two States of treaty relations under this Convention.

2. At the time of deposit of its instrument of ratification or accession, or at any time thereafter, each State shall deposit with the depository a copy of its declarations concerning all Contracting States with which the State will enter into treaty relations under the Convention. A Contracting State may withdraw or modify a declaration at any time.

3. The depository shall circulate all declarations received to all Contracting States and to Member States of the Hague Conference.

4. The Hague Conference on Private International Law shall regularly publish information reporting on the declarations that have been deposited pursuant to this Article.]

[Alternative B

1. The Convention shall be open for signature by the States which were Members of the Hague Conference on Private International Law at the time of its Nineteenth Session.[189]

2. It shall be ratified, accepted or approved and the instruments of ratification, acceptance or approval shall be deposited with the Ministry of Foreign Affairs of the Kingdom of the Netherlands.

3. Any other State may accede to the Convention.

---

[188] It was agreed that the two following proposals be included in this document in order to facilitate future discussion of this subject. There was no decision on whether there should be a provision dealing with bilateralisation and, if so, what form such a provision should take and how far bilateralisation should extend.

[189] It was requested that consideration be given to a method whereby the European Community could become a party to the Convention.

4. The instrument of accession shall be deposited with the Ministry of Foreign Affairs of the Kingdom of the Netherlands.

5. The Convention shall enter into force for a State acceding to it on the first day of the third calendar month after the deposit of its instrument of accession.

6. The accession will have effect only as regards the relations between the acceding State and such Contracting States as will have declared their acceptance of the accession. Such a declaration will also have to be made by any Member State ratifying, accepting or approving the Convention after an accession. Such declaration shall be deposited at the Ministry of Foreign Affairs of the Kingdom of the Netherlands; this Ministry shall forward, through diplomatic channels, a certified copy to each of the Contracting States.

7. The Convention will enter into force as between the acceding State and the State that has declared its acceptance of the accession on the first day of the third calendar month after the deposit of the declaration of acceptance.] [190]]

ANNEX I[191]

Article 37 Relationship with other Conventions

Proposal 1

1. The Convention does not affect any international instrument to which Contracting States are or become Parties and which contains provisions on matters governed by the Convention, unless a contrary declaration is made by the States Parties to such instrument.

2. However, the Convention prevails over such instruments to the extent that they provide for fora not authorised under the provisions of Article 18 of the Convention.

---

[190] This proposal follows the language of Articles 37 and 38 of the *Hague Convention of 1980 on the Civil Aspects of International Child Abduction*.

[191] Proposals 1-3 were annexed to the preliminary draft Convention of October 1999. Proposal 4 was introduced and discussed at the June 2001 Session.

3. The preceding paragraphs also apply to uniform laws based on special ties of a regional or other nature between the States concerned and to instruments adopted by a community of States.

Proposal 2

1. *a)* In this Article, the Brussels Convention [as amended], Regulation [...] of the European Union, and the Lugano Convention [as amended] shall be collectively referred to as "the European instruments".

    b) A State Party to either of the above Conventions or a Member State of the European Union to which the above Regulation applies shall be collectively referred to as "European instrument States".

2. Subject to the following provisions [of this Article], a European instrument State shall apply the European instruments, and not the Convention, whenever the European instruments are applicable according to their terms.

3. Except where the provisions of the European instruments on—

    a) exclusive jurisdiction;

    b) prorogation of jurisdiction;

    c) *lis pendens* and related actions;

    d) protective jurisdiction for consumers or employees;

are applicable, a European instrument State shall apply Articles 3, 5 to 11, 14 to 16 and 18 of the Convention whenever the defendant is not domiciled in a European instrument State.

4. Even if the defendant is domiciled in a European instrument State, a court of such a State shall apply—

    a) Article 4 of the Convention whenever the court chosen is not in a European instrument State;

    b) Article 12 of the Convention whenever the court with exclusive jurisdiction under that provision is not in a European instrument State; and *c)* Articles 21 and 22 of this Convention whenever the court in whose favour the proceedings are stayed or jurisdiction is declined is not a court of a European instrument State.

<u>Note</u>: Another provision will be needed for other conventions and instruments.

Proposal 3

Judgments of courts of a Contracting State to this Convention based on jurisdiction granted under the terms of a different international convention ("other Convention") shall be recognised and enforced in courts of Contracting States to this Convention which are also Contracting States to the other Convention. This provision shall not apply if, by reservation under Article . . ., a Contracting State chooses—

a) not to be governed by this provision, or

b) not to be governed by this provision as to certain designated other conventions.

Proposal 4[192]

Article 2   Territorial scope

Insert the words shown in brackets in the chapeau of paragraph 1, as follows:

1. The provisions of Chapter II shall apply in the courts of a Contracting State unless all the parties are habitually resident in that State [or in the territory of a regional economic integration organisation that is a Contracting Party under Article []]. However, even if all the parties are habitually resident in that [Contracting] State [or Party]—

[. . .]

---

[192] It was pointed out to facilitate future discussions that Article 37A and Article X could in principle also be extended to cover regional economic integration organisations.

Article 37A   Relationship with Conventions
in particular matters

This Convention shall not affect any conventions to which the Contracting States are or will be parties and which, in relation to particular matters, govern jurisdiction or the recognition or enforcement of judgments.

Article 37A   Relationship with Conventions
in particular matters

This Convention shall not affect the application of any other convention to which the Contracting States are or will be parties and which, in relation to particular matters, governs jurisdiction or the recognition or enforcement of judgments, provided that the application of such other convention shall not affect the rights and obligations under this Convention of any State Party that is not a Party to such other convention.

Article X   Allocation of jurisdiction under
this Convention

Nothing in this Convention shall affect any rule of a Contracting State regarding the internal allocation of jurisdiction among the courts of that State.

ANNEX II (Art. 8)

Proposal 1

Article 8   Individual contracts of employment

1. An employee may bring a claim in matters relating to individual contracts of employment against the employer

    a) in the courts of the State where the employer has its habitual residence;

b) in the courts of the State in which the employee habitually carries out or carried out his work, [unless it was not reasonably foreseeable by the employer that the employee would habitually carry out his work in that State]; or

c) if the employee does not or did not habitually carry out his work in any one State, in the courts of the State in which the establishment that engaged the employee is or was situated or in the courts of the State in which the employee carried out the work which has given rise to the dispute.

2. An employer may bring a claim in matters relating to individual contracts of employment against the employee only in the courts of the State in which the employee is habitually resident or in which the employee habitually carries out his work.

3. However, proceedings may be brought before the courts referred to in an agreement which conforms with the requirements of Article 4, paragraphs 1 and 2—

a) if the agreement is entered into after the dispute has arisen;

b) to the extent that the agreement allows the employee to choose whether to bring proceedings in the courts referred to in the agreement or in the courts of the State referred to in paragraph 1; or

c) to the extent that the agreement is binding on both parties under the law of the State in which the employee carried out the work which has given rise to the dispute and provided that it meets the requirements specified in the declaration made by such State as contemplated in Article X.

Proposal 2

Article 8   *Individual contracts of employment*

1. In matters relating to individual contracts of employment, an employee may bring a claim against the employer,

a) in the courts of the State in which the employee habitually carries out or carried out his work, [unless it was not reasonably foreseeable by the employer that the employee would habitually carry out his work in that State]; or

b) if the employee does not or did not habitually carry out his work in any one State, in the courts of the State in which the establishment that engaged the employee is or was situated.

2. An employer may bring a claim against the employee under this Convention only—

    a) in the courts of the State:

        i) in which the employee is habitually resident; or

        ii) in which the employee habitually carries out his work; or

    b) if the employee and the employer have entered into an agreement to which paragraph 4 b) or c) applies, in the court designated in that agreement.

3. Article 4 applies to an agreement between an employee and an employer only:

    a) to the extent that it allows the employee to bring proceedings in the courts of a State other than the State referred to in paragraph 2; or

    b) if the agreement is entered into after the dispute has arisen; or

    c) to the extent that the agreement is binding on the employee under the law of the State in which the employee is resident at the time the agreement is entered into.

Proposal 3

Article X   *Reservation in respect of consumer contracts and employment contracts*

1. A Contracting State may declare at the time of signature, ratification, acceptance, approval or accession that it will not be bound by Article 7 or 8 of this Convention.

2. A Contracting State which makes a declaration in accordance with the pre-ceding paragraph may also declare that it will not be bound by Chapter III of this Convention in respect of judgments rendered under Article 7 or 8.

3. A Contracting State which makes a declaration in accordance with the preceding paragraphs is not to be considered a Contracting State of this Convention in respect of matters to which the declaration applies.

Note: This proposal is an alternative to Article 25 *bis* in the Edinburgh Draft Annex III A and Article 8, paragraph 4 c). It could also work well with the present wording of Articles 7 and 8 in the 1999 draft Convention. However, some modifications of the rules of jurisdiction will have to be modified in the Edinburgh Draft.

The purpose of this reservation is to make it possible for States that do not accept special rules about consumers or employees, to opt out from the Convention in this respect.

Under the first paragraph a State can opt out from the jurisdictional rules but not the rules on recognition and enforcement under Chapter III. Consequently, such a State is bound to recognise and enforce judgments rendered under Article 7 or 8. However, the State is not obliged to apply Articles 7 and 8 in relation to jurisdiction.

Under the second paragraph, a Contracting State has the possibility to opt out completely in respect of consumer contracts and/or employment contracts. A State can only make a declaration under this paragraph if it has also made a declaration under paragraph 1. A State that has decided to make declarations under paragraphs 1 and 2 will be regarded as having opted out completely in respect of consumer contracts and employment contracts under the Convention. Therefore such a State cannot apply Articles 7 and 8, and judgments rendered in other Contracting States under Articles 7 and 8 will not be recognised under the Convention in the State that has taken this reservation.

Paragraph 3 makes it clear that a State making reservations under paragraphs 1 and 2 is to be considered a non-Contracting State in respect of matters covered by the reservation.

Proposal 4   *"Edinburgh Solution"*

Article 8   *Individual contracts of employment*

1. This Article applies in matters relating to individual contracts of employment.

2. An employee may bring a claim against the employer

    a) in the courts of the State in which the employee habitually carries out or carried out his work, [unless it was not reasonably foreseeable by the employer that the employee would habitually carry out his work in that State]; or

    b) if the employee does not or did not habitually carry out his work in any one State, in the courts of the State in which the establishment that engaged the employee is or was situated.

3. An employer may bring a claim against the employee under this Convention only—

    a) in the courts of the State:

        i)   in which the employee is habitually resident; or

        ii) in which the employee habitually carries out his work; or

    b) if the employee and the employer have entered into an agreement to which paragraph 4 b) or c) applies, in the court designated in that agreement.

4. Article 4 applies to an agreement between an employee and an employer only:

    a) to the extent that it allows the employee to bring proceedings in the courts of a State other than the State referred to in paragraph 2; or

    b) if the agreement is entered into after the dispute has arisen; or *c)* to the extent that the agreement is binding on the employee under the law of the State in which the employee is resident at the time the agreement is entered into.

Article 25   Judgments to be recognised or enforced

"Subject to Article 25 *bis* . . ."

[Article 25 *bis*

1. A Contracting State may make a declaration that it will not recognise or enforce a judgment under this Chapter, or a declaration specifying the conditions under which it will recognise or enforce a judgment under this Chapter, where:

   a) the judgment was rendered by the court of origin under Article 7(2) or Article 8(2); and

   b) the parties had entered into an agreement which conforms with the requirements of Article 4 designating a court other than the court of origin.

2. [A declaration under this Article may not deny recognition and enforcement of a judgment given under Article 7(2) or Article 8(2) if the Contracting State making the declaration would exercise jurisdiction under the relevant Article in a corresponding case.]

3. Recognition or enforcement of a judgment may be refused by a Contracting State that has made a declaration contemplated by paragraph 1 in accordance with the terms of that declaration.]

ANNEX III

Proposal by the Informal Working Group on Forms

Annex to the Convention

Forms

FORM A

CONFIRMATION OF JUDGMENT

(Sample form confirming the issuance of a judgment by the Court of Origin for the purposes of recognition and enforcement under the Convention on Jurisdiction and Foreign Judgments in Civil and Commercial Matters (the "Convention"))

(THE COURT OF ORIGIN)

(ADDRESS OF THE COURT OF ORIGIN)

(CONTACT PERSON AT THE COURT OF ORIGIN)

(TEL./FAX/EMAIL OF THE COURT OF ORIGIN)

(PLAINTIFF)

Case / Docket Number:

v.

(DEFENDANT)

(THE COURT OF ORIGIN) hereby confirms that it rendered a judgment in the above captioned matter on (DATE) in (CITY, STATE, COUNTRY), which is a Contracting State to the Convention. Attached to this form is a complete and certified copy of the judgment rendered by (THE COURT OF ORIGIN).[193]

---

[193] Article 29(1)(a).

1. *Select one or more of the following options:*[194]

    A. This Court based its jurisdiction over the defendant(s) on the following article(s) of the Convention, as implemented under the law governing the proceedings of this Court:

    ....

    ....

    B. This Court based its jurisdiction over the defendant(s) on the following ground of jurisdiction provided for by national law:

    ....

    ....

    C. This Court did not identify in the judgment a ground for jurisdiction over the defendant(s):

    YES _____ NO _____

2. *This Court based its jurisdiction over the defendant(s) on the following findings of fact (If the findings of fact are stated in the judgment or accompanying decision, indicate the relevant passages of the judgment and the decision):*[195]

    ....

    ....

    ....

---

[194] Article 27 (1)—The court addressed shall verify the jurisdiction of the court of origin.

[195] Article 27(2)—The court addressed shall be bound by the findings of fact on which the court of origin based its jurisdiction.

3. This Court awarded the following payment of money *(Please indicate any relevant categories of damages):*[196]

    ....

    ....

    ....

4. This Court awarded interest as follows *(Please specify the rate of interest, the portion(s) of the award to which interest applies, and the date from which interest is computed):*

    ....

    ....

    ....

5. This Court included within the judgment the following court costs and expenses (including attorneys fees) related to the proceedings *(Please specify the amounts of any such awards, including where applicable, any amount(s) intended to cover costs and expenses relating to the proceedings within a monetary award)*[197]

    ....

    ....

    ....

6. This Court awarded, in whole or in part, the following non-monetary remedy *(Please describe the nature of the remedy):*

    ....

    ....

    ....

---

[196] Refer to Article 33.
[197] Article 33 (3).

7. This judgment was rendered by default:

                YES_____ NO_____

(If this judgment was rendered by default, please attach the original or a certified copy of the document verifying notice to the defendant of the proceedings.)[198,199]

8. This judgment (or some part thereof) is currently the subject of review in (COUNTRY OF THE COURT OF ORIGIN):[200]

                YES_____ NO_____

9. This judgment (or some part thereof) is presently enforceable in (COUNTRY OF THE COURT OF ORIGIN):[201]

                YES_____ NO_____

List of documents:

....

....

....

....

....

Dated this .... day of ...., 20 ....

....
Signature and/or stamp by an officer of the Court

---

[198] Article 27(2)—If the judgment was by default, then the Court being addressed by this form is not bound by the findings of fact on which the court of origin based its jurisdiction.

[199] Article 29(1)(b).

[200] Article 25(4).

[201] Article 25(3).

Appendix D

2005 Hague Convention on Choice of Court Agreements

CONVENTION ON CHOICE OF COURT AGREEMENTS
(Concluded 30 June 2005)

The States Parties to the present Convention,

Desiring to promote international trade and investment through enhanced judicial co-operation,

Believing that such co-operation can be enhanced by uniform rules on jurisdiction and on recognition and enforcement of foreign judgments in civil or commercial matters,

Believing that such enhanced co-operation requires in particular an international legal regime that provides certainty and ensures the effectiveness of exclusive choice of court agreements between parties to commercial transactions and that governs the recognition and enforcement of judgments resulting from proceedings based on such agreements,

Have resolved to conclude this Convention and have agreed upon the following provisions—

Chapter I—Scope and Definitions

Article 1   Scope

1. This Convention shall apply in international cases to exclusive choice of court agreements concluded in civil or commercial matters.

2. For the purposes of Chapter II, a case is international unless the parties are resident in the same Contracting State and the relationship of the parties and all other elements relevant to the dispute, regardless of the location of the chosen court, are connected only with that State.

3. For the purposes of Chapter III, a case is international where recognition or enforcement of a foreign judgment is sought.

Article 2   Exclusions from scope

1. This Convention shall not apply to exclusive choice of court agreements—

    a) to which a natural person acting primarily for personal, family or house-hold purposes (a consumer) is a party;

    b) relating to contracts of employment, including collective agreements.

2. This Convention shall not apply to the following matters—

    a) the status and legal capacity of natural persons;

    b) maintenance obligations;

    c) other family law matters, including matrimonial property regimes and other rights or obligations arising out of marriage or similar relationships;

    d) wills and succession;

    e) insolvency, composition and analogous matters;

f) the carriage of passengers and goods;

g) marine pollution, limitation of liability for maritime claims, general average, and emergency towage and salvage;

h) anti-trust (competition) matters;

i) liability for nuclear damage;

j) claims for personal injury brought by or on behalf of natural persons;

k) tort or delict claims for damage to tangible property that do not arise from a contractual relationship;

l) rights in rem in immovable property, and tenancies of immovable property;

m) the validity, nullity, or dissolution of legal persons, and the validity of decisions of their organs;

n) the validity of intellectual property rights other than copyright and related rights;

o) infringement of intellectual property rights other than copyright and related rights, except where infringement proceedings are brought for breach of a contract between the parties relating to such rights, or could have been brought for breach of that contract;

p) the validity of entries in public registers.

3. Notwithstanding paragraph 2, proceedings are not excluded from the scope of this Convention where a matter excluded under that paragraph arises merely as a preliminary question and not as an object of the proceedings. In particular, the mere fact that a matter excluded under paragraph 2 arises by way of defence does not exclude proceedings from the Convention, if that matter is not an object of the proceedings.

4. This Convention shall not apply to arbitration and related proceedings.

5. Proceedings are not excluded from the scope of this Convention by the mere fact that a State, including a government, a governmental agency or any person acting for a State, is a party thereto.

6. Nothing in this Convention shall affect privileges and immunities of States or of international organisations, in respect of themselves and of their property.

Article 3   Exclusive choice of court agreements

For the purposes of this Convention—

a) "exclusive choice of court agreement" means an agreement concluded by two or more parties that meets the requirements of paragraph *c)* and designates, for the purpose of deciding disputes which have arisen or may arise in connection with a particular legal relationship, the courts of one Contracting State or one or more specific courts of one Contracting State to the exclusion of the jurisdiction of any other courts;

b) a choice of court agreement which designates the courts of one Contracting State or one or more specific courts of one Contracting State shall be deemed to be exclusive unless the parties have expressly provided otherwise;

c) an exclusive choice of court agreement must be concluded or documented—

  i) in writing; or

  ii) by any other means of communication which renders information accessible so as to be usable for subsequent reference;

d) an exclusive choice of court agreement that forms part of a contract shall be treated as an agreement independent of the other terms of the contract. The validity of the exclusive choice of court agreement cannot be contested solely on the ground that the contract is not valid.

Article 4   Other definitions

1. In this Convention, "judgment" means any decision on the merits given by a court, whatever it may be called, including a decree or order, and a determination

of costs or expenses by the court (including an officer of the court), provided that the determination relates to a decision on the merits which may be recognised or enforced under this Convention. An interim measure of protection is not a judgment.

2. For the purposes of this Convention, an entity or person other than a natural person shall be considered to be resident in the State—

   a) where it has its statutory seat;

   b) under whose law it was incorporated or formed;

   c) where it has its central administration; or

   d) where it has its principal place of business.

Chapter II—Jurisdiction

Article 5   Jurisdiction of the chosen court

1. The court or courts of a Contracting State designated in an exclusive choice of court agreement shall have jurisdiction to decide a dispute to which the agreement applies, unless the agreement is null and void under the law of that State.

2. A court that has jurisdiction under paragraph 1 shall not decline to exercise jurisdiction on the ground that the dispute should be decided in a court of another State.

3. The preceding paragraphs shall not affect rules—

   a) on jurisdiction related to subject matter or to the value of the claim;

   b) on the internal allocation of jurisdiction among the courts of a Contracting State. However, where the chosen court has discretion as to whether to transfer a case, due consideration should be given to the choice of the parties.

Article 6   Obligations of a court not chosen

A court of a Contracting State other than that of the chosen court shall suspend or dismiss proceedings to which an exclusive choice of court agreement applies unless—

a) the agreement is null and void under the law of the State of the chosen court;

b) a party lacked the capacity to conclude the agreement under the law of the State of the court seised;

c) giving effect to the agreement would lead to a manifest injustice or would be manifestly contrary to the public policy of the State of the court seised;

d) for exceptional reasons beyond the control of the parties, the agreement cannot reasonably be performed; or

e) the chosen court has decided not to hear the case.

Article 7   Interim measures of protection

Interim measures of protection are not governed by this Convention. This Convention neither requires nor precludes the grant, refusal or termination of interim measures of protection by a court of a Contracting State and does not affect whether or not a party may request or a court should grant, refuse or terminate such measures.

Chapter III—Recognition and Enforcement

Article 8   Recognition and enforcement

1.   A judgment given by a court of a Contracting State designated in an exclusive choice of court agreement shall be recognised and enforced in other Contracting

States in accordance with this Chapter. Recognition or enforcement may be refused only on the grounds specified in this Convention.

2. Without prejudice to such review as is necessary for the application of the provisions of this Chapter, there shall be no review of the merits of the judgment given by the court of origin. The court addressed shall be bound by the findings of fact on which the court of origin based its jurisdiction, unless the judgment was given by default.

3. A judgment shall be recognised only if it has effect in the State of origin, and shall be enforced only if it is enforceable in the State of origin.

4. Recognition or enforcement may be postponed or refused if the judgment is the subject of review in the State of origin or if the time limit for seeking ordinary review has not expired. A refusal does not prevent a subsequent application for recognition or enforcement of the judgment.

5. This Article shall also apply to a judgment given by a court of a Contracting State pursuant to a transfer of the case from the chosen court in that Contracting State as permitted by Article 5, paragraph 3. However, where the chosen court had discretion as to whether to transfer the case to another court, recognition or enforcement of the judgment may be refused against a party who objected to the transfer in a timely manner in the State of origin.

Article 9 *Refusal of recognition or enforcement*

Recognition or enforcement may be refused if—

a) the agreement was null and void under the law of the State of the chosen court, unless the chosen court has determined that the agreement is valid;

b) a party lacked the capacity to conclude the agreement under the law of the requested State;

c) the document which instituted the proceedings or an equivalent document, including the essential elements of the claim, *i)*   was not notified to the defendant in sufficient time and in such a way as to enable him to arrange for his defence, unless the defendant entered an appearance and presented his case without contesting notification in the court of origin, provided that the law of the State of origin permitted notification to be contested; or

     ii) was notified to the defendant in the requested State in a manner that is incompatible with fundamental principles of the requested State concerning service of documents;

d) the judgment was obtained by fraud in connection with a matter of procedure;

e) recognition or enforcement would be manifestly incompatible with the public policy of the requested State, including situations where the specific proceedings leading to the judgment were incompatible with fundamental principles of procedural fairness of that State;

f) the judgment is inconsistent with a judgment given in the requested State in a dispute between the same parties; or

g) the judgment is inconsistent with an earlier judgment given in another State between the same parties on the same cause of action, provided that the earlier judgment fulfils the conditions necessary for its recognition in the requested State.

Article 10   Preliminary questions

1.   Where a matter excluded under Article 2, paragraph 2, or under Article 21, arose as a preliminary question, the ruling on that question shall not be recognised or enforced under this Convention.

2.   Recognition or enforcement of a judgment may be refused if, and to the extent that, the judgment was based on a ruling on a matter excluded under Article 2, paragraph 2.

3.   However, in the case of a ruling on the validity of an intellectual property right other than copyright or a related right, recognition or enforcement of a

judgment may be refused or postponed under the preceding paragraph only where—

a) that ruling is inconsistent with a judgment or a decision of a competent authority on that matter given in the State under the law of which the intellectual property right arose; or

b) proceedings concerning the validity of the intellectual property right are pending in that State.

4. Recognition or enforcement of a judgment may be refused if, and to the extent that, the judgment was based on a ruling on a matter excluded pursuant to a declaration made by the requested State under Article 21.

Article 11   Damages

1. Recognition or enforcement of a judgment may be refused if, and to the extent that, the judgment awards damages, including exemplary or punitive damages, that do not compensate a party for actual loss or harm suffered.

2. The court addressed shall take into account whether and to what extent the damages awarded by the court of origin serve to cover costs and expenses relating to the proceedings.

Article 12   Judicial settlements (transactions judiciaires)

Judicial settlements (transactions judiciaires) which a court of a Contracting State designated in an exclusive choice of court agreement has approved, or which have been concluded before that court in the course of proceedings, and which are enforceable in the same manner as a judgment in the State of origin, shall be enforced under this Convention in the same manner as a judgment.

Article 13   Documents to be produced

1. The party seeking recognition or applying for enforcement shall produce—

a) a complete and certified copy of the judgment;

    b) the exclusive choice of court agreement, a certified copy thereof, or other evidence of its existence;

    c) if the judgment was given by default, the original or a certified copy of a document establishing that the document which instituted the proceedings or an equivalent document was notified to the defaulting party;

    d) any documents necessary to establish that the judgment has effect or, where applicable, is enforceable in the State of origin;

    e) in the case referred to in Article 12, a certificate of a court of the State of origin that the judicial settlement or a part of it is enforceable in the same manner as a judgment in the State of origin.

2. If the terms of the judgment do not permit the court addressed to verify whether the conditions of this Chapter have been complied with, that court may require any necessary documents.

3. An application for recognition or enforcement may be accompanied by a document, issued by a court (including an officer of the court) of the State of origin, in the form recommended and published by the Hague Conference on Private International Law.

4. If the documents referred to in this Article are not in an official language of the requested State, they shall be accompanied by a certified translation into an official language, unless the law of the requested State provides otherwise.

Article 14   Procedure

The procedure for recognition, declaration of enforceability or registration for enforcement, and the enforcement of the judgment, are governed by the law of the requested State unless this Convention provides otherwise. The court addressed shall act expeditiously.

Article 15   Severability

Recognition or enforcement of a severable part of a judgment shall be granted where recognition or enforcement of that part is applied for, or only part of the judgment is capable of being recognised or enforced under this Convention.

Chapter IV—General Clauses

Article 16   Transitional provisions

1. This Convention shall apply to exclusive choice of court agreements concluded after its entry into force for the State of the chosen court.

2. This Convention shall not apply to proceedings instituted before its entry into force for the State of the court seised.

Article 17   Contracts of insurance and reinsurance

1. Proceedings under a contract of insurance or reinsurance are not excluded from the scope of this Convention on the ground that the contract of insurance or reinsurance relates to a matter to which this Convention does not apply.

2. Recognition and enforcement of a judgment in respect of liability under the terms of a contract of insurance or reinsurance may not be limited or refused on the ground that the liability under that contract includes liability to indemnify the insured or reinsured in respect of—

    a)   a matter to which this Convention does not apply; or

    b)   an award of damages to which Article 11 might apply.

Article 18   No legalisation

All documents forwarded or delivered under this Convention shall be exempt from legalisation or any analogous formality, including an Apostille.

Article 19   Declarations limiting jurisdiction

A State may declare that its courts may refuse to determine disputes to which an exclusive choice of court agreement applies if, except for the location of the chosen court, there is no connection between that State and the parties or the dispute.

Article 20   Declarations limiting recognition and enforcement

A State may declare that its courts may refuse to recognise or enforce a judgment given by a court of another Contracting State if the parties were resident in the requested State, and the relationship of the parties and all other elements relevant to the dispute, other than the location of the chosen court, were connected only with the requested State.

Article 21   Declarations with respect to specific matters

1. Where a State has a strong interest in not applying this Convention to a specific matter, that State may declare that it will not apply the Convention to that matter. The State making such a declaration shall ensure that the declaration is no broader than necessary and that the specific matter excluded is clearly and precisely defined.

2. With regard to that matter, the Convention shall not apply—

   a) in the Contracting State that made the declaration;

   b) in other Contracting States, where an exclusive choice of court agreement designates the courts, or one or more specific courts, of the State that made the declaration.

Article 22   Reciprocal declarations on non-exclusive choice of court agreements

1. A Contracting State may declare that its courts will recognise and enforce judgments given by courts of other Contracting States designated in a choice

of court agreement concluded by two or more parties that meets the requirements of Article 3, paragraph *c)*, and designates, for the purpose of deciding disputes which have arisen or may arise in connection with a particular legal relationship, a court or courts of one or more Contracting States (a non-exclusive choice of court agreement).

2. Where recognition or enforcement of a judgment given in a Contracting State that has made such a declaration is sought in another Contracting State that has made such a declaration, the judgment shall be recognised and enforced under this Convention, if—

    a) the court of origin was designated in a non-exclusive choice of court agreement;

    b) there exists neither a judgment given by any other court before which proceedings could be brought in accordance with the non-exclusive choice of court agreement, nor a proceeding pending between the same parties in any other such court on the same cause of action; and

    c) the court of origin was the court first seised.

Article 23   Uniform interpretation

In the interpretation of this Convention, regard shall be had to its international character and to the need to promote uniformity in its application.

Article 24   Review of operation of the Convention

The Secretary General of the Hague Conference on Private International Law shall at regular intervals make arrangements for—

    a) review of the operation of this Convention, including any declarations; and

    b) consideration of whether any amendments to this Convention are desirable.

Article 25   Non-unified legal systems

1. In relation to a Contracting State in which two or more systems of law apply in different territorial units with regard to any matter dealt with in this Convention—

   a) any reference to the law or procedure of a State shall be construed as referring, where appropriate, to the law or procedure in force in the relevant territorial unit;

   b) any reference to residence in a State shall be construed as referring, where appropriate, to residence in the relevant territorial unit;

   c) any reference to the court or courts of a State shall be construed as referring, where appropriate, to the court or courts in the relevant territorial unit;

   d) any reference to a connection with a State shall be construed as referring, where appropriate, to a connection with the relevant territorial unit.

2. Notwithstanding the preceding paragraph, a Contracting State with two or more territorial units in which different systems of law apply shall not be bound to apply this Convention to situations which involve solely such different territorial units.

3. A court in a territorial unit of a Contracting State with two or more territorial units in which different systems of law apply shall not be bound to recognise or enforce a judgment from another Contracting State solely because the judgment has been recognised or enforced in another territorial unit of the same Contracting State under this Convention.

4. This Article shall not apply to a Regional Economic Integration Organisation.

Article 26   Relationship with other international instruments

1. This Convention shall be interpreted so far as possible to be compatible with other treaties in force for Contracting States, whether concluded before or after this Convention.

2. This Convention shall not affect the application by a Contracting State of a treaty, whether concluded before or after this Convention, in cases where none of the parties is resident in a Contracting State that is not a Party to the treaty.

3. This Convention shall not affect the application by a Contracting State of a treaty that was concluded before this Convention entered into force for that Contracting State, if applying this Convention would be inconsistent with the obligations of that Contracting State to any non-Contracting State. This paragraph shall also apply to treaties that revise or replace a treaty concluded before this Convention entered into force for that Contracting State, except to the extent that the revision or replacement creates new inconsistencies with this Convention.

4. This Convention shall not affect the application by a Contracting State of a treaty, whether concluded before or after this Convention, for the purposes of obtaining recognition or enforcement of a judgment given by a court of a Contracting State that is also a Party to that treaty. However, the judgment shall not be recognised or enforced to a lesser extent than under this Convention.

5. This Convention shall not affect the application by a Contracting State of a treaty which, in relation to a specific matter, governs jurisdiction or the recognition or enforcement of judgments, even if concluded after this Convention and even if all States concerned are Parties to this Convention. This paragraph shall apply only if the Contracting State has made a declaration in respect of the treaty under this paragraph. In the case of such a declaration, other Contracting States shall not be obliged to apply this Convention to that specific matter to the extent of any inconsistency, where an exclusive choice of court agreement designates the courts, or one or more specific courts, of the Contracting State that made the declaration.

6. This Convention shall not affect the application of the rules of a Regional Economic Integration Organisation that is a Party to this Convention, whether adopted before or after this Convention—

   a) where none of the parties is resident in a Contracting State that is not a Member State of the Regional Economic Integration Organisation;

b) as concerns the recognition or enforcement of judgments as between Member States of the Regional Economic Integration Organisation.

Chapter V—Final Clauses

Article 27   *Signature, ratification, acceptance, approval or accession*

1. This Convention is open for signature by all States.

2. This Convention is subject to ratification, acceptance or approval by the signatory States.

3. This Convention is open for accession by all States.

4. Instruments of ratification, acceptance, approval or accession shall be deposited with the Ministry of Foreign Affairs of the Kingdom of the Netherlands, depositary of the Convention.

Article 28   *Declarations with respect to non-unified legal systems*

1. If a State has two or more territorial units in which different systems of law apply in relation to matters dealt with in this Convention, it may at the time of signature, ratification, acceptance, approval or accession declare that the Convention shall extend to all its territorial units or only to one or more of them and may modify this declaration by submitting another declaration at any time.

2. A declaration shall be notified to the depositary and shall state expressly the territorial units to which the Convention applies.

3. If a State makes no declaration under this Article, the Convention shall extend to all territorial units of that State.

4. This Article shall not apply to a Regional Economic Integration Organisation.

Article 29   Regional Economic Integration Organisations

1. A Regional Economic Integration Organisation which is constituted solely by sovereign States and has competence over some or all of the matters governed by this Convention may similarly sign, accept, approve or accede to this Convention. The Regional Economic Integration Organisation shall in that case have the rights and obligations of a Contracting State, to the extent that the Organisation has competence over matters governed by this Convention.

2. The Regional Economic Integration Organisation shall, at the time of signature, acceptance, approval or accession, notify the depositary in writing of the matters governed by this Convention in respect of which competence has been transferred to that Organisation by its Member States. The Organisation shall promptly notify the depositary in writing of any changes to its competence as specified in the most recent notice given under this paragraph.

3. For the purposes of the entry into force of this Convention, any instrument deposited by a Regional Economic Integration Organisation shall not be counted unless the Regional Economic Integration Organisation declares in accordance with Article 30 that its Member States will not be Parties to this Convention.

4. Any reference to a "Contracting State" or "State" in this Convention shall apply equally, where appropriate, to a Regional Economic Integration Organisation that is a Party to it.

Article 30   Accession by a Regional Economic Integration Organisation without its Member States

1. At the time of signature, acceptance, approval or accession, a Regional Economic Integration Organisation may declare that it exercises competence

over all the matters governed by this Convention and that its Member States will not be Parties to this Convention but shall be bound by virtue of the signature, acceptance, approval or accession of the Organisation.

2. In the event that a declaration is made by a Regional Economic Integration Organisation in accordance with paragraph 1, any reference to a "Contracting State" or "State" in this Convention shall apply equally, where appropriate, to the Member States of the Organisation.

Article 31   Entry into force

1. This Convention shall enter into force on the first day of the month following the expiration of three months after the deposit of the second instrument of ratification, acceptance, approval or accession referred to in Article 27.

2. Thereafter this Convention shall enter into force—

   a) for each State or Regional Economic Integration Organisation subsequently ratifying, accepting, approving or acceding to it, on the first day of the month following the expiration of three months after the deposit of its instrument of ratification, acceptance, approval or accession;

   b) for a territorial unit to which this Convention has been extended in accordance with Article 28, paragraph 1, on the first day of the month following the expiration of three months after the notification of the declaration referred to in that Article.

Article 32   Declarations

1. Declarations referred to in Articles 19, 20, 21, 22 and 26 may be made upon signature, ratification, acceptance, approval or accession or at any time thereafter, and may be modified or withdrawn at any time.

2. Declarations, modifications and withdrawals shall be notified to the depositary.

3. A declaration made at the time of signature, ratification, acceptance, approval or accession shall take effect simultaneously with the entry into force of this Convention for the State concerned.

4. A declaration made at a subsequent time, and any modification or withdrawal of a declaration, shall take effect on the first day of the month following the expiration of three months after the date on which the notification is received by the depositary.

5. A declaration under Articles 19, 20, 21 and 26 shall not apply to exclusive choice of court agreements concluded before it takes effect.

Article 33   Denunciation

1. This Convention may be denounced by notification in writing to the depositary. The denunciation may be limited to certain territorial units of a non-unified legal system to which this Convention applies.

2. The denunciation shall take effect on the first day of the month following the expiration of twelve months after the date on which the notification is received by the depositary. Where a longer period for the denunciation to take effect is specified in the notification, the denunciation shall take effect upon the expiration of such longer period after the date on which the notification is received by the depositary.

Article 34   Notifications by the depositary

The depositary shall notify the Members of the Hague Conference on Private International Law, and other States and Regional Economic Integration Organisations which have signed, ratified, accepted, approved or acceded in accordance with Articles 27, 29 and 30 of the following—

a) the signatures, ratifications, acceptances, approvals and accessions referred to in Articles 27, 29 and 30;

b) the date on which this Convention enters into force in accordance with Article 31;

c) the notifications, declarations, modifications and withdrawals of declarations referred to in Articles 19, 20, 21, 22, 26, 28, 29 and 30;

d) the denunciations referred to in Article 33.

In witness whereof the undersigned, being duly authorised thereto, have signed this Convention. Done at The Hague, on 30 June 2005, in the English and French languages, both texts being equally authentic, in a single copy which shall be deposited in the archives of the Government of the Kingdom of the Netherlands, and of which a certified copy shall be sent, through diplomatic channels, to each of the Member States of the Hague Conference on Private International Law as of the date of its Twentieth Session and to each State which participated in that Session.

RECOMMENDED FORM
UNDER THE CONVENTION ON
CHOICE OF COURT AGREEMENTS
("THE CONVENTION")

(Sample form confirming the issuance and content of a judgment
given by the court of origin for the purposes of recognition
and enforcement under the Convention)

1. (THE COURT OF ORIGIN) ....

   ADDRESS ....

   TEL. ....

   FAX ....

   E-MAIL ....

2. CASE / DOCKET NUMBER ....

3. .... (PLAINTIFF)

   v.

   .... (DEFENDANT)

4. (THE COURT OF ORIGIN) gave a judgment in the above-captioned matter
   on (DATE) in (CITY, STATE).

5. This court was designated in an exclusive choice of court agreement within
   the meaning of Article 3 of the Convention:

   YES   NO

   UNABLE TO CONFIRM

6. If yes, the exclusive choice of court agreement was concluded or documented in the following manner:

7. This court awarded the following payment of money *(please indicate, where applicable, any relevant categories of damages included)*:

8. This court awarded interest as follows *(please specify the rate(s) of interest, the portion(s) of the award to which interest applies, the date from which interest is computed, and any further information regarding interest that would assist the court addressed)*:

9. This court included within the judgment the following costs and expenses relating to the proceedings *(please specify the amounts of any such awards, including, where applicable, any amount(s) within a monetary award intended to cover costs and expenses relating to the proceedings)*:

10. This court awarded the following non-monetary relief *(please describe the nature of such relief)*:

11. This judgment is enforceable in the State of origin:

    YES   NO

    UNABLE TO CONFIRM

12. This judgment (or a part thereof) is currently the subject of review in the State of origin:

    YES   NO

    UNABLE TO CONFIRM

    If "yes" please specify the nature and status of such review:

13. Any other relevant information:

14. Attached to this form are the documents marked in the following list *(if available)*:

     a complete and certified copy of the judgment;

     the exclusive choice of court agreement, a certified copy thereof, or other evidence of its existence;

     if the judgment was given by default, the original or a certified copy of a document establishing that the document which instituted the proceedings or an equivalent document was notified to the defaulting party;

     any documents necessary to establish that the judgment has effect or, where applicable, is enforceable in the State of origin;

     (list if applicable):

     in the case referred to in Article 12 of the Convention, a certificate of a court of the State of origin that the judicial settlement or a part of it is enforceable in the same manner as a judgment in the State of origin;

     other documents: ....

15. Dated this ....day of ...., 20... at ....

16. Signature and / or stamp by the court or officer of the court:

CONTACT PERSON:

TEL.:

FAX:

E-MAIL:

Index

interest of the state, 179
in Michigan, 72
in *Piper Aircraft*, 52

Q

Québec *Civil Code*, 83–85

R

race to courthouse in civil law, 2, 126, 149, 206
race to judgment in common law, 149, 206
Radeljak v. DaimlerChrysler Corp. (2006), 72
related litigation, existence of, 34
Reno, Janet, 130
restrictions to application of forum non
   conveniens
   in United Kingdom
      by *Brussels Regulation*, 25–27
      by *Owusu* decision, 29–30
   in United States, 48–50
Rivas v. Ford Motor Co. (2004), 137–38
Rogers v. Guaranty Trust Co. of N.Y. (1933), 42–43
Rome Convention, 180
Ruhrgas AG v. Marathon Oil Co. (1999), 69

S

Scotland, 7–10. *See also* United Kingdom
Sei Mukoda v. Boeing (Japan, 1986), 124–25
service ex juris
   and burden of proof, 22–23, 117–18
   forum non conveniens analysis applied to
      in Australia, 94
      in Canada, 76–77, 80
      in England, 21–23
      in United Kingdom, 33
      in *Spiliada*, 21
Shaffer v. Heitner (1977), 50
Shevill v. Presse Alliance S.A. (European Court of
   Justice, 1995), 175
Sibaja v. Dow Chemical Co. (1985), 66
similarities in forum non conveniens doctrines,
   101–6
   benefits of, 106
Sim v. Robinow (Scotland, 1892), 8–9
*Sinochem Int'l Co. Ltd. v. Malaysia Int'l Shipping
   Corp.* (2007), 61–62, 69–71
Slater v. Mexican National R.R. Co. (1904), 41
*La Société du Gaz de Paris v. La Société Anonyme de
   Navigation "Les Armateurs Français"* (England,
   1926), 9–10

"special circumstances," Japanese doctrine of, 124–25
Spiliada Maritime Corp. v. Cansulex Ltd.
   (United Kingdom, 1987)
   and alternative forum requirement, 102
   and Australia, 91, 94
   basis of English current application of forum non
      conveniens, 3, 21–23
   on judicial discretion, 105
   on plaintiff's juridical advantage, 109
   private interest factors, 104
   test adopted in Canada by *Amchem*, 79–80
   two-stage process of analysis, 110
      and burden of proof, 117
*St. Pierre v. South American Stores (Goth & Chaves),
   Ltd.* (England, 1936)
   as base for the Australian clearly inappropriate
      forum test, 88–89
   reiteration of *Logan* test, 13
state systems influence on global conventions,
   172–73
statute of limitation, waiver of, 51
   in Australia, 95, 106
   in United States, 51, 106
Steel Co. v. Citizens for a Better Env't (1998), 69
Story, Joseph, 54
*Swift & Co. Packers v. Compania Colombiana del
   Caribe* (1950), 58

T

Taruffo, Michele, 159
Texas, 71–72
third parties, joining of, 34
Treaties of Friendship, Commerce and Navigation
   (FCN treaties), 62, 129–30

U

U.N. Sales Convention. *See United Nations
   Convention on Contracts for the International
   Sale of Goods*
Uniform Foreign Money-Judgments Recognition Act
   (2002), 163
Uniform Interstate and International Procedure Act
   (U.S., 1986), 57
United Kingdom, 7–35
   alternative forum requirement, 102
   and *Brussels Regulation*, 119
   burden of proof
      on the defendant, 103
      shifting of, 116–17